FINANCIAL MANAGEMENT FOR NONPROFITS

THE COMPLETE GUIDE TO MAXIMIZING RESOURCES AND MANAGING ASSETS

JAE K. SHIM, PH.D.
JOEL G. SIEGEL, PH.D., CPA

McGraw-Hill

New York   San Francisco   Washington, D.C.   Auckland   Bogotá
Caracas   Lisbon   London   Madrid   Mexico City   Milan
Montreal   New Delhi   San Juan   Singapore
Sydney   Tokyo   Toronto

McGraw-Hill

A Division of The **McGraw·Hill** *Companies*

FINANCIAL MANAGEMENT FOR NONPROFITS: THE COMPLETE GUIDE TO
MAXIMIZING RESOURCES AND MANAGING ASSETS

This publication is designed to provide accurate and
authoritative information in regard to the subject matter
covered. It is sold with the understanding that neither the
author or the publisher is engaged in rendering legal, accounting,
or other profiessional service. If legal advice or other expert
assistance is required, the services of a competent professional
person should be sought.

*From a Declaration of Principles jointly adopted by a Committee
of the American Bar Association and a Committee of Publishers.*

1 2 3 4 5 6 7 9 0 DOC/DOC 9 1 0 9 8 7

ISBN 0-7863-0850-8

Library of Congress Cataloging-in-Publication Data

Shim, Jae K.
    Financial management for nonprofits: the complete guide to
maximizing resources and managing assets / Jae K. Shim, Joel G. Siegel.
        p.   cm.
    Includes index.
    ISBN 0–7863–0850–8
    1. Nonprofit organizations—Finance. I.Siegel, Joel G.
II. Title.
HG4027.65.S538
658.15—dc20   96–41902

ABOUT THE AUTHORS

JAE K. SHIM, Ph.D., is professor of business at California State University, Long Beach, and chief financial officer (CFO) of a Los Angeles-based nonprofit health care provider.

Dr. Shim received his M.B.A. and Ph.D. degrees from the University of California at Berkeley. He is a certified cost analyst. Dr. Shim has published numerous refereed articles in such journals as *Financial Management*, *Long Range Planning*, *Decision Sciences*, *Management Accounting*, *Econometrica*, *Management Science*, *OMEGA*, *Journal of Operational Research Society*, *Journal of Systems Management*, and *CMA Magazine*.

He has over 40 professional books to his credit, including *Financial Management*, *Handbook of Financial Analysis, Forecasting and Modeling*, *Managerial Accounting*, *Strategic Business Forecasting*, *The Vest-Pocket CFO*, *The Vest-Pocket CPA*, and the best selling *Vest-Pocket MBA*.

Dr. Shim was the 1982 recipient of the *Credit Research Foundation Outstanding Paper Award* for an article he published in *Financial Management*. Dr. Shim is a member of Decision Science Institute, the Institute of Management Science, Financial Management Association, and the American Accounting Association.

JOEL G. SIEGEL, Ph.D., CPA, is professor of accounting and finance at Queens College of the City University of New York. Dr. Siegel is a financial consultant to nonprofit entities. He was previously associated with Coopers and Lybrand, CPAs, and Arthur Andersen, CPAs. Professor Siegel has acted as a consultant to many organizations, including the City of New York, International Telephone and Telegraph, Citicorp, Carrier Corporation, and Person-Wolinsky Associates. Dr. Siegel is the author of 50 books and about 200 articles. His books have been published by Probus/Irwin, Prentice-Hall, McGraw-Hill, John Wiley, International Publishing, HarperCollins, Macmillan, Barron's, and the American Institute of CPAs.

He has published in numerous journals, including *The CPA Journal*, *The Financial Executive*, *The Financial Analysts Journal*, *Managerial Planning*, *Long Range Planning*, *Decision Sciences*, *Credit and Financial Management*, and *International Journal of Systems Science*.

In 1972, he was the recipient of the Outstanding Educator of America Award. He is listed in *Who's Who in the World, Who's Where among Writers,* and *Personalities of America*. He formerly served as chairperson of the National Oversight Board.

PREFACE

Managers of nonprofit organizations (NPOs) generally are not skilled in financial matters; or, often preoccupied with the NPO's welfare objectives, they ignore operations efficiency and operating cost controls. A series of appropriate questions that nonprofit financial managers must address in connection with an organization's financial condition and activity include:

1. Do we have a profit or a loss?
2. Do we have sufficient reserves?
3. Are we liquid?
4. Do we have strong internal controls?
5. Are we operating efficiently?
6. Are we meeting our budget?
7. Are our programs valid?
8. Are we competing successfully?
9. Is our prioritizing of programs and activities reasonable?

This book is an effort to help answer these questions. Also, it attempts to address recent management planning tools—time series forecasting, aggregate production planning, ABC analysis, and material requirements planning—to facilitate better demand and resource management.

The book will be quite different from other books in many ways:

1. It is practical and reader friendly.
2. It is up-to-date and comprehensive, covering all *new* developments in finance pertinent to the nonprofit sector.
3. There are many case studies, examples, and illustrations.
4. There is heavy emphasis on the use of financial software.
5. It is directed toward the practitioner.
6. It applies to all nonprofit organizations including colleges, hospitals and health care organizations, libraries, charities, performing arts, religious institutions, community services, professional societies, fraternities, private foundations, museums, and research and scientific organizations.
7. It can be used by all people directly or indirectly involved with nonprofit entities including general managers, accountants, controllers, treasurers, financial managers, CFOs, attorneys, fund raisers, and politicians.

Jae K. Shim
Joel G. Siegel

CONTENTS

Chapter 3

Break-Even and Cost-Volume-Revenue Analysis   47

Chapter 4

Financial Statement Analysis and Avoiding Financial Distress   63

Chapter 5

Financial Planning and Forecasting   105

Chapter 6

Budgeting: A Tool for Planning and Control   139

Chapter 7

Zero Base Budgeting and Program Budgeting   167

Chapter 8

Analysis of Cost Behavior and Flexible Budgeting   179

Chapter 9

Improving Managerial and Departmental Performance   193

Chapter 10

Short-Term and Long-Term Financing   203

APPENDIXES

CHAPTER 1

Introduction

Since 1993, annual increases in corporate contributions have lagged the inflation rate.

Ann Kaplan
Research Director for the American Association of
Fund-Raising Consultants in New York City
Rochester Business Journal, *April 14, 1995*

More than half of San Diego's 64 performing arts organizations ended last year in the red. Attendance at arts and cultural events was down to 3.7 million in 1991, from a high of 4.1 million in 1988.

Alan Ziter
Executive Director of the San Diego Theatre League
San Diego Business Journal, *August 24, 1992*

These days, managers in the not-for-profit sector sound an awful lot like managers in the for-profit sector. Faced with dwindling resources and greater demand, they talk about flattening management, surveying customers, educating donors, and creating strategic alliances. They talk about packaging, delivery, and cost cutting. They talk about things like total quality management (TQM).

Nonprofit organizations (NPOs) are among the most influential and powerful institutions in our free society. These organizations range in size from small local organizations to large national and international ones. Their scope covers almost every activity imaginable—health and welfare, research, education, religion, and the like. It is estimated that there are more than one million nonprofit organizations in the United States and they own property representing from 10 to 50 percent of the tax roll in many large cities. The role of nonprofit organizations in our economy has become increasingly prominent over the last several decades. A lot of money is involved. Nonprofits raise nearly $700 billion annually, about 10 percent of the gross domestic product (GDP), according to the IRS.

CHARACTERISTICS OF NONPROFIT ORGANIZATIONS

Nonprofit organizations provide socially desirable services without the intention of realizing a profit. They have no ownership shares that can be sold or traded by individuals, and any excess of revenues over expenses or expenditures is used to enlarge the service capability of the organization. They are financed, at least partially, by taxes and/or contributions based on some measure of ability to pay, and some or all of their services are distributed on the basis of need rather than effective demand. Within this definition, governmental entities such as cities and counties, colleges and universities, most hospitals, health and welfare agencies, churches, performing arts associations such as symphony orchestras, and foundations are all nonprofit enterprise units. Figure 1.1 shows different categories of nonprofit organizations.

Public nonprofit organizations are created by formal community action for the purpose of providing community services. They have the sanction of law, allowing them to levy taxes as a source of support and typically include such entities as federal, state, and municipal governing units.

Typically, these organizations are controlled by boards of directors composed of leading citizens who volunteer their time. If an organization is large or complex enough in operation to require it, the board may delegate limited or broad operating responsibility to a part-time or full-time paid executive, who may be given any one of many alternative titles—executive secretary, administrator, manager, and so on. Regardless of the size, the board will usually appoint one of its own part-time volunteer members as treasurer, and in most cases this person is the second most important person after the chairman of the board, simply because its programs revolve around finances.

How Do Nonprofits Differ from For-Profits?

A nonprofit can run itself in a businesslike way, but there remain several critical distinctions between the for-profit and the nonprofit worlds:

1. A nonprofit has no owner. There are no private shareholders, and the organization is governed by a board of directors or trustees who may

F I G U R E   1.1

Categories of Nonprofit Organizations

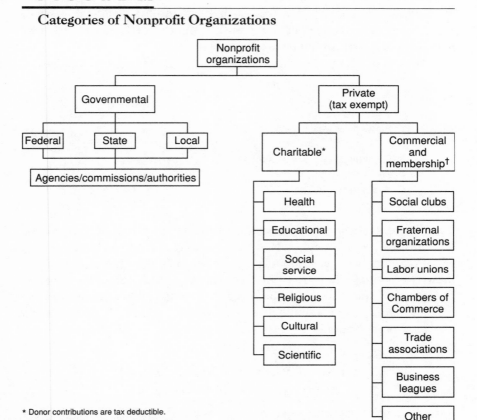

* Donor contributions are tax deductible.
† Donor contributions are not tax deductible.

Source: Anthony, R. and D. Young, *Management Control in Non-Profit Organizations*. 5th ed. (Burr Ridge, IL: Richard D. Irwin, Inc., 1994), p. 49.

not receive any individual benefit—direct or indirect—from the organization. There can be no transfer of ownership. For this reason, nonprofits are called "nonstock corporations."

2. A nonprofit is set up to carry out a designated mission or specific purposes, and its Internal Revenue Service (IRS) classification confers special tax-exempt status. Nonprofits are chartered by the states, which may also grant exemption from property, sales, use, and income taxes.

3. Nonprofits may generate profits (or "surplus"), but they may not distribute them. All the assets of a nonprofit must be dedicated to its exempt purposes. You may give incentive compensation based on productivity, but you may not give compensation based on the profitability of the organization.

4. All nonprofits have mission statements, and the IRS forbids such organizations to engage in businesses unrelated to their original mission. Business income unrelated to a nonprofit's mission, called unrelated business income (UBI), would be taxable.

The following table summarizes the differences between the two.

For-profits	Nonprofits
1. Stockholder wealth maximization	1. Stability
2. Profit maximization	2. Mission responsibility
3. Managerial reward maximization	3. Behavioral goals
4. Behavioral goals	4. Social responsibility
5. Social responsibility	

Success in nonprofits is primarily measured by how much service the organization provides and by how well the service is done. Despite apparent differences between nonprofit and for-profit entities, there's much that these two entities can learn from each other to create more robust organizations. Put it another way, to be successful, nonprofit entities need to use a blended approach, combining the best practices from both for-profit and nonprofit organizations.

Goals of Financial Management in Nonprofit Organizations

For-profit and nonprofit organizations often embrace distinctly different missions—a fact that can impact virtually every aspect of their operations. For-profits typically place the highest priority on maximizing shareholder value. Nonprofits generally consider service to the community to be their ultimate, overriding charter.

Because for-profits are continually accountable to their shareholders, and because they carefully guard their assets, they tend to focus on short-term objectives that will have an immediate impact on their balance sheets and income statements. By pursuing a quarter-to-quarter strategy, for-profits run the risk of losing sight of their long-term business visions.

Largely free of public scrutiny on a quarterly basis, nonprofits are more inclined to make long-term investments that support their service-oriented missions.

1. For-profits often excel in financial planning, information systems, strategic planning, and management practices.

2. Nonprofits are mission-driven, service-oriented, and more fully integrated into the communities they serve. Social responsibility is a primary concern.

Looking at how these organizations respond in times of crisis also reveals differences. In a crisis, for-profit companies tend to attack and solve a problem as quickly as possible, doing all they can to protect their assets. Nonprofits, because they often aren't fiscally focused, tend to rely on their cash reserves as their first line of defense when a crisis occurs.

From a management perspective, there's a tendency among nonprofits to preserve employee positions even when overstaffing might be apparent. The opposite is often true at for-profits, where labor reductions are frequently made too swiftly as quick fixes for financial problems.

To be well-positioned for long-term growth, nonprofit organizations need to become more fiscally focused, as those companies with the strongest balance sheets are the most likely to succeed in the years ahead.

Nonprofits also need to devote as much attention to systems as they do service. Sophisticated information and management systems are key to achieving efficiency and cost effectiveness—both of which are mandatory characteristics in today's competitive marketplace.

For-profit companies must embrace service with the same vigor they have given to systems and financial stability. In a highly competitive environment, the edge often goes to those companies that are perceived as customer-driven and conscientious corporate citizens. Both nonprofit and for-profit organizations should craft a balance between serving their communities and refining their business systems and financial goals. Nonprofits, for instance, still must compete with for-profits to secure financing. They must also realize that without adequate capital, and without access to their capital, they will be unable to either carry out or expand their community service charters. For-profits must recognize that strong commitment to community service is as critical in today's world as is a strong balance sheet. For all practical purposes, both entities should work toward goals that reflect altruism as well as profitability.

What Is Finance?

Finance is a form of applied economics. It covers areas that involve: (1) financial analysis and planning, (2) investment decisions, (3) financing decisions, and (4) management of financial resources. As discussed earlier, the goals of nonprofits are quite different from those of for-profit organizations. Nonprofits are mission-driven, they emphasize service, and they are community-directed. Therefore, financial management for nonprofits must be directed toward achieving their major mission or goal, that is, long-term stability.

ROLE OF THE FINANCIAL MANAGER

The financial manager of a nonprofit entity plays an important role in the organization's goals, policies, and financial success. The financial manager's responsibilities include:

1. Determining the proper amount of funds to employ in the agency, i.e., designating the size of the agency and its rate of growth.
2. Efficiently allocating funds to specific assets.
3. Obtaining low-cost capital.
4. Managing working capital such as cash, inventory, and receivables.
5. Controlling risk.
6. Reducing excessive costs.
7. Fundraising.
8. Conducting overall financial planning and budgeting.

In a large agency, these financial responsibilities are carried out by the treasurer, the controller, and the financial vice president (chief financial officer). The treasurer is responsible for managing corporate assets and liabilities, planning the finances, budgeting capital, finding funds for the agency, and managing the investment portfolio. He or she basically handles external financing matters. The controller is basically concerned with internal matters, namely, financial and cost accounting, budgeting, and control functions. The financial vice president, better known as the chief financial officer (CFO), supervises all phases of financial activity and serves as the financial adviser to the board of directors.

Financing for Nonprofits

Unlike for-profit firms, nonprofits are very limited in having access to financial markets. This appears to be changing, thanks to the change in laws governing bond issuance. In general, the financial markets are composed of *money markets* and *capital markets*. *Money markets* (credit markets) are the markets for short-term (less than one year) debt securities. Examples of money market securities include bankers' acceptances, commercial paper, and negotiable certificates of deposit issued by financial institutions. Capital markets are the markets in which long-term securities issued by the government and corporations are traded. Nonprofits may gain access to bond financing. Other financing ideas available to nonprofits include (1) pooled bond issue, (2) private bond offerings, (3) pooled pension funds, and (4) private foundation loan programs. The financial manager of nonprofts needs to have an increased understanding of financial markets and various financing sources and ideas.

MORE ON FOR-PROFIT AND NONPROFIT CHARACTERISTICS

While there are some particular aspects that are unique, in many respects, the budgeting concerns and priorities of nonprofit organizations are also similar to those of for-profit organizations. To fully appreciate the entire budgeting process and the ramifications of the choices that are made by management, we will review some of the basic characteristics of various nonprofit enterprises. Our discussion, however, will not be limited to only those aspects that make the nonprofit organizations atypical in the business world; we will also review some of the organizational characteristics that they share in common with for-profit organizations.

Investors and Contributors

Investors and contributors support the organization of their choice with financial resources that can be used to meet the goals of the entity. One of the major differences between the investors in a commercial enterprise and the contributors to a nonprofit organization, however, is the expectation of a profit. Investors assume the for-profit business will maximize *their* profits and improve *their* financial position, giving them a good return on their investment. The investors build an equity based on the size of their investment and the profitability of the firm. The stockholders' control over corporate activities is directly related to the number of ownership shares that are held. In the nonprofit organization, however, contributors do not own a share of the entity. The operations of a nonprofit are controlled by its constituency, which in governmental units are citizens and in voluntarily supported units are contributors. Each constituent has *one* vote regardless of the amount he or she contributes to the organization. While the voice impact in the decision-making process is not related to resources contributed for each contributor, the nonprofit is subject to externally imposed constraints of the community.

Contributors to a nonprofit organization do not expect to build an equity, but the enterprise is expected to provide a quality product or service to the public. A contributor to a nonprofit wants to know whether the organization has spent the resources it has received, whether it has spent its resources as it has promised, whether the services performed are of high quality, and whether it has any resources left.

While contributors have no expectation of profits, they do have an interest in the future commitments of the organization. Conventional accounting practices in for-profit businesses discourage the use of forecasts in financial statements. Investors, in fact, who relied on financial statements that were forecasts to make an investment decision would have a basis for litigation, as the statements would be perceived as misleading. Commitments may become future liabilities for the nonprofit organization and may seriously impact the budgeting process when resources are being allocated.

Commitments made by the nonprofit organization are incurred in a number of ways. For example, a grant might establish new computer training facilities at a school, but not provide for the continued maintenance expense (e.g., repairs of equipment) of the program or for the teachers' salaries for instruction. The nonprofit would then be required to allocate its resources to continue the program, and often would have to return repeatedly to its supporters for new contributions or services in order to continue its programs from year to year.

In general, nonprofit commitments can be separated into four areas: debt, program, facilities, and investment. Accounting rules under Generally Accepted Accounting Principles (GAAP) do not require that these kinds of obligations be recognized as liabilities in a balance sheet; however, an annual statement should be prepared detailing each area for the nonprofit organization. The deliberate understatement of commitments for the nonprofit entity is comparable to intentionally overstating income for a commercial business.

Contributors to nonprofits want to provide the resources to the organization so that a service can be provided to the community. The organization may view the making of a profit as irrelevant, or even detrimental, if government regulations or grant provisions require them to utilize their total revenue directly for services. Some nonprofits, such as performing arts organizations, may be able to use a year-end surplus to augment contribution income or endowment funds, thus increasing their ability to create services.

Assets and Liabilities/Revenues and Expenses

Nonprofit organizations require inflow/outflow statements that reveal the extent to which the organization's service objectives have been met. The accounting system for a nonprofit organization should provide information in two areas: (1) operational accountability and (2) the resource obligation position of the entity. Also, because most of these organizations operate under externally imposed constraints, it is important to have financial statements that disclose the extent to which these constraints have been met.

On the balance sheet, unconditional pledges from members of the community are recorded as an asset. Membership and subscription fees may also be viewed as contributions if they do not give an economic benefit other than a tax deduction. Other contributions or donations to nonprofit organizations may sometimes include noncash items, such as donated facilities and other fixed assets, donated materials, volunteer labor, and donated services. All of these are generally recorded as assets at fair market value. If volunteer labor is controlled in the same way as paid labor, however, it must be expended in the same way as paid labor.

Revenues, or inflows, are the realization of resources capable of being expended in meeting the service objectives of the agency. The expenses of providing the services should then be matched against those revenues. Both revenues and expenditures should be reported on a modified accrual basis to provide statement users with an objective measurement of resource inflows and outflows. The statement of revenues and expenditures will disclose the sources from which spendable resources have been realized and the ways in which they have been used. This statement is known as a "dollar-accountability statement," rather than an "operational-accountability statement," as it would be called in a for-profit business enterprise.

In dollar-accountability accounting systems, which emphasize the inflows and outflows of spendable resources, the inflows are revenues and the outflows are expenditures. The basic accounting equation is then stated as:

Assets + Expenditures = Liabilities + Fund Balance + Revenues

The balance sheets of nonprofit organizations will disclose only readily spendable resources and claims against those resources. Cash and receivables are reflected on the asset side of the statements, while payables constitute the major liability. The equity section of the balance sheet includes an account called "fund balance," since no capital stock or other equity documents are being sold or traded. The fund balance is equal to the difference between the assets and the liabilities.

In reporting assets and liabilities, many nonprofits will own the facilities and equipment used in providing their services. Though a school district may own several buildings or schools where its activities are conducted, are these assets? The building may look like an asset; however, because its existence implies substantial future expenditures, it cannot be considered one. No commercial enterprise would include as an asset a property that ensured a negative cash flow indefinitely into the future.

The nature of the nonprofit might require using facilities to provide its services with no expectation of recovering the full cost of those services from the people who receive them. Are these facilities a liability? The cash outflow created by the operation of a high school is not required to be reported as a liability. Moreover, church buildings and public office buildings are examples of a large group of properties currently classified as assets. When they appear on the financial statements of the nonprofit business, however, they produce a distorted picture of the entity's financial situation. Instead of capitalizing and depreciating their facilities, nonprofits should expense their costs and report the facilities as commitments. Long-term assets, available for operations, are shown in separate funds or account groups. Additionally, because the primary product (service) of the nonprofit cannot be inventoried, these organizations rarely need to budget for target inventory levels and units to be produced.

Besides the balance sheet, another financial statement that is used by nonprofit organizations is called a "statement of changes in fund balance." Comparable to the statement of retained earnings, it shows the increases and decreases in the fund balance resulting from resource influx and outflow activity for the period.

The actual relationship between the expenses a nonprofit organization incurs and the benefits it provides is difficult to measure. To illustrate, in a performing arts organization, the measure might be the amount of ticket sales and contributions it is able to generate with its programs. Unlike a government-sponsored health facility, its benefit to the community is not easily calculated. Nevertheless, if the programs produced are not considered valuable enough to the members of the community it serves, it will not generate enough revenue to cover expenses and it will have to cease operations.

Gifts, contributions, and endowments can be difficult to estimate when planning for the coming year's activities. An economic downturn or unforeseen circumstances may result in a severe curtailment of funds that are urgently needed to cover operating expenses. For example, in May 1992, the Joffrey Ballet, which had recently been running in the black, announced that an expected donation of $1 million had been revoked, and that problems due to the recession had left them $1,200,000 in debt. Joffrey Ballet decided to cancel its New York spring season and cut back on its commitments in Los Angeles.

Besides receiving contributions, there are some nonprofits that have other resources to fall back on to prevent the collapse of the organization. For example, radio station KCRW of Santa Monica College is associated with the National Public Radio (NPR) network and thus receives federal funding, as well as listener contributions. If the federal funds are insufficient, funds are also available from Santa Monica College, to which the station is licensed. This is an unusual nonprofit situation, and KCRW must keep records and budgets for two separate fiscal years for accounting purposes.

Some small nonprofits do their record keeping on a cash basis rather than an accrual basis, because they have little in the way of accounts due or payable. They may also expense the purchase of a fixed asset, rather than capitalizing it and recording depreciation. Larger organizations, however, must use the accrual system, especially if they accept grants, and if they wish to present financial statements that conform to GAAP.

Restricted and Unrestricted Funds

Another characteristic that distinguishes the nonprofit from the for-profit organization is accounting for restricted and unrestricted funds. Many nonprofit organizations are funded exclusively by private contributions from community members. Americans gave an estimated $124.8 billion to charity in 1991. These gifts helped to save or change the lives of millions of people throughout the United States and abroad. However, these gifts are often given to nonprofit organizations with various restrictions and can be used only for specified purposes. This means that financial statements for nonprofit businesses must also be able to show how the different resources, restricted and unrestricted, were used. Equity sections on the balance sheet are typically divided into reserved and unreserved segments, with the reserved portion representing the amount of assets already contractually committed to be used for specified purposes.

Some of the grants and private donations may be restricted, or given for specific purposes, and the spending of these funds must be strictly accounted for. For example, restricted funding may be given for building a performance hall, or for creating a new staging of an opera. Other large donations, or revenues from other unrestricted income sources, may be usable for general operating expenses or special projects as decided by the organization's board of directors. Some funds may be given to the nonprofit as an endowment, in which case only the income from the gift may be used, not the principal. Endowment income may be the only truly predictable revenue source that a nonprofit receives.

The accounting profession has developed four different, and occasionally conflicting, industry accounting guides to address the unique nature of the nonprofits' financial reporting needs.[1] The distribution of overhead costs must be done carefully because the way in which the financial reports show the matching of applicable overhead costs to these funds can sometimes handicap the nonprofit organization's ability to raise future contributions from charitable sources.

What is clearly apparent is that the information the investors in for-profit organizations need and expect is different from the information contributors to nonprofit businesses want and expect. These dissimilarities between the two types of organizations means that managers must seriously review their accounting, financial planning, and budgeting requirements, and must consider these distinctions as they implement their planning processes. The essential needs of the nonprofit organization and its supporters must be satisfied.

Operations Control and Motivating Managers

Budgeting is important in a nonprofit organization because of the control factor. In a nonprofit agency, especially in one with fixed income, managers must closely follow the budget plan because the budget represents the programs and services to be provided for the year. In a for-profit organization, operations managers can, within parameters, be allowed to modify certain manufacturing or service plans as conditions change during the year, if they can show that the revision will increase profits. For example, there can be a greater effort in marketing promotions or advertising to increase sales if revenues are not meeting forecasts, or managers can make product line changes or increase distribution efforts to increase sales.

In a nonprofit setting, however, there is little room to increase revenues if costs are exceeding estimates. Therefore, a more careful estimate of revenues and expenditures must be made during the budgeting process for the nonprofit, and there must be greater control during the year to make sure managers are not exceeding the estimated costs for their programs. Usually, expenditure cuts must be made to other programs or services in order to close any gaps that develop between revenues and expenditures during the year. If expenses are below revenues by more than the amount needed for reserves, the organization is not delivering the services that the funding agencies have a right to expect.

Conformance to the nonprofit budget is not only encouraged but controlled with the appropriate audit and internal control procedures. Senior administrators are well aware of the natural tendency for managers to spend 100 percent of their budget, whether needed or not, for fear that the program's budget will be decreased in the next year. Many nonprofit agencies are finding ways to reward managers who provide the planned services but do so below the estimated cost. There is an urgent need in nonprofit organizations to encourage and motivate managers without stifling their creativity or initiative.

The measuring of output is a bit more complicated in the nonprofit than in the for-profit organization. The usual measures of revenues, gross margins or net incomes, are not relevant to the nonprofit, so other measures must be developed. There are several types that can be used; namely, results measures, process measures, and social indicators. The *results measures* will show whether the organization is accomplishing its objectives, and the *process indicators* will indicate the quantity of work. The *social indicators* are not control measures per se, but may be used for strategic planning during the budgeting planning process. Both quantity and quality measures should be devised, even though measures of the quality of service are highly subjective.

There are several areas in today's nonprofit controls that can be improved upon. One of the most important is that there must be a more active interest in the functioning of the organization by its governing board, including legislative committees. Additionally, senior management levels need to be involved in operations and program performance evaluations, in systems improvements, and in the budgeting process. There must be suitable rewards and motivations to encourage managers to provide services below cost estimates, and output measures must be included in program budgets. Reports on performance must be structured to be consistent with budgets, and there must be a regular evaluation of operations with a more thorough attention to programming. Finally, there must be more attention to the selling prices for services and the importance of using the "full" cost of services.

Nonprofit organization administrators must take seriously the demands for improved management control. During the 1980s and the 1990s, nonprofits have been seeing significant cutbacks in all phases of funding, at the federal, state, and local levels. During this same period, however, there have been increasing demands for services from clients and other users. By meeting the requirements for better control, managers will ensure the continued life and growth of the organization.

Budgetary System and Accounts

Annual budgets of estimated revenues and estimated expenditures are prepared for most governmental funds. Approval of the budget by legislative units provides the legal authority to spend for fund activities, within the limitation of the budget. (The estimated expenditures authorized by the legislative body are called *appropriations*.) The approved budgets of such funds are recorded in *budgetary accounts* in the accounting system to provide control over fund revenues and expenditures. *Proprietary Funds* and *Fiduciary Funds*—and most *Special Assessment Funds* and *Capital Projects Funds*—are not contingent on annual budgets and legislative appropriations of resources. Thus, budgets need not be integrated into their formal accounting records. The type of budget prepared by a nongovernmental nonprofit entity will more closely resemble a budget prepared by a business enterprise than a budget prepared by a governmental unit, except when a state legislature or a local council appropriates funds for an entity (e.g., a public college or a hospital).

More Need for Sound Information Systems

One way nonprofit organizations can keep their costs down is to implement an information-management system. Such a system cuts costs by reducing the amount of time and effort employees spend creating, updating, and maintaining files. However, nonprofit organizations have the least amount of money to spend on establishing the systems. Raising the capital to purchase the necessary hardware and software is not an easy task, and justifying that cost to a board of directors is sometimes a hard sell. Nonprofits are in dire need of financial-management systems, database systems, and so on.

COST CONCEPTS AND TERMINOLOGY

> It is important to understand actual costs. Nonprofits have a tendency not to know how much things cost. But maybe they have capacity that isn't being used.
>
> Oregonian, *July 16, 1995*

In financial accounting, the term "cost" is defined as a measurement, in monetary terms, of the amount of resources used for some purpose. In managerial accounting, the term "cost" is used in many different ways. Cost is not a unidimensional concept. That is, there are different types of costs used for different purposes. Some costs are useful and required for surplus/deficit determination. Some costs are useful for planning, budgeting, and cost control. Still others are useful for making both short-term and long-term decisions. In this section, we will cover various cost concepts useful for financial management and distinguish between variable costs and fixed costs.

Cost Classifications

Costs can be classified into various categories, according to:

1. Their managerial functions.
   a. Materials.
   b. Labor.
   c. Contractual services.
   d. Overhead.
2. Their ease of traceability.
   a. Direct costs.
   b. Indirect costs.
3. Their behavior in accordance with changes in activity.
   a. Variable costs.
   b. Fixed costs.
   c. Mixed (semivariable) costs.
4. Their relevance to planning, control, and decision making.
   a. Sunk costs.
   b. Incremental costs.
   c. Relevant costs.
   d. Out-of-pocket costs.
   e. Opportunity costs.
   f. Controllable and noncontrollable costs.
   g. Standard costs.

We will discuss each of the cost categories in the remainder of this section.

Costs by Managerial Functions

Four basic cost components can be generally identified in any program, project, operation, or activity: (*a*) materials and supplies; (*b*) labor or personnel services such as wages, salaries, and fringe benefits; (*c*) contractual services resulting from outsourcing; and (*d*) overhead. Overhead includes various costs such as insurance, rent, property taxes, and depreciation.

Direct Costs and Indirect Costs

Costs may be viewed as either direct or indirect in terms of the extent to which they are traceable to a particular object of costing, such as a program or a department. Direct costs can be directly traceable to the costing object. For example, the salary of the manager of a day-care center would be a direct cost of that center. Overhead items are generally indirect costs since they are not directly identifiable to any particular program. A fundraising campaign that benefits more than one activity or program is an example of an indirect cost.

Variable Costs, Fixed Costs, and Mixed Costs

From a planning and control standpoint, perhaps the most important way to classify costs is by how they behave in accordance with changes in some measure of activity—for example, number of patient-days or number of labor-hours required to complete some task. By behavior, costs can be classified into the following three basic categories:

1. Variable costs are costs that vary in total in direct proportion to changes in activity. Examples are direct materials and direct labor.
2. Fixed costs are costs that remain constant in total regardless of changes in activity. Examples are rent and insurance.
3. Mixed (or semivariable) costs are costs that vary with changes in volume but, unlike variable costs, do not vary in direct proportion. In other words, these costs contain both a variable component and a fixed component. Examples are the rental of a delivery truck, where a fixed rental fee plus a variable charge based on mileage is made; and utilities costs, where the expense consists of a fixed amount plus a variable charge based on consumption.

Costs by behavior will be examined further in a later chapter. The breakdown of costs into variable components and fixed components is important in many areas of flexible budgeting, break-even analysis, and short-term decision making.

Costs for Planning, Control, and Decision Making

Sunk Costs
Sunk costs are the costs of resources that have already been incurred whose total will not be affected by any decision made now or in the future. Sunk costs are considered irrelevant to future decisions since they are past or historical costs.

EXAMPLE 1.1
Suppose you acquired an asset for $50,000 three years ago which is now listed at a book value of $20,000. The $20,000 book value is a sunk cost which does not affect a future decision.

Incremental (or Differential) Costs

The incremental cost is the difference in costs between two or more alternatives. Incremental costs are increases or decreases in total costs; or changes in specific elements of cost (e.g., direct labor cost) that result from any variation in operations.

EXAMPLE 1.2

Consider the two alternatives A and B, whose costs are as follows:

	A	B	Difference (B – A)
Direct materials	$10,000	$10,000	$ 0
Direct labor	10,000	15,000	5,000

The incremental costs are simply B – A (or A – B) as shown in the last column. The incremental costs are relevant to future decisions.

Relevant Costs

Relevant costs are expected future costs that will differ between alternatives. This concept, a key to short- and long-term decisions, is discussed in detail later in the book.

EXAMPLE 1.3

The incremental cost is said to be relevant to the future decision. The sunk cost is considered irrelevant.

Out-of-Pocket Costs

Out-of-pocket costs, also known as "outlay costs," are costs that require expenditures of cash or other resources. Noncash charges such as depreciation and amortization are not out-of-pocket costs. Out-of-pocket costs are usually relevant to a particular decision.

EXAMPLE 1.4

A capital investment project requires $120,000 in cash outlays. The $120,000 is an out-of-pocket cost.

Opportunity Costs

An opportunity cost is the net benefit forgone by rejecting an alternative. There is always an opportunity cost involved in making a choice decision. It is a cost incurred relative to the alternative given up.

EXAMPLE 1.5
Suppose a child-care center has a choice of using its capacity to provide 100 units of services or renting the facility out for $20,000. The opportunity cost of using the capacity is $20,000.

Controllable and Noncontrollable Costs

A cost is said to be controllable when the amount of the cost is assigned to the head of a department and the level of the cost is significantly under the manager's influence. Noncontrollable costs are those costs not subject to influence at a given level of managerial supervision.

EXAMPLE 1.6
The supervisor of an emergency room in a hospital might exercise significant control over the costs of supplies, maintenance, and nursing. On the other hand, fixed costs such as depreciation of medical equipment and insurance, or the cost of doctors, would not be controllable by the supervisor, since he or she would have no power to authorize the purchase of the equipment and insurance, or hire doctors.

Standard Costs

Standard costs are the costs established in advance to serve as goals, norms, or yardsticks to be achieved and, after the fact, to determine how well those goals were met. They are based on the quantities and prices of the various inputs (e.g., direct materials, labor, and overhead) needed to output efficiently. Standard costs are better known as "budgeted costs" set for nonprofit organizations. The differences between standard costs and actual costs are referred to as "variances." If actual costs exceed standard costs, this is an unfavorable variance. In the opposite case, the variance is favorable. Any unfavorable variance must be determined and evaluated. Is the variance controllable or uncontrollable? If controllable, who is responsible and why did it occur? Immediate corrective action may be needed. On the other hand, we could learn from a favorable variance and improve performance in other areas as well.

More on Fixed and Variable Costs

Most of the costs for NPOs are fixed. The majority of expenses are for the salaries and benefits of their employees, whose contracts represent a liability to the organization. After program activities are budgeted for the year, staffing evaluations are done to determine whether enough employee talent is available or whether recruitment efforts need to be budgeted for more staff and volunteers. Staffing budgets are prepared, and then a comparison of the expected service levels to current staffing is done to ascertain whether sufficient staff is available. Based on this review, decisions to increase the number of employees or to recruit additional volunteers are then implemented.

There are many ways to calculate or estimate costs; some are simple and others can be quite complex. In budgeting for government defense contracts, direct costs are estimated using a cost analysis on the price previously paid for an item that is adjusted for quantity, reduction or increase in technical scope, economic adjustments in overhead, direct labor rates, and inflation and currency fluctuations between nations of the world. Another method is parametric modeling, which utilizes the technical characteristics of many programs to determine a probability cost range to prepare budgets for many programs presently in development where specific performance history is unavailable.

Indirect costs are used by both profit and nonprofit organizations to offset some of the central administrative costs provided by the parent agency to various activities. Although estimating indirect costs often involves complex calculations, the parent agency provides vital services to each program, including basic resources for administering the program itself, and indirect allowances must be made to fund the parent agency as well as its programs.

The parent agency may handle such things as personnel matters, and may provide legal and auditing services, data processing, accounting services, and so on. Most nonprofit supporters expect that all indirect costs will be specified and subject to possible audit, that only allowable costs will be represented, and that the subtotal of these costs will not exceed a fixed percentage level. Some watchdog groups insist that nonprofit organizations should spend no more than 40 percent of their funds on administration and fund raising. Another method for budgeting indirect costs requires specifying and costing out every element the agency wants to include in its indirect cost request.

Break-Even and Cost-Volume-Revenue Analysis

Break-even and cost-volume-profit (CVP) analysis is not limited to profit firms. CVP analysis in a NPO is more appropriately called *cost-volume-revenue (CVR) analysis*. The CVR model not only calculates the break-even service level, but helps answer a variety of "what-if" decision questions. This is covered in Chapter 3.

ENDNOTE

1. See *Audits of Certain Non-Profit Organizations, Audits of Voluntary Health and Welfare Organizations, Hospital Audit Guide,* and *Audits of Colleges and Universities,* published by the American Institute of CPAs. New York, 1973–1974.

C H A P T E R 2*

Nonprofit Financial and Managerial Accounting

The surrogate owner of the nonprofit organization (NPO) is society. The NPO provides services and programs to its members or to the public at large without concern for profits. Success is measured in terms of what quality of services and activities is provided, and whether objectives are being accomplished.

An NPO requires up-to-date, reliable, and meaningful financial data to evaluate operating position and financial status. Financial information should be recorded, reviewed, summarized, and reported. The books of account and records must be accurate. Internal controls must exist to protect assets.

The accounting and reporting requirements for NPOs are provided by Financial Accounting Standards Board (FASB) 116 (Accounting for Contributions Received and Contributions Made) and FASB 117 (Financial Statements of Not-for-Profit Organizations). FASB 117 is designed to improve the usefulness, understandability, and comparability of financial statements.

The financial statements must focus on the organization as an integrated whole. Presenting information by fund is no longer required by the FASB. However, NPOs will continue fund accounting for internal purposes.

---

*This chapter was coauthored by Abraham J. Simon, Ph. D., CPA, Professor of Nonprofit Accounting at Queens College and consultant to nonprofit organizations. Dr. Simon is former Chairperson of the Government and Nonprofit Section of the American Accounting Association.

External reports issued by NPOs should conform to Generally Accepted Accounting Principles (GAAP). NPOs must prepare for outsiders the following financial statements: Statement of Financial Position (Balance Sheet), Statement of Activities (similar to an Income Statement prepared by commercial businesses), and the Statement of Cash Flows.

Information about the existence of donor-imposed restrictions must be reported. FASB 117 sets forth the following three *classes* (previously called funds) of net assets (fund balance): unrestricted, temporarily restricted, and permanently restricted. Unrestricted net assets are resources that can be used for any purpose. They are *not* donor-restricted. Board-designated assets are classified as unrestricted, since the restrictions are self-imposed and can be lifted at any time. Temporarily restricted net assets are resources with a donor stipulation that the resources can be used for a specific purpose. The restriction or condition can be met either by the passage of time or by actions of the organization. Permanently restricted net assets are resources with donor-imposed restrictions which stipulate that resources must be maintained permanently but allow the entity to use all or part of the income obtained from the donated assets. The donors' restrictions are permanent in nature, meaning they can never be met and can never expire. Financial reporting should show how different resources, restricted and unrestricted, were used.

Internal reports for management decision-making purposes may be in the format managers believe is most useful. For example, reports may be prepared on a functional basis. Functional reporting is an effective means of communication because the NPO identifies its programs and determines the income and costs of such. A single transaction may be classified in more than one way, including by program, by responsibility unit, by source, and by object of expenditure. Financial information should be timely for control and to make up-to-date decisions. Budget and actual amounts may be compared for variance determination and analysis.

A manual should be retained including: (1) information regarding financial statement presentation, timing, and distribution; (2) check-signing policies; (3) expense incurrence policy; (4) revenue collection policy; (5) insurance; (6) travel policy; and (7) internal controls.

CHART OF ACCOUNTS

The chart of accounts depends on the size of the NPO, the volume of activities, the nature of services, the financial structure, and the competency of staff. The chart of accounts allows for expanding or deleting to satisfy the NPO's requirements, while maintaining uniformity in the recording and reporting of financial information.

STATEMENT OF FINANCIAL POSITION (BALANCE SHEET)

FASB 117 requires that the Statement of Financial Position (Balance Sheet) present assets according to their nearness to cash and sequencing of liabilities according to the nearness of their maturity. Alternatively, NPOs can provide a classified Balance Sheet which shows assets and liabilities as current and noncurrent. FASB 117 recommends having a total column for assets, liabilities, and net assets (fund balance). The total change in net assets for all classes, including unrestricted, temporarily restricted (will ultimately expire over time or be satisfied by the NPO), and permanently restricted (will not expire or be fulfilled) should be presented.

The Balance Sheet should present the total of unrestricted funds and the balance of major restricted funds. The unrestricted funds may be shown in subcategories. Some NPOs detail restricted funds into separate funds by major donor. Temporarily and permanently restricted net assets result from donor-dictated restrictions. Temporarily restricted net assets may be for unspent gifts limited to specific operating purposes, future pledges, and unspent funds to be used only to buy equipment. Permanently restricted net assets may be permanent endowments or funds on which a perpetual restriction exists.

The previous practice of presenting financial statements for only certain funds has been eliminated. Fund accounting will continue to be used for *internal reporting* only. FASB 117 allows flexibility in reporting. Organizations can continue to present financial position by fund (e.g., operating, plant), as long as the net assets are classified as either unrestricted or restricted.

Assets

Assets support the NPO's activities and will ultimately be consumed by them. Some specific assets are now discussed.

Cash   A very important asset because it indicates whether enough money exists to pay bills when due.

Pledges Receivable (Net)   Promises by outsiders to make donations that have not yet been received. Under FASB 116, nonprofits recognize unconditional pledges as assets when made even though the actual cash is still not received.

Grants Receivable (Net)   Similar to pledges, except that grants are received from foundations, companies, and government agencies.

Inventories   The accumulation of raw materials, supplies, and so on, used to deliver services.

Prepaid Expenses   The prepayment of expenditures having future benefit, such as prepaid insurance.

Investments   Debt and equity securities that generate income. Often, endowments consist of securities.

NPOs may report investments at cost or at market value. Investment securities donated to the NPO should be recorded at their fair market value at the date received.

Unrestricted or restricted realized gains or losses on sale of investments are presented in the Statement of Activities. However, unrestricted realized gains or losses are presented in the unrestricted fund class, while restricted realized gains or losses are shown in the restricted fund class. Further, capital gains or losses on endowment investments are classified as unrestricted even though the *endowment* is donor-restricted.

FASB 117 requires unrealized losses on noncurrent investments to be presented in the Statement of Activities after the "excess of revenue over expenses" line but before the "change in net assets" line.

Unrestricted investment income (interest and dividends) are presented in the current unrestricted fund of the Statement of Activities. If the investment income is restricted (e.g., if it is an endowment fund), it should be presented in the restricted fund.

Fixed Assets   Under GAAP and to receive an unqualified audit opinion, NPOs should record fixed assets at cost and depreciate them (FASB 93). If a small purchase is involved (e.g., $100), practicality may support immediate write-off.

Donated fixed assets may be reported as either unrestricted or temporarily restricted income when the asset is received. If the gift is treated as temporarily restricted, the restriction expires proportionately over the useful life of the asset. The expiration is treated as a reclassification from the temporarily restricted to the unrestricted class of net assets. Land, which is not subject to depreciation, continues in the temporarily restricted class indefinitely until sold.

Liabilities

Liabilities are amounts owed to others in money or future services. Some liabilities are discussed below.

Accounts Payable   Amounts owed to suppliers.

Accrued Expenses Payable   Bills owed that will have to be paid (e.g., utilities).

Grants Payable   Applicable to granting agencies for amounts promised but not yet paid.

Unearned Revenue   Revenue received in advance before being earned, such as advance membership fees for three years.

Mortgages Payable   Mortgage on real property such as on a day-care center. Restrictions may be placed on borrowed funds.

Net Assets (Fund Balance)

Net assets (fund balance) equals total assets less total liabilities. Net assets is the net worth of the NPO. "Positive net assets" (credit balance) is a net accumulation of surpluses. "Negative net assets" (debit balance) is a net accumulated deficit.

An appropriation is shown in the Net Assets (Fund Balance) section of the Balance Sheet, as shown below:

Net Assets
Designated by the Board for Project X
Undesignated, available for current purposes
Total

As amounts are expended for Project X, they are recorded as expenses in the Statement of Activities. The amount expended, of course, reduces the appropriated amount.

A simplified balance sheet for an NPO is shown in Exhibit 2.1. A detailed illustrative balance sheet is shown in Exhibit 2.2.

E X H I B I T 2.1

Simplified Balance Sheet

Assets	
Cash	$ 500,000
Accounts Receivable	200,000
Securities	150,000
Land, Building, and Equipment	350,000
Total Assets	$1,200,000
Liabilities	
Accounts Payable	200,000
Notes Payable	50,000
Long-term Debt	100,000
Total Liabilities	$ 350,000
Net Assets	
Unrestricted	400,000
Temporarily Restricted	350,000
Permanently Restricted	100,000
Total Net Assets	$ 850,000
Total Liabilities and Net Assets	$1,200,000

ACCRUAL VERSUS CASH BASIS

There are three bases on which NPOs may keep their records: the accrual basis, the cash basis, and the modified accrual basis. Most small NPOs use the cash basis, but most larger NPOs use the accrual basis. Government NPOs often use the modified accrual basis.

The accrual method recognizes operating and nonoperating transactions not only when cash is impacted but when the NPO is involved in receiving or extending credit. The accrual basis expenditure represents the using up of financial resources for the purchase of goods, services, or other financial resources. An expense constitutes the consuming of goods or services for operating purposes. The accrual basis is ordinarily needed for fair presentation of the financial statements.

The cash basis is often used by NPOs when: (1) no significant difference exists between the cash and the accrual bases, or (2) NPOs spend in the year what they receive as revenue from all sources (there are no significant unpaid bills, nor is there uncollected income).

E X H I B I T 2.2

Balance Sheet
June 30, 19X2

	Unrestricted		Temporarily Restricted	Permanently Restricted	Total
	General Fund	Investment Fund			
Assets					
Current assets:					
Cash	$ 100,000	$ 2,000	$ 21,000	$ 17,000	$ 140,000
Marketable securities, at cost (market value $2,000,000)		300,000	400,000	1,100,000	1,800,000
Contract receivables	$ 40,000				40,000
Inventories of supplies	20,000				20,000
Total current assets	$ 160,000	$302,000	$421,000	$1,117,000	$2,000,000
Fixed assets:					
Fixed assets at cost	$1,500,000				$1,500,000
Less: Accumulated depreciation	(1,000,000)				(1,000,000)
Net fixed assets	$ 500,000				$ 500,000
Total assets	$ 660,000	$302,000	$421,000	$1,117,000	$2,500,000
Liabilities and Net Assets					
Accounts payable	$ 70,000				$ 70,000
Unearned grants revenue	$ 50,000				$ 50,000
Total liabilities	$ 120,000				$ 120,000
Net assets:					
Restricted			$421,000	$1,117,000	$1,538,000
Unrestricted	$ 540,000	$302,000			$ 842,000
Total	$ 660,000	$302,000	$421,000	$1,117,000	$2,380,000
Total liabilities and net assets	$ 660,000	$302,000	$421,000	$1,117,000	$2,500,000

The cash basis is simple. It recognizes and records both operating and nonoperating revenue and expense transactions only when *cash* is received or paid.

Under the modified accrual accounting basis, revenue is recognized when available and measurable. Expenditures are recognized in the period the liability is incurred (accrued) except for:

- Use of encumbrances.
- Interest on general long-term debt, which is recognized when due.
- Inventories of materials and supplies are considered expenditures either when bought or when used.

Under the modified accural basis, unpaid bills are accrued but uncollected income is on the cash basis.

STATEMENT OF ACTIVITIES

The NPO's Statement of Activities is analogous to the Income Statement of a commercial business. The Statement of Activities may also correctly be called by other names, including "Statement of Revenue, Expenses, and Changes in Net Assets," and "Statement of Changes in Net Assets." It shows all the NPO's financial activity over the year.

The "bottom line" of the Statement of Activities is the change in net assets. It may be positive or negative. This is the change in *all* types of net assets (unrestricted, temporarily restricted, and permanently restricted). The change in net assets is the final change after all items of revenue, expense, gain/loss, and reclassification have been shown. This measure includes such items as restricted contributions to the permanent endowment or plant fund contributions which do not reflect operations.

An illustrative columnar Statement of Activities (Statement of Revenue, Expenses, and Changes in Net Assets) is presented in Exhibit 2.3.

For internal management reports or restricted donor purposes, revenue and expenses may be shown by individual funds for greater detail. Also, internal reports may present revenue and expenses by program, service, activity, or function.

Cost allocation is important so that program costs have been fairly determined. An example is personnel costs for workers performing duties on a number of programs.

E X H I B I T 2.3

Statement of Activities
For the Year Ended June 30, 19X2

	Unrestricted	Temporarily Restricted	Permanently Restricted	Total
Income:				
Contributions	$ 42,500	$12,000	$ 12,500	$ 67,000
Contracts	55,000			55,000
Investment income from endowments	10,000			10,000
Gains on sale of investments	20,000		3,000	23,000
Other	6,500			6,500
Total	$134,000	$12,000	$ 15,500	$161,500
Net assets released from restrictions	11,500	(11,500)		
Total income	$145,500	$ 500	$ 15,500	$161,500
Expenses:				
Administration	$ 81,500			$ 81,500
Program services	21,500			21,500
Fund raising	6,000			6,000
Total expenses	$109,000			$109,000
Excess of income over expenses	$ 36,500	$ 500	$ 15,500	$ 52,500
Net assets, beginning of year	28,500	5,000	125,000	158,500
Net assets, end of year	$ 65,000	$ 5,500	$140,500	$211,000

Revenue

Revenue must be spent consistent with regulations, limitations, or restrictions. Revenue is segregated as to restricted and unrestricted. Revenue includes dues and membership fees, admission fees, donations and contributions, grants, contract fees, conference registrations, advertising, sales of publications and merchandise, special event fees, royalties, and investment income.

Membership and subscription fees received in advance are deferred and should be allocated over the years the services will be provided as income. Life membership and initiation fees are prepaid dues and are deferred and allocated over the years services are provided as income. In a large NPO, the initiation fee may be amortized based on the average life expectancy of members. If the initiation fee is not a prepayment, it should be immediately recognized as income.

Revenue from a sponsored event is recorded as earned (when the performance occurs). Revenue must exceed the costs related to the event to earn a profit. The audience must be able to cover the costs (e.g., fund raising, marketing, insurance, rent, and production).

Expenses

FASB 117 requires the reporting of expenses in the unrestricted class of net assets, irrespective of the financing source. Expenses cannot be shown in the temporarily or permanently restricted classes. NPOs must report expenses by functional categories (program, fund-raising, management). Voluntary health and welfare entities must also present expenses by natural categories (e.g., rent, wages, insurance, travel).

Membership development costs are expensed. Straight line depreciation is usually used.

Fund-raising costs include a fair allocation of overhead. Fund-raising costs are recorded as expense as incurred. However, such costs are deferred if the related donor contribution is treated as deferred income and the donor has stipulated that the donation may be used to pay the fund-raising costs to obtain the gift.

Cost control requires program identification and classification. It is easier to control variable costs than fixed costs, because variable costs can be changed whereas fixed costs are constant. It is easier to control direct costs than indirect costs, because their sources are more identifiable. It is easiest to control direct variable costs, because you know exactly what program or service is responsible and you can adjust the costs. The most difficult cost to control is indirect fixed costs.

STATEMENT OF CASH FLOWS

FASB 117 requires the preparation of the Statement of Cash Flows. It shows where the NPO received and used its cash. Cash flows are reported in three sections: operating cash flows, investing cash flows, and financing cash flows (including receipt on nonexpendable contributions). Restricted cash flows are also indicated.

The statement shows the NPO's ability to generate cash flows, and its ability to pay obligations. Cash flows from financing activities will include donor-restricted gifts (e.g., gifts restricted to use in buying equipment or establishing a permanent endowment) of a long-term nature. Also included in the financing activity category is interest and dividend income restricted for long-term purposes. Such items are not included in operating cash flows. Significant noncash investing and financing transactions are disclosed in a supplementary schedule accompanying the statement. An example is a substantial noncash gift such as equipment.

The statement may be prepared under either the direct or indirect methods. The direct method is preferred by the FASB in which NPOs report cash flows from operating activities by major classes of receipts and payments and the resulting net amount. Less preferable, but acceptable, is the indirect method. Here, the NPO reports net cash flows from operating activities indirectly, by adjusting change in net assets (used in place of net income for a commercial business) to net cash flow from operating activities. This method is commonly used by NPOs because it is simpler to prepare.

An illustrative Statement of Cash Flows is presented in Exhibit 2.4.

Supplementary cash-flow data may also be presented. For example, cash inflows may be classified as to (1) estimated or actual, (2) restricted or unrestricted, (3) source (e.g., grant, contribution, loan), and (4) operating or nonoperating. Cash outflows may be classified as to (1) object of expenditure, (2) program or activity, (3) estimated or actual, (4) operating or nonoperating, (5) responsibility center, and (6) restricted or unrestricted.

DISCLOSURES

NPOs should provide disclosures to make the financial statements meaningful and informative. These include unrestricted and restricted revenue by major category or source, amount of gifts, and expenses by type. Related-party transactions should be disclosed, such as when the manager of the NPO also personally owns real estate rented to the NPO.

EXHIBIT 2.4

Statement of Cash Flows
(Indirect Method)

Cash flows from operating activities:	
Change in net assets	$100,000
Adjustments to reconcile change in net assets to net cash used by operating activities:	
Depreciation	10,000
Increase in pledges receivable	(30,000)
Decrease in inventories	20,000
Increase in accounts payable	15,000
Decrease in grants payable	(5,000)
Contributions restricted for long-term investment	(2,000)
Net unrealized and realized gains on long-term investments	(1,000)
Net cash received from operating activities	$107,000
Cash flows from investing activities:	
Purchase of equipment	($ 40,000)
Proceeds from sale of investments	35,000
Net cash flows used by investing activities	($ 5,000)
Cash flows from financing activities:	
Proceeds from restricted contributions to be invested in endowments and equipment	$ 50,000
Long-term loan proceeds	22,000
Payments on long-term debt	(12,000)
Net cash received from financing activities	$ 60,000
Net increase in cash and cash equivalents*	$162,000
Cash and cash equivalents (beginning of year)	80,000
Cash and cash equivalents (end of year)	$242,000
Noncash investing and financing activities:	
Gifts of furniture	$ 16,000

* A cash equivalent is a short-term, highly liquid investment with an initial maturity of three months or less.

SUPPLEMENTARY STATEMENTS

Supplementary (optional) statements include:

- Statement of Changes in Fund Balance.
- Statement of Functional Expenses (optional in some nonprofits but required by voluntary health and welfare agencies). It details expenses by program or support area.

RESTRICTED RESOURCES

Restricted resources may be accounted for either in their own special accounts or in restricted funds. A fund is an accounting entity (it may also be a legal entity) with its own self-balancing set of accounts, including its own ledgers, journals, and so on. Special accounts are used if restricted resources are of no major importance for the NPO. Funds are used if the restricted resources are important, normal, and recurring financing sources.

Under FASB 116, restricted resources are considered used when an expense is incurred that satisfies the donor's restriction, unless the expense is for a reason directly related to another specific outside revenue source.

GRANTS

Grants may have mandates as well as matching requirements. For example, foundation grants are usually restricted. Some NPOs receive grants from third parties for a specific project or activity (e.g., research).

FASB 116 requires that an unconditional pledge be immediately recorded as revenue, not deferred revenue. In the case of an unrestricted grant, advance payments must be immediately recognized as revenue when received. Reimbursement grants are recognized as revenue as reimbursements are due.

Restricted grants should be treated as Deferred Revenue until the restrictions have been satisfied, at which time they are recognized as income. Typically, this occurs when expenses have been incurred.

In an endowment grant, the principal received must be invested to generate current income to fund a specified activity. An example is an "endowed chair" at a college where the grant's principal can never be used but forever invested. Only the interest earned is used to pay the "endowed chair."

CONTRIBUTIONS

FASB 116 provides for the recognition of unrestricted or restricted contributions at fair value regardless of form (e.g., cash, gifts-in-kind, securities) as revenue or gains when received with the concurrent recognition of assets or decrease in liabilities depending on the nature of the benefit received. Unrestricted contributions should be included in the unrestricted class of net assets, while restricted contributions should be included in the temporarily restricted class of net assets. Current restricted contributions can be used to satisfy current expenses even though they are restricted as to use for some specific purpose or some specified time period. Note that restricted contributions are *not* deferred until the restriction is met. Footnote disclosure of the nature of the restriction and the amount of contribution is required. Contributions should also be recorded in the appropriate fund.

Unrestricted contributions should be presented in the unrestricted class of net assets in the Statement of Activities. Contributions preferably should be segregated from service fee income in the following manner:

Service fees	$260,000
Less: Expenses	210,000
Excess of service fees over expenses	$ 50,000
Contributions	80,000
Excess of income over expenses	$130,000

Donor-restricted endowment fund contributions are recognized as revenue when received in either a temporarily or a permanently restricted class of net assets, depending on the term.

Donated materials should be recorded at fair market value.

Volunteer contributed services are recorded both as an expense and as revenue at fair market value if *either* of the following criteria is met.

• The services enhance nonfinancial assets.

• The services are of specialized skill and would normally be paid for if not donated.

If neither of these criteria is met, only footnote disclosures need be made.

Contributed services are presented separately as unrestricted income in the Statement of Activities. Such services should also be allocated to the appropriate program or activity.

FASB 116 allows for alternative accounting policies for unrestricted contributions of *long-lived assets*. Contributions of plant and equipment with no donor restrictions can be accounted for in two ways:

• The entire gift may be treated as unrestricted revenue in the year received.

• A time restriction may be implied that expires over the asset's estimated service life. The gift would be initially recorded as temporarily restricted revenue, and in each year of the asset's useful life, the NPO would reclassify the amount of depreciation for the year from temporarily restricted net assets to unrestricted net assets. In either policy, depreciation is recorded.

If facilities are donated, they should be valued at no more than what the facilities would be worth if rented. Such value should be recorded both as income and as an expense. If the donation is reduced rent, only the excess amount the NPO would normally pay over the reduced rent should be recorded.

A "split-interest" gift is an irrevocable trust or similar arrangement in which the gift is split between the donor and the NPO (e.g., charity).

PLEDGES

A pledge may or may not be legally enforceable. According to FASB 116, an unconditional pledge should be recorded as an asset at fair value when the promise to give is made if the NPO expects to collect upon it. Prior experience helps in making this determination. Pledges due beyond one year must be discounted to their present value using an appropriate interest rate. This interest rate is often the NPO's borrowing rate or the average return rate the NPO earns on its investments. The accretion in value of the discounted pledge receivable should be recorded each year as contribution income.

A pledge received is a legal obligation of the donor if it is in writing, if the NPO spends money relying on receipt of the funds, or if the NPO would suffer economic hardship if the promised funds were not received. However, as a practical matter, the NPO will rarely sue the potential donor for the promise because such a suit would create bad publicity and might hurt future donations from others.

A donor may make a pledge *contingent* on a matching pledge by another. The match need not be equal, it may be a percentage. A conditional pledge should not be accrued until the condition is satisfied. Unrecorded conditional pledges should be footnoted.

An allowance should be recognized for anticipated uncollectible pledges based on past experience and in light of the current economic conditions. If a donor is delinquent on an installment of the promised pledge, an allowance must be established for the *entire* pledged amount, not just the delinquent installment.

A conditional pledge is different from a restriction of how the funds may be used. The donor may stipulate that he will not provide the gift unless some happening occurs. This is conditional. On the other hand, a restriction means the funds donated may only be used for a specified purpose.

FASB 116 considers *all* pledges (short-term and long-term) *time restricted* until collected. As such, time-restricted pledges are presented in the temporarily restricted class of net assets in the balance sheet. When collected, pledges are reclassified to the unrestricted classification of net assets in the balance sheet.

FASB 116 requires that donors use the same guidelines for recognition of the expense of making a gift as recipients do for the income. It is accrued at the time of the unconditional pledge.

BARGAIN PURCHASES OF GOODS OR SERVICES

An NPO may be allowed to buy goods or services at a lower than usual price. In this case, FASB 117 provides that the seller is basically giving the buyer a gift for the difference between the going market value and price charged. For example, a charity buys an item for $800 that sells for $1,000. The purchase should be recorded at $800, with $200 recognized as a contribution.

BEQUESTS

A bequest is a special type of pledge. It is conditional on an uncertain future occurrence that must take place to be payable. Bequests cannot be recorded prior to the donor's death because an individual can always change his or her will and give the NPO (e.g., the charity) nothing.

The bequest should not be treated as a gift until the estate has been probated by the court, so that the amount is known. If an NPO is definitely informed it will receive a bequest of a specific amount (e.g., $200,000), it can record it as an asset. On the other hand, if the NPO is informed that it will receive 20 percent of the estate, the total being unknown, it cannot yet record the asset, but footnote disclosure should be made.

FUND ACCOUNTING

A *fund* is any part of the NPO's assets for which separate accounting records are maintained. A fund meets specified purposes. It may be unrestricted or restricted.

Fund accounting segregates assets, liabilities, net assets (fund balance), revenue, and expenses into several separate entities (classes or funds). Each fund is a self-balancing accounting unit. Each fund may be listed along with a total column for all funds. Different types of NPOs may practice their own versions of fund accounting.

Amounts are categorized based on donor or governing board restrictions to comply with legal requirements and to show management steward-

E X H I B I T 2.5

Current Unrestricted Fund
Statement of Income, Expenses, and Changes in Net Assets

Income:		
Contributions	$100,000	
Service fees	200,000	
Investment income	30,000	
Other income	70,000	
Total income		$400,000
Expenses:		
Administration	$ 90,000	
Program services	110,000	
Fund raising	50,000	
Total expenses		250,000
Excess of income over expenses		$150,000
Net assets (beginning of year)		60,000
Less: Transfer to Plant Fund		(40,000)
Net assets (end of year)		$170,000

ship. Some NPOs break funds down even further by major donor. An example is the endowment fund further subdivided by donor.

Funds may be expendable or nonexpendable. Expendable funds may have all monies spent. Unexpendable funds can usually spend only the income earned, not the principal. An example is an endowment. Endowment income may be unrestricted or restricted.

The major types of funds are described below.

Current Unrestricted Fund (General Fund, Operating Fund)

The funds are used for the general primary operating activities and services of the NPO. There are no restricted resources, and all funds may be used as the board desires to accomplish objectives. All transactions are recorded in this fund, unless another fund is applicable. The fund includes all unrestricted contributions, gifts, and other income. The amount in the fund is reported in the unrestricted class of net assets.

Each fund may be reported in a separate statement. An illustrative Statement of Income, Expenses, and Changes in Net Assets for a current unrestricted fund is shown in Exhibit 2.5.

Current Restricted Fund

The funds are donor-restricted as to use for specified purposes in performing normal activites. This amount is reported in the temporarily restricted class of net assets.

Endowment Fund

A *permanent (perpetual) endowment fund* requires that the principal remain intact, but interest earned may or may not be spent for a specific or general purpose. Net assets of the fund are reported in the permanently restricted class of net assets. The provisions of the endowment must be footnoted.

A *term endowment* allows for the principal to be spent after the passage of time (e.g., after 10 years) or occurrence of a specific event (e.g., the college becomes ranked in the "top 20" in the United States). Net assets are reported in the temporarily restricted class of net assets.

In a *quasi-endowment*, the board rather than the donor has set aside unrestricted amounts to be used as an endowment.

The asset accounts of the endowment fund include cash, permanent investments, real estate, and interfund receivables. Any mortgage on the real estate should be shown separately as a liability.

Illustrative entries in the endowment fund follow.

1. Investments
        Cash—Unrestricted
   For purchase of investment
2. Cash—Unrestricted
   Endowment Fund Principal—Income Unrestricted (for Loss)
        Investments
   For sale of investment at loss

Fixed Asset (Plant) Fund

The fund includes fixed assets (net of accumulated depreciation) used to house the NPO's activities. It includes liabilities associated with the purchase and upkeep of the fixed assets such as accounts payable and mortgage payable. Amounts must be set aside to pay debt service (principal and interest). The fund includes revenue received from third parties specifying it is to be used for plant additions.

The fund includes assets to be improved, renewed, replaced, or for plant expansion. Before actually used to buy or construct fixed assets, the Fixed Asset Fund may include cash, investments, and pledges receivable.

Reclassifications (Transfers)

Reclassifications are often made between net assets (funds). One type of reclassification is the release of temporary restrictions because of the elapse of time or because of satisfaction of a restricted purpose. Another type of reclassification may be for the use of unrestricted resources to meet matching requirements of a grant. Reclassifications are shown after the "Excess of Revenue over Expenses" caption in the Statement of Activities.

ENCUMBRANCES

Encumbrance accounting is designed not to spend more or less than the amount appropriated. It reflects contractual obligations. In an encumbrance, the entity becomes obligated to pay for goods and services. This occurs when a contract is signed, when a purchase order is made, or when personnel work. The entry is to debit Encumbrances and credit Reserve for Encumbrances. When the item is received, this entry is reversed. Expenditures are charged and Cash is credited.

BUDGET RECORDING
AND ACCOUNTABILITY

Budgets are adopted and recorded in the accounts of the applicable fund. Recording both the budget and actual transactions helps assign responsibility. Budgets usually cover both unrestricted resource inflows anticipated to be available and restricted resource inflows expected to become available on an unrestricted basis.

The entry to record the adoption of a budget is:

Estimated Revenues	xx	
Fund Balance	xx	
Appropriations		xx

Estimated Revenues is the authorization to raise funds, while Appropriations are the setting aside of part of fund balance for designated (special) purposes, such as future expenditures. An appropriation is neither an expenditure nor an obligation incurred. It is solely an internal authorization to spend. It is not reported as a liability. The Fund Balance is similar to an equity account.

Estimated Revenues and Appropriations budget lines are itemized by specific sources of revenue and expenditure categories.

The entry to record the closing of the budget is:

Revenues	xx	
Fund Balance	xx	
Appropriations		xx
Estimated Revenues		xx
Expenditures		xx
Encumbrances		xx

Budgetary and actual accounts affect fund balance.

Budgetary information may or may not be incorporated into the financial statements depending upon the circumstances.

AUDITING

An internal audit examines the strengths and weaknesses of the nonprofit entity. Questions to be answered include: Is the staff competent? Is the NPO technologically up-to-date? Are procedures sound? Can the organization change quickly to changing developments? Is the NPO financially viable? Does the NPO break even?

Donor constraints include dollar ceilings on program support, forms of funding, length and timing of funding, application forms and formats, program performance tracking, and like-item costs.

An external audit by a CPA looks at the opportunities and threats critical to the NPO. The audit assures that the financial statements are accurate and that fiduciary responsibilities are being carried out. The audit tests the accounting system, determines the adequacy of internal checks and balances, checks on compliance with proper accounting principles, confirms account balances, and evaluates documentation.

An unqualified audit opinion states that the NPO's financial statements present the balance sheet and operating results fairly. Such an opinion is crucial in fund raising, borrowing, and obtaining grants.

INTERNAL CONTROLS

Internal controls are needed to protect the NPO's assets and assure proper record keeping. Such controls include:

- Duties should be segregated. One person should not be in control of all the major accounting responsibilities. For example, the person having custody of assets should be different from the one handling the record keeping. The one preparing a bank reconciliation should be different from the one keeping the cash books.

- Checks received should be restrictively endorsed upon receipt.
- Checks should be deposited the same day they are received.
- Invoices should be approved before payment.
- *Only* original invoices should be paid to avoid duplication.
- Each invoice should be marked "paid" when the check is prepared.
- Checks should have accompanying documentation.
- Two signatures should be required for large checks.
- Assets should be safeguarded (e.g., proper security should be used).
- Internal control policies and procedures should be documented.
- Supporting documentation should exist for transactions such as deeds for buildings and loan agreements for debt incurrence.
- Authorized levels of staffing and budgeting should exist.
- Policies should be communicated throughout the entity.

ACCOUNTING BY SPECIFIC NONPROFIT ORGANIZATIONS

Voluntary Health and Welfare

Voluntary health and welfare entities have as their principal revenue source voluntary contributions from the public to be spent for general or specific purposes.

Accrual accounting is followed. Revenue is recognized as accrued in the financial statements when the provider has met the contractual terms. Patient service revenue is recognized when services are provided, not when the patient is discharged. Such revenue may be based on per occasion, per case, or per diem. Premium revenue is recognized when coverage is provided to an enrollee in a prepaid health care program. An allowance should be provided for the expected difference between the prevailing rate for covered services and the amounts received from third parties. This net revenue difference is reported in the Statement of Activities. Other operating revenue is indirectly related to patient services (e.g., gift shop, cafeteria, tuition from education, parking fees, research grants). Nonoperating gains and losses are incidental transactions to operations such as investment income, unrestricted income from endowment funds, general contributions, and rental income. Expenses must be reported by functional categories such as program, management, and fund raising. A Statement of Functional Expenses is required. Salaries are allocated to programs based on time reports. Rent, utilities, and maintenance are allocated based on floor space. Fund-raising expenses include direct costs and indirect costs (allocated overhead). Fund-raising costs are recognized as incurred. Another expense accrued, bad debts, should be shown as a separate item. Depreciation expense should also be recorded. Expected malpractice claims should be accrued.

Receivables from patients involves a patient record including date of admission and discharge, balance due, charges, credits, itemization of services rendered, and medical information. The balance due may be paid in full by the patient but in most cases will be paid mostly by the third-party insurance company. The billing procedure and the amount received vary with the insurance carrier (e.g., Medicare, Medicaid, Blue Cross/Blue Shield, and Health Insurance Plan [HIP]). Thus, it is advisable for there to be a subsidiary ledger for patient receivables, depending on source of payment, which can be a private insurance carrier, Blue Cross/Blue Shield, Medicare, or Medicaid.

The entry to bill a patient is:

Inpatient Receivables	xx	
Revenue from Patient Services		xx

The entry to record a reduction in rate due to a contractual stipulation follows:

Contractual Adjustments	xx	
Inpatient Receivables—Group Health Insurance (GHI)		xx

Footnote disclosure should be made for charity care.

College or University

Fund accounting is used by colleges and universities. Accrual accounting is followed. Funds used by colleges include:

• *Current funds.* Funds available for the primary educational operations of the institution. Such funds may be unrestricted (e.g., tuition, student fees) or restricted. Current restricted funds must be used for donor-designated purposes and are included in the temporarily restricted class of net assets. Restricted funds usually come from gifts, grants, and contracts.

• *Endowment funds*. Discussed previously, in the "Fund Accounting" section.

• *Plant funds*. Funds for building, restoring, or buying physical properties, such as a new building for classrooms. Included in this category are unexpended, renewal and replacement, retirement of debt, and investment-in-plant.

• *Loan funds*. Monies loaned to students, faculty, and staff. Repayment of principal and interest paid are returned to the fund and again made available. Interest earned on the loan funds is used to pay expenses associated with the loans, including bad debts.

• *Agency or custodian funds*. Funds held by the college but not legally owned by it. The college is acting as an agent for others to collect, maintain custody, or disburse assets. An example is student organization fees held by the institution.

• *Annuity and life income funds*. Principal and *not* current income earned is given to the college. The donor keeps the income for a stated time period. Income is funds received from gifts or bequests providing life income to a beneficiary (or beneficiaries), or income from living trusts or annuities. In an *annuity fund*, the college must pay a specified amount. In a *life income fund*, the college will only pay the income earned by the assets of the fund.

Colleges can record investments at cost or at market value. If cost is used, market value must be footnoted. Fixed assets must be depreciated.

Tuition received in advance is credited to Unearned Revenue. Expenses should be shown by function, program, or activity.

Control accounts in the general ledger are supported by subsidiary accounts in the subsidiary ledger showing detail information so as to better manage and control the college's activities and to comply with laws, regulations, gifts, and grants.

Library

If library books are recorded as assets, they should be depreciated. Books decline in value because they become out of date. A 3- to 10-year life might be appropriate. An exception is a rare-book collection which retains or increases in value. However, a rare-book collection should be retained at cost, *not* written up.

Religious Institution

Most religious institutions (e.g., churches, synagogues) report on the cash or the modified cash basis. Support is in the form of contributions directly from the membership. Fixed assets and depreciation are recorded.

Performing Arts

The major source of revenue is ticket sales. Ticket revenue should be recorded as *earned* when the performance occurs. Advance ticket sales are deferred revenue and recognized as revenue when the show occurs. Revenue from "season ticket sales" and subscriptions should be prorated over the performances subscribed to. Contributions are received to support the organization.

Production costs should be deferred until the performance takes place, at which time the costs are matched against the revenue obtained from the show. However, if a loss is expected from the future performance, the loss should be recognized immediately, based on conservatism. Thus, the only costs to be deferred are those expected to be recovered from the future revenue.

Costumes and stage scenery should be recorded as assets if the production will be given again the next season or in subsequent seasons. These items should then be charged to fixed assets and depreciated. If the production is just for this season, which is usually the case, the costumes and stage scenery should be expensed in the current year.

A typical financial statement presentation follows:

Ticket sales		$600,000
Less: Expenses		
Production costs	$300,000	
Administration and general	100,000	
Total expenses		400,000
Income from operations		$200,000
Contribution income, net of fund-raising costs of $30,000		120,000
Excess for the year		$320,000

The accounting period should preferably be the end of the season.

Community Service

A community service organization presents as revenue service fees, grants, membership dues, contributions, dividends, and interest. Expenses are reported by program and by supporting service (e.g., general management, fund raising, and membership development).

Professional Society or Association

A professional society has separate sections, groups, or local units operating within specified geographical regions or within particular disciplines. These limits operate autonomously but are legally part of the main organization.

Fraternity

A fraternity collects dues, recruits members, socializes, and caters to the needs of the college student. Revenue includes membership fees, donations, college support funds, endowment income, and investment income. Expenses include food, rent, insurance, property taxes, stationery, postage, utilities, social events and entertainment, repairs and maintenance, salaries (e.g., for the chef), uncollectible membership fees (bad debts), fund-raising expenses, newsletters, uniforms, registration fees for conferences, travel, tournament fees, and supplies.

Private Foundation

A private foundation is mostly supported through endowment income. These foundations usually do not solicit funds from the general public.

Many foundations give awards payable in installments over a number of years. Often, future payments are contingent on satisfactory performance or on compliance with contractual arrangements.

Grants should be recorded as expenses and liabilities when recipients are entitled to them. This is typically at the time the grant is awarded. Grants payable in future years subject to routine performance requirements by the grantee and not requiring later appraisal and approval for continuance should be recorded as expenses and liabilities when the grants are first made. However, if a foundation has not made a final determination on future payments, these future grants should not be recorded.

Museum

Museums typically do *not* record their collections as assets. The cost or contributed value of the works should be reported in the financial statements or footnotes. Except for collections, museums should record fixed assets and depreciation.

Research and Scientific

Contract revenue is recorded when the contract terms are satisfied. This is usually when expenses incurred can be charged to the contract. Unrestricted grant revenue is recorded proportionately over the period the grant stipulates. If a grant is received in advance, it should be credited to Deferred Grant Revenue in the balance sheet. If the grant is paid in arrears, a Receivable account should be established when revenue is being recognized, since grant payment is due. Future grants should not be recorded. If the grantor, however, makes the grant *unconditional* and legally enforceable, and only the passage of time is the condition, a Receivable and Deferred Grant Revenue may be recorded.

CHAPTER 3*

Break-Even and Cost-Volume-Revenue Analysis

The Salvation Army, one of most efficient nonprofits in the state, keeps costs down largely because its officers are not paid. The officers are pastors. This is their calling in life, and they aren't paid a salary.

Christy Ziemba
Public-Relations Director for the Salvation Army
Denver Business Journal, *December 2, 1994*

By definition, the goal of a nonprofit entity is *not* to earn a profit. The NPO's objective is to render as much suitable service as possible, with as little human and physical services as needed. Ideally, the performance in a nonprofit organization is to break even. This means that, by and large and on a short-term basis, revenues should equal costs. If you generate a surplus, a possibility is that you may not receive the same amount from the funding agency as last year. On the other hand, if you produce a deficit, you may run into insolvency, a danger for survival. Chances are that you may not be able to borrow money from the bank, as not-for-profit entities often can, because of your weak financial stance. One thing is clear; over the long run, nonprofit entities cannot survive without reserves and cannot sustain persistent deficits.

Cost-volume-revenue (CVR) analysis, together with cost behavior information, helps nonprofit managers perform many useful analyses. CVR analysis deals with how revenue and costs change with a change in

---

*Throughout the book, the symbol appears where the reader is referred to material on the diskette.

the service level. More specifically, it looks at the effects on revenues of changes in such factors as variable costs, fixed costs, prices, service level, and mix of services offered. By studying the relationships of costs, service volume, and revenue, nonprofit management is better able to cope with many planning decisions.

Break-even analysis, a branch of CVR analysis, determines the break-even service level. The break-even point—the financial crossover point where revenues exactly match costs—does not show up in financial reports, but nonprofit financial managers find it an extremely useful measurement in a variety of ways. It reveals which programs are self-supporting and which are subsidized.

QUESTIONS ANSWERED BY CVR ANALYSIS

CVR analysis tries to answer the following questions:

1. What service level is (or what units of service are) required to break even?
2. How would changes in price, variable costs, fixed costs, and service volume affect a surplus?
3. How do changes in program levels and mix affect aggregate surplus/deficit?
4. What alternative break-even strategies are available?

Analysis of Revenues

Revenues for nonprofit entities are typically classified into the following categories:

- Grants from governments.
- Grants from private sources.
- Cost reimbursements and sales.
- Membership fees.
- Public contributions received directly or indirectly.
- Legacies and memorials.
- Other revenues such as investment income (e.g., interest, dividends).

For managerial purposes, however, each type of revenue is grouped into its fixed and variable parts. Fixed revenues are those that remain unchanged regardless of the level of service, such as gifts, grants, and contracts., In colleges, for example, donations, gifts, and grants have no relationship to enrollment. Variable revenues are the ones that vary in proportion to the volume of activity. Examples are cost reimbursements and membership fees. In colleges, tuition and fees are variable in relation to the number of students. Different nonprofit entities may have different sources of revenue: variable revenue only, fixed revenue only, or a combination of both. In this chapter, we will cover all three cases in treating break-even and CVR questions.

Analysis of Cost Behavior

For external reporting purposes, costs are classified by managerial function (such as payroll, occupancy, and office) and also by programs and supporting services. A model functional classification is IRS Form 990 Part II—Statement Of Functional Expenses, an excerpt from which is shown below.

IRS Form 990 Line No.	Functional expense category
26	Salaries and wages
27	Pension plan contributions
28	Other employee benefits
29	Payroll taxes
30	Professional fundraising fees
31	Accounting fees
32	Legal fees
33	Supplies
34	Telephone
35	Postage and shipping
36	Occupancy
37	Equipment rental and maintenance
38	Printing and publications
39	Travel
40	Conferences, conventions, meetings
41	Interest
42	Depreciation, depletion, etc.
43	Other expenses (itemize)

For managerial purposes (such as planning, control, and decision making), further classification of costs is desirable. One such classification is by behavior. Depending on how a cost will react or respond to changes in the level of activity, costs may be viewed as variable or fixed. This classification is made within a specified range of activity, called the "relevant range." The relevant range is the volume zone within which the behavior of variable costs, fixed costs, and prices can be predicted with reasonable accuracy.

Typical activity measures are summarized below.

Measures of the Service Level

Nonprofit Types	Units of Service
Hospital or health care	Bed-days, patient contact-hours, patient-days, service-hours
Educational	Number of enrollments, class size, full-time equivalent (FTE) hours
Social clubs	Number of members served

Variable Costs

Variable costs vary in total with changes in volume or level of activity. Examples of variable costs include supplies, printing and publications, telephone, and postage and shipping.

Fixed Costs

Fixed costs do not change in total, regardless of the volume or level of activity. Examples include salaries, accounting and consulting fees, and depreciation.

The following table shows the fixed/variable breakdown of IRS Form 990 functional expenses.

IRS Form 990 Line No	Expense Category
Fixed Costs	
26	Salaries and wages
27	Pension plan
28	Other benefits
29	Payroll taxes
30	Fund-raising fees
31	Accounting fees
32	Legal fees

IRS Form 990 Line No	Expense Category
36	Occupancy
37	Equipment rental/maintenance
41	Interest
42	Depreciation
43	Other
Variable Costs	
33	Supplies
34	Telephone
35	Postage and shipping
38	Printing and publications
39	Travel
40	Conferences, meetings
43	Other

Types of Fixed Costs—Program-Specific or Common

Fixed costs of nonprofit entities are subdivided into two groups. Direct or program-specific fixed costs are those that can be directly identified with individual programs. These costs are avoidable or escapable if the program is dropped. Examples include the salaries of the staff whose services can be used only in a given program, and depreciation of equipment used exclusively for the program. Common fixed costs would continue even if an individual program were discontinued.

CVR ANALYSIS WITH VARIABLE REVENUE ONLY

For accurate CVR analysis, a distinction must be made between costs as either variable or fixed. In order to compute the break-even point and perform various CVR analyses, note the following important concepts.

Contribution Margin (CM)   The contribution margin is the excess of revenue (R) over the variable costs (VC) of the service. It is the amount of money available to cover fixed costs (FC) and to generate surplus. Symbolically, $CM = R - VC$.

Unit CM   The unit CM is the excess of the unit price (P) over the unit variable cost (V). Symbolically, unit $CM = P - V$.

CM Ratio   The CM ratio is the contribution margin as a percentage of revenue, i.e.,

$$\text{CM ratio} = \frac{CM}{R} = \frac{R - VC}{R} = 1 - \frac{VC}{R}$$

The CM ratio can also be computed using per-unit data as follows:

$$\text{CM ratio} = \frac{\text{Unit CM}}{P} = \frac{P - V}{P} = 1 - \frac{V}{P}$$

Note that the CM ratio is 1 minus the variable cost ratio. For example, if variable costs are 40 percent of revenue, then the variable cost ratio is 40 percent and the CM ratio is 60 percent.

EXAMPLE 3.1

To illustrate the various concepts of CM, assume that Los Altos Community Hospital has an average revenue of $250 per patient-day. Variable costs are $50 per patient-day. Total fixed costs per year are $650,000. Expected number of patient-days is 4,000. The projected statement of revenue and expenditures follows.

	Total	Per Unit	Percentage
Revenue (4,000 days)	$1,000,000	$250	100%
Less: Variable costs	200,000	50	20
Contribution margin	$ 800,000	$200	80%
Less: Fixed costs	650,000		
Net income	$ 150,000		

From the data listed above, CM, unit CM, and the CM ratio are computed as:

$$CM = R - VC = \$1,000,000 - \$200,000 = \$8,000$$
$$\text{Unit CM} = P - V = \$250 - \$50 - \$200$$
$$\text{CM ratio} = \frac{CM}{R} = \frac{\$800,000}{\$1,000,000} = 1 - \frac{\$200,000}{\$1,000,000}$$
$$= 0.8 = 80\%$$
$$\text{or} = \frac{\text{Unit CM}}{P} = \frac{\$200}{\$250} = 0.8 = 80\%$$

BREAK-EVEN ANALYSIS

The break-even point represents the level of revenue that equals the total of the variable and the fixed costs for a given volume of output service at a particular capacity use rate. Generally, the lower the break-even point, the higher the surplus and the less the operating risk, other things being equal. The break-even point also provides nonprofit managers with insights into surplus/deficit planning. To develop the formula for the break-even units of service, use the following variables:

R = Total revenue
P = Price or average revenue per unit
U = Units of service
VC = Total variable costs
V = Unit variable cost
FC = Total fixed costs

To break even means: Total revenue – total costs = 0

$$R - VC - FC = 0 \quad \text{or} \quad PU - VU - FC = 0$$

To solve, factor U out to get $(P - V)U - FC = 0$. Rearrange as $(P - V)U = FC$ and divide by $(P - V)$ to isolate U.

$$U = \frac{FC}{(P - V)}$$

In words,

$$\text{Break-even point in units} = \frac{\text{Fixed costs}}{\text{Unit CM}}$$

If you want break-even point in dollars, use

$$\text{Break-even point in dollars} = \frac{\text{Fixed Costs}}{\text{CM ratio}}$$

EXAMPLE 3.2

Using the same data as given in Example 1, where unit CM = $250 – $50 = $200 and CM ratio = 80%, we get:

Break-even point in units = $650,000/$200 = 3,250 patient-days
Break-even point in dollars = $650,000/0.8 = $812,500

Or, alternatively,

3,250 patient-days × $250 = $812,500.

The hospital needs 3,250 patient-days to break even.

F I G U R E   3.1

Break-Even Chart

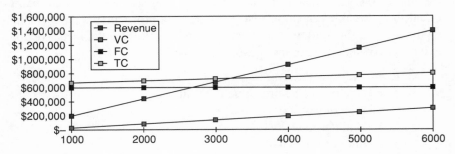

Graphical Approach in a Spreadsheet Format

The graphical approach to obtaining the break-even point is based on the so-called *break-even (B-E) chart,* as shown in Figure 3.1. Sales revenue, variable costs, and fixed costs are plotted on the vertical axis while volume, x, is plotted on the horizontal axis. The break-even point is the point where the total revenue line intersects the total cost line. The chart can effectively report surplus potentials over a wide range of activity and therefore can be used as a tool for discussion and presentation.

The *surplus-volume (S-V) chart,* as shown in Figure 3.2, focuses on how surplus varies with changes in volume. Surplus is plotted on the vertical axis, while units of output are shown on the horizontal axis. The S-V chart provides a quick condensed comparison of how alternatives on pricing, variable costs, or fixed costs may affect surplus (or deficit) as volume changes. The S-V chart can be easily constructed from the B-E chart. Note that the slope of the chart is the unit CM.

Determination of Target Surplus Volume

Besides determining the break-even point, CVR analysis determines the volume to attain a particular level of surplus. The formula is:

$$\text{Target surplus level} = \frac{\text{Fixed costs plus target surplus}}{\text{Unit CM}}$$

FIGURE 3.2

Surplus-Volume (S-V) Chart

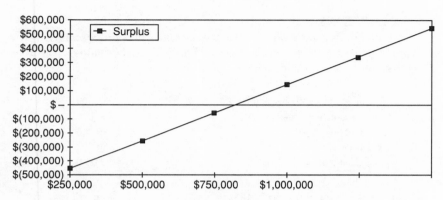

EXAMPLE 3.3

Using the same data as given in Example 3.1, assume the hospital wishes to accumulate a surplus of $250,000 per year. Then, the target surplus service level would be:

$$\frac{\$650,000 + \$250,000}{\$250 - \$50} = \frac{\$900,000}{\$200} = 4,500 \text{ patient-days}$$

Margin of Safety

The margin of safety is a measure of difference between the actual level of service and the break-even service level. It is the amount by which revenue may drop before deficits begin, and is expressed as a percentage of expected service level:

$$\text{Margin of safety} = \frac{\text{Expected level} - \text{Break-even level}}{\text{Expected level}}$$

The margin of safety is used as a measure of operating risk. The larger the ratio, the safer the situation since there is less risk of reaching the break-even point.

EXAMPLE 3.4

Assume that Los Altos Hospital projects 4,000 patient-days with a break-even level of 3,250. The projected margin of safety is

$$\frac{4,000 - 3,250}{4,000} = 18.75\%$$

EXAMPLE 3.5

A nonprofit college offers a program in management for executives. The program has been experiencing financial difficulties. Operating data for the most recent year are shown below.

Tuition revenue (40 participants @$7,000)	$280,000
Less variable expenses (@$4,000)	160,000
Contribution margin	$120,000
Less fixed expenses	150,000
Operating deficit	$(30,000)

The break-even point is $150,000/($7,000 − $4,000) = 50 participants.

EXAMPLE 3.6

In Example 3.5, the dean of the school is convinced that the class size can be increased to more economical levels without lowering the quality. He is prepared to spend $15,000 per year in additional promotional and other support expenses. If that is the case, the new break-even point is 55 participants ($165,000/($7,000 − $4,000)).

To generate a surplus of $30,000, the school must get 60 participants [($150,000 + $30,000)/$3,000].

Some Applications of CVR Analysis and What-If Analysis

The concepts of contribution margin and the contribution income statement have many applications in surplus/deficit planning and short-term decision making. Many "what-if" scenarios can be evaluated using them as planning tools, especially utilizing a spreadsheet program such as Microsoft Excel or Lotus 1-2-3. Some applications are illustrated below, using the same data as in Example 3.1.

EXAMPLE 3.7

Recall from Example 3.1 that Los Altos Hospital has unit CM = $250–$50 = $200, CM ratio = 80%, and fixed costs of $650,000. Assume that the hospital expects revenues to go up by $250,000 for the next period. How much will surplus increase?

Using the CM concepts, we can quickly compute the impact of a change in the service level on surplus or deficit. The formula for computing the impact is:

Change in surplus = Dollar change in revenue × CM ratio

Thus:

Increase in surplus = \$250,000 × 80% = \$200,000

Therefore, the income will go up by \$200,000, assuming there is no change in fixed costs. If we are given a change in service units (e.g., patient-days) instead of dollars, then the formula becomes:

Change in surplus = Change in units × Unit CM

EXAMPLE 3.8

Assume that the hospital expects patient-days to go up by 500 units. How much will surplus increase? From Example 3.1, the hospital's unit CM is \$200. Again, assuming there is no change in fixed costs, the surplus will increase by \$100,000, as computed below:

500 additional patient-days × \$200 CM per day = \$100,000

EXAMPLE 3.9

Referring back to Example 3.5, another alternative under consideration is to hold the present program without any change in the regular campus facilities instead of in rented outside facilities that are better located. If adopted, this proposal will reduce fixed costs by \$60,000. The variable costs will decrease by \$100 per participant. Is the move to campus facilities advisable if it leads to a decline in the number of participants by five?

	Present		**Proposed**
S(40 × \$7,000)	\$280,000	(35 × \$7,000)	\$245,000
VC(40 × \$4,000)	160,000	(35 × \$3,900)	136,500
CM	120,000		\$108,500
FC	150,000		90,000
Surplus	\$(30,000)		\$ 18,500

The answer is yes, since the move will turn into a surplus.

CVR Analysis with Variable and Fixed Revenues

Many nonprofit organizations derive two types of revenue: fixed and variable. In this situation, the formulas developed previously need to be modified. The following example illustrates this.

EXAMPLE 3.10

ACM, Inc., a mental rehabilitation provider, has a $1,200,000 lump-sum annual budget appropriation to help rehabilitate mentally ill clients. The agency charges each client $600 a month for board and care. All the appropriation must be spent. The variable costs for rehabilitation activity average $700 per patient per month. The agency's annual fixed costs are $800,000. The agency manager wishes to know how many clients can be served.

Let:

U = units of service = number of clients to be served

We set up:

Total revenue − Total expenses = 0
Lump sum appropriation + R − VC − FC = 0
Lump sum appropriation + PU − VC − FC = 0

$$\$1,200,000 + \$7,200\ U - \$8,400\ U - \$800,000 = 0$$
$$(\$7,200 - \$8,400)U = \$800,000 - \$1,200,000$$
$$-\$1,200\ U = -\$400,000$$
$$U = \$400,000/\$1,200$$
$$U = 333\ \text{clients}$$

Alternatively, you may use the following formula:

$$\text{Break-even point in units} = \frac{\text{Fixed costs} - \text{Fixed revenue}}{\text{Unit CM}}$$

Thus,

$$\text{Break-even number of patients} = \frac{\$800,000 - \$1,200,000}{-\$1,200}$$
$$= \$400,000/\$1,200 = 333\ \text{clients}$$

We will investigate the following two "what-if" scenarios:

EXAMPLE 3.11

In Example 3.10, suppose the manager of the agency is concerned that the total budget for the coming year will be cut by 10 percent to $1,080,000. All other things remain unchanged. The manager wants to know how this budget cut affects the next year's service level. Using the formula yields:

$$\text{Break-even number of clients} = \frac{\$800,000 - \$1,080,000}{-\$1,200}$$
$$U = -\$280,000/-\$1,200$$
$$U = 233\ \text{clients}$$

EXAMPLE 3.12

In Example 3.10, the manager does not reduce the number of clients served despite a budget cut of 10 percent. All other things remain unchanged. How much more does he or she have to charge clients for board and care? We let V = board and care charge per year and set up:

$1,200,000 + $7,200 U – $8,400 U – $800,000 = 0

($7,200 – $8,400)U = $800,000 – $1,200,000

–$1,200 U = –$4,000,000

U = $400,000/$1,200

U = 333 clients

$1,080,000 + 333V – $8,400(333) – $800,000 = 0

333V = $2,797,200 + $800,000 – $1,080,000

333V = $2,517,200

V = $2,517,200/333 clients

V = $7,559

Thus, the monthly board and care charge must be increased to $630 (7,559/ 12 months).

Use of Spreadsheet Software

"What-If" scenarios can be easily analyzed using popular spreadsheet software such as Microsoft Excel, Lotus 1-2-3, or QuattroPro. Examples 3.11 and 3.12 are illustrated in 03-EX-11.XLS and 03-EX-12.XLS, using the GoalSeek command (see Appendix D). For example, in Excel, you find this command under Tools Bar.

CVR Analysis with Fixed Revenue Only

Some nonprofit entities may have only one source of revenue, typically a government budget appropriation. In this case, the break-even formula becomes:

$$\text{Break-even point in units} = \frac{\text{Fixed revenue} - \text{Fixed costs}}{\text{Unit variable cost}}$$

EXAMPLE 3.13

A social service agency has a government budget appropriation of $750,000. The agency's main mission is to assist handicapped people who are unable to seek or hold jobs. On the average, the agency supplements each individual's income by $6,000 annually. The agency's fixed costs are

$150,000. The agency CEO wishes to know how many people could be served in a given year. The break-even point can be computed as follows:

$$\frac{\$750,000 - \$150,000}{\$6,000} = 100$$

EXAMPLE 3.14
In Example 3.13, assume that the CEO is concerned that the total budget for the year will be reduced by 10 percent to a new amount of 90%($750,000) = $675,000. The new break-even point is:

$$\frac{\$675,000 - \$150,000}{\$6,000} = 88 \text{ (rounded)}$$

The CEO has the options of cutting the budget in one or more of three ways: (1) cut the service level, as computed above, (2) reduce the variable cost, the supplement per person, and (3) seek to cut down on the total fixed costs.

PROGRAM MIX ANALYSIS

Previously, our main concern was to determine program-specific break-even volume. But as we are aware, most nonprofit companies are involved in multiservice, multiprogram activities. One major concern is how to plan aggregate break-even volume, surplus, and deficits. Break-even analysis and cost-volume-revenue analysis require additional computations and assumptions when an organization offers more than one program. In multiprogram organizations, program mix is an important factor in calculating an overall break-even point. Different rates and different variable costs result in different unit CMs. As a result, break-even points and cost-volume-revenue relationships vary with the relative proportions of the programs offered, called the *program mix*.

When the product is defined as a package, the multiprogram problem is converted into a single-program problem. The first step is to determine the number of packages that need to be served to break even. The following example illustrates a multiprogram, multiservice situation.

EXAMPLE 3.15
The Cypress Counseling Services is a nonprofit agency offering two programs: psychological counseling (PC) and alcohol addiction control (AAC). The agency charges individual clients an average of $10 per hour of counseling provided under the PC program. The local Chamber of Commerce reimburses the company at the rate of $20 per hour of direct service provided

under the AAC program. The nonprofit agency believes that this billing variable rate is low enough to be affordable for most clients and also high enough to derive clients' commitment to the program objectives. Costs of administering the two programs are given below.

	PC	AAC
Variable costs	$4.6	$11.5
Direct fixed costs	$120,000	$180,000

There are other fixed costs that are common to the two programs, including general and administrative and fund raising, of $255,100 per year. The projected surplus for the coming year, segmented by programs, follows:

	PC	AAC	Total
Revenue	$ 500,000	$ 800,000	$1,300,000
Program mix in hours	(50,000)	(40,000)	
Less: VC	(230,000)	(460,000)	(690,000)
Contribution margin	$ 270,000	$ 340,000	$ 610,000
Less: Direct FC	(120,000)	(180,000)	(300,000)
Program margin	$ 150,000	$ 160,000	$ 310,000
Less: Common FC			(255,100)
Surplus			$ 54,900

First, based on program-specific data on the rates, the variable costs, and the program mix, we can compute the package (aggregate) value as follows:

Program	P	V	Unit CM	Mix*	Package CM
PC	$10	$ 4.6	$5.4	5	$27
AAC	20	11.5	8.5	4	34
Package total					$61

*The mix ratio is 5:4 (50,000 hours for PC and 40,000 hours for AAC).

We know that the total fixed costs for the agency are $555,100. Thus, the package (aggregate) break-even point is

$$\frac{\$555,100}{\$61} = 9,100 \text{ packages}$$

The agency must provide 45,500 hours of PC (5 x 9,100) and 36,400 hours of AAC (4 x 9,100) to avoid a deficit. To prove:

	PC	AAC	Total
Revenue	$ 455,000[a]	$ 728,000[b]	$1,183,000
Program mix in hours	(45,500)	(36,400)	
Less: VC	(209,300)[c]	(418,600)[d]	(627,900)
Contribution margin	$ 245,700	$ 309,400	$ 555,100
Less: Direct FC	(120,000)	(180,000)	(300,000)
Program margin	$ 125,700	$ 129,400	$ 255,100
Less: Common FC			(255,100)
Surplus			$ 0

[a]45,500 × $10   [c]45,500 × $4.60
[b]36,400 × $20   [d]36,400 × $11.50

EXAMPLE 3.16

Assume in Example 3.15 that 56,000 hours of PC services are budgeted for the next period. The agency wants to know how many hours of AAC services are necessary during that period to avoid an overall deficit. Again, once a spreadsheet is set up properly (as shown in 03-EX-16.XLS), we can answer the question using the GoalSeek command. The answer is 29,729 hours.

MANAGEMENT OPTIONS

Cost-volume-revenue analysis is useful as a frame of reference, as a vehicle for expressing overall managerial performance, and as a planning device via break-even techniques and "what-if" scenarios. In many practical situations, management will have to resort to a combination of approaches to reverse a deficit, including:

1. Selected changes in volume of activity.
2. Planned savings in fixed costs at all levels.
3. Some savings in variable costs.
4. Additional fund drives or grant seeking.
5. Upward adjustments in pricing.
6. Cost reimbursement contracts.

All these approaches will have to be mixed to form a feasible planning package. Many nonprofit managements fail to develop such analytical approaches to the economics of their operations. Further, the accounting system is not designed to provide information to investigate cost-volume-revenue relations.

CHAPTER 4

Financial Statement Analysis and Avoiding Financial Distress

In analyzing the financial statements of an NPO, do the following:

- Appraise the balance sheet for financial position and flexibility.
- Analyze the Statement of Activities for operating performance.
- Evaluate the Statement of Cash Flows for cash position.
- Refer to footnote information.
- Evaluate the auditor's opinion.
- Review internal documents related to financial health.
- Review budgets to determine whether plans are practical and to assess future directions.

Financial statement analysis reveals how well the NPO did in meeting its targets. Interrelated ratios reveal the NPO's financial standing and areas of financial trouble. Each ratio should be compared over the years to a trend, to an industry norm (e.g., a health care standard ratio), and to comparable NPOs to obtain a *relative* standing. Ratios vary depending on the service provided, the complexity of operations, funding sources, and donor restrictions.

A cost/benefit analysis should be undertaken for new programs. Risk/return analysis is also essential.

When evaluating the service efforts of an NPO, look to see how much of every dollar goes to the primary mission as opposed to the fund raiser's commissions and the executive director's salary. Carefully monitor the relationship of supporting services to program services expenses.

Financial statement analysis is undertaken by those working within the NPO, such as managers and outsiders evaluating the NPO's financial statements. Financial statement preparers are provided with "red flags" as to impending financial problems that need to be identified and corrected. Areas of strength are also identified and taken further advantage of. Financial statement users include resource providers such as contributors and grantors, who want to know how well their funds are being spent for the purposes solicited. Financial statements reveal this fiduciary trust. Further, donors do not want to pour money into a sinking ship. Suppliers and loan officers analyze the financial statements to determine whether to give credit, and if so, how much and for what time period. Companies and government (federal and local) agencies awarding contracts appraise financial statements as to whether contractual provisions are being adhered to. Government regulators (watchdogs) evaluate the financial statements to ascertain whether compliance is being made to prescribed regulations and limitations. An NPO serves the public, so concerned citizens may want to analyze the financial statements to determine whether service goals are being met.

A case study, presented at the end of this chapter, analyzes a nonprofit organization, including trend analysis, ratio computations, and analytical evaluation.

TREND ANALYSIS

Trend (horizontal) analysis is a time series analysis of financial statements of the NPO, covering more than one accounting period. It looks at the percentage change in an account or category over time. The percentage change equals the change over the prior year. For example, if salaries expense increased from $140,000 to $165,000 from 19X1 to 19X2, the percentage increase is 18 percent ($25,000 ÷ $140,000). The reason (or reasons) for such an increase should be determined. Does the increase indicate more staff were needed because operations improved, or does it indicate a lack of cost control, or is there some other cause? Is the situation an unfavorable one requiring management attention? By evaluating the magnitude of direction of a financial statement item over the years, the analyst can appraise its reasonableness.

EXAMPLE 4.1
Membership fee revenue declined from $100,000 to $80,000 over the last year. The percentage decline equals:

$$\frac{\text{Amount of Change}}{\text{Base Year Amount}} = \frac{\$20,000}{\$100,000} = 20\%$$

Why such a significant decline in membership fees? Is this a problem peculiar just to this NPO, or does it affect all NPOs in the industry? Is the problem controllable or uncontrollable by management? Is the decline due to dissatisfaction among members of the NPO, who object to its policies, or was it caused by overall poor economic conditions? Trend analysis reveals direction, positive or negative, requiring further study of the causes. The decline may indicate a problem requiring corrective action.

ANALYSIS OF THE BALANCE SHEET

An evaluation of the balance sheet considers the NPO's liquidity, asset utilization, solvency, financial flexibility, and capital structure. Assets, liabilities, and fund balance must be scrutinized. Book values may be used for ratio computations, and market values may be used to express current values.

Liquidity Analysis

FASB 117 requires NPOs to present information about their liquidity. Liquidity is the ability of the NPO to pay current debts as they come due. Liquidity is how fast the NPO's assets turn into *cash*. A liquid asset has less risk than an illiquid one. In evaluating liquidity, exclude restricted funds because they are unavailable for use.

Liquidity considers the seasonality of cash flows. Wide fluctuations in cash flows may result in a liquidity problem.

Working Capital   Working capital equals current assets less current liabilities. The higher the working capital amount, the better the liquidity.

Current Ratio   The current ratio is a measure of liquidity equal to:

$$\text{Current Ratio} = \frac{\text{Current Assets}}{\text{Current Liabilities}}$$

Current assets are those assets to be converted to cash within one year or within the normal operating cycle of the NPO, whichever is greater. Current liabilities are due within one year.

In general, the current ratio should be a minimum of 2 : 1. A low ratio means poor liquidity.

An excessively high ratio may also be a negative sign because it may indicate too much money is being tied up in current assets rather than invested in noncurrent assets for a higher return.

A limitation of the current ratio is that not all current assets have the same degree of liquidity. For example, accounts receivable is more liquid than inventories of supplies. Prepaid expenses (e.g., prepaid advertising) are not redeemable for cash but rather are prepayments for future benefit.

Current unrestricted assets include cash and cash equivalents (marketable securities), accounts receivable, grants receivable, notes receivable, inventories of supplies, and prepaid expenses. Current unrestricted liabilities include accounts payable, prepaid services, and the current portion of mortgage payable.

$$\frac{\text{Current Ratio for Unrestricted}}{\text{Current Assets and Current Liabilities}} = \frac{\text{Current Unrestricted Assets}}{\text{Current Unrestricted Liabilties}}$$

Temporarily restricted assets should also be considered. An example is Pledges Receivable arising from gifts to finance operating activities. However, another type of Pledges Receivable exists, namely unconditional and unrestricted Pledges Receivable. Another temporarily restricted asset is Grants Receivable.

With respect to temporarily restricted net assets, determine *when* the resources will be available. For example, if temporarily restricted net assets include term endowments and annuities, it may be best to consider them permanently restricted.

$$\frac{\text{Current Ratio for Unrestricted}}{\text{and Temporarily Restricted Assets}} = \frac{\substack{\text{Current Unrestricted Assets +} \\ \text{Current Temporarily Restricted} \\ \text{Assets for Operations}}}{\text{Current Unrestricted Liabilities}}$$

A determination should be made as to the nature of the restrictions on pledges receivable.

Acid-Test (Quick) Ratio   The quick unrestricted assets are the most liquid assets. Excluded are inventories of supplies and prepaid expenses. The quick unrestricted assets include cash and cash equivalents, accounts receivable, and investment income receivable.

$$\text{Quick Ratio} = \frac{\text{Quick Unrestricted Assets}}{\text{Current Unrestricted Liabilities}}$$

A higher ratio is better. It should be at least 1 : 1.

Accounts Receivable Ratios   Useful ratios are turnover and the collection period.

$$\text{Accounts Receivable Turnover} = \frac{\text{Fees for Services on Credit}}{\text{Average Net Accounts Receivable}}$$

$$\text{Net Accounts Receivable} = \frac{\text{Accounts Receivable less Allowance}}{\text{for Uncollectible Accounts}}$$

The ratio shows the number of times average net accounts receivable turn over relative to fees generated. The more turnover, the better.

$$\text{Days to Collect on Receivables} = \frac{365}{\text{Turnover}}$$

The ratio indicates the amounts owed the NPO as well as its accounts receivable management success. A lower ratio is better because it takes fewer days to collect on receivables. Cash received earlier can be reinvested for a return. A high ratio is bad because money is being tied up in receivables that could be invested elsewhere. Further, the longer receivables are held, the greater is the chance of uncollectibility. Perhaps billing is deficient. Receivables must be kept under control.

In looking at the collection period, consider terms of sale, account profile, service mix, collection policies, and the collection period of comparable NPOs.

An aging of receivable balances should be prepared broken down by current, past due (0–30 days), past due (31–60 days), past due (61–90 days), and past due (91–120 days). The aging listing should be both in alphabetical order and by magnitude of receivable balances outstanding. The older the receivables are, the less the chance of collection. A determination should be made of both time distribution and size distribution. How many billing periods has a particular account been unpaid?

A determination should be made of what percent receivables are to total assets, equal to:

$$\frac{\text{Total Accounts Receivable}}{\text{Total Assets}}$$

A high ratio is a problem, especially if most of the accounts receivable are from a few sources.

Pledges Receivable and Turnover   The turnover ratio for pledges receivable is similar to that of accounts receivable.

$$\text{Turnover} = \frac{\text{Net Contributions from Pledges}}{\text{Average Net Pledges Receivable}}$$

A lower turnover for pledges' receivables means a longer collection period.

$$\text{Collection Period} = \frac{365}{\text{Turnover}}$$

Is the collection period for pledges less than expected? If so, is it because of inadequate collection efforts? Compare to industry averages. Determine the reasonableness of the provision for uncollectible pledges. Analyze pledges receivable in terms of time and size diversification.

The turnover and age of grants receivable should be determined in a similar way.

Inventory   Inventory may have a low turnover because it is too costly, is of poor quality, or lacks appeal.

Days in Cash   The ratio equals:

$$\text{Days} = \frac{(\text{Cash} + \text{Cash Equivalents}) \times 365}{\text{Operating Expenses} - \text{Depreciation}}$$

The days' cash is the number of days the NPO can continue in operation if cash inflow stops. It is the number of days of average cash payments the NPO can manage without cash inflow. The more days, the better.

EXAMPLE 4.2
An NPO expends $30,000 daily on average in a one year period. If it has $900,000 of cash and cash equivalents on hand, it has 30 days' cash.

Cash Flow to Total Debt   The ratio equals:

$$\frac{\text{Net Income} + \text{Depreciation}}{\text{Total Liabilities}}$$

The ratio indicates how much of internally generated cash is available to pay debt. A higher ratio is better because there is better liquidity, in that cash flow from operations is being generated.

Days Purchases Unpaid   The ratio equals:

$$\frac{\text{Accounts Payable}}{\text{Daily Purchases}}$$

$$\text{Daily Purchases} = \frac{\text{Purchases}}{360}$$

The ratio is used to evaluate trade credit. It shows how long (how many days) trade credit remains unpaid.

If the suppliers' payment terms are 30 days and the NPO pays in 90 days on average, it may mean there are liquidity problems.

Current Liability Coverage   The ratio equals:

$$\frac{\text{Cash} + \text{Marketable Securities (unrestricted)}}{\text{Current Liabilities}}$$

The ratio reveals how much of current liabilities can be paid from cash and short-term investments if cash inflows cease.

Financial Flexibility

The greater the amount of unrestricted net assets, the greater the amount of financial flexibility. NPOs with huge permanently restricted endowments and minimal unrestricted net assets may not enjoy much flexibility. Can the NPO respond and adapt to financial adversity and unexpected needs and opportunities? Which resources are available when needed?

Asset Utilization

Asset utilization applies to the efficiency with which the assets are used in the operating activities of the NPO. For example, a higher ratio of revenue to assets indicates more efficiency of assets in generating profit. What assets are excessive relative to the optimal level?

The efficiency usage of supplies may be determined as follows:

$$\text{Turnover of Supplies} = \frac{\text{Annual Total Supplies Expense}}{\text{Average Total Inventory of Supplies}}$$

A low turnover is a negative sign because it means supplies are excessive and are not being used efficiently.

The available days of supplies' use equals 365 ÷ Turnover. What is the rate of supplies' usage? How fast would the current usage level deplete supplies inventory?

Average Daily Total Supplies Expense equals:

$$\frac{\text{Annual Total Supplies Expense}}{\text{Average Number of Days of Supplies' Use}}$$

The ratio shows how often supplies are used, for instance, in a particular program.

Analysis of Fixed Assets

In the long run, buying assets is cheaper than renting. The NPO also achieves more control by buying because it doesn't have to concern itself with lessor unexpectedly raising rental rates or demanding certain prohibitions on use of the property.

The average accounting age of equipment (e.g., computers) may be determined as follows:

$$\frac{\text{Accumulated Depreciation}}{\text{Depreciation Expense}}$$

The ratio reveals how old the equipment is. It shows the rate at which equipment is being used and replaced. A lower ratio is better.

The ratio is of particular interest to hospitals because it must buy expensive up-to-date technological medical equipment and must keep facilities in good working order, for the best patient care.

A low depreciation charge may indicate the NPO is making signficant use of rentals.

Does a reduction in fixed assets mean there is less capacity and less utilization?

Analysis of Liabilities

Short-term borrowing may be used to fill the gap resulting from the temporary shortfall in contributions or other sources of cash inflow.

If long-term debt is used to finance fixed assets, the NPO has greater financial leverage risk. The NPO must be able to pay principal and interest.

Analyze the long-term indebtedness of the NPO including:

- Interest rate being charged.
- Excessiveness of debt.
- Reason for borrowings. How is the money to be used?
- Maturity dates of debt. Are debt payments staggered? Can the debt be repaid?
- Lines of credit.
- Loan restrictions such as collateral requirements. Are such restrictions tying the hands of the manager?
- Understated liabilities, such as the liability for severance payments or for earned but unused vacation time.

Appraisal of Solvency, Capital Structure, and Fund Balance

A healthy capital structure will help to assure the NPO's ability to engage in its daily activities. High leverage (debt to fund balance) means risk. The debt ratio will increase if the NPO must finance fixed asset expansion with borrowed funds.

The ratio of long-term debt to total unrestricted fund balance reveals the NPO's long-term credit commitments to its ability to pay the debt. It relates borrowed funds to owned funds. A ratio over 1 may indicate a problem in handling additional debt. Can the NPO pay existing interest and principal payments?

Analysis of the fund balance depends on the facts and circumstances. A surplus indicates better financial health than a deficit. An increasing trend in the surplus is a favorable sign. Surpluses provide savings for financing the future and the ability to pay off debt.

EVALUATION OF THE STATEMENT OF ACTIVITIES

An NPO should communicate to the users of the financial statements which specific revenues and expenses are included in the operating measure. If the NPO's use of the term "operating" is not clear from the details on the face of the statement, FASB 117 requires a footnote describing the nature of the measure of operating performance. The financial analyst should carefully review the NPO's definition of the operating measure. A comparison should be made with similar NPOs and the definition should be consistently applied. Generally, the operating income measure is a subtotal in arriving at the net change in unrestricted net assets.

In analyzing the Statement of Activities, determine:

- Whether the entity is self-sustaining and operating well.
- Whether service efforts are being successful.
- Whether management has discharged its stewardship responsibilities.

In the long run, if an NPO does not spend all its revenues, it is not funding as much service as possible to the public. On the other hand, if it continues to spend more than its revenues, it will go bankrupt.

In analyzing an NPO, consider "operating capital maintenance," which means whether the NPO is maintaining its capital by having its revenues at least equal to its expenses. Why did a surplus or a deficit occur?

An NPO should not report a surplus consistently each year. If it always shows a surplus, the NPO may not be accomplishing its objective of providing as much service as possible with available resources. Either It should provide more service and thereby increase its costs, or it should reduce the prices it charges for services. The objective of an NPO's financial policy should be to break even over the long haul.

An NPO (such as a membership organization) may have a policy of having an operating excess one year but a deficit in another year, which balances out. For example, member dues may be increased only once each three years. In the year of the dues increase, an operating surplus may arise. In the second year, there may be a break-even, and in the third year, a deficit may exist. Dues will then be increased again.

In a similar vein, an NPO may want an operating excess one year to eliminate a deficit from the previous year.

An operating surplus may also be desired so as to have adequate funding for expansion, to subsidize programs, or as a result of a lawsuit. A surplus may be desired as a contingency for unexpected problems, and to replace assets.

An NPO may want to operate at a deficit in one year to reduce an accumulated surplus or to meet a special need.

In conclusion, an NPO does not have to break even each year. It may have a surplus in one or more years and a deficit in another year or years, to meet its unique circumstances. What is important is that the NPO's funds balance out over a number of years.

Revenue

The revenue base should be diversified to reduce risk. For example, overdependence on one revenue source (e.g., grants) may be dangerous.

A decline in revenue may indicate ineffectiveness. For example, a decline in college tuition may mean problems in attracting students to a college. How does actual revenue compare to expected revenue?

Total revenue needed daily on average equals:

$$\frac{\text{Total Revenue (prior year)}}{365}$$

Costs

Expenses should be analyzed in terms of program and object of expense. Variances between actual and budgeted expenses should be investigated.

Determine the reason for a sizable increase or decrease in an expense. For example, a significant increase in a specific expense may not be due to a change in organizational plan but may reflect contributed services instead.

A determination should be made of the cost per unit of service. A lower rate means better cost containment. When costs need to be reduced, the first thing to cut is lower-priority programs—the programs that contribute least toward accomplishing the NPO's goals. However, consider how changes in program activities would affect donor contributions and volunteer support. Identify controllable and uncontrollable costs. Ask these questions:

- Can costs be reduced by replacing obsolete and/or inactive equipment?
- Can costs be reduced by improved technology?
- Will an improved repairs and maintenance program lower costs?
- Can staff improvements be made to lower costs?
- Can energy costs be reduced through improved traffic management?
- Can productivity be improved?

Ratios include:

$$\frac{\text{Operating Expenses}}{\text{Total Revenue}}$$

A lower ratio indicates better cost control.

$$\frac{\text{Fund Raising Costs}}{\text{Total Donations}}$$

The ratio evaluates the effectiveness of fund-raising efforts. Are fund-raising costs excessive for funds obtained?

The Statement of Functional Expenses is required of voluntary and health organizations. The statement is helpful to the financial analyst because it provides a detailed breakdown of expenses by program. It is analogous to segment reporting in business enterprises.

Profitability

Profitability is needed, for NPOs try to expand, enter new areas, are unstable, and are ever-changing. Profitability measures include:

$$\text{Profit Margin} = \frac{\text{Revenue} - \text{Expenses}}{\text{Revenue}}$$

A higher ratio shows better operational performance (profit).

$$\text{Operating Margin} = \frac{\text{Operating Revenue} - \text{Operating Expenses}}{\text{Operating Revenue}}$$

Operating revenue excludes nonoperating sources such as fundraising revenue, dividends, and extraordinary items. The operating surplus is derived solely from operating activities without having to rely on contributors. A higher ratio is better.

$$\text{Return on Fund Balance (Net Assets)} = \frac{\text{Total Revenue} - \text{Total Expenses}}{\text{Average Net Assets}}$$

The ratio shows how efficiently the fund balance has created the year's surplus.

Ratios of investment performance include:

$$\frac{\text{Interest and/or Dividend Income}}{\text{Investments at Cost}}$$

$$\frac{\text{Interest and/or Dividend Income}}{\text{Investments at Market Value}}$$

Higher ratios indicate better returns on investments.

DISCLOSURES

In examining footnote disclosures, identify contingencies, including positive and negative developments affecting the NPO. Disclosure of possible future funding problems is a "red light." An example is changing political policies directed toward reducing government funding.

A lawsuit against an NPO is a negative sign, particularly if it is reasonably possible that the NPO will lose.

PERFORMANCE MEASURES

Examine the quality of the services and programs offered by the NPO in other ways, not just by looking at dollars. The NPO's objective is to render an amount and a quality of services. For example, measures of performance for a college include number of courses, and the ratio of faculty to students. Some general performance measures to keep in mind include:

- Capital per unit of service.
- Number of patients treated daily by a doctor.
- Number of welfare cases handled by a social worker.
- Input/output relationships, such as the cost and time of performing a service, and the quality and quantity of the service provided.
- Number of complaints.

FUND-RAISING ABILITY

Creditors evaluate an NPO's fund-raising ability as a major source of debt repayment for non-revenue-generating projects. Donated funds are important to consider in appraising the NPO's creditworthiness. Refunding is issuing new debt to replace existing debt and may occur if (1) market interest rates have decreased, (2) excessive restrictions exist in current debt, or (3) there is a desire to lengthen debt maturity.

ANALYSIS OF PLEDGES

In appraising pledges, consider:

- Are pledges decreasing among a particular category of donors or among all donors?
- Does poor economic activity result in fewer pledges?
- Have new tax laws made gift giving less advisable?
- Do donors feel the objectives of the NPO no longer match with their views?

Creditors may not assign a value to pledges receivable, in analyzing the NPO, because donors are not legally bound to honor either their dollar pledges or time they have promised to donate. For example, if a donor goes bankrupt (although this is unlikely), the promise will not be kept. Donors may change their minds about giving because of a change in circumstances. The creditor should examine who the donors are, their past history of giving, their current financial status, and their reliability. If donors' profiles indicate a high probability that they will give the amounts promised, creditors will give loans based on security or the pledges receivable. For example, pledges may be used to secure debt service or construction loans.

The analyst considers pledges due within one year of higher quality than pledges due in five years. The shorter the time period associated with the pledge, the less risk is involved.

ANALYSIS OF CONTRIBUTIONS

A potential cash problem is indicated when actual contributions fall significantly short of expectations. Restricted contributions are unavailable for operating purposes and to pay short-term debt. What amount of funds is available, and when? What are the restrictions (e.g., on a scholarship fund or a building fund)? Are the restrictions specific or excessive?

It is better to have a higher ratio of unrestricted contributions to total contributions, because unrestricted contributions are available to be used by the NPO in its regular activities. Restricted contributions do little to improve the NPO's liquidity unless the terms of the donor allow for the transfer of funds for operating purposes.

NPOs with substantial contributed services need special attention. The footnote on contributed services should be read closely, because it describes the program or activities that use volunteer services, the nature and extent of contributed services in monetary and nonmonetary terms, and the amount of contributed services recognized as revenue for the year.

LOOKING AT ENDOWMENTS

An endowment represents long-term investments. Investment income from the endowment may be unrestricted and available to finance operating activities, or it may be restricted as to use. Donors want financial feedback about whether the NPO has expended resources received, whether expenditures are in accord with promises made, whether services and activities provided are of high quality, and what balance remains in resources. Constraints and commitments made to donors regarding a fund's use and status are disclosed in the financial statements. Are legal requirements being met?

A decrease in endowments is a negative sign, because it may indicate potential donors are becoming less interested in or dissatisfied with the NPO. However, poor economic conditions may be the reason.

Answer the following questions about the portfolio in which endowment funds are invested:

- How much fluctuation exists in the securities portfolio?
- Is the diversification of the portfolio adequate?

- Are the securities negatively or positively correlated?

Total return on endowment investments may be estimated by computing it as a percentage of the average balance of endowment investments.

EXAMPLE 4.3
The return on an endowment portfolio is $60,000. The beginning and ending balances are $1,000,000 and $1,200,000, respectively.

$$\text{Return Rate} = \frac{\text{Return}}{\text{Average Balance}} = \frac{\$60,000}{\$1,100,000} = 5.5\%$$

A low return rate is a negative sign. The return on the endowment investment should become higher as the risk of the investment increases.

EVALUATION OF GRANTS

In analyzing grants, answer the following questions:

- Has the NPO made sufficient attempts to obtain public and private grants?
- In making grant applications, was reference made to suitable sources, such as *The Foundation Directory*?[1]
- Do the foundation's objectives match the grant proposals?
- Are matching funds required for any grants that were received?
- Were the proposals well done (i.e., was detailed information included, along with a clear discussion of how the funds would be used)?
- Were due date filings met?

RISK/RETURN ANALYSIS

Is the return sufficient to justify the risk? The greater the risk, the greater should be the return. Risk means the probability that an activity will accomplish its objective. For example, there may be a high degree of risk associated with a new, specialized academic program in a university or a new medical procedure at a hospital. There is always risk in allocating human and financial resources to new programs.

Ways to control or reduce risk include:

- Use agents and representatives, including volunteers to reduce exposure to lawsuits from employees' actions.
- Carry adequate insurance protection. For example, insurance carried should be adequate relative to the value of the insured property.

- Take care to hire qualified staff, so as to avoid damages and injuries to staff and others.
- Provide written policies, and make sure they are communicated clearly throughout the organization.
- Provide proper supervision for new hirees.
- Have protective provisions in contracts, to limit the NPO's liability for contractor malfeasance.
- Provide appropriate security for assets, to guard against theft or destruction.
- Diversify operations.
- Avoid dealings with selected groups that may result in legal liability problems (e.g., young children should not be allowed access to hazardous items).

AUDIT RELIABILITY

Many state and local governments require that NPOs be audited. Has the NPO's financial statements been subject to an audit, a review, or a compilation? A big difference exists between these processes in terms of the reliability of the NPO's financial statements. The highest level of reliability and testing is in an audit. In a review, no testing exists; rather, a determination is made about whether the financial statements make sense. A compilation, the least reliable of these processes, involves collecting and reformatting financial records.

In looking at the audit opinion, an "except-for" qualification or a disclaimer may indicate a problem. An unqualified opinion is best.

SOFTWARE

Software exists for analyzing NPOs. For example, The Functional Cost Analysis Program develops credit union income and cost information along functional lines and gives comparisons of data among credit unions and banks.

SPOTTING POTENTIAL BANKRUPTCY AND AVOIDING FINANCIAL PROBLEMS

A negative fund balance (a balance in which total liabilities exceed total assets) indicates a worrisome deficit position that is an indicator of potential bankruptcy. Cash forecasts showing that expected cash out-flows exceed expected cash inflows may point to financial distress. If cash is a problem, timely steps may be needed to improve cash flow and solve problems. How long would the current cash position last if all cash inflows were to cease?

A balanced budget, using conservative revenue estimates, is one way to avoid financial ruin. Balancing a budget requires making difficult choices, such as curtailing or eliminating certain services or programs.

Answer the following questions to gauge the probability of potential failure:

- Does the NPO have adequate insurance?
- Does excessive legal exposure exist? What is the nature of pending lawsuits? Is the NPO abreast of all current laws and regulations affecting it?
- What government adjustments are expected regarding rate charges and reimbursements?
- Are the NPO's controls over expenditures inadequate?
- Has the organization been deferring maintenance that can no longer be postponed?
- Are loan restrictions excessive?
- What effect will contractual violations have?
- Are costs skyrocketing? Why?
- Are bills past due?
- Is debt excessive?
- Are debt repayment schedules staggered?
- Should maturity dates be extended?
- Is the public or the government criticizing the NPO?
- Is there a decreasing trend in donor interest?
- To what extent are donor contributions restricted? Remember that restricted donations cannot be used to pay current expenses unless the restriction is satisfied or lifted.
- Is there less community interest in the NPO (e.g., are there fewer members or patients)?
- Are fewer volunteers available?
- Are more grant applications being rejected?
- Is there a cash shortage?

- Is the NPO anticipating future social, political, or technological trends?
- Does the NPO have sufficient expertise in the areas it is involved in?
- Is there a buildup in assets (e.g., receivables)?
- Is a hedging approach used to finance assets by matching them against the maturity dates of liabilities?
- Are long-term fixed-fee contracts hurting the NPO?
- Is there a sharp increase in the number of employees per unit of service?
- Does the NPO have open lines of credit?
- Does a lack of communication exist within the NPO?

Ways to avoid financial problems include:

- Merge with another financially stronger similar NPO. Will a merger aid in financing, lead to lower overall operating costs, increase synergy and efficiency, and enhance program expansion?
- Restructure the organization.
- Sell off unproductive assets.
- Defer paying bills.
- Discard programs and activities that are no longer financially viable.
- Implement a cost reduction program including layoffs and attrition. First, however, evaluate whether such a program would eliminate operations that would be hard to start up again. Would you be getting rid of scarce talents? Such measures are referred to as "irreversible reductions" and in the long run they may not be wise.
- Increase service fees.
- Increase fund-raising efforts and contributions.
- Apply for grants.
- Stimulate contracts.

EXAMPLE 4.4

A nonprofit organization provides the following financial information:

Summary of Income, Expenses, and Cash Balances

	19X1	19X2	Percentage Change
Income:			
Membership and program fees	$125,000	$130,000	4%
Contributions	126,000	130,000	3
Other	13,000	35,000	169
Total income	$254,000	$295,000	12
Expenses:			
Salaries	$100,000	$160,000	60
Rent	40,000	70,000	43
Insurance	10,000	20,000	100
Supplies	20,000	40,000	100
Total expenses	$170,000	$290,000	71
Excess of income over expenses	$ 94,000	$ 5,000	95
Cash balance, beginning of year	50,000	144,000	
Cash balance, end of year	$144,000	$149,000	

From 19X1 to 19X2, total expenses have increased 71 percent while total revenue has increased only 12 percent. This is a very negative sign. Among the things it may indicate are a failure to control costs, or declining fees for services, possibly due to membership dissatisfaction. Then too, why have contributions increased by only 3 percent? Are donors upset with the NPO's policies, objectives, or management?

It is particularly alarming that profitability has declined by a stunning 95 percent. The sharp increase in each expense category must be closely scrutinized for cause, and corrective action must be taken immediately. Unless something is done to correct this unfavorable trend, the NPO is in serious trouble!

CASE STUDY IN FINANCIAL STATEMENT ANALYSIS: FAMILY SERVICE AGENCY OF UTOPIA

This case study is based on a sample NPO provided by the Internal Revenue Service in Form 990. The completed tax return, as prepared by the IRS for illustrative purposes, is presented in the appendix to this chapter.

Trend Analysis

All line references in the table below are to Form 990

	12/31/93	12/31/94	Percent Change
Total Cash (lines 45 and 46)	$248,700	$228,500	(8.1)
Pledges Receivable (line 48c)	46,000	58,900	28.0
Grants Receivable (line 49)	4,600	5,800	26.1
Inventories (line 52)	6,100	7,000	14.8
Fixed Assets (line 57c)	168,500	174,800	3.7
Total Assets (line 59)	916,000	964,800	5.3
Total Liabilities (line 66)	111,200	112,300	1.0
Current Unrestricted Fund (line 67a)	446,300	485,100	8.7
Current Restricted Fund (line 67b)	10,000	6,400	(36.0)
Land, Buildings, and Equipment Fund (line 68)	156,800	116,200	6.0
Endowment Fund (line 69)	191,700	194,800	1.6
Total Fund Balances (Net Assets) (line 74)	$804,800	$852,500	5.9

For the Year Ended		
	1993	1994	Percent Change
---	---	---	---
Contributions, gifts, and similar amounts (1994 from line 1; 1993 from Schedule A, line 15)	$742,300	$710,800	(4.2)
Membership dues (1994 from Line 3; 1993 from Schedule A, Line 16)	1,100	1,600	45.5

An analysis of the trends from 1993 to 1994 reveals the following:

- The cash position declined, with a negative effect on liquidity.
- Both pledges and grants receivable increased significantly, reflecting success in obtaining pledges and grants to the NPO. A favorable sign. However, it may be that there is a problem in collecting the pledges and grants due to higher receivable balances.
- The buildup in inventories may mean greater realization risk.

- Fixed assets were fairly constant.
- The increase in total assets is a favorable indicator.
- Total liabilities were about the same.
- While the balance in current unrestricted funds increased, a favorable sign, there was a decline in the current restricted fund. However, the dollar amount of the decline was small even though the percentage was higher.
- More funds became available for fixed asset expansion.
- The NPO was successful in attracting more endowment funds.
- The increase in total fund balances (net assets) of about 6 percent is a positive sign.
- Contributions, gifts, grants, and similar items decreased by about 5 percent. The reasons for the decrease should be determined. Is there less interest in the NPO among donors? If so, why?
- The membership revenue almost doubled, reflecting greater interest in the NPO's policies as indicated by more enrollments or an increase in per-member fees. Perhaps there was a successful membership drive.

Liquidity Analysis

$$\frac{\text{Total Current Assets (Balance Sheet [BS]} - 12/31/94)}{\text{Total Assets (BS)}}$$

$$\frac{\$315,600}{\$964,800} = 0.33$$

Each $1 of total assets is composed of $0.33 of current assets.

$$\text{Current Ratio} = \frac{\text{Current Assets (BS)}}{\text{Current Liabilities (BS)}} = \frac{\$315,600}{\$98,900} = 3.2$$

The high ratio means good liquidity.

$$\begin{array}{l}\text{Current Ratio for Unrestricted} \\ \text{Current Assets and Current} \\ \text{Unrestricted Liabilities}\end{array} = \frac{\text{Current Unrestricted Assets (BS)}}{\text{Current Unrestricted Liabilities (BS)}}$$

$$= \frac{\$304,400}{\$98,900} = 3.1$$

The high ratio further indicates good liquidity.

$$\text{Quick Ratio} = \frac{\text{Quick Unrestricted Current Assets (BS)}}{\text{Current Unrestricted Liabilities (BS)}}$$

$$= \frac{\$283,600}{\$98,900} = 2.87$$

Quick Unrestricted Current Assets

$= \text{Total Current Assets} - \text{Inventories} - \text{Prepaid Expenses}$

$= \$304,400 - \$7,000 - \$13,800 = \$283,600$

Because the quick ratio (2.87) exceeds the norm of 1.0, good liquidity is evident.

Accounts Receivable Turnover

$$= \frac{\text{Program Service Revenue (Form 990, line 2)}}{\text{Average Net Accounts Receivable (Form 990, line 47c)}}$$

$$= \frac{\$2,600}{\$1,700} = 1.5$$

Receivables turn over 1.5 times per year relative to fees generated. The low turnover rate indicates less liquidity. Perhaps there is risk in collecting.

$$\text{Days to Collect on Receivables} = \frac{365}{\text{Turnover}} = \frac{365}{1.5} = 243 \text{ days}$$

It takes 243 days to collect on receivables, indicating a possible collection problem.

$$\frac{\text{Total Accounts Receivable (Form 990, line 47c)}}{\text{Total Assets (Form 990, line 59)}} = \frac{\$1,600}{\$964,800} = 0.2\%$$

The very low ratio means receivables are insignificant relative to total assets.

Pledges Turnover = Net Contributions from Pledges (From
Statement of Revenue, Expenses, and
Changes in Fund Balance [SRECF])

$$\frac{}{\text{Average Net Pledges Receivable (Form 990, line 48c)}}$$

$$= \frac{\$473,700}{\$52,450} = 9 \text{ times}$$

The high turnover rate means faster collection on pledges, which is a favorable liquidity indicator.

$$\text{Collection Period on Pledges} = \frac{365}{\text{Turnover}} = \frac{365}{9} = 40.6 \text{ days}$$

It takes about 41 days to collect on pledges. This is favorable.

$$\text{Cash Flow to Total Debt} = \frac{\text{Net Income} + \text{Depreciation}}{\text{Total Liabilities}}$$

$$= \frac{\text{Form 990, line 18} + \text{line 42}}{\text{Form 990, line 66}}$$

$$= \frac{\$47,700 + \$5,200}{\$112,300} = 0.47$$

This computation indicates that $0.47 of internally generated cash is available to pay $1 of debt.

Current Liability Coverage

$$= \frac{\text{Cash} + \text{Marketable Securities (Unrestricted) (BS)}}{\text{Total Current Liabilities (BS)}}$$

$$= \frac{\$221,100}{\$98,900} = 2.2$$

For each $1 in current liabilities, there is $2.20 of cash and short-term investments available to pay it.

$$\frac{\text{Total Current Liabilities (BS)}}{\text{Total Liabilities (BS)}} = \frac{\$98,900}{\$112,300} = 0.88$$

Current debt is a high proportion of total liabilities. This is an unfavorable liquidity indicator.

Analysis of Solvency

$$\frac{\text{Total Assets (Form 990, line 59)}}{\text{Total Liabilities (Form 990, line 66)}} = \frac{\$964,800}{\$112,300} = 8.6$$

There is $8.60 in assets for each $1 in liabilities, indicating a good solvency position.

$$\frac{\text{Total Liabilities (Form 990, line 66)}}{\text{Total Fund Balance (Net Assets) (Form 990, line 74)}} = \frac{\$112,300}{\$852,500}$$

$$= 0.13$$

The low ratio of debt to fund balance is a favorable indicator of the ability of the NPO to meet its obligations. It indicates less risk.

$$\frac{\text{Long-Term Debt (BS)}}{\text{Total Unrestricted Fund Balance (BS)}} = \frac{\$13,400}{\$485,100} = 2.8\%$$

This ratio is a further indication of a solid solvency position. The NPO is able to fulfill its long-term debt commitments.

Analysis of the Statement of Activities

$$\text{Daily Revenue (1994)} = \frac{\text{Total Revenue for Current Year}}{365}$$

$$= \frac{\text{Form 990, line 12}}{365} = \frac{\$760,300}{365} = \$2,083$$

$$\text{Daily Revenue (1993)} = \frac{\text{Total Revenue for Prior Year}}{365}$$

$$= \frac{\text{Form 990, Schedule A, line 23}}{365}$$

$$= \frac{\$800,600}{365} = \$2,193$$

The declining revenue per day from 1993 to 1994 is a negative sign for operating performance.

$$\frac{\text{Total Expenses (Form 990, line 17)}}{\text{Total Revenue (Form 990, line 12)}} = \frac{\$712,600}{\$760,300} = 93.7\%$$

Total expenses are a high percentage of total revenue, cutting into surplus.

$$\frac{\text{Fund-raising Costs (Form 990, line 15)}}{\text{Total Donations (SRECF)}} = \frac{\$65,400}{\$473,700} = 13.8\%$$

Fund-raising costs as a percentage of contributions are reasonable, indicating an effective fund-raising campaign.

$$\text{Profit Margin} = \frac{\text{Excess of Revenue over Expenses}}{\text{Total Revenue}}$$

$$\frac{\text{Form 990, line 18}}{\text{Form 990, line 12}} = \frac{\$47,700}{\$760,300} = 6.3\%$$

The profit margin should be compared to other similar NPOs. If it is lower, it indicates less operational performance.

Return on Fund Balance (Net Assets)

$$\frac{\text{Excess of Revenue over Expenses}}{\text{Average Net Assets}} = \frac{\text{Form 990, line 18}}{\text{Form 990, line 59}}$$

$$= \frac{\$47,700}{\$940,400} = 5.1\%$$

This ratio reflects reasonable efficiency of the fund balance in generating yearly surplus for the year.

$$\frac{\text{Dividends and Interest from Securities}}{\text{Investments}} = \frac{\text{Form 990, line 5}}{\text{Form 990, line 54}}$$

$$= \frac{\$16,400}{\$474,400} = 3.5\%$$

The rate of return earned on the investment portfolio is low.

$$\frac{\text{Return Rate on}}{\text{Endowment Funds}} = \frac{\text{Total Revenue on Endowment Fund}}{\text{Total Assets in Endowment Fund}}$$

$$= \frac{\text{SRECF}}{\text{BS}} = \frac{\$3,100}{\$194,800} = 1.6\%$$

The return rate on endowment funds is very low.

Conclusion

The NPO's liquidity is favorable, meaning the organization is able to pay its short-term obligations. Its solvency is also favorable, meaning it can satisfy its long-term debt when due. The NPO is having difficulty in its operating performance, as indicated by declining daily revenue, high expenses to revenue, and low investment return. However, fund-raising costs are being controlled, resulting in successful fund-raising efforts. Profit margin and return on fund balance appears reasonable.

There is more interest in the NPO as indicated by the increasing membership base.

ENDNOTE

1. (1995) *The Foundation Center,* 79 Fifth Ave., N. Y., N. Y. 10003 (202-620-4230).

APPENDIX TO CHAPTER 4

Form **990**	**Return of Organization Exempt From Income Tax**	OMB No. 1545-0047
	Under section 501(c) of the Internal Revenue Code (except black lung benefit trust or private foundation) or section 4947(a)(1) nonexempt charitable trust	19**94**
Department of the Treasury Internal Revenue Service	Note: *The organization may have to use a copy of this return to satisfy state reporting requirements.*	This Form is Open to Public Inspection

A For the 1994 calendar year, OR tax year period beginning _____, 1994, and ending _____, 19__

B Check if:	Please use IRS label or print or type. See Specific Instructions.	**C** Name of organization		**D** Employer identification number
☐ Change of address		Family Service Agency of Utopia, Inc.		12 : 3456789
☐ Initial return		Number and street (or P.O. box if mail is not delivered to street address)	Room/suite	**E** State registration number
☐ Final return		1414 West Ash Drive		567890
☐ Amended return (required also for State reporting)		City, town, or post office, state, and ZIP code		**F** Check ▶ ☐ if exemption application is pending
		Utopia, PA 11111		

G Type of organization—▶ ☒ Exempt under section 501(c)(**3**) ◀ (insert number) OR ▶ ☐ section 4947(a)(1) nonexempt charitable trust

Note: *Section 501(c)(3) exempt organizations and 4947(a)(1) nonexempt charitable trusts MUST attach a completed Schedule A (Form 990).*

H(a) Is this a group return filed for affiliates? . . . . ☐ Yes ☒ No   **I** If either box in H is checked "Yes," enter four-digit group exemption number (GEN) ▶ ....

(b) If "Yes," enter the number of affiliates for which this return is filed: . ▶ _____

(c) Is this a separate return filed by an organization covered by a group ruling? ☐ Yes ☒ No

J Accounting method: ☐ Cash ☒ Accrual ☐ Other (specify) ▶

K Check here ▶ ☐ if the organization's gross receipts are normally not more than $25,000. The organization need not file a return with the IRS; but if it received a Form 990 Package in the mail, it should file a return without financial data. **Some states require a complete return.**

Note: *Form 990-EZ may be used by organizations with gross receipts less than $100,000 and total assets less than $250,000 at end of year.*

Part I	**Statement of Revenue, Expenses, and Changes in Net Assets or Fund Balances**				
1	Contributions, gifts, grants, and similar amounts received:				
a	Direct public support	1a	$483,300		
b	Indirect public support	1b	227,500		
c	Government contributions (grants)	1c			
d	Total (add lines 1a through 1c) (attach schedule—see instructions) (cash $ 710,800 noncash $ _____)			1d	$710,800
2	Program service revenue including government fees and contracts (from Part VII, line 93)			2	2,600
3	Membership dues and assessments (see instructions)			3	1,600
4	Interest on savings and temporary cash investments			4	14,800
5	Dividends and interest from securities			5	16,400
6a	Gross rents	6a			
b	Less: rental expenses	6b			
c	Net rental income or (loss) (subtract line 6b from line 6a)			6c	
7	Other investment income (describe ▶ _____)			7	
8a	Gross amount from sale of assets other than inventory	(A) Securities 24,200	8a	(B) Other	
b	Less: cost or other basis and sales expenses.	23,700	8b		
c	Gain or (loss) (attach schedule)	500	8c		
d	Net gain or (loss) (combine line 8c, columns (A) and (B))			8d	500
9	Special events and activities (attach schedule—see instructions):				
a	Gross revenue (not including $ -0- of contributions reported on line 1a)	9a	28,400		
b	Less: direct expenses other than fundraising expenses	9b	18,000		
c	Net income or (loss) from special events (subtract line 9b from line 9a) .			9c	10,400
10a	Gross sales of inventory, less returns and allowances . .	10a	1,400		
b	Less: cost of goods sold	10b	1,000		
c	Gross profit or (loss) from sales of inventory (attach schedule) (subtract line 10b from line 10a) .			10c	400
11	Other revenue (from Part VII, line 103)			11	2,800
12	Total revenue (add lines 1d, 2, 3, 4, 5, 6c, 7, 8d, 9c, 10c, and 11)			12	$760,300
13	Program services (from line 44, column (B)—see instructions)			13	$577,400
14	Management and general (from line 44, column (C)—see instructions)			14	57,400
15	Fundraising (from line 44, column (D)—see instructions)			15	65,400
16	Payments to affiliates (attach schedule—see instructions)			16	12,400
17	Total expenses (add lines 16 and 44, column (A))			17	$712,600
18	Excess or (deficit) for the year (subtract line 17 from line 12)			18	$ 47,700
19	Net assets or fund balances at beginning of year (from line 74, column (A)) . .			19	804,800
20	Other changes in net assets or fund balances (attach explanation)			20	-0-
21	Net assets or fund balances at end of year (combine lines 18, 19, and 20)			21	$852,500

(Left margin labels: Revenue / Expenses / Net Assets)

For Paperwork Reduction Act Notice, see page 1 of the separate instructions.   Cat. No. 11282Y   Form **990** (1994)

Appendix to Chapter 4

89

Form 990 (1994)
Page 2

Part II — Statement of Functional Expenses

All organizations must complete column (A). Columns (B), (C), and (D) are required for section 501(c)(3) and (4) organizations and section 4947(a)(1) nonexempt charitable trusts but optional for others. (See instructions.)

Do not include amounts reported on line 6b, 8b, 9b, 10b, or 16 of Part I.		(A) Total	(B) Program services	(C) Management and general	(D) Fundraising
22 Grants and allocations (attach schedule) . . (cash $ 35,900 noncash $ _____)	22	$ 35,900	$ 35,900		
23 Specific assistance to individuals (attach schedule)	23	45,800	45,800		
24 Benefits paid to or for members (attach schedule)	24				
25 Compensation of officers, directors, etc. . .	25	62,800	46,600	$ 8,800	$ 7,400
26 Other salaries and wages	26	184,700	131,000	24,300	29,400
27 Pension plan contributions	27	300	200	100	
28 Other employee benefits	28	13,000	9,400	2,100	1,500
29 Payroll taxes	29	23,800	17,700	3,000	3,100
30 Professional fundraising fees	30				
31 Accounting fees	31				
32 Legal fees	32				
33 Supplies	33	30,000	26,500	1,800	1,700
34 Telephone	34	15,400	11,600	1,500	2,300
35 Postage and shipping	35	23,100	13,100	1,000	9,000
36 Occupancy	36	37,750	34,900	1,500	1,350
37 Equipment rental and maintenance . . .	37	8,750	5,900	1,500	1,350
38 Printing and publications	38	14,100	12,200	300	1,600
39 Travel	39	22,000	16,700	2,300	3,000
40 Conferences, conventions, and meetings . .	40	17,700	12,800	4,500	400
41 Interest	41	900		100	800
42 Depreciation, depletion, etc. (attach schedule)	42	5,200	4,200	600	400
43 Other expenses (itemize): a ..... Dues	43a	500	500		
b .... Professional Fees	43b	127,900	124,500	2,600	800
c .... Insurance	43c	26,300	25,650	600	50
d .... Miscellaneous	43d	4,300	2,150	100	2,050
e	43e				
44 Total functional expenses (add lines 22 through 43) Organizations completing columns (B)-(D), carry these totals to lines 13-15 .	44	$700,200	$577,400	$57,400	$65,400

Reporting of Joint Costs.—Did you report in column (B) (Program services) any joint costs from a combined educational campaign and fundraising solicitation? . . . . ▶ ☒ Yes ☐ No
If "Yes," enter (i) the aggregate amount of these joint costs $ 9,600 ; (ii) the amount allocated to Program services $ 2,800 ;
(iii) the amount allocated to Management and general $ 700 ; and (iv) the amount allocated to Fundraising $ 6,000

Part III — Statement of Program Service Accomplishments (See instructions.)

What is the organization's primary exempt purpose? ▶ Family counseling

	Program Service Expenses (Required for 501(c)(3) and (4) orgs., and 4947(a)(1) trusts; but optional for others.)
All organizations must describe their exempt purpose achievements. State the number of clients served, publications issued, etc. Discuss achievements that are not measurable. (Section 501(c)(3) and (4) organizations and 4947(a)(1) nonexempt charitable trusts must also enter the amount of grants and allocations to others.)	
a Counseling - The organization provided 5,954 hours of counseling to individuals and families. A total of 635 cases were assisted involving 2,426 individuals. The agency also made a grant to its national affiliate for a research project. (Grants and allocations $ 3,000)	$257,800
b Adoption Services - The agency placed 50 children in adoptive families. This included counseling for 189 birth parents. Five adoptions involved children from foreign countries. There were 65 home studies completed during this year. (This program was assisted (Grants and allocations $)	
c by $8,000 of donated services in 1994.) Under the Adoption Services program, the agency made grants to three organizations for related services. (Grants and allocations $ 21,000)	187,800
d Foster Care - The agency placed 28 children in 16 foster homes. The agency also made grants to two other organizations providing foster home care for hard-to-place children. (Grants and allocations $ 11,900)	131,800
e Other program services (attach schedule) (Grants and allocations $)	
f Total of Program Service Expenses (should equal line 44, column (B), Program services). . . . . ▶	$577,400

Form 990 (1994)   Page **3**

Part IV	**Balance Sheets**						

Note: *Where required, attached schedules and amounts within the description column should be for end-of-year amounts only.*

				(A) Beginning of year		(B) End of year
	Assets					
45	Cash—non-interest-bearing			$ 4,000	**45**	$ 6,400
46	Savings and temporary cash investments			244,700	**46**	222,100
47a	Accounts receivable	**47a**	$ 1,800			
b	Less: allowance for doubtful accounts . . .	**47b**	200	1,800	**47c**	1,600
48a	Pledges receivable	**48a**	70,100			
b	Less: allowance for doubtful accounts . . .	**48b**	11,200	46,000	**48c**	58,900
49	Grants receivable			4,600	**49**	5,800
50	Receivables due from officers, directors, trustees, and key employees (attach schedule)				**50**	
51a	Other notes and loans receivable (attach schedule)	**51a**				
b	Less: allowance for doubtful accounts . . .	**51b**			**51c**	
52	Inventories for sale or use			6,100	**52**	7,000
53	Prepaid expenses and deferred charges			9,600	**53**	13,800
54	Investments—securities (attach schedule)			430,700	**54**	474,400
55a	Investments—land, buildings, and equipment: basis	**55a**				
b	Less: accumulated depreciation (attach schedule)	**55b**			**55c**	
56	Investments—other (attach schedule)				**56**	
57a	Land, buildings, and equipment: basis . . .	**57a**	188,000			
b	Less: accumulated depreciation (attach schedule)	**57b**	13,200	168,500	**57c**	174,800
58	Other assets (describe ▶ _____)				**58**	
59	**Total assets** (add lines 45 through 58) (must equal line 75)			$916,000	**59**	$964,800
	Liabilities					
60	Accounts payable and accrued expenses			$ 46,000	**60**	$ 39,300
61	Grants payable				**61**	
62	Support and revenue designated for future periods (attach schedule) . .			61,600	**62**	59,600
63	Loans from officers, directors, trustees, and key employees (attach schedule)				**63**	
64a	Tax-exempt bond liabilities (attach schedule)				**64a**	
b	Mortgages and other notes payable (attach schedule)			3,600	**64b**	3,200
65	Other liabilities (describe ▶ Payable under capital lease)				**65**	10,200
66	**Total liabilities** (add lines 60 through 65)			$111,200	**66**	$112,300
	Fund Balances or Net Assets					
	Organizations that use fund accounting, check here ▶ X and complete lines 67 through 70 and lines 74 and 75 (see instructions).					
67a	Current unrestricted fund			$446,300	**67a**	$485,100
b	Current restricted fund			10,000	**67b**	6,400
68	Land, buildings, and equipment fund			156,800	**68**	166,200
69	Endowment fund			191,700	**69**	194,800
70	Other funds (describe ▶ _____)			-0-	**70**	-0-
	Organizations that do not use fund accounting, check here ▶ ☐ and complete lines 71 through 75 (see instructions).					
71	Capital stock or trust principal				**71**	
72	Paid-in or capital surplus				**72**	
73	Retained earnings or accumulated income				**73**	
74	**Total fund balances or net assets** (add lines 67a through 70 OR lines 71 through 73; column (A) must equal line 19 and column (B) must equal line 21)			$804,800	**74**	$852,500
75	**Total liabilities and fund balances/net assets** (add lines 66 and 74) . .			$916,000	**75**	$964,800

Form 990 is available for public inspection and, for some people, serves as the primary or sole source of information about a particular organization. How the public perceives an organization in such cases may be determined by the information presented on its return. Therefore, please make sure the return is complete and accurate and fully describes the organization's programs and accomplishments.

Form 990 (1994)

Part V   List of Officers, Directors, Trustees, and Key Employees (List each one even if not compensated; see instructions.)

(A) Name and address	(B) Title and average hours per week devoted to position	(C) Compensation (if not paid, enter -0-)	(D) Contributions to employee benefit plans & deferred compensation	(E) Expense account and other allowances
Anita Hurlimann 10 Paradise Drive, Utopia, PA 11111	President 10 hrs./wk.	-0-	-0-	-0-
John S. Brown, Ph.D. 15 Heavenly Place, Utopia, PA 11111	Executive Director 50 hrs./wk.	$62,800	$1,810	-0-
Janet Newhouse 20 Musical Drive, Utopia, PA 11111	Vice President 10 hrs./wk.	-0-	-0-	-0-
Jim Jones 5 Scenic Rd., Utopia, PA 11111	Treasurer 2 hrs./wk.	-0-	-0-	-0-

Did any officer, director, trustee, or key employee receive aggregate compensation of more than $100,000 from your organization and all elated organizations, of which more than $10,000 was provided by the related organizations?. ▶ ☐ Yes ☒ No
If "Yes," attach schedule—see instructions.

Part VI   Other Information

		Yes	No
76	Did the organization engage in any activity not previously reported to the IRS? If "Yes," attach a detailed description of each activity.	76	X
77	Were any changes made in the organizing or governing documents, but not reported to the IRS? . . .	77	X
	If "Yes," attach a conformed copy of the changes.		
78a	Did the organization have unrelated business gross income of $1,000 or more during the year covered by this return?	78a	X
b	If "Yes," has it filed a tax return on **Form 990-T**, Exempt Organization Business Income Tax Return, for this year?	78b	N/A
79	Was there a liquidation, dissolution, termination, or substantial contraction during the year? If "Yes," attach a statement; see instructions.	79	X
80a	Is the organization related (other than by association with a statewide or nationwide organization) through common membership, governing bodies, trustees, officers, etc., to any other exempt or nonexempt organization? (See instructions.)	80a	X
b	If "Yes," enter the name of the organization ▶ .... and check whether it is ☐ exempt **OR** ☐ nonexempt.		
81a	Enter the amount of political expenditures, direct or indirect, as described in the instructions . |81a| -0-		
b	Did the organization file **Form 1120-POL**, U.S. Income Tax Return for Certain Political Organizations, for this year? .	81b	X
82a	Did the organization receive donated services or the use of materials, equipment, or facilities at no charge or at substantially less than fair rental value?	82a	X
b	If "Yes," you may indicate the value of these items here. Do not include this amount as revenue in Part I or as an expense in Part II. (See instructions for reporting in Part III.) . |82b| $8,000		
83	Did the organization comply with the public inspection requirements for returns and exemption applications?	83	X
84a	Did the organization solicit any contributions or gifts that were not tax deductible?	84a	N/A
b	If "Yes," did the organization include with every solicitation an express statement that such contributions or gifts were not tax deductible? (See General Instruction M.)	84b	N/A
85	Section 501(c)(4), (5), or (6) organizations.—**a** Were substantially all dues nondeductible by members?	85a	N/A
b	Did the organization make only in-house lobbying expenditures of $2,000 or less?	85b	N/A
	If "Yes" to either 85a or 85b, do not complete 85c through 85h below unless the organization received a waiver for proxy tax owed for the prior year.		
c	Dues, assessments, and similar amounts from members . . . . |85c| N/A		
d	Section 162(e) lobbying and political expenditures . . . . |85d| N/A		
e	Aggregate nondeductible amount of section 6033(e)(1)(A) dues notices . . . . . |85e| N/A		
f	Taxable amount of lobbying and political expenditures (line 85d less 85e; see instructions) . |85f| N/A		
g	Does the organization elect to pay the section 6033(e) tax on the amount in 85f?	85g	N/A
h	If section 6033(e)(1)(A) dues notices were sent, does the organization agree to add the amount in 85f to its reasonable estimate of dues allocable to nondeductible lobbying and political expenditures for the following tax year? . . .	85h	N/A
86	Section 501(c)(7) organizations.—Enter:		
a	Initiation fees and capital contributions included on line 12 . . . . |86a| N/A		
b	Gross receipts, included on line 12, for public use of club facilities (See instructions.) |86b| N/A		
87	Section 501(c)(12) organizations.—Enter: **a** Gross income from members or shareholders |87a| N/A		
b	Gross income from other sources. (Do not net amounts due or paid to other sources against amounts due or received from them.) . . . . |87b| N/A		
88	At any time during the year, did the organization own a 50% or greater interest in a taxable corporation or partnership? If "Yes," complete Part IX	88	X
89	Public interest law firms.—Attach information described in the instructions.		
90	List the states with which a copy of this return is filed ▶ .....Pennsylvania.....		
91	The books are in care of ▶ .Nancy Ward......Telephone no. ▶ (123) 456-7899		
	Located at ▶ .1414 West Ash Drive, Utopia, PA....... ZIP code ▶ .11111.		
92	Section 4947(a)(1) nonexempt charitable trusts filing Form 990 in lieu of **Form 1041**, U.S. Income Tax Return for Estates and Trusts, check here ▶ ☐ and enter the amount of tax-exempt interest received or accrued during the tax year . . ▶ |92| N/A		

Form 990 (1994)   Page **5**

Part VII Analysis of Income-Producing Activities

Enter gross amounts unless otherwise indicated.	Unrelated business income		Excluded by section 512, 513, or 514		(E)
	(A) Business code	(B) Amount	(C) Exclusion code	(D) Amount	Related or exempt function income (See instructions.)
93 Program service revenue:					
a Consultation fees					$2,300
b					
c					
d					
e					
f					
g Fees and contracts from government agencies					300
94 Membership dues and assessments . . .					1,600
95 Interest on savings and temporary cash investments			14	$14,800	
96 Dividends and interest from securities . . .			14	16,400	
97 Net rental income or (loss) from real estate:					
a debt-financed property					
b not debt-financed property					
98 Net rental income or (loss) from personal property					
99 Other investment income					
100 Gain or (loss) from sales of assets other than inventory			18	500	
101 Net income or (loss) from special events . .			1	10,400	
102 Gross profit or (loss) from sales of inventory .					400
103 Other revenue: a Sale of easement			18	2,800	
b					
c					
d					
e					
104 Subtotal (add columns (B), (D), and (E))		-0-		$44,900	$4,600
105 **Total** (add line 104, columns (B), (D), and (E)) . . . . ▶					$49,500

Note: (Line 105 plus line 1d, Part I, should equal the amount on line 12, Part I.)

Part VIII Relationship of Activities to the Accomplishment of Exempt Purposes

Line No. ▼	Explain how each activity for which income is reported in column (E) of Part VII contributed importantly to the accomplishment of the organization's exempt purposes (other than by providing funds for such purposes). (See instructions.)
93a	Fees for marriage counseling--one of our exempt purposes.
93g	Fee from county for finding foster homes for 2 children--this furthers our exempt purpose of ensuring quality care for foster children.
94	Members are social service workers who receive information and advice on problem cases from our staff as part of our counseling, adoption, and foster care programs.
102	Sale of educational materials to members and persons receiving counseling--part of our overall counseling program.

Part IX Information Regarding Taxable Subsidiaries (Complete this Part if the "Yes" box on line 88 is checked.)

Name, address, and employer identification number of corporation or partnership	Percentage of ownership interest	Nature of business activities	Total income	End-of-year assets
N/A	%			
	%			
	%			
	%			

Please Sign Here	Under penalties of perjury, I declare that I have examined this return, including accompanying schedules and statements, and to the best of my knowledge and belief, it is true, correct, and complete. Declaration of preparer (other than officer) is based on all information of which preparer has any knowledge.		
▶	*John S. Brown* Signature of officer	3/23/95 Date	**Executive Director** Title

Paid Preparer's Use Only	Preparer's signature ▶		Date		Check if self-employed ▶ ☐	Preparer's social security no.
	Firm's name (or yours if self-employed) and address ▶				E.I. No. ▶	
					ZIP code ▶	

SCHEDULE A (Form 990) Department of the Treasury Internal Revenue Service	**Organization Exempt Under Section 501(c)(3)** (Except Private Foundation), and Section 501(e), 501(f), 501(k), or Section 4947(a)(1) Nonexempt Charitable Trust **Supplementary Information** ▶ **Must be completed by the above organizations and attached to their Form 990 (or 990-EZ).**	OMB No. 1545-0047 19**94**

Name of the organization	Employer identification number
Family Service Agency of Utopia, Inc.	12 ⋮ 3456789

Part I Compensation of the Five Highest Paid Employees Other Than Officers, Directors, and Trustees
(See instructions.) (List each one. If there are none, enter "None.")

(a) Name and address of each employee paid more than $50,000	(b) Title and average hours per week devoted to position	(c) Compensation	(d) Contributions to employee benefit plans & deferred compensation	(e) Expense account and other allowances
Roshan Contractor, M.S.W. 41 Allegro Way, Utopia, PA	Dep. to the Director 45 hrs./wk.	$56,000	$1,634	-0-
Mehroo Aziz 50 Mountain View, Utopia, PA	Ch. Counseling Services 45 hrs./wk.	52,000	1,490	-0-

Total number of other employees paid over $50,000 . . . . ▶ | -0- |

Part II Compensation of the Five Highest Paid Independent Contractors for Professional Services
(See instructions.) (List each one (whether individuals or firms.) (If there are none, enter "None.")

(a) Name and address of each independent contractor paid more than $50,000	(b) Type of service	(c) Compensation
None		

Total number of others receiving over $50,000 for professional services . . . . ▶

Part III Statements About Activities

		Yes	No
1	During the year, has the organization attempted to influence national, state, or local legislation, including any attempt to influence public opinion on a legislative matter or referendum? . . . . ▶ $ _____ If "Yes," enter the total expenses paid or incurred in connection with the lobbying activities. ▶ $ _____ Organizations that made an election under section 501(h) by filing Form 5768 must complete Part VI-A. Other organizations checking "Yes," must complete Part VI-B AND attach a statement giving a detailed description of the lobbying activities.	1		X
2	During the year, has the organization, either directly or indirectly, engaged in any of the following acts with any of its trustees, directors, officers, creators, key employees, or members of their families, or with any taxable organization with which any such person is affiliated as an officer, director, trustee, majority owner, or principal beneficiary:			
a	Sale, exchange, or leasing of property?	2a		X
b	Lending of money or other extension of credit?	2b		X
c	Furnishing of goods, services, or facilities?	2c		X
d	Payment of compensation (or payment or reimbursement of expenses if more than $1,000)? See Part V,	2d	X	
e	Transfer of any part of its income or assets? . . . . Form 990 . .	2e		X
	If the answer to any question is "Yes," attach a detailed statement explaining the transactions.			
3	Does the organization make grants for scholarships, fellowships, student loans, etc.?	3		X
4	Attach a statement explaining how the organization determines that individuals or organizations receiving grants or loans from it in furtherance of its charitable programs qualify to receive payments. (See instructions.)			

For Paperwork Reduction Act Notice, see page 1 of the Instructions to Form 990 (or Form 990-EZ). Cat. No. 11285F Schedule A (Form 990) 1994

Part IV Reason for Non-Private Foundation Status (See instructions for definitions.)

The organization is not a private foundation because it is (please check only **ONE** applicable box):

5 ☐ A church, convention of churches, or association of churches. Section 170(b)(1)(A)(i).

6 ☐ A school. Section 170(b)(1)(A)(ii). (Also complete Part V, page 3.)

7 ☐ A hospital or a cooperative hospital service organization. Section 170(b)(1)(A)(iii).

8 ☐ A Federal, state, or local government or governmental unit. Section 170(b)(1)(A)(v).

9 ☐ A medical research organization operated in conjunction with a hospital. Section 170(b)(1)(A)(iii). **Enter the hospital's name, city, and state ▶** ....

10 ☐ An organization operated for the benefit of a college or university owned or operated by a governmental unit. Section 170(b)(1)(A)(iv). (Also complete the **Support Schedule** below.)

11a ☒ An organization that normally receives a substantial part of its support from a governmental unit or from the general public. Section 170(b)(1)(A)(vi). (Also complete the **Support Schedule** below.)

11b ☐ A community trust. Section 170(b)(1)(A)(vi). (Also complete the **Support Schedule** below.)

12 ☐ An organization that normally receives: **(a) no more than 33⅓%** of its support from gross investment income and unrelated business taxable income (less section 511 tax) from businesses acquired by the organization after June 30, 1975, and **(b) more than 33⅓%** of its support from contributions, membership fees, and gross receipts from activities related to its charitable, etc., functions—subject to certain exceptions. See section 509(a)(2). (Also complete the **Support Schedule** below.)

13 ☐ An organization that is not controlled by any disqualified persons (other than foundation managers) and supports organizations described in: **(1)** lines 5 through 12 above; or **(2) section** 501(c)(4), (5), or (6), if they meet the test of section 509(a)(2). (See section 509(a)(3).)

Provide the following information about the supported organizations. (See instructions for Part IV, line 13.)

(a) Name(s) of supported organization(s)	(b) Line number from above

14 ☐ An organization organized and operated to test for public safety. Section 509(a)(4). (See instructions.)

Support Schedule (Complete only if you checked a box on line 10, 11, or 12 above.) **Use cash method of accounting.**

Note: *You may use the worksheet in the instructions for converting from the accrual to the cash method of accounting.*

Calendar year (or fiscal year beginning in) ▶	(a) 1993	(b) 1992	(c) 1991	(d) 1990	(e) Total
15 Gifts, grants, and contributions received. (Do not include unusual grants. See line 28.)	$742,300	$696,800	$640,600	$594,300	$2,674,000
16 Membership fees received	1,100	1,500	1,500	1,400	5,500
17 Gross receipts from admissions, merchandise sold or services performed, or furnishing of facilities in any activity that is not a business unrelated to the organization's charitable, etc., purpose	31,200	26,400	30,600	24,900	113,100
18 Gross income from interest, dividends, amounts received from payments on securities loans (section 512(a)(5)), rents, royalties, and unrelated business taxable income (less section 511 taxes) from businesses acquired by the organization after June 30, 1975.	26,000	27,700	22,100	20,400	96,200
19 Net income from unrelated business activities not included in line 18					
20 Tax revenues levied for the organization's benefit and either paid to it or expended on its behalf					
21 The value of services or facilities furnished to the organization by a governmental unit without charge. Do not include the value of services or facilities generally furnished to the public without charge.					
22 Other income. Attach a schedule. Do not include gain or (loss) from sale of capital assets					
23 Total of lines 15 through 22	$800,600	$752,400	$694,800	$641,000	$2,888,800
24 Line 23 minus line 17	$769,400	$726,000	$664,200	$616,100	$2,775,700
25 Enter 1% of line 23	$ 8,006	$ 7,524	$ 6,948	$ 6,410	

26 Organizations described in lines 10 or 11:

a Enter 2% of amount in column (e), line 24 . . . . $ 55,514

b Attach a list (which is not open to public inspection) showing the name of and amount contributed by each person (other than a governmental unit or publicly supported organization) whose total gifts for 1990 through 1993 exceeded the amount shown in line 26a. Enter the sum of all these excess amounts here . . . . ▶ -0-

(Support Schedule continued on page 3)

Part IV Support Schedule (continued) (Complete only if you checked a box on line 10, 11, or 12.)

27 Organizations described on line 12:   **N/A**

a Attach a list, for amounts shown on lines 15, 16, and 17, to show the name of, and total amounts received in each year from, each "disqualified person." Enter the sum of such amounts for each year:

(1993) .... (1992) .... (1991) .... (1990) ....

b Attach a list to show, for 1990 through 1993, the name of, and amount included in line 17 for, each person (other than a "disqualified person") from whom the organization received, during that year, an amount that was more than the larger of **(1)** the amount on line 25 for the year or **(2)** $5,000. Include organizations described in lines 5 through 11, as well as individuals. After computing the difference between the amount received and the larger amount described in **(1)** or **(2)**, enter the sum of all these differences (the excess amounts) for each year:

(1993) .... (1992) .... (1991) .... (1990) ....

28 For an organization described in line 10, 11, or 12, that received any unusual grants during 1990 through 1993, attach a list (which is not open to public inspection) for each year showing the name of the contributor, the date and amount of the grant, and a brief description of the nature of the grant. Do not include these grants in line 15. (See instructions.)   **N/A**

Part V Private School Questionnaire
(To be completed ONLY by schools that checked the box on line 6 in Part IV)   **N/A**

		Yes	No
29	Does the organization have a racially nondiscriminatory policy toward students by statement in its charter, bylaws, other governing instrument, or in a resolution of its governing body? **29**		
30	Does the organization include a statement of its racially nondiscriminatory policy toward students in all its brochures, catalogues, and other written communications with the public dealing with student admissions, programs, and scholarships? **30**		
31	Has the organization publicized its racially nondiscriminatory policy through newspaper or broadcast media during the period of solicitation for students, or during the registration period if it has no solicitation program, in a way that makes the policy known to all parts of the general community it serves? **31**		

If "Yes," please describe; if "No," please explain. (If you need more space, attach a separate statement.)

....
....
....
....

32	Does the organization maintain the following:		
a	Records indicating the racial composition of the student body, faculty, and administrative staff? **32a**		
b	Records documenting that scholarships and other financial assistance are awarded on a racially nondiscriminatory basis? **32b**		
c	Copies of all catalogues, brochures, announcements, and other written communications to the public dealing with student admissions, programs, and scholarships? **32c**		
d	Copies of all material used by the organization or on its behalf to solicit contributions? **32d**		

If you answered "No" to any of the above, please explain. (If you need more space, attach a separate statement.)

....

33	Does the organization discriminate by race in any way with respect to:		
a	Students' rights or privileges? **33a**		
b	Admissions policies? **33b**		
c	Employment of faculty or administrative staff? **33c**		
d	Scholarships or other financial assistance? (See instructions.) **33d**		
e	Educational policies? **33e**		
f	Use of facilities? **33f**		
g	Athletic programs? **33g**		
h	Other extracurricular activities? **33h**		

If you answered "Yes" to any of the above, please explain. (If you need more space, attach a separate statement.)

....
....

34a	Does the organization receive any financial aid or assistance from a governmental agency? **34a**		
b	Has the organization's right to such aid ever been revoked or suspended? **34b**		

If you answered "Yes" to either 34a or b, please explain using an attached statement.

35	Does the organization certify that it has complied with the applicable requirements of sections 4.01 through 4.05 of Rev. Proc. 75-50, 1975-2 C.B. 587, covering racial nondiscrimination? If "No," attach an explanation. (See instructions for Part V.) . . **35**		

Schedule A (Form 990) 1994   Page **4**

Part VI-A **Lobbying Expenditures by Electing Public Charities** (See instructions.)
              (To be completed **ONLY** by an eligible organization that filed Form 5768)

Check here ▶ **a** ☐ If the organization belongs to an affiliated group (see instructions).

Check here ▶ **b** ☐ If you checked **a** and "limited control" provisions apply (see instructions).   **N/A**

Limits on Lobbying Expenditures (The term "expenditures" means amounts paid or incurred)		**(a)** Affiliated group totals	**(b)** To be completed for ALL electing organizations
36	Total lobbying expenditures to influence public opinion (grassroots lobbying)	36	
37	Total lobbying expenditures to influence a legislative body (direct lobbying)	37	
38	Total lobbying expenditures (add lines 36 and 37)	38	
39	Other exempt purpose expenditures (see Part VI-A instructions)	39	
40	Total exempt purpose expenditures (add lines 38 and 39) (see instructions)	40	
41	Lobbying nontaxable amount. Enter the amount from the following table—		
	If the amount on line 40 is— **The lobbying nontaxable amount is—**		
	Not over $500,000 . . . . 20% of the amount on line 40 . . . . . ⎫		
	Over $500,000 but not over $1,000,000 . . $100,000 plus 15% of the excess over $500,000 ⎪		
	Over $1,000,000 but not over $1,500,000 . $175,000 plus 10% of the excess over $1,000,000 ⎬ 41		
	Over $1,500,000 but not over $17,000,000 . $225,000 plus 5% of the excess over $1,500,000 ⎪		
	Over $17,000,000 . . . . $1,000,000 . . . . ⎭		
42	Grassroots nontaxable amount (enter 25% of line 41)	42	
43	Subtract line 42 from line 36. Enter -0- if line 42 is more than line 36	43	
44	Subtract line 41 from line 38. Enter -0- if line 41 is more than line 38	44	

Caution: File Form 4720 if there is an amount on either line 43 or line 44.

4-Year Averaging Period Under Section 501(h)
(Some organizations that made a section 501(h) election do not have to complete all of the five columns below.
See the instructions for lines 45 through 50.)

	Lobbying Expenditures During 4-Year Averaging Period				
Calendar year (or **fiscal year beginning in)** ▶	**(a)** 1994	**(b)** 1993	**(c)** 1992	**(d)** 1991	**(e)** Total
45 Lobbying nontaxable amount (see instructions)					
46 Lobbying ceiling amount (150% of line 45(e))					
47 Total lobbying expenditures (see instructions)					
48 Grassroots nontaxable amount (see instructions)					
49 Grassroots ceiling amount (150% of line 48(e))					
50 Grassroots lobbying expenditures (see instructions)					

Part VI-B **Lobbying Activity by Nonelecting Public Charities**
              (For reporting by organizations that did not complete Part VI-A)   **N/A**

During the year, did the organization attempt to influence national, state or local legislation, including any
attempt to influence public opinion on a legislative matter or referendum, through the use of:

		Yes	No	Amount
a	Volunteers			
b	Paid staff or management (include compensation in expenses reported on lines c through h) . . .			
c	Media advertisements			
d	Mailings to members, legislators, or the public			
e	Publications, or published or broadcast statements			
f	Grants to other organizations for lobbying purposes			
g	Direct contact with legislators, their staffs, government officials, or a legislative body			
h	Rallies, demonstrations, seminars, conventions, speeches, lectures, or any other means			
i	Total lobbying expenditures (add lines c through h)			

If "Yes" to any of the above, also attach a statement giving a detailed description of the lobbying activities.

Schedule A (Form 990) 1994

Part VII	Information Regarding Transfers To and Transactions and Relationships With Noncharitable Exempt Organizations

51 Did the reporting organization directly or indirectly engage in any of the following with any other organization described in section 501(c) of the Code (other than section 501(c)(3) organizations) or in section 527, relating to political organizations?

		Yes	No
a Transfers from the reporting organization to a noncharitable exempt organization of:			
(i) Cash	**51a(i)**		X
(ii) Other assets	**a(ii)**		X
b Other transactions:			
(i) Sales of assets to a noncharitable exempt organization	**b(i)**		X
(ii) Purchases of assets from a noncharitable exempt organization	**b(ii)**		X
(iii) Rental of facilities or equipment	**b(iii)**	X	
(iv) Reimbursement arrangements	**b(iv)**		X
(v) Loans or loan guarantees	**b(v)**		X
(vi) Performance of services or membership or fundraising solicitations	**b(vi)**		X
c Sharing of facilities, equipment, mailing lists, other assets, or paid employees	**c**		X

d If the answer to any of the above is "Yes," complete the following schedule. Column (b) should always show the fair market value of the goods, other assets, or services given by the reporting organization. If the organization received less than fair market value in any transaction or sharing arrangement, show in column (d) the value of the goods, other assets, or services received.

(a) Line no.	(b) Amount involved	(c) Name of noncharitable exempt organization	(d) Description of transfers, transactions, and sharing arrangements
b(iii)	$800	Fraternal Society of Utopia	Rental of hall, kitchen, dining room equipment and supplies for the agency's annual dinner/dance.

52a Is the organization directly or indirectly affiliated with, or related to, one or more tax-exempt organizations described in section 501(c) of the Code (other than section 501(c)(3)) or in section 527? . . . . ☐ Yes ☒ No

b If "Yes," complete the following schedule.

(a) Name of organization	(b) Type of organization	(c) Description of relationship
None		

FAMILY SERVICE AGENCY OF UTOPIA, INC.
EIN: 12-3456789
Form 990 (1994) Schedule Attachment

Part I, line 1d: Contributions, gifts, grants, etc.

No single contributor gave $5,000 or more during the year.

Part I, line 8c: Sale of assets other than inventory

Proceeds from sales of:
Publicly traded securities	$24,200
Cost and sales expenses	23,700
Gain	$ 500

Part I, line 9: Special events and activities

	Dinner/ dance	Celebrity auction	Raffle	Total
Gross revenue	$14,500	$9,200	$4,700	$28,400
Less:				
Direct expenses	11,200	3,700	3,100	18,000
Net income	$ 3,300	$5,500	$1,600	$10,400

Part I, line 10: Sales

Proceeds from sale of educational publications	$1,400
Cost of publications sold	$1,000
Gross profit	$ 400

Part I, line 16:

Payments to affiliates	$12,400

Two percent (2%) of unrestricted contributions collected
were paid to the National Association of Family Service
Agencies for its general operations, as required by our
affiliation agreement with that organization.

Part II, line 22: Grants and allocations

Family Counseling:
National Association of Family Service Agencies Milwaukee, Wisconsin 53226	$ 3,000

Adoption Services:
National Association of Family Service Agencies	$10,000
Utopia Adolescent Center Utopia, Pennsylvania 11111	5,000
Utopia Children's Services Utopia, Pennsylvania 11111	6,000
Total	$21,000

Foster Home Care:
Utopia Children's Services	$ 5,000
Utopia Adolescent Center	6,900
Total	$11,900

FAMILY SERVICE AGENCY OF UTOPIA, INC.
EIN: 12-3456789
Form 990 (1994) Schedule Attachment

Part II, line 23: Specific assistance to individuals

Adoption assistance to low-income families $20,400

Reimbursement of out-of-pocket expenses
for foster home care 25,400
Total $45,800

Part II, line 42: Depreciation AND Part IV, line 57 -- Land, buildings, equipment

Asset	Date acquired	Cost	Prior years' depreciation	Method	Useful life	Current depreciation
Land	1992	$ 45,500	--	--	--	--
Office equip.	1987	3,000	$2,450	S.L.	8 years	$ 350
Office equip.	1994	11,500	--	S.L.	8 years	1,150
Building	1992	128,000	5,550	S.L.	30 years	3,700
Total		$188,000	$8,000			$5,200

Part IV, line 54: Investments - securities (end of year)

Common stock	Number of shares	Book value (cost)
A Corporation	4,000	$ 98,000
B Corporation	1,600	17,400
C Corporation	1,000	22,100
D Corporation	1,200	58,200
E Corporation	800	43,700
F Corporation	2,000	109,200
G Corporation	1,000	62,400
H Corporation	600	16,500
I Corporation	900	46,900
Total		$474,400

Part IV, line 62: Support and revenue designated for future periods

		Designated for Year		
	1994	1995	1996	Total
Received prior to 1994	$20,000	$20,800	$20,800	$61,600
Received in 1994		9,000	9,000	18,000
Expended (earned) in 1994	(20,000)			(20,000)
Balance at end of 1994	$ -0-	$29,800	$29,800	$59,600

All of the above represent grants designated by contributors to support adoption services
in future periods.

FAMILY SERVICE AGENCY OF UTOPIA, INC.
EIN: 12-3456789
Form 990 (1994) Schedule Attachment

Part IV, line 64b: Mortgages and other notes payable

Mortgage payable to State Bank of Utopia
@6% per annum $3,200

Part V: List of Officers, Directors, Trustees, and Key Employees (Continued)

(A)	(B)	(C)	(D)	(E)
	Title & avg. hrs. per week		Cont. to employee benefit plans	
Name & address	devoted to position	Compensation	& deferred compensation	Expense account & other allowances
Zenobia Boyce 23 Wonderful Way Utopia, PA 11111	Secretary 3 hrs./wk.	-0-	-0-	-0-

FAMILY SERVICE AGENCY OF UTOPIA, INC.
EIN: 12-3456789
Attachment for Schedule A (Form 990) (1994)

Part III, Item 4

Organizations receiving grants are required to furnish:

1. A copy of their section 501(c)(3) determination letter from the IRS.

2. Audited financial statements for the 2 preceding years.

3. Evidence of service quality and effectiveness in reaching poverty level population.

4. Quarterly report of services delivered.

Supplemental Instructions and a Completed Sample of Form 990 and Schedule A (Form 990)

This part of the instructions provides a set of facts and a filled-in example to help you prepare a complete and accurate Form 990 and Schedule A (Form 990) for 1994.

To avoid having to respond to requests for missing information, complete all applicable line items; answer "Yes," "No," or "N/A" (not applicable) to each question on the return; make an entry (including a "-0-" when appropriate) on all **total** lines; and enter "None" or "N/A" if an entire part of Form 990 does not apply. If one or more applicable line items are not completed, we will consider the return incomplete and contact the organization for the missing information. The penalty of $10 a day for not filing a return under section 6652(c) also applies if a return is submitted without required information.

The illustrated example of a completed Form 990 and Schedule A (Form 990) for 1994 was prepared using the following facts.

The Family Service Agency of Utopia, Inc., a not-for-profit organization, is exempt from income tax under section 501(c)(3) of the Internal Revenue Code. The agency is a member of the National Association of Family Service Agencies. Its principal programs include: (1) adoption of infants and children; (2) foster home care; and (3) counseling individuals and families.

The agency was incorporated September 16, 1968. It received a letter from the IRS dated January 25, 1971, notifying it that it had been determined not to be a private foundation within the meaning of section 509(a).

The agency uses the fund method of accounting and is on the accrual- and calendar-year basis. The books are in the custody of the bookkeeper, Ms. Nancy Ward at 1414 West Ash Drive, Utopia, PA 11111.

All contributions are considered available for unrestricted use, unless specifically restricted by the donor. Pledges are recorded in the books of account whenever the agency is notified of the pledge, and allowances are provided for amounts estimated to be uncollectible. Bequests are recorded as income at the time the agency has established a right to the bequest and the proceeds are measurable.

A substantial number of volunteers have donated significant amounts of their time to the organization's adoption program. No amounts have been reflected in the financial statements, however, for donated services.

In accordance with the affiliation agreement with the national organization, a portion of the unrestricted support from the public is remitted to the national organization for its use as determined by its board of directors. Additional grants are made to individuals and organizations as determined by the agency's board of directors.

For its annual dinner/dance, the agency paid $800 (fair rental value) to rent a hall, kitchen, tables, dishes, etc., from the Fraternal Society of Utopia, an unrelated section 501(c)(10) fraternal lodge. This was the agency's only transaction with exempt organizations not described in section 501(c)(3). The agency is not affiliated with or related to any such organization.

Depreciation of $5,200 was computed for buildings and equipment on a straight line basis.

In 1994, the agency incurred joint costs of $9,600 for informational materials and activities that included fundraising appeals. Of those costs, $6,100 was allocated to fundraising expense, $400 was allocated to adoption services expense, $2,400 was allocated to counseling services expense, and $700 was allocated to management and general expense.

The expenses for the year are allocable as follows:

Statement of Functional Expenses

	Program Services			Supporting Services		
	Adoption	Foster Home Care	Counseling	Mgmt. & General	Fund Raising	TOTAL
Salaries . . .	$ 25,600	$ 25,100	$126,900	$33,100	$36,800	$247,500
Pension plan cont. .	100	.....	100	100	.....	300
Other emp. benefits .	1,700	1,400	6,300	2,100	1,500	13,000
Payroll taxes, etc. .	3,000	2,300	12,400	3,000	3,100	23,800
Professional fees .	63,000	300	61,200	2,600	800	127,900
Supplies	3,900	21,300	1,300	1,800	1,700	30,000
Telephone	9,500	1,000	1,100	1,500	2,300	15,400
Postage & shipping .	2,900	1,300	8,900	1,000	9,000	23,100
Occupancy . . .	2,550	21,100	11,250	1,500	1,350	37,750
Interest	.....	.....	100	800	.....	900
Rental & maintenance of equipment .	3,550	1,100	1,250	1,500	1,350	8,750
Prtg. & publications .	5,400	400	6,400	300	1,600	14,100
Travel & trans. .	12,500	2,000	2,200	2,300	3,000	22,000
Conferences, etc. . .	3,700	7,100	2,000	4,500	400	17,700
Specific assistance to individuals .	16,500	24,300	5,000	.....	.....	45,800
Membership dues .	500	.....	.....	.....	.....	500
Awards & grants—						
To national org. .	10,000	.....	3,000	.....	.....	13,000
To indvs./other organizations .	11,000	11,900	.....	.....	.....	22,900
Insurance . . .	10,450	10,100	5,100	600	50	26,300
Other expenses .	1,250	500	400	100	2,050	4,300
Depr.-bldgs./equip.	700	600	2,900	600	400	5,200
Total functional expenses:	$187,800	$131,800	$257,800	$57,400	$65,400	$700,200
Payments to national org.						12,400
Total expenses						$712,600

The financial statements for the Family Service Agency of Utopia are given on the following pages.

We made the following entries on Form 990 and Schedule A (Form 990) and have attached explanatory schedules.

Form 990

Part I—Line 1a.—We have entered the $473,700 of direct contributions received from the public and the $9,600 received from legacies and bequests.

Line 1b.—We have entered the amount of $223,500 received through the United Way organization and the $4,000 collected through the local auxiliary.

Line 2.—We have entered the total of program service revenue from Part VII, lines 93(a) and (g). This included $2,300 in consultation fees and $300 in fees from government agencies.

Line 3.—We have entered $1,600 of membership dues and assessments. These dues are not equivalent to contributions because members receive benefits and privileges (educational programs and counseling services) which have a monetary value in excess of their dues payment. Therefore, they are reported on line 3. (See the discussion of this principle in the instructions for line 3 of Form 990.)

Lines 4 and 5.—We have entered the $14,800 received in interest income and $16,400 received in dividends for the year.

Line 8.—We have entered $24,200, the selling price of securities sold, and subtracted their cost basis and the sales expense. We entered the $500 gain on line 8d.

Family Service Agency of Utopia, Inc.

Statement of Revenue, Expenses, and Changes in Fund Balances

For the Year Ended December 31, 1994

	Current Funds		Land, Bldg., & Equip. Fund	Endow- ment Fund	TOTAL
	Unrestricted	Restricted			
Revenue:					
Public support—					
Received directly—					
Contributions (net of estimated uncollectible pledges of $19,500)	$460,100	$ 6,200	$ 7,200	$ 200	$473,700
Special events (net of costs of direct benefit to participants of $18,000)	10,400				10,400
Legacies & bequests	9,200			400	9,600
Received indirectly—					
Collected through local auxiliary	4,000				4,000
Allocated by federated fundraising organizations (net of their related fundraising expenses estimated at $12,300)	223,500				223,500
Total public support	707,200	6,200	7,200	600	721,200
Revenue and grants from governmental agencies		300			300
Other revenue:					
Membership dues—individuals	1,600				1,600
Program service fees	2,300				2,300
Sales of materials and services (net of direct expenses of $1,000)	400				400
Endowment and other investment income	30,500	700			31,200
Miscellaneous revenue	2,800				2,800
Gains (losses) on investments	(2,000)			2,500	500
Total other revenue	35,600	700		2,500	38,800
Total revenue	742,800	7,200	7,200	3,100	760,300
Expenses:					
Program services—					
Adoption	187,100		700		187,800
Foster home care	131,200		600		131,800
Counseling	244,100	10,800	2,900		257,800
Total program services	562,400	10,800	4,200		577,400
Supporting services—					
Management & general	56,800		600		57,400
Fundraising	65,000		400		65,400
Total supporting services	121,800		1,000		122,800
Payments to national organization	12,400				12,400
Total expenses	696,600	10,800	5,200		712,600
Excess (deficiency) of revenue over expenses	46,200	(3,600)	2,000	3,100	47,700
Fund balances, beginning of year	446,300	10,000	156,800	191,700	804,800
Other changes in fund balances:					
Acquisition of fixed assets	(7,000)		7,000		
Mortgage payment	(400)		400		
Fund balances, end of year	$485,100	$ 6,400	$166,200	$194,800	$852,500

Family Service Agency of Utopia, Inc.
BALANCE SHEET
December 31, 1994

ASSETS	Current Funds Unrestricted	Current Funds Restricted	Land, Bldg., & Equip. Fund	Endowment Fund	TOTAL
Current assets:					
Cash, including $115,000 in interest-bearing accounts	$121,100	$ 300			$121,400
Short-term investments, at cost (approximates market)	100,000	7,100			107,100
Receivables:					
Program service fees, less allowance of $200	600				600
Pledges, less allowance of $11,200	58,900				58,900
Grants		1,000	$ 4,800		5,800
From affiliated organizations	1,000				1,000
Interfund receivable (payable)	2,000	(2,000)			
Inventory, at lower of cost or market	7,000				7,000
Prepaid expenses and deferred charges	13,800				13,800
Total current assets	304,400	6,400	4,800		315,600
Noncurrent investments	279,600			$194,800	474,400
Land, buildings, and equipment, at cost, less accumulated depreciation			174,800		174,800
Total assets	$584,000	$6,400	$179,600	$194,800	$964,800

LIABILITIES AND FUND BALANCES

	Current Funds Unrestricted	Current Funds Restricted	Land, Bldg., & Equip. Fund	Endowment Fund	TOTAL
Current liabilities:					
Accounts payable and accrued expenses	$ 39,300				$ 39,300
Support & revenue designated for subsequent period	59,600				59,600
Total current liabilities	98,900				98,900
Mortgage payable, 6%, due 1996			$ 3,200		3,200
Amounts payable under capital lease			10,200		10,200
Total liabilities	98,900		13,400		112,300
Fund balances:					
Current unrestricted:					
Designated by the governing board for—					
Long-term investment	279,600				279,600
Purchase of new equipment	10,400				10,400
Undesignated—available for general activities	195,100				195,100
Current restricted for:					
Professional education		$4,000			4,000
Expansion of services		2,400			2,400
Land, building, and equipment:					
Unexpended restricted			4,800		4,800
Equity in fixed assets			161,400		161,400
Endowment				$194,800	194,800
Total fund balances	485,100	6,400	166,200	194,800	852,500
Total liabilities and fund balances	$584,000	$6,400	$179,600	$194,800	$964,800

Line 9.—We have reported the revenue of $28,400 less direct expenses of $18,000 from special events and activities. As there were no contributions included in gross revenue from these events, we entered "-0-" within the parentheses on line 9a. All of the $18,000 of expenses attributable to this function are reportable here and none in Part II.

Line 10.—We have reported, on line 10a, $2,000 in gross sales of educational publications, less $600 of returns and allowances. On line 10b, we entered $1,000, the cost of goods sold, and entered the $400 gross profit on line 10c.

Line 11.—We have entered the gross amount of other revenue received from the sale of an easement. This amount was also reported in Part VII on line 103(a).

Line 13.—We have entered the program services expenses from line 44, column (B) of Part II.

Line 14.—We have entered the management and general expenses from line 44, column (C) of Part II.

Line 15.—We have entered the fundraising expenses from line 44, column (D) of Part II.

Line 16.—We have entered the portion of the unrestricted support from the public that was remitted to the national organization.

Lines 17 and 18 are self-explanatory.

Line 19.—We have entered the net asset balance at the beginning of the year from line 74, column (A) of Part IV.

Line 21.—We have entered the total of lines 18, 19, and 20. This computed net asset figure agrees with the end-of-year net asset balance from line 74, column (B) of Part IV.

Part II.—From the breakdown of the expenses provided, we have listed the organization's expenses attributable to program services; management and general; and fundraising functions. In column (A), we reported the total expenses for each line of columns (B), (C), and (D). The total for column (A) was included on line 17, "Total expenses," of Part I. The expenses in Part II include only those that are not reported on lines 6b, 8b, 9b, or 10b of Part I. (The expenses of the special events and activities are reported on line 9b of Part I and, therefore, are not also reported in Part II. In this example, the expenses listed in the program service column include those attributable to adoption services, foster home care, and family counseling.) In the space below line 44, the joint costs incurred in combined fundraising and educational campaigns are reported in accordance with the facts given.

Part III.—We have listed and described the organization's three program services and indicated the expenses attributable to each. Statistical information regarding the number of individuals, families, and organizations served is also provided. We have entered the amount attributable to donated services in the narrative section for "Adoption Services."

Part IV.—We have completed beginning- and end-of-year balance sheets. **Note:** *For the sake of brevity, the beginning-of-year balance sheet was not given in the statement of facts.*

Part V.—We have entered, in Part V and in an attachment, the name, address, and other required information for each officer, director, and key employee during the year even though some of them serve without compensation. We entered "-0-" when there were no amounts to enter. No compensation was provided by a related organization.

Note: *For the sake of brevity, specific names, addresses, titles, and hours worked were not given in the statement of facts.*

Part VI—Lines 76 through 81.—From the facts given, the appropriate answer to each of these questions was either "No," "N/A," or "-0-."

Line 82b.—We have entered the amount of $8,000 in donated services that was also reported in the narrative section of Part III.

Line 92.—We have entered "N/A" because the organization is not a section 4947(a)(1) nonexempt charitable trust.

Part VII.—We have listed both consultation fees and fees from government agencies as the organization's only source of program service revenue for the year. None of the organization's other receipts constitute program service revenue as defined in the instructions for line 2 of Part I.

In column (D), we have entered the amounts received from income-producing activities that do not further the charitable purposes of the agency (other than by providing funds for such purposes) and the income from which would be taxable as unrelated business income but for specific provisions in the Code that render such income nontaxable. We have also entered the appropriate exclusion codes (from the Instructions for Form 990) to indicate the Code provision that excludes each amount from classification as unrelated business income.

In column (E), we have entered the amounts received from activities that contributed to the agency's related or exempt purposes.

Part VIII.—We indicated the line number for the related or exempt function amounts we entered in column (E) and explained how each reported activity contributed importantly to the accomplishment of the agency's exempt purposes.

Part IX.—We entered "N/A" because we answered "No" to question 88 of Part VI.

Schedule A (Form 990)

Part I.—We have entered the compensation and contribution to employee benefit plans for each employee listed.

Part IV.—We have checked the box on line 11a, based on our sample facts, and entered the appropriate information on lines 15 through 28. The amounts shown on these lines are from returns for previous years that are not part of this example.

Parts VI-A and VI-B.—We have entered "N/A" in both Parts VI-A and VI-B as the agency did not engage in any lobbying activity during the year and did not file Form 5768 to make a section 501(h) election.

Part VII.—We have entered the required information regarding the agency's rental of facilities and equipment from a fraternal organization for the annual dinner/dance. Note that this does not constitute a "sharing of facilities or equipment" (line 51c) which connotes a continuing arrangement and joint or alternating use of the same assets (sharing of office space and equipment, for example). Because there was no such sharing and because the agency was not otherwise affiliated with or related to the fraternal organization, we answered "No" to question 52a.

CHAPTER 5

Financial Planning and Forecasting

Never be sure you are totally right because you are not. Never be too disappointed when you are wrong because it happens all the time.

Advice to fellow forecasters from Clifton Clarke
Assistant to the Dean for Academic Affairs
LaGuardia Community College, CUNY
The Journal of Business Forecasting, *Summer 1993*

Management in both private and public organizations typically operate under conditions of uncertainty or risk. Probably the most important function of a nonprofit entity is forecasting. A forecast is a starting point for planning. The objective of forecasting is to reduce risk in decision making.

Forecasts are needed for many planning activities, such as purchasing, manpower, and financial planning. The forecasting of personnel and operating expenses is also vital for effective planning and control. Further, top management needs forecasts to plan and implement long-term strategic objectives and to plan for capital expenditures.

Managers of nonprofit institutions must make forecasts for revenues and expenditures. Hospital administrators face the problem of forecasting the health care needs of the community. In order to do this efficiently, a projection has to be made of:

- The growth in absolute size of population.
- The changes in the number of people in various age groupings.
- The varying medical needs these different age groups will have.

Forecasting costs in hospitals is also important for effective planning and control. Forecasts are used to determine such basic things as workload and to develop plans for meal production. Other applications include using forecasts as devices for cash-flow analysis, improving fund raising, cost control, marketing, streamlining, ordering, improving operational efficiency, and planning capital expenditures.

Universities need to forecast student enrollments; facility requirements (classrooms, staff, rental space availability, etc.); cost of operations; and, in many cases, what level of funds will be provided by tuition and by government appropriations.

In the context of cash management and future viability of the agency, the ultimate test for a forecast is to guide proper and timely managerial action toward improved control of cash flow. A sound forecast for cash inflows and outlays will eliminate the need (or minimize the cost) of short-term borrowing and extra fund-raising efforts. It will also help to determine the amount of money for investment. More specifically, cash-flow forecasting can serve a number of goals, including:

1. Avoidance of financial distress or bankruptcy.
2. Escape from costly mistakes such as ill-conceived ventures.
3. Aid in cash management and control.
4. Increased confidence in the agency on the part of creditors and donors.
5. Improved use of capital, such as investment of surplus funds.

FORECASTING METHODOLOGY

There is a wide range of forecasting techniques which the nonprofit manager may choose from. There are basically two approaches to forecasting: qualitative and quantitative. They are as follows:

1. Qualitative approach—forecasts based on judgment and opinion.
   Executive opinions.
   Delphi technique.
2. Quantitative approach.
   a. Forecasts based on historical data.
   Naive methods.
   Moving averages.
   Exponential smoothing.
   Trend analysis.
   Classical decomposition.

Life-cycle analysis.

Box-Jenkins.

   b. Associative (causal) forecasts.

Simple regression.

Multiple regression.

Note: Discussions on techniques such as classical decomposition, life-cycle analysis, and Box-Jenkins are reserved for advanced forecasting literature.

What technique or techniques to select depends on the following criteria:

1. What is the cost associated with developing the forecasting model as compared to potential gains resulting from its use? The choice is one of benefit/cost tradeoff.
2. How complicated are the relationships that are being forecast?
3. Is the forecast being made for short-run or long-run purposes?
4. How much accuracy is desired?
5. Is there a minimum tolerance level of errors?
6. What amount of data is available? Techniques vary in the amount of data they require.

THE QUALITATIVE APPROACH

The qualitative (or judgmental) approach can be useful in formulating short-term forecasts and also can supplement the projections based on the use of any of the qualitative methods. Two of the better-known qualitative forecasting methods are Executive Opinions and the Delphi Method.

Executive Opinions

In this approach, the subjective views of executives or experts from various functional areas are averaged to generate a forecast about future revenues. Usually this method is used in conjunction with some quantitative method, such as trend extrapolation. The management team modifies the resulting forecast based on their expectations.

The advantage of this approach is that the forecasting is done quickly and easily, without need of elaborate statistics. Also, the jury of executive opinions may be the only feasible means of forecasting in the absence of adequate data. The disadvantage of this method is that it leads to "group think." This is a set of problems inherent to those who meet as a group. Foremost among these problems are high cohesiveness, strong leadership, and insulation of the group. With high cohesiveness, the group becomes increasingly conforming through group pressure which helps stifle dissension and critical thought. Strong leadership fosters group pressure for unanimous opinion. Insulation of the group tends to separate the group from outside opinions, if given.

The Delphi Method

The Delphi Method is a group technique in which a panel of experts are individually questioned about their perceptions of future events. The experts do not meet as a group in order to reduce the possibility that consensus is reached because of dominant personality factors. Instead, the forecasts and accompanying arguments are summarized by an outside party and returned to the experts along with further questions. This continues until a consensus is reached by the group, especially after only a few rounds. This type of method is useful and quite effective for long-range forecasting. The technique uses a "questionnaire" format and thus eliminates the disadvantages of group think. There is no committee, and no debate. The experts are not influenced by peer pressure to forecast a certain way, as the answer is not intended to be reached by consensus or unanimity. Low reliability and lack of consensus from the returns are cited as the main disadvantages of the Delphi Method. (See Table 5.1.)

T A B L E 5.1

An Example of the Use of the Delphi Method

1	2	3	4	5
Population (in millions)	Midpoint	Number of Panelists	Probability Distribution of Panelists	Weighted Average (2 × 4)
30 and above	—	0	0.00	0
20–30	25	1	0.05	1.25
15–19	17	2	0.10	1.70
10–14	12	2	0.10	1.20
5–9	7	7	0.35	2.45
2–4	3	8	0.40	1.20
Less than 2	1	0	0.00	0
Total		20	1.00	7.80

Case example: "In 1982, a panel of 20 representatives, with college educations, from different parts of the U.S.A., were asked to estimate the population of Bombay, India. None of the panelists had been to India since World War I.
    "The population was estimated to be 7.8 million, which is very close to the actual population."
Source: Singhvi, Surendra. "Financial Forecast: Why and How?" *Managerial Planning*. March–April 1984.

A Word of Caution

It is important to realize that forecasting is not an exact science like mathematics; it is an art. The quality of forecasts tends to improve over time as a forecaster gains more experience. Evidence, however, shows that forecasts using qualitative techniques are not as accurate as those using quantitative techniques:

> Humans possess unique knowledge and inside information not available to quantitative methods. Surprisingly, however, empirical studies and laboratory experiments have shown that their [humans'] forecasts are not more accurate than those of quantitative methods. Humans tend to be optimistic and underestimate the future uncertainty. In addition, the cost of forecasting with judgmental methods is often considerably higher than when quantitative methods are used.[1]

Note: Because of the lack of accuracy of qualitative forecasts, a forecaster must use both qualitative and quantitative techniques to create a reasonable forecast.

COMMON FEATURES AND ASSUMPTIONS INHERENT IN FORECASTING

As previously pointed out, forecasting techniques are quite different from each other. But there are certain features and assumptions that underlie the business of forecasting. They are:

1. Forecasting techniques generally assume that the same underlying causal relationship that existed in the past will continue to prevail in the future. In other words, most of our techniques are based on historical data.

2. Forecasts are very rarely perfect. Therefore, for planning purposes, allowances should be made for inaccuracies. For example, the nonprofit manager should always maintain a cash cushion in anticipation of unexpected cash outlays.

3. Forecast accuracy decreases as the time period covered by the forecast (that is, the time horizon) increases. Generally speaking, a long-term forecast tends to be more inaccurate than a short-term forecast, because of the greater uncertainty.

4. Forecasts for groups of items tend to be more accurate than forecasts for individual items, since forecasting errors among items in a group tend to cancel each other out. For example, industry forecasting is more accurate than an individual nonprofit entity's forecasting.

Steps in the Forecasting Process

There are five basic steps in the forecasting process. They are:

1. Determine the what and the why of the forecast, as well as what will be needed. This will indicate the level of detail required in the forecast (forecast by region, forecast by service, etc.), the amount of resources (computer hardware and software, personnel, etc.) that can be justified, and the level of accuracy desired.

2. Establish a time horizon, short-term or long-term. More specifically, for example, project for the next year or the next five years.

3. Select a forecasting technique. Refer to the criteria discussed before.

4. Gather the data and develop a forecast.

5. Identify any assumptions that had to be made in preparing the forecast, and that must be made using it.

6. Monitor the forecast to see whether it is performing in a manner desired. Develop an evaluation system for this purpose. If not, go to step 1. (See Figure 5.1.)

MOVING AVERAGES AND SMOOTHING METHODS

Several forecasting methods fall into the quantitative approach category. These include naive models, moving averages, and exponential smoothing.

Naive Models

Naive forecasting models may be based exclusively on historical observation of revenue, or on other variables, such as costs and cash flows. They do not attempt to explain the underlying causal relationships which produce the variable being forecast.

Naive models may be classified into two groups. One group consists of simple projection models. These models require inputs of data from recent observations, but no statistical analysis is performed. The second group are made up of models which, while naive, are complex enough to require a computer. Traditional methods, such as classical decomposition, moving average, and exponential smoothing models, are some examples.

F I G U R E 5.1

The Forecasting Process

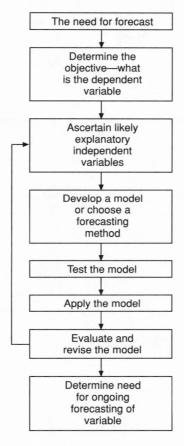

Advantages: Naive models are inexpensive to develop, to store data in, and to operate.

Disadvantages: Naive models do not consider possible causal relationships that underlie the forecasted variable.

1. A simplest example of a naive model type would be to use the actual revenue of the current period as the forecast for the next period. Let us use the symbol Y'_{t+1} as the forecast value and the symbol Y_t as the actual value. Then, $Y'_{t+1} = Y_t$.

2. If you consider trends, then $Y'_{t+1} = Y_t + (Y_t - Y_{t-1})$. This model adds the latest observed absolute period-to-period change to the most recent observed level of the variable.

3. If you want to incorporate the rate of change rather than the absolute amount, then

$$Y'_{t+1} = Y_t \frac{Y_t}{Y_{t-1}}$$

EXAMPLE 5.1

Consider the following data for monthly program fees for the Center for Global Peace:

19X1

Month	Monthly Program Fees
1	$3,050
2	2,980
3	3,670
4	2,910
5	3,340
6	4,060
7	4,750
8	5,510
9	5,280
10	5,504
11	5,810
12	6,100

We will develop forecasts for January 19X2 based on the aforementioned three models.

1. $Y'_{t+1} = Y_t = \$6,100$

2. $Y'_{t+1} = Y_t + (Y_t - Y_{t-1}) = \$6,100 + (\$5,810 - \$5,504) = \$6,100 + \$306$
$= \$6,406$

3. $Y'_{t+1} = Y_t \dfrac{Y_t}{Y_{t-1}}$

$= \$6,100 \times \dfrac{\$6,100}{\$5,810} = \$6,100 \,(1.05)$

$= \$6,405$

The naive models can be applied, with very little need of a computer, to develop forecasts for revenue, costs, and cash flows. They must be compared with more sophisticated models such as the regression for forecasting efficiency.

Smoothing Techniques

Smoothing techniques are a higher form of naive models. There are two typical forms: moving average and exponential smoothing. Moving averages are the simpler of the two.

Moving Averages

Moving averages are averages that are updated as new information is received. With the moving average, a manager simply employs the most recent observations to calculate an average, which is used as the forecast for the next period.

EXAMPLE 5.2
Assume that the nonprofit manager has the following revenue data.

Date	Actual Revenue (Y_t) (in thousands)
Jan. 1	46
2	54
3	53
4	46
5	58
6	49
7	54

In order to predict the revenue for the seventh and eighth days of January, the manager has to pick the number of observations for averaging purposes. Let us consider two cases: one is a six-day moving average and the other is a three-day average.

Case 1

$$Y'_7 = \frac{46 + 54 + 53 + 46 + 58 + 49}{6} = 51$$

$$Y'_8 = \frac{54 + 53 + 46 + 58 + 49 + 54}{6} = 52.3$$

where Y' = predicted

Case 2

$$Y'_7 = \frac{46 + 58 + 49}{3} = 51$$

$$Y'_8 = \frac{58 + 49 + 54}{3} = 53.6$$

Moving Average Calculations

Date	Acual Revenue	Predicted Revenue (Y'_t) Case 1	Case 2
Jan. 1	46		
2	54		
3	53		
4	46		
5	58		51
6	49		53.6
7	54	51	
8		52.3	

In terms of weights given to observations, in case 1, the old data received a weight of 5/6, and the current observation got a weight of 1/6. In case 2, the old data received a weight of only 2/3 while the current observation received a weight of 1/3.

Thus, the manager's choice of the number of periods to use in a moving average is a measure of the relative importance attached to old versus current data.

Advantages and Disadvantages

The moving average is simple to use and easy to understand. However, it has two shortcomings.

- It requires you to retain a great deal of data and carry it along with you from forecast period to forecast period.
- All data in the sample are weighted equally. If more recent data are more valid than older data, why not give them greater weight?

The forecasting method known as "exponential smoothing" gets around these disadvantages.

EXPONENTIAL SMOOTHING

Exponential smoothing is a popular technique for short-run forecasting by managers. It uses a weighted average of past data as the basis for a forecast. The procedure gives heaviest weight to more recent information and smaller weights to observations in the more distant past. The reason for this is that the future is more dependent upon the recent past than on the distant past. The method is known to be effective when there is randomness and no seasonal fluctuations in the data. One disadvantage of the method, however, is that it does not include economic or industry factors such as market conditions, prices, unemployment levels, and the effects of competitors' actions.

The Model

The formula for exponential smoothing is:

$$Y'_{t+1} = \alpha Y_t + (1 - \alpha) Y'_t$$

or in words,

$$Y'_{new} = \alpha Y_{old} + (1 - \alpha) Y'_{old}$$

where Y'_{new} = Exponentially smoothed average to be used as the forecast

Y_{old} = Most recent actual data

Y'_{old} = Most recent smoothed forecast

α = Smoothing constant

The higher the α, the higher the weight given to the more recent information.

EXAMPLE 5.3

The data on donations for a public broadcasting station are given below.

Time period (t)	Donations (in thousands) (Y_t)
1	$60.0
2	64.0
3	58.0
4	66.0
5	70.0
6	60.0
7	70.0
8	74.0
9	62.0
10	74.0
11	68.0
12	66.0
13	60.0
14	66.0
15	62.0

To initialize the exponential smoothing process, we must have the initial forecast. The first smoothed forecast to be used can be:

1. First actual observations.

2. An average of the actual data for a few periods.

For illustrative purposes, let us use a six-period average as the initial forecast Y'_7 with a smoothing constant of $= 0.40$.

Then

$$Y'_7 = \frac{Y_1 + Y_2 + Y_3 + Y_4 + Y_5 + Y_6}{6}$$

$$= \frac{60 + 64 + 58 + 66 + 70 + 60}{6} = 63$$

Note that $Y_7 = 70$. Then Y'_8 is computed as follows:

$$Y'_8 = \alpha Y_7 + (1 - \alpha)Y'_7$$

$$= (0.40)(70) + (0.60)(63)$$

$$= 28.0 + 37.80 = 65.80$$

Similarly,

$$Y'_9 = \alpha Y_8 + (1 - \alpha)Y'_8$$

$$= (0.40)(74) + (0.60)(65.80)$$

$$= 29.60 + 39.48 = 69.08$$

and

$$Y'_{10} = \alpha Y_9 + (1 - \alpha)Y'_9$$

$$= (0.40)(62) + (0.60)(69.08)$$

$$= 24.80 + 41.45 = 66.25$$

By using the same procedure, the values of Y'_{11}, Y'_{12}, Y'_{13}, Y'_{14}, and Y'_{15} can be calculated. Table 5.2 shows a comparison between the actual donations and predicted donations by the exponential smoothing method.

Due to the negative and positive differences between actual donations and predicted donations, the forecaster can use a higher or lower smoothing constant (α), in order to adjust the prediction as quickly as possible to large fluctuations in the data series. For example, if the forecast is slow in reacting to increased donations (that is to say, if the difference is negative), the forecaster might want to try a higher value. For practical purposes, the optimal may be picked by minimizing what is known as the *mean squared error* (MSE).

$$MSE = (Y_t - Y'_t)^2/(n - i)$$

T A B L E 5.2

Comparison of Actual Donations and Predicted Donations
(In Thousands of Dollars)

Time Period (t)	Actual Donations (Y_t)	Predicted Donations (Y'_t)	Difference ($Y_t - Y'_t$)	Difference^2 ($Y_t - Y'_t)^2$
1	$60.0			
2	64.0			
3	58.0			
4	66.0			
5	70.0			
6	60.0			
7	70.0	63.00	7.00	49.00
8	74.0	65.80	8.20	67.24
9	62.0	69.08	−7.08	50.13
10	74.0	66.25	7.75	60.06
11	68.0	69.35	−1.35	1.82
12	66.0	68.81	−2.81	7.90
13	60.0	67.69	−7.69	59.14
14	66.0	64.61	1.39	1.93
15	62.0	65.17	−3.17	10.05
				307.27

where i = the number of observations used to determine the initial forecast
(in our example, $i = 6$).
In our example,

$$MSE = 307.27/(15 - 6) = 307.27/9 = 34.14$$

The idea is to select the α that minimizes MSE, which is the average sum
of the variations between the historical donations data and the forecast values for the corresponding periods.

The Computer and Smoothing Techniques

As a manager, you will be confronted with complex problems requiring
large sample data. You will also need to try different values of α for exponential smoothing. Virtually all forecasting software have an exponential
smoothing routine. In addition, spreadsheet programs such as Excel have
add-in commands for moving average and exponential smoothing analysis.

REGRESSION ANALYSIS

Regression analysis is a statistical procedure for estimating mathematically the average relationship between the dependent variable and one or more independent variables. *Simple regression* involves one independent variable (for example, total employment costs in hospitals as a function of patient-days), whereas *multiple regression* involves two or more variables (for example, patient-days and time together). In this section, we will discuss *simple (linear) regression* to illustrate the *least-squares method*, which means that we will assume the $Y = a + bX$ relationship.

The Least-Squares Method

The least-squares method is widely used in regression analysis for estimating the parameter values in a regression equation. The regression method includes all the observed data and attempts to find a line of best fit. To find this line, a technique called the least-squares method is used.

To explain the least-squares method, we define the error as the difference between the observed value and the estimated one and denote it with u. Symbolically,

$$u = Y - Y'$$

where Y = observed value of the dependent variable
  Y' = estimated value based on $Y' = a + bX$

The least-squares criterion requires that the line of best fit be such that the sum of the squares of the errors (or the vertical distance in Figure 5.2 from the observed data points to the line) is a minimum, that is,

$$\text{Minimum: } \Sigma u^2 = \Sigma(Y - a - bX)^2$$

Using differential calculus we obtain the following equations, called normal equations:

$$\Sigma Y = na + b\Sigma X$$
$$\Sigma XY = a\Sigma X + b\Sigma X^2$$

Solving the equations for b and a yields

$$b = \frac{n\Sigma XY - (\Sigma X)(\Sigma Y)}{n\Sigma X^2 - (\Sigma X)^2}$$

$$a = \bar{Y} - b\bar{X}$$

where $\bar{Y} = \Sigma Y/n$ and $\bar{X} = \Sigma X/n$

F I G U R E 5.2

Y and Y'

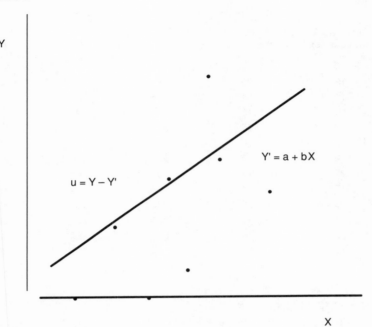

EXAMPLE 5.4

To illustrate the computations of b and a, we will refer to the data in Table 5.3. All the sums required are computed and shown below.

From Table 5.3:

$$\Sigma X = 174 \qquad \Sigma Y = 225 \qquad \Sigma XY = 3,414 \qquad \Sigma X^2 = 2,792$$
$$\bar{X} = \Sigma X/n = 174/12 = 14.5 \qquad \bar{Y} = \Sigma Y/n = 225/12 = 18.75$$

Substituting these values into the formulas:

$$b = \frac{n\Sigma XY - (\Sigma X)(\Sigma Y)}{n\Sigma X^2 - (\Sigma X)^2} = \frac{(12)(3,414) - (174)(225)}{(12)(2,792) - (174)^2} = \frac{1,818}{3,228} = 0.5632$$

$$a = \bar{Y} - b\bar{X} = 18.75 - (0.5632)(14.5) = 18.75 - 8.1664 = 10.5836$$

Thus, $Y' = 10.5836 + 0.5632X$

T A B L E 5.3

Computed Sums

Advertising X (in thousands)	Revenue Y (in thousands)	XY	X^2	Y^2
$ 9	$ 15	$ 135	$ 81	$ 225
19	20	380	361	400
11	14	154	121	196
14	16	224	196	256
23	25	575	529	625
12	20	240	144	400
12	20	240	144	400
22	23	506	484	529
7	14	98	49	196
13	22	286	169	484
15	18	270	225	324
17	18	306	289	324
$174	$225	$3,414	$2,792	$4,359

EXAMPLE 5.5
Assume that the advertising of $10 is to be expended for next year; the projected revenue for the next year will be computed as follows:

$$Y' = 10.5836 + 0.5632X$$
$$= 10.5836 + 0.5632(10)$$
$$= \$16.2156$$

Note that ΣY^2 is not used here but rather is computed for R squared (R^2).

Use of Lotus 1-2-3 (DOS) for Regression

Spreadsheet programs such as Lotus and Excel have a regression routine which you can use without any difficulty. As a matter of fact, in reality, you do not compute the parameter values a and b manually. Figure 5.3 shows the Lotus regression output. Note: The Quattro Pro regression output is very similar.

At this juncture of our discussion, we note from the output:

$$a = 10.58364$$
$$b = 0.563197$$

F I G U R E   5.3

Lotus 1-2-3 Regression Output

Constant	10.58364	(a = 10.58364)
Standard error of Y, estimated	2.343622	
R squared	0.608373	
No. of observations	12	
Degrees of freedom	10	
X coefficients	0.563197	(b = 0.563197)
Standard error of coefficient	0.142893	

The result shows:

$$Y' = 10.58364 + 0.563197$$

That is, $Y' = 10.58364 + 0.563197\ X$.

Other statistics shown on the printout are discussed later in the chapter.

Using Regression on Excel

To utilize Excel for regression analysis, the following procedure needs to be followed:

1. Click the Tools menu.
2. Click Add-Ins.
3. Click Analysis ToolPak. (If Analysis ToolPak is not listed among your available add-ins, exit Excel, double-click the MS Excel Setup icon, click Add/Remove, double-click Add-Ins, and select Analysis ToolPak. Then restart Excel and repeat the above instructions.)

After ensuring that the Analysis ToolPak is available, you can access the regression tool by completing the following steps:

1. Click the Tools menu.
2. Click Data Analysis.
3. Click Regression.

Note: To create a scatter graph, use Excel's Chart Wizard.

Scatter Graph

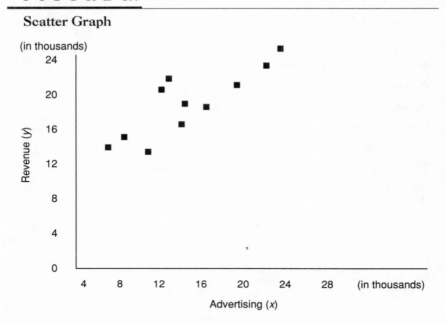

A Word of Caution

Before attempting a least-squares regression approach, it is extremely important to plot the observed data on a diagram called a "scatter graph." (See Figure 5.4.) The reason is that you might want to make sure that a linear (straight-line) relationship existed between Y and X in the past sample.

If for any reason there was a nonlinear relationship detected in the sample, the linear relationship we assumed—$Y = a + bX$—would not give a good fit.

In order to obtain a good fit and achieve a high degree of accuracy, you should be familiar with statistics relating to regression such as R squared (R^2) and t value, which are discussed below.

Regression Statistics

Regression analysis is a statistical method. Hence, it uses a variety of statistics to tell about the accuracy and reliability of the regression results. They include:

1. Correlation coefficient (R) and coefficient of determination (R^2).

2. Standard error of the estimate (S_e) and prediction confidence interval.

3. Standard error of the regression coefficient (S_b) and t statistic.

Each of these statistics is explained below.

1. Correlation Coefficient (R) and Coefficient of Determination (R^2)

The correlation coefficient R measures the degree of correlation between Y and X. The range of values it takes on is between -1 and $+1$. More widely used, however, is the coefficient of determination, designated R^2. Simply put, R^2 tells us how good the estimated regression equation is. In other words, it is a measure of "goodness of fit" in the regression. Therefore, the higher the R^2, the more confidence we have in our estimated equation.

More specifically, the coefficient of determination represents the proportion of the total variation in Y that is explained by the regression equation. It has the range of values between 0 and 1.

EXAMPLE 5.6

The statement "Revenue is a function of advertising expenditure with $R^2 =$ "70 percent," can be interpreted as, "70 percent of the total variation of revenue is explained by the regression equation or the change in advertising, and the remaining 30 percent is accounted for by something other than advertising, such as price and income."

The coefficient of determination is computed as:

$$R^2 = 1 - \frac{\Sigma(Y - Y')^2}{\Sigma(Y - \bar{Y})^2}$$

In a simple regression situation, however, there is a shortcut method available:

$$R^2 = \frac{[n\Sigma XY - (\Sigma X)(\Sigma Y)]^2}{[n\Sigma X^2 - (\Sigma X)^2][n\Sigma Y^2 - (\Sigma Y)^2]}$$

Comparing this formula with the one for b, we see that the only additional information we need to compute R^2 is ΣY^2.

EXAMPLE 5.7

To illustrate the computations of various regression statistics, we will refer to the data in Table 5.3. Using the shortcut method for R^2,

$$R^2 = \frac{(1,818)^2}{(3,228)[(12)(4,359) - (225)^2]} = \frac{3,305,124}{(3,228)(52,308 - 50,625)}$$

$$= \frac{3,305,124}{(3,228)(1,683)} = \frac{3,305,124}{5,432,724} = 0.6084 = 60.84\%$$

This means that about 60.84 percent of the total variation in revenue is explained by advertising and the remaining 39.16 percent is still unexplained. A relatively low R^2 indicates that there is a lot of room for improvement in our estimated forecasting formula ($Y' = \$10.5836 + \$0.5632X$). Price or a combination of advertising and price might improve R^2.

2. Standard Error of the Estimate (S_e) and Prediction Confidence Interval

The standard error of the estimate, designated S_e, is defined as the standard deviation of the regression. It is computed as:

$$S_e = \sqrt{\frac{\Sigma(Y - Y')^2}{n - 2}} = \sqrt{\frac{\Sigma Y^2 - a\Sigma Y - b\Sigma XY}{n - 2}}$$

This statistic can be used to gain some idea of the accuracy of our predictions.

EXAMPLE 5.8

Going back to our example data, S_e is calculated as :

$$S_e = \sqrt{\frac{4,359 - (10.5836)(225) - (0.5632)(3,414)}{12 - 2}}$$

$$= \sqrt{\frac{54.9252}{10}} = 2.3436$$

Suppose you wish to make a prediction regarding an individual Y value—such as a prediction about the revenue when an advertising expense = \$10. Usually, we would like to have some objective measure of the confidence we can place in our prediction, and one such measure is a *confidence (or prediction) interval* constructed for Y.

A confidence interval for a predicted Y, *given a value for X*, can be constructed in the following manner.

$$Y' \pm tS_e \sqrt{1 + \frac{1}{n} + \frac{(X_p - \bar{X})^2}{\Sigma X^2 - \frac{(\Sigma X)^2}{n}}}$$

where Y' = the predicted value of Y given a value for X

X_p = the value of independent variable used as the basis for prediction

Note: t is the critical value for the level of significance employed. For example, for a significant level of 0.025 (which is equivalent to a 95 percent confidence level in a two-tailed test), the critical value of t for 10 degrees of freedom is 2.228 (see Table 3 in Appendix E). As can be seen, the confidence interval is the linear distance bounded by limits on either side of the prediction.

EXAMPLE 5.9
If you want to have a 95 percent confidence interval in your prediction, the range for the prediction, given an advertising expense of $10, will be between $10,595.10 and $21,836.10. This range is determined as follows: Note that from Example 5.5, $Y' = \$16.2156$. The confidence interval is therefore established as follows:

$$\$16.2156 \pm (2.228)(2.3436) \sqrt{1 + \frac{1}{12} + \frac{(10 - 14.5)^2}{2792 - (174)^2 / 12}}$$

$$= \$16.2156 \pm (2.228)(2.3436)(1.0764)$$

$$= \$16.2156 \pm 5.6205$$

which means the range for the prediction, given an advertising expense of $10, will be between $10.5951 and $21.8361. Note that $10.5951 (= $16.2156 − 5.6205) and $21.8361 (= $16.2156 + 5.6205).

3. Standard Error of the Regression Coefficient (S_b) and t Statistic

The standard error of the regression coefficient, designated S_b, and the t statistic are closely related. S_b is calculated as:

$$S_b = \frac{S_e}{\sqrt{\Sigma(X - \bar{X})^2}}$$

or, in short-cut form:

$$S_b = \frac{S_e}{\sqrt{\Sigma X^2 - X \Sigma \bar{X}}}$$

S_b gives an estimate of the range where the true coefficient will "actually" fall. The t statistic (or t value) is a measure of the statistical significance of an independent variable X in explaining the dependent variable Y. It is determined by dividing the estimated regression coefficient b by its standard error S_b. It is then compared with the table t value (see Table 3 in Appendix E). Thus, the t statistic measures how many standard errors the coefficient is away from zero.

Rule of thumb: Any t value greater than +2 or less than –2 is acceptable. The higher the t value, the greater the confidence we have in the coefficient as a predictor. Low t values are indications of low reliability of the predictive power of that coefficient.

EXAMPLE 5.10

The S_b for our example is:

$$S_b = \frac{2.3436}{\sqrt{2,792 - (14.5)(174)}}$$

$$= \frac{2.3436}{\sqrt{2,792 - 2,523}} = \frac{2.3436}{\sqrt{269}} = 0.143$$

Thus,

$$t \text{ statistic} = \frac{b}{S_b} = \frac{0.5632}{0.143} = 3.94$$

Since $t = 3.94 > 2$, we conclude that the b coefficient is statistically significant. As was indicated previously, the table's critical value (cutoff value) for 10 degrees of freedom is 2.228 (from Table 3 in Appendix E).
Note:

1. The t statistic is more relevant to multiple regressions which have more than one b.

2. R^2 tells you how good the forest (overall fit) is, while t statistic tells you how good an individual tree (an independent variable) is.

Note: In summary, the table t value, based on a degree of freedom and a level of significance, is used:

1. To set the prediction range—upper and lower limits—for the predicted value of the dependent variable.

2. To set the confidence range for regression coefficients.

3. As a cutoff value for the t test.

Lotus and Excel Regression Output

Figure 5.5 shows a Lotus 1-2-3 output that contains the statistics we discussed so far.

Figure 5.6 presents Excel's regression output, which is more informative than either Lotus's or Quatrro Pro's.

F I G U R E 5.5

Lotus 1-2-3 Regression Result

Constant	10.58364
Standard error of Y estimated	2.343622 (S_e)
R squared	0.608373 (R^2)
No. of observations	12
Degree of freedom	10
X coefficients	0.563197
Standard error of coefficient	0.142893 (S_b)
t value	0.394138 (calculated independently)

The result shows:

$$Y' = 10.58364 + 0.563197X$$

with:

1. R squared ($R^2 = 0.608373 = 60.84\%$).
2. Standard error of the estimate ($S_e = 2.343622$).
3. Standard error of the coefficient ($S_b = 0.142893$).
4. t value = 3.94.

All the above are the same as the ones manually obtained.

F I G U R E 5.6

Excel Regression Result
Summary Output

Regression Statistics

Multiple R	0.7800
R squared	0.6084
Adjusted R Square	0.5692
Standard error	2.3436
Observations	12

F I G U R E   5.6—*Continued*

			Anova		
	df	SS	MS	F	Significance F
Regression	1	85.3243	85.3243	15.5345	0.0028
Residual	10	54.9257	5.4926		
Total	11	140.25			

	Coefficients	Standard Error	t Statistic	P Value*	Lower 95%	Upper 95%	Lower 95.000%
Intercept	10.583643	2.1796	4.8558	0.0007	5.7272	15.4401	5.7272
X variable 1	0.563197	0.1429	3.9414	0.0028	0.2448	0.8816	0.2448

*The P value for X variable = 0.0028 indicates that we have a 0.28% chance that the true value coefficient is equal to 0, implying a high level of accuracy about the estimated value of 0.563197.

TREND ANALYSIS

Trends are the general upward or downward movements of the average over time. Data on these movements may have to be collected over many years before they can be determined or described. They can be described by a straight line or a curve. The basic forces underlying the trend include technological advances, productivity changes, inflation, and population change.

Trend analysis is a special type of simple regression. This method involves a regression whereby a trend line is fitted to a time series of data.

The *linear* trend line equation can be shown as:

$$Y = a + b\,t$$

where t = time

The formula for the coefficients a and b are essentially the same as the cases for simple regression, except X is now t. However, for regression purposes, a time period can be given a number so that $\Sigma t = 0$. When there is an odd number of periods, the period in the middle is assigned a zero value. If there is an even number, then -1 and $+1$ are assigned the two periods in the middle, so that again $\Sigma t = 0$.

With $\Sigma t = 0$, the formula for b and a reduces to the following:

$$b = \frac{n\Sigma tY}{n\Sigma t^2}$$

$$a = \frac{\Sigma Y}{n}$$

EXAMPLE 5.11
Case 1 (odd number):

	19*X*1	19*X*2	19*X*3	19*X*4	19*X*5
t =	−2	−1	0	+1	+2

Case 2 (even number):

	19*X*1	19*X*2	19*X*3	19*X*4	19*X*5	19*X*6
t =	−3	−2	−1	+1	+2	+3

In each case $\Sigma t = 0$.

EXAMPLE 5.12
Consider ABC College, whose historical revenues (student tuition and fees, state appropriation, contract and grants, gifts, investment income, etc.) follow.

Year	Revenues (in millions)
19*X*1	$10
19*X*2	12
19*X*3	13
19*X*4	16
19*X*5	17

Since the college has five years' data, which is an odd number, the year in the middle is assigned a zero value.

Year	*t*	Revenues(*Y*)	*tY*	t^2	Y^2
19*X*1	−2	$ 10	−20	4	100
19*X*2	−1	12	−12	1	144
19*X*3	0	13	0	0	169
19*X*4	+1	16	16	1	256
19*X*5	+2	17	34	4	289
	0	68	18	10	958

$$b = \frac{(5)(18)}{(5)(10)} = \frac{90}{50} = 1.8$$

$$a = \frac{68}{5} = 13.6$$

Therefore, the estimated trend equation is

$$Y' = \$13.6 + \$1.8t$$

To project 19X6 revenues, we assign +3 to the t value for the year 19X6.

$$Y' = \$13.6 + \$1.8(3)$$
$$= \$19$$

The Computer and Trend Analysis

Again, virtually all forecasting software has an extensive trend analysis routine. Furthermore, spreadsheet programs such as Excel offer many ways of analyzing trends in the time-series data. The Excel spreadsheet program includes: (1) the Insert Trendline command that lets you select from among six trend/regression types (linear, logarithmic, polynomial, power, exponential, and moving average), along with its forecast option, (2) the Regression Analysis Toolpack command, and (3) many useful built-in functions such as Growth, Linest, and Trend.

MULTIPLE REGRESSION

Multiple regression analysis, a powerful statistical technique, is perhaps the one most widely used by forecasters. Multiple regression attempts to statistically estimate the average relationship between the dependent variable and two or more independent variables (or explanatory factors). Examples are numerous, including:

1. **Student enrollments** (full-time equivalents) may be determined by a host of factors such as demographic changes, military draft, educational fee increases, unemployment levels, inflation, and recession.
2. **Hospital labor costs** may be explained by such factors as patient-days, time, supply of health care professionals, and seasonal dummies.
3. **Donations and contributions** may be a function of such variables as local economy, interest rates, competition, community support, and number of volunteers.
4. **Program fees and membership dues** may be determined by prices or rates, promotion and advertising, membership drive, and foundation grants.

In reality, forecasters will face more multiple regression situations than simple regression. In order to obtain a good fit and achieve a high degree of accuracy, they should be familiar with statistics relating to regression such as R squared (R^2) and t value. (Note: Look beyond the statistics discussed here.) Furthermore, forecasters will have to perform additional tests unique to multiple regression.

The Model

The model takes the following form:

$$Y = b_0 + b_1 X_1 + b_2 X_2 \ldots + b_k X_k + u$$

where Y = dependent variable
$\quad\quad X$'s = independent (explanatory) variables
$\quad\quad b$'s = regression coefficients
$\quad\quad u$ = error term

Two examples are in order. An Excel regression printout is shown in Figure 5.7.

EXAMPLE 5.13

When a simple regression is not good enough to provide a satisfactory fit (as indicated typically by a low R squared), the manager should use multiple regression. Presented below is an example of both simple and multiple regressions, with the relevant Excel spreadsheet printouts. The Vice President of Planning of Pep University is trying to develop a model for forecasting annual enrollments for the university using advertising budgets for the current year and for two previous years. Assume the data in Table 5.4.

T A B L E 5.4

Annual Enrollment Data for Pep University with Current and Previous Advertising Budgets

Year	Enrollments (Y_t)	Advertising Budget (X_t) (in thousands of dollars)	$X_t - 1$	$X_t - 2$
19X0	11,375	15.000		
19X1	12,415	14.000	15.000	
19X2	13,300	15.400	14.000	15.000
19X3	12,600	18.250	15.400	14.000
19X4	16,200	17.300	18.250	15.400
19X5	19,163	23.000	17.300	18.250
19X6	18,900	19.250	23.000	17.300
19X7	21,000	23.056	19.250	23.000
19X8	22,425	26.000	23.056	19.250
19X9	24,500	28.000	26.000	23.056

Figure 5.7 presents two regression results.

FIGURE 5.7a

Simple Regression

Summary Output

Regression Statistics

Multiple R	0.9458
R square	0.8946
Adjusted R square	0.8814
Standard error	1,607
Observations	10

Anova

	df	SS	MS	F	Significance F
Regression	1	$1.75E+08$	$1.75E+08$	67.888	$3.529E-05$
Residual	8	20658692	2582336		
Total	9	$1.96E+08$			

	Coefficient	Standard Error	t Stat	P-value	Lower 95%	Upper 95%	Lower 95.000%	Upper 95.000%
Intercept	-959.22	2260.322	-0.42438	0.6825	-6171.54	4253.09	-6171.53984	4253.09081
X variable 1	910.74	110.5341	8.239441	4E-05	655.84693	1165.63	655.8469283	1165.63142

F I G U R E 5.7b

Multiple Regression

Summary Output

Regression Statistics

Multiple R	0.97
R square	0.941
Adjusted R square	0.9174
Standard error	1216.6
Observations	8

Anova

	df	SS	MS	F	Significance F
Regression	2	117993430	$5.9E+07$	39.858	0.00084626
Residual	5	7400796.1	1480159		
Total	7	125394226			

	Coefficient	Standard Error	t Stat	P-Value	Lower 95%	Upper 95%	Lower 95.000%	Upper 95.000%
Intercept	−3788	2544.21818	−1.4887	0.1967	−10327.678	2752.542	−10327.6785	2752.542238
X variable 1	497.02	152.233588	3.26487	0.0223	105.694547	888.3511	105.6945468	888.3510583
X variable 2	693.44	182.193982	3.80603	0.0126	225.092294	1161.78	225.092294	1161.779847

The simple regression model shows:

$$Y_t = -959.22 + 910.74X_t \qquad R^2 = 89.46\%$$

$$(110.53)*$$

The multiple regression model with advertising budgets for two previous years is:

$$Y_t = -3,787.57 + 497.02X_{t-1} + 693.44X_{t-2} \qquad R^2 = 94.10\%$$

$$(152.23) \qquad (182.19)$$

This model has two advantages:

1. The explanatory power has increased from 89.46 percent to 94.10 percent.
2. From the forecaster's point of view, using only lagged variables does not require any assumptions about actual future budgets.

EVALUATION OF FORECASTS

The cost of a prediction error can be substantial. For example, with improved accuracy, the California State University (CSU) System could have saved over $1 million a year. The state legislature has even formalized the importance of forecasting through legislation, which causes funds to be transferred if the percentage enrollment forecast error exceeds 2 percent in either direction. It is important to note that 13 out of 22 times (in the period 1963–84), the forecast error exceeded 2 percent, the accuracy standard. Perttula[2] showed, however, that even the use of simple, inexpensive forecasting methods such as exponential smoothing and time series analysis would have saved the CSU System $1,197,652 per year due to reduced forecasting error.

The forecaster must continually find ways to improve forecasts in an effort to enhance efficiency and reduce cost. That means that the forecaster might want to examine some objective evaluations of alternative forecasting techniques. This section presents the necessary guidelines. Two evaluation techniques are presented here. The first is in the form of a checklist. A forecaster could use it to evaluate either a new model in the process of development or an existing model. The second is a statistical technique for evaluating a model.

---

*Standard error of regression coefficient S_b.

CHECKLIST

Two main items to be checked are the data and the model with its accompanying assumptions. The questions to be raised are the following:

1. Is the source reliable and accurate?
2. In the case of use of more than one source that is reliable and accurate, is the source used the best?
3. Are the data the most recent available?
4. If the answer to question 3 is yes, are the data subject to subsequent revision?
5. Is there any known systematic bias in the data which may be dealt with?

The model and its accompanying assumptions should be similarly examined. Among other things, the model has to make sense from a theoretical standpoint. The assumptions should be clearly stated and well tested.

MEASURING ACCURACY OF FORECASTS

The performance of a forecast should be checked against its own record or against that of other forecasts. There are various statistical measures that can be used to measure performance of the model. Of course, the performance is measured in terms of forecasting error, where error is defined as the difference between a predicted value and the actual result.

$$\text{Error } (e) = \text{Actual } (A) - \text{Forecast } (F)$$

MAD, MSE, RMSE, and MAPE

The commonly used measures for summarizing historical errors include the *mean absolute deviation* (MAD), the *mean squared error* (MSE), the *root mean squared error* (RMSE), and the *mean absolute percentage error* (MAPE). The formulas used to calculate MAD, MSE, and RMSE are

$$\text{MAD} = \Sigma |e| / n$$
$$\text{MSE} = \Sigma e^2 / (n - 1)$$
$$\text{RMSE} = \sqrt{(\Sigma e^2 / n)}$$

Sometimes it is more useful to compute forecasting errors in percentages than in amounts. The MAPE is calculated by finding the absolute error in each period, dividing this by the actual value of that period, and then averaging these absolute percentage errors, as shown below:

$$\text{MAPE} = \Sigma|e|/A/n$$

The following example illustrates the computation of MAD, MSE, and RMSE, and of MAPE.

EXAMPLE 5.14

Operating expense data (in thousands) of United Gospel Church are given below:

Period	Actual (A)	Forecast (F)	e (A – F)	|e|	e²	Absolute Percent Error |e|/A
1	217	215	2	2	4	.0092
2	213	216	–3	3	9	.0014
3	216	215	1	1	1	.0046
4	210	214	–4	4	16	.0190
5	213	211	2	2	4	.0094
6	219	214	5	5	25	.0023
7	216	217	–1	1	1	.0046
8	212	216	<u>–4</u>	<u>4</u>	<u>16</u>	<u>.0019</u>
			–2	22	76	.0524

Using the figures,

$$\text{MAD} = \Sigma|e|/n = 22/8 = 2.75$$

$$\text{MSE} = \Sigma e^2/(n-1) = 76/7 = 10.86$$

$$\text{RMSE} = \sqrt{\Sigma e^2/n} = \sqrt{76/8} = \sqrt{9.5} = 3.08$$

$$\text{MAPE} = \Sigma|e|/A/n = .0524/8 = .0066$$

One way these measures are used is to evaluate forecasting ability of alternative forecasting methods. For example, using either MAD or MSE, a forecaster could compare the results of exponential smoothing with alphas and select the one that performed best in terms of the lowest MAD or the lowest MSE for a given set of data. These measures can also help select the best initial forecast value for exponential smoothing.

T A B L E 5.5

Forecasting Techniques in the Health Care Industry

Method	No. of Respondents
Gut feeling	28
Population-based method	21
Moving average	13
Exponential smoothing	4
Trend analysis	4
Regression	1
Simulation	1
Life-cycle analysis	1
Classical decomposition	0
Box-Jenkins	0
Total	73

SURVEY OF FORECASTING METHODS USED[3]

Table 5.5 presents the result of a survey made on the health care industry in connection with the use of forecasting techniques. The result is limited to the health care area and should be interpreted as such. Nonetheless, the result should give you an idea for other nonprofit organizations.

None of the respondents uses sophisticated techniques such as Box-Jenkins and regression. Many seem to use their gut feeling based on past experience to prepare forecasts. A large portion of the respondents use formal methods such as the population-based method, trend analysis, moving averages, and exponential smoothing. On average, each respondent uses two or three different methods.

ENDNOTES

1. S. Makridakis, "The Art and Science of Forecasting," *International Journal of Forecasting,* vol. 2, 1986, p. 17.

2. L. William Perttula, "Enrollment Forecasts—California State University System's Experience," *The Journal of Business Forecasting,* Spring, 1987, p. 20.

3. Sandy Reyna, K. Keru, K. Kwong, and Cheng Li, "Forecasting Practices in the Healthcare Industry," *The Journal of Business Forecasting,* Spring 1991, pp. 26–27.

C H A P T E R 6*

Budgeting: A Tool for Planning and Control

Nonprofit organizations (NPOs) range from small, community-related (such as local schools, churches, social clubs, library) to large, national (such as American Management Association). The NPO's purpose is to render services. The NPO is usually funded by the community or group it serves, or by an outside agency (e.g., government).

Budgets are a tool and a means to an end. They are used for planning and control. Planning considers the physical and human resources required. Budgets may be in monetary and nonmonetary terms such as dollars, number of personnel, service units, manpower, space, number of donors and size of contribution, and volunteers required. Programs and services should be prioritized. The starting point for a budget is prior year figures. Budgets should be flexible and adapt to changes as needed. The financial effects of alternative plans may be shown. A budget is an approved plan for raising funds and spending. Budgets are primarily for internal use. The longer the time period of the budget, the more uncertainty is involved.

Budgets must conform to the long-term goals and objectives of the NPO. Budgeting includes a comprehensive integrated plan for all phases of the NPO's operations such as responsibility centers, programs, and activities. It shows how the units contribute to the overall organization. There must be goal congruence. It is a coordinated effort.

---

*This chapter was coauthored by Anique Qureshi, Ph.D., CPA, CIA, a consultant and assistant professor of accounting at Queens College.

A monthly budget is better than a quarterly budget so as to reduce the time lag before corrective action may be implemented.

Budgets should be participatory to encourage teamwork. The budget preparer should work closely with managers and employees to assure budgeted figures are realistic and accurate, and useful for control. Budget participants might include community leaders, funding sources, and regulatory agencies.

If the budget is being prepared for the first time, obtain information from similar NPOs. Contact foundations, government, funding agencies, and consultants.

The budget has a total column for the whole NPO and separate columns for the budget for each responsibility unit.

Revenue and cost norms depend on quantitative and qualitative measurements.

Budgets should distinguish between restricted and unrestricted sources and uses of funds. Any expected transfers between restricted and unrestricted, or vice versa should be presented. Restricted funds must be used for the specific purposes stated. To do otherwise is a contractual violation. Restricted funds may be restricted by donors or the board of directors for a special reason.

Performance budgeting relates the input of resources to the output of services for each unit of the NPO. It shows work performance and efficiency. Quotas may be set such as for donor contributions based on fund-raising costs.

Budgets may be used by external parties. Bankers may request budgets in support of credit applications so as to gauge the NPO's future financial status and its ability to pay back the loan. Prospective donors may insist on reviewing budget amounts before making a contribution. They may also want to see variance reports for prior periods between budget and actual amounts.

The method used to present budget reports depends on the purposes management want them to serve. They may present year-to-year comparisons, expenditures as percentage of revenues, expenditures and revenues as a percentage of budgeted amounts, or any of several variations.

Detailed supplementary information that will not be used should be avoided because it requires cost and time to obtain.

STRATEGIC PLANNING

Strategic planning involves the following steps:

- Identify and define the mission.
- Formulate goals and objectives.

- Conduct an external audit.
- Perform an internal audit.
- Set strategies.
- Formulate priorities including any needed changes.
- Allocate resources to achieve objectives.
- Appraise operations on an ongoing basis.

Establishment of goals should take into account how successful current programs have been and changes in the current environment or in the entity's mission. Broad goals should be further specified and defined.

"WHAT-IF" ANALYSIS

Spreadsheets may be used in budget preparation based on "what-if" scenarios. The impact of changes in one or more assumptions on related budget amounts are quickly shown. It also considers various possibilities. For example, the effect of a change in expected contributions on related financial items, such as costs, can be seen.

Questions can be answered with spreadsheet software doing "what-if" analysis, such as "What incremental income will arise if donations increase by 10 percent?"

CONTINGENCY PLANNING

Contingency plans should be in place in case of a significant revenue shortfall. A contingency account may be added as a final item in the budget in case unexpected occurrences take place. For example, a 5 percent provision may be appropriate.

TYPES OF BUDGETS

Budgets may be classified based on their flexibility in planning and control. A flexible budget is appropriate when operating costs are variable at different activity levels or when it is difficult to estimate service demand. Budgeted figures are adjusted to actual activity. It allows for variation from original estimates by revising revenue, cost, and cash-flow forecasts based on changing circumstances. On the other hand, a fixed (static) budget is set at a fixed amount not subject to change during the budget period. It may be used when costs are highly predictable. Such budgets may be applied to such areas as fund raising, research, and capital expenditures.

T A B L E   6.1

Line-Item Budget

Expense	Actual 19X5	Percent of Increase	Budget 19X6
Salaries	$100,000	8	$108,000
Supplies	70,000	10	77,000
Telephone	3,000	6	3,180
Rent	20,000	7	21,400
Total expenses	$193,000		$209,580

A line-item budget (LIB), also called an incremental budget, may also be prepared. LIBs are simple and widely used. They emphasize the past. Historical amounts are adjusted at a predetermined rate. For example, the inflation rate may be used to adjust figures upward. Projected increases are referred to as *increments*. The increment adjustment may be applied to some or all items. This process aids in making meaningful comparisons over the years. Of course, budget figures may be downwardly adjusted if appropriate such as in a recessionary environment.

The line-item budget lists the source of revenue and categories of expenses (object accounts). It is done by organization unit rather than by program. Where did the money come from, how much, where did it go, and how much was spent?

An illustrative line-item budget is shown in Table 6.1.

A program budget focuses on programs representing activities for which the funds are spent. (See Chapter 7.)

Zero base budgeting (ZBB) starts fresh each year and all activities, new and old, must be justified. (See Chapter 7.)

A grant or contract proposal budget is for a specific grant, program, or activity.

A social accountability budget may be prepared showing community service activities including charity care and free health care clinics to justify tax-exempt status for federal and state. Such a budget will help the NPO facility counteract any possible challenges from tax authorities. The social accountability budget should include:

- Community needs being satisfied and not being satisfied.
- Community benefits provided.

In imposed budgeting, budgets are prepared by top-level administrators and then imposed on managers. In participatory budgeting, managers at the lower levels provide input to budget formulation. This is a better approach; it motivates managers and staff because they feel part of the process. They also internalize the goals and strive to achieve them.

An NPO may integrate (mix) a number of budgeting methods to achieve the best results such as combining the features of line-item budgets, program budgeting, and zero base budgeting using the favorable attributes of each to the particular setting.

The budget per unit of service is computed after considering the relative usage value. Such value is determined based on the standard cost per each unit. Total cost is allocated to each cost center based on expected volume and relative usage value for the current period.

CASH BASIS VERSUS ACCRUAL BASIS BUDGETS

It is preferable to prepare both cash basis and accrual basis budgets. Cash basis and accrual basis accounting were discussed in Chapter 2.

Whether an item is shown on the cash basis budget or the accrual basis budget is a timing consideration. Timing is important if there is concern over possible overspending during the reporting period. In general, the accrual basis makes the budget superior for monitoring and controlling spending.

Permanent differences also occur between cash basis and accrual basis budgets. Contributions of nonmonetary items (e.g., donated equipment and materials, volunteer services) give rise to permanent differences between the two types of budgets. These permanent differences show up in accrual basis budgets, but not in cash basis ones.

CAPITAL BUDGET

After the revenue budget is formulated, a capital budget is prepared. The capital budget lists and describes planned capital acquisitions and improvements, such as expenditures to maintain facilities. It looks at the timing and cost of major capital assets (minimum life of five years) and their financing source. It is prepared for the purchase and disposition of property, equipment, and other fixed assets. If disposed of, the selling price of the fixed asset or replacement information is given.

The capital budget involves the following:

- A listing of what is needed, why it's needed, its cost, and expected income to be derived.
- A statement of whether needed for technological update.
- The amount of total capital budget based on sources of funding (e.g., donor contributions, patient revenue, investment income).

The capital budget comes before the operating budget. The capital budget helps in approving capital outlays, and shows expenditures by responsibility or cost center.

OPERATING BUDGET

The operating budget is a plan for current operations including estimating revenues from all sources and estimating expenses for all programs, activities, or services. It is based on prior experience. Expense/revenue relationships are considered. If revenues do not relate to costs, guidelines may be established in nonmonetary, service-related terms. For example, in patient-oriented NPOs, budget guidelines may be based on the number of patients served and the identification of type of service provided by type.

The operating budget reveals what programs and services may be performed. An illustrative operating budget is shown in Table 6.2, and a typical operating budget solely estimating expenses is shown in Table 6.3.

T A B L E 6.3

Operating Budget for Expenses

Expense	General Management	Contracts	Fund Raising	Grant Proposal
Salaries	$ 30,300	$ 40,600	$ 60,800	$ 50,100
Fringe benefits	6,200	7,000	8,400	7,600
Professional fees	20,100	23,600	28,500	15,300
Telephone	10,600	9,400	15,000	6,800
Rent	7,300	8,700	10,100	9,500
Supplies	12,200	10,100	11,500	8,200
Postage	4,300	4,200	6,000	5,600
Travel	5,100	8,700	10,200	11,100
Printing	3,000	5,200	4,600	8,900
Insurance	7,000	2,000	3,500	4,600
Interest	2,300	2,400	2,700	2,600
Total expenses	$108,400	$121,900	$161,300	$130,300

T A B L E 6.2

Operating Budget

	Second Quarter Actual	Second Quarter Budget	Second Quarter Variance	Year to Date			Explanation for Variance	Responsible Individual
				Actual	Budget	Variance		
Income:								
Membership fees	$ 20,000	$ 22,500	$ 2,500 U[a]	$200,000	$250,000	$50,000 U[a]		
Donations	10,000	8,000	2,000 F[b]	115,000	100,000	15,000 F[b]		
Special events	60,000	70,000	10,000 U	65,000	80,000	15,000 U		
Sale of materials	6,000	5,700	300 F	32,000	30,000	2,000 F		
Investment income	7,000	6,500	500 F	40,000	36,000	4,000 F		
Total income	$103,000	$112,700	$ 9,700 U	$452,000	$496,000	$44,000 U		
Expenses:								
General and administrative	$ 25,000	$ 24,000	$ 1,000 U	$140,000	$125,000	$15,000 U		
Travel	2,000	3,500	1,500 F	18,000	17,000	1,000 U		
Supplies	6,000	5,200	800 U	43,000	40,000	3,000 U		
Rent	4,000	4,000	–0–	48,000	48,000	–0–		
Printing and publications	1,000	600	400 U	8,000	9,000	1,000 F		
Fund-raising costs	13,000	12,500	500 U	42,000	40,000	2,000 U		
Telephone	1,500	1,400	100 U	5,300	5,100	200 U		
Salaries	10,000	10,000	–0–	41,600	40,000	1,600 U		
Utilities	2,000	1,800	200 U	9,000	8,100	900 U		
Postage	1,200	1,300	100 F	4,000	4,500	500 F		
Conference meetings	6,000	7,000	1,000 F	25,000	27,000	2,000 F		
Award and grants	5,200	4,900	300 U	21,000	19,400	1,600 U		
Total expenses	$76,900	$76,200	$ 700 U	$404,900	$383,100	$21,800 U		
Excess of income over expenses	$26,100	$36,500	$10,400 U	$ 47,100	$112,900	$65,800 U		

[a]U = Unfavorable.
[b]F = Favorable

A detailed operating budget showing revenue and expenses is presented in Table 6.4.

T A B L E 6.4

Detailed Operating Budget

Revenue:		
Contributions		$ 800,000
Special events		100,000
Grants:		
Foundations	$600,000	
Government		
Total grants	<u>300,000</u>	900,000
Membership dues		30,000
Fees for services		40,000
Contractual revenue		60,000
Concession revenue		15,000
Rental income		25,000
Auxiliary activities		6,000
Investment income		41,000
Miscellaneous income		<u>7,000</u>
Total revenue		<u>$2,024,000</u>
Expenses:		
Salaries	$260,000	
Fringe benefits	50,000	
Payroll taxes	16,000	
Materials and supplies	240,000	
Communication	190,000	
Professional fees	130,000	
Publications	240,000	
Exhibits and displays	70,000	
Conferences	30,000	
Grants and awards	25,000	
Prizes	16,000	
Rentals	55,000	
Repairs and maintenance	28,000	
Printing and promotion	181,000	
Travel and lodging	49,000	
Royalties	53,000	
Licenses	21,000	
Insurance	16,000	
Depreciation	20,000	
Dues to affiliates	4,000	
Interest expense	2,000	
Miscellaneous expenses	<u>1,000</u>	
Total expenses		<u>$1,697,000</u>
Excess (deficit) on operations		<u>$ 327,000</u>

Budgeting Revenue

The initial step for an NPO is to estimate revenue and then expenses. (However, in some NPOs, program expenditures may be estimated first and revenue raised accordingly.) Budgeted revenue may be based on past experience and changed in light of the current environment. The price for services should take into account member or community needs. Revenue may be budgeted by department, program, function, and service.

The revenue budget depends on many factors, including consistency and timing of donations, fund drives, stability of income generated, capacity of the institution, demographics, social conditions, community relationship, risk, legal requirements, new services to be provided, competition, economic climate (e.g., recession, unemployment, tight money), political environment (e.g., government regulations, government reimbursement policy), professional reputation, and changes in tax law.

The NPO may project revenue levels under alternative assumptions such as best-case, worst-case, and normal-case. Expected revenue equals the quantity of services times price. Expected units of service depend on a number of considerations including unit price and promotion.

EXAMPLE 6.1
A child-care center is licensed to care for up to 30 children. The expected number of students is 80 percent. Thus, 24 children are actually expected on average. The center operates 50 weeks a year. It is open 35 hours a week. The hourly rate charged is $6.

$$\text{Gross Revenue} = 24 \text{ Children} \times 50 \text{ Weeks} \times 35 \text{ hours} \times \$6$$
$$= \underline{\$252,000}$$

In estimating revenue, a simple average and a weighted average over a five-year period may be calculated. A simple average equals:

$$\frac{\text{Total revenue for 5 years}}{5 \text{ years}}$$

A weighted average is more desirable, because it gives more weight to the most recent years, reflecting higher current fees or prices. If a five-year weighted average is used, the current year is given a weight of 5 while the first year is assigned a weight of 1.

EXAMPLE 6.2

A charity is estimating its donations for 19X6. The donations over the last five years were:

Year	Donation
19X5	$15 million
19X4	12
19X3	11
19X2	9
19X1	10
Total	$57 million

If the donation for 19X6 were budgeted based on a simple average, it would equal:

$$\text{Simple Average} = \frac{\text{Total for 5 Years}}{5} = \frac{\$57 \text{ Million}}{5}$$

$$= \$11.4 \text{ Million}$$

If the donation for 19X6 were estimated using a weighted average, it would equal:

Year	Donation	×	Weight	=	Total
19X5	$15 million		5		$ 75 million
19X4	12		4		48
19X3	11		3		33
19X2	9		2		18
19X1	10		1		10
	$57 million		15		$184 million

$$\text{Weighted Average} = \frac{\$184 \text{ Million}}{15} = \$12.3 \text{ Million}$$

Primary sources of revenue provide most of the NPO's revenue such as patient care services in a health care facility received directly from patients and insurance carriers. *Secondary* sources of revenue include interest income, dividend income, and royalties. A religious institution's major source of revenue is its weekly offerings from members. A college's primary source of revenue includes tuition, alumni grants, and admission fees. A nonprofit trade association's major revenue source is membership dues. A nonprofit periodical's primary revenue source is subscription fees.

After overall revenue for the entire organization is planned, individual revenue for the responsibility units are estimated. The unit's budget report should specify revenue by category, costs by type, service output measures, and unit cost for the service.

Revenue may be predictable such as contract revenue on a long-term contract. However, it is difficult to estimate many revenue sources because they do not directly relate to services rendered. An example is interest and dividend income on investments of endowment funds, which is difficult to measure. Estimated investment income equals expected return rate times the amount invested in the portfolio. Interest income varies with changing interest rates in the economy. Dividend income may be sharply cut if an investment does poorly. A decline in stock price may also occur. Uncertainty exists with government, foundation, and third-party grants. Most grant proposals are rejected. If accepted, the amount of grant might be substantially below that requested. How long will the grant be for? Uncertainty exists in fund raising. Will fund raising decline? How long will it take to get the funds and will there be prohibitive restrictions?

The greater the degree of soft revenue sources (e.g., one-time nonrenewable promotional efforts), the greater the risk of not accomplishing it.

Some NPOs rely principally on sales of services (e.g., college tuition, hospital fees, government funding of research). If estimated revenue does not cover estimated costs, costs must be reduced such as by cutting services. Another way to balance revenue and expenses is to increase revenue by having special fund drives.

Sometimes revenue falls below that which is based on fair market rates. For example, doctors and hospitals are often underpaid by state Medicaid and federal Medicare programs. However, in general, Medicaid payments are assured and are substantial.

Revenue reports update administrators on the current status of revenue receipts by source relative to budgeted amounts.

Estimating Costs

After the activity (service) level and revenues are estimated, expenses are forecasted. Expenses are segregated into categories such as personnel and staffing, and supplies. Budgeting expenditures is usually easier than budgeting revenue. It may be difficult, however, to match expenses to a program, a service, an operation, a department, or a particular revenue source. It is easier to budget expenditures when they are grouped into categories such as travel, fund raising, and utilities. Estimated cost per unit of service should be determined.

Expenses are budgeted based on past experience incorporating the current environment. The trend in each cost over time should be considered. In budgeting costs, units must evaluate how costs change with the different service levels. Some costs are constant irrespective of activity level (i.e., fixed costs such as rent), while other costs change with varying activity levels (i.e., variable costs such as materials). Expenses may also be estimated using regression analysis and modeling.

Some budget items equal quantity times cost per unit. An example is personnel wages being equal to the number of workers times average salary. Overtime payments may be estimated at a multiple of the normal rate. Salaries may be expressed in full-time equivalents (FTEs). This expresses the cost of a worker working full-time for 52 weeks. For example, assume a worker works two days in a five-day week. The FTE is .40 multiplied by 40 hours, or 16 hours. The wages for part-time workers may be estimated at the hours worked times the hourly rate. Fringe benefits and payroll taxes are typically expressed as a percentage of salaries. Personnel costs must be controlled closely because of their high amount.

Utility costs (e.g., electric, heat, telephone, water) are estimated, based on expected usage.

To lower professional fees, pay honorariums (token amounts) and give recognition. Very successful people will work for honorariums just for the privilege.

For each program or unit, add to direct costs (e.g., salaries) the allocated indirect costs (e.g., rent based on square footage). Salaries may be allocated to two or more programs based on time spent in each program.

Some costs are discretionary, and the optimum amount is not evident or unknown. How much will it cost to feed the homeless?

Payroll taxes may be avoided by paying individuals as independent contractors instead of salaried wage earners. However, the circumstances and employment relationship must support this treatment. It has to pass IRS and Department of Labor scrutiny. Misclassification can result in severe penalties. Generally, independent contractors (consultants) are in control of how they do the job, the contractor can do the work where he wants, there is *not* a continuing relationship, and the contractor can work any hours he or she wishes.

Expenditure reports are very useful for managers. Information is obtained from current expenditure accounts and should include the names of the budget category, the amounts budgeted, encumbrances on the current budget, actual expenditures, and the balance in the current budget.

An illustrative expenditure budget report is shown in Table 6.5.

T A B L E 6.5

Nonprofit Expenditure Report

Budget Unit	Budget Amount	Expenditures	Encumbrances	Balance
Administration	$185,000	$120,000	$50,000	$15,000
Personnel	160,000	100,000	40,000	20,000
Fund raising	300,000	170,000	60,000	70,000
Mailing	35,000	21,000	8,000	6,000
Visitation	12,000	6,000	3,000	3,000

CASH BUDGET

The cash budget shows future cash inflows and cash outflows. Cash budgets usually include both operating and nonoperating transactions. A cash budget identifies possible cash shortages and overages. Shortages may require borrowing. Overages may mean there is extra money available to invest for a return. The cash budget also indicates whether anticipated cash resources are adequate to finance operations. If not, external financing may be needed for which the budget estimates the amount and timing.

The cash budget focuses on short-term cash flows, including receipts, disbursements, loans, repayments of debt, and purchases. Expenditures may be timed to match cash receipts or cash availability.

Probability analysis to predict cash flows may be used. For income, the probabilities should be conservative. An example follows, showing the determination of the expected cash inflow from donations.

EXAMPLE 6.3

Donor	Probability of Donation	Expected Value
1	$60,000 × 90%	$ 54,000
2	80,000 × 80	64,000
3	85,000 × 75	63,750
4	90,000 × 50	45,000
Total		$226,750

The cash budget period depends to some degree on the stability of the NPO's major operations. For example, a shorter period is suggested when the NPO's activities are erratic.

T A B L E 6.6

Cash Budget

Cash inflows:		
Membership fees	$ 900,000	
Guest fees	60,000	
Rental income	200,000	
Contributions	1,000,000	
Grants	800,000	
Contracts	400,000	
Investment income	80,000	
Loan proceeds	150,000	
Sale of assets	50,000	
Total cash inflows		$3,640,000
Cash outflows:		
Salaries	$ 350,000	
Rent	220,000	
Supplies	160,000	
Insurance	40,000	
Utilities	80,000	
Telephone	30,000	
Maintenance	20,000	
Accounting and legal fees	190,000	
Travel	60,000	
Payment on debt	300,000	
Purchase of fixed assets	500,000	
Total cash outflows		1,950,000
Net cash inflows		$1,690,000
Beginning cash balance		230,000
Ending cash balance		$1,920,000

A cash-flow budget should have columns for expected and actual. The more predictable the entity's cash flow, the more accurate and valuable the cash flow analysis. Review data available in contracts and other documents calling for payments.

An illustrative cash budget is shown in Table 6.6.

BUDGET APPRAISAL

A goal is general while an objective is specific and measurable. Progress toward achieving goals and objectives should be evaluated. Priorities should be established. The least costly method to achieve objectives should be used. Areas should be identified where cost reductions can occur. Objectives should be attainable, challenging, documented, flexible, up-to-date, and timely.

Senior administrators are aware of managers' tendencies to spend 100 percent of their budget, even if not needed, for fear the program's budget will be decreased in the next year. Ways must be designed to reward managers having actual costs below budgeted costs provided quality services are still provided. Managers should *not* be penalized for coming in under budgeted costs. Future budgets should not be adjusted downward arbitrarily or unreasonably.

Under functional reporting, expenditures are accumulated by program purpose for which costs were incurred instead of by object of expenditure (e.g., research program).

In evaluating a department, efficiency measures are emphasized. In appraising a program, effectiveness measures are relied on to appraise the quality of services rendered. The best possible service should be provided given resource constraints. A problem may arise in providing a service at a particular time. As a result, problems may arise in scheduling and capacity planning. Measuring (quantifying) and controlling service quality is difficult. Objective standards must be set. Is the NPO making a contribution to society?

The program structure emphasizes outputs and usually crosses departmental responsibility lines. Program costs are difficult to quantify and consistently record. Specific actions (functions) for each program should be clearly expressed. Does the program meet its objective? What groups benefit?

Do sufficient unrestricted financial and human resources exist? If not, the program objective should be modified or an alternative method chosen. What risks do the programs generate? How long will the program take? Does a new program make sense?

Recurring programs should be periodically reviewed. Older programs may be out of date or may have lost community interest. Should a program be restructured or merged to better achieve goals and improve efficiency?

Have there been major changes in responsibilities of funders, government, clients, patients, media, and community? Are new directions called for?

In staffing budgets, a comparison is made between expected service levels and current staffing to determine whether adequate staff exists. After this review, a decision is made about whether to add or delete staff, and how much staff change is needed.

VARIANCE DETERMINATION
AND ANALYSIS

Budgeted revenue and costs are what they *should* be. Actual revenue and costs are what they *are*. A variance is the difference between the two. Such difference must be investigated as to cause and who is responsible, if controllable. Sometimes the variance is due to incorrect forecasting (e.g., outdated standards, deficient planning) other times it is due to poor performance. Budget figures should be adjusted when circumstances have changed (e.g., increased competition, new technology). Computerized models and quantitative techniques may be used in this regard.

Immediate corrective action must be undertaken for unfavorable variances. Favorable variances should be further taken advantage of. However, even favorable variances may reflect a problem. For example, if actual spending is below planned amounts, this may be due to laggard program performance. Variances may be determined and evaluated by program, service, cost center, or department.

Variances are interrelated, so an unfavorable variance in one responsibility unit may result in a favorable one in another segment.

Insignificant variances need not be considered unless they recur repeatedly and/or reflect potential problems. For example, even a variance below a cutoff dollar or percent amount may need analysis if the variance is continually unfavorable because it indicates a problem (e.g., poor supervision). The cumulative effect of a repeated minor unfavorable variance may be just as harmful as an occasional one.

Variances should be thorough and as detailed as needed. They may be expressed in total dollars, per unit fee, per unit cost, service units, volume, and percentages. They may be computed yearly, quarterly, monthly, daily, or hourly, depending on how important it is to identify the problem.

Variance analysis shows whether resources (physical and human) have been effectively used. It may result in rearranging resources to result in cost savings and efficiencies.

The objective of cost control is to result in the least possible cost based on predetermined quality standards. Variances indicating cost overruns can be a problem in contracts because the excess costs may not be reimbursable.

If responsibility for a variance is joint, corrective steps should also be joint. If correcting for an unfavorable variance conflicts with organizational policy, the policy should be reappraised and perhaps changed. If the policy is not changed, the variance should be considered uncontrollable.

A measure of materiality is to divide the variance by the budgeted cost. A 10 percent deviation would typically be considered significant and require corrective action especially when the NPO is using tight standards. Materiality may be considered in terms of dollars or service units. Stricter materiality guidelines should be set for crucial items such as laboratory equipment and x-ray machines in hospitals.

The efficiency variance is the difference between actual costs and budgeted costs that are not explained by the volume (quantity), price, or mix variances.

Effectiveness is the extent to which the NPO achieves its objectives. It is measured by the difference between planned and actual output. Effectiveness measures emphasize the program's results instead of the operation of a program.

If there is a long-term program, variances determined when the program is completed may be too late for prompt corrective steps to be taken. In such a case, analysis may be conducted at "key" points during the program. This allows problems to be corrected at early stages.

Budgets should be *realistic*. Standards are based on the situation being evaluated. For example, a "tight" standard should be set for cost reduction. A "perfection" standard should be used for high-quality services. However, tight standards may discourage workers, while loose standards may cause inefficiency.

Revenue Variances

Revenue variances examine the difference between actual revenue and budgeted revenue in total dollars, per-unit fee, and service units. If actual revenue exceeds expected revenue, a favorable variance arises. In the opposite case, there is an unfavorable variance. Such unfavorable variance points to a need for corrective steps such as increasing user fees, increasing membership, and so on.

Membership and fund-raising quotas may be set. Such quotas may be stated in dollars and units (e.g., number of members, new donors, retaining existing donors).

Cost Variances

Cost variances look at the difference between actual cost and budgeted cost and may be expressed in total dollars, per unit cost, and service units. If actual cost exceeds budgeted cost, an unfavorable variance arises. Identification of the problem is needed, including whether the variance is controllable or uncontrollable. If controllable, corrective actions must be implemented and the responsible party taken to task.

Fund-Raising Costs

Some fund-raising costs can be standardized, such as presentations for which a standard time call can be established. Call frequency should be determined. If percentages are tied to charitable contributions obtained, standards can be based on a percentage of those contributions.

Actual funds raised may not be the best measure of fund raisers' performance. They do not take into account different territory potentials. Also, a high volume fund raiser may have to cover a high promotion cost. What has been the trend in funds raised over the years in total and as a percentage of related fund raising costs?

Standards for fund raisers' automobile expenses may be expressed in cost per mile traveled and cost per day. The standard may relate to cost per donor or cost per dollar of funds raised.

The fund raisers' effectiveness with a territory should be considered, including hours spent and expenses incurred.

The control variance is broken down between fund raisers' days and fund raisers' costs.

Variance in Days = (Actual Days versus Standard Days) × Standard Rate per Day

Variance in Cost = (Actual Rate versus Standard Rate) × Actual Days

Total variance equals:

Actual Calls × Actual Amount Raised
Standard Calls × Standard Amount Raised

The elements of the total variance above equals:

Variance in Calls = (Actual Calls versus Standard Calls) × Standard Amount Raised

Variance in Funds Raised = (Actual Amount Raised versus Standard Amount Raised) × Actual Calls

Joint variance equals:

(Actual Calls versus Standard Calls) × (Actual Amount Raised versus Standard Amount Raised)

Performance measures of fund raisers' effectiveness include relationship between costs and dollar donations obtained, number of donor contributions from current and new donors, and meeting quotas.

An evaluation should be made of whether fund-raising expenses are realistic, taking into account contributions generated.

Are excessive costs (cost above limits set) due to the failure of controls or deficient management?

Labor Costs

Standard labor rates may be based on the current rates adjusted for future changes in the following factors: union contracts, changes in the environment, and average experience of staff.

Worker hours may be set by administrators by observing and timing workers. When salary rates are established by union contract, the labor rate variance will usually be minimal.

Worker time standards should include only the elements controllable by the employee or the work center. The standard time may include allowances for normal breaks and personal needs.

The causes of an unfavorable labor price variance might be poor scheduling resulting in overtime, use of workers receiving higher hourly rates than budgeted, and increase in wages. An unfavorable labor efficiency variance may arise from poor supervision, use of poor quality resources, inadequately trained staff, and employee unrest.

Variances may be by service category. Standards may be used for office personnel performing clerical work, and a standard unit cost for processing a form (e.g., a welfare application). The variance between the actual cost of processing a form versus the standard cost can be analyzed by administrators, and corrective action can be implemented.

Variances may be in physical and dollar measures. Examples of physical measures are the number of employees, the number of welfare recipients serviced, and the number of files handled.

Cost variances may be presented to administrators in special reports. For example, the variance in time and cost of processing payments to retirees may be evaluated.

Variance Analysis Reports

Variance analysis reports include examining the difference between actual and budget figures for (1) revenue, (2) costs, (3) quality, and (4) growth. For example, revenue volume may be declining because of inadequacy in fund raising. Variance analysis reports may be expressed in dollars, ratios, graphs, percentages, and narrative. Variance analysis reports should be broken down between that resulting from providing more or less services than initially budgeted, and that due to efficiency (inefficiency) or unplanned changes in input prices.

An illustrative variance report would be set-up as shown in Table 6.7.

T A B L E 6.7

Budget by Activity

| | Current Month | | | Year to Date | | |
Activity	Budget	Actual	Variance	Actual	Budget	Variance

T A B L E 6.8

Variance Report of Costs

	Current Month			Cumulative		
	Actual	Budget	Variance	Actual	Budget	Variance
Number of staff	110	105	5 U	230	215	15 U
Expenses:						
Salaries	$10,000	$ 9,000	$1,000 U	$112,000	$100,000	$12,000 U
Rent	2,000	2,000	–0–	25,000	24,000	1,000 U
Utilities	300	350	50 F	3,200	3,500	300 F
Insurance	400	380	20 U	4,300	4,200	100 U
Travel	1,000	1,250	250 F	12,600	13,000	400 F
Depreciation	600	500	100 U	7,200	6,000	1,200 U
Total expenses	$14,300	$13,480	$ 820 U	$164,300	$150,700	$13,600 U
Percentage of net sales	38%	36%	2%	38.2%	37.6%	.6%

A typical variance report of costs is shown in Table 6.8. A typical variance analysis report for a service activity is shown in Table 6.9.

BUDGETARY CONTROL

Budgetary control should exist over revenue and expenses. Cost controls should be established. Spending limits may be placed on personnel, time, funds, and assets. Any expenditures above the preset amount must be authorized. A cost containment report should be prepared, identifying above-average costs.

T A B L E   6.9

Variance Analysis Report for a Service Activity

Function	Time Variance	Cost Variance
Processing orders	120 hours	$1,200
Processing reports	65	800
Processing invoices	12	300
Preparing checks	18	500
Filing paid invoices and related documentation	23	610

Budget cuts, when needed (e.g., because of a poor economy or political factors), should be in the areas that are of the least importance and/or that will have the least severe consequences (e.g., on quality of service performed).

Some programs may be downgraded, where the same level of service or comparable results are sought through less expensive ways. The community may be invited to give input to program cuts. Is it better to make cuts in the areas served, to raise membership requirements, or to reduce service hours? What effect do budget cuts have on the scope, volume, quality, and character of programs and services?

Improved productivity results in lower unit cost. This may be achieved through volunteers who are very motivated. Administrative costs may be lowered by improving work office procedures so as to increase productivity. Automating administrative work enhances efficiency.

Distribution costs may be lowered by using commercial mailing services to reduce mailing costs, by utilizing bulk zone mailing and other methods, and by combining appropriate mailings at specific times.

Demographically targeted fund-raising campaigns may be more cost-effective than wide distributions. Costs can be reduced by updating mailing lists for people who have moved or not responded. Word-of-mouth solicitation should be encouraged because little or no cost is involved. Computer bulletin boards can be very cost-effective. This reduces the need for mailings of fund-raising material.

Publicity costs may be reduced by using in-house desktop publishing to produce the NPO's own flyers and promotional material.

Financial control includes procedures designed to collect, categorize, and report information on daily activities.

Revenue and cost information should be provided by service line, patient, program, and activity.

Resource utilization performance measures should be established. Performance reports should discuss potential problems and opportunities. Timely and analytical information should be provided. Strengths and weaknesses should be included.

Effectiveness measures should be used for fund raisers by donation obtained, call frequency, cost per donor, dollar amount of contributions per hour spent, and incentives. Less reliance on professional fund raisers will lower costs. Perhaps the same funds can be raised by internal staff (for example, clergy). Fund-raising activities have to be looked at in terms of net return.

Budget allocation procedures may have to be adjusted. The reasons for a change in budget allotment in whole or between major elements should be determined.

Managers preparing program or department budgets must have operating authority over their responsibility units and must be accountable for performance. Otherwise, there is deficient planning and control.

SUPPORT OR CAPITAL ADDITIONS

Grants, gifts, and bequests are usually accounted for as support or capital additions. The principal source is typically nonreciprocal giving to support activities. Support may be donor-restricted or unrestricted. Restrictions may exist as to how the resource may be used; a time limitation may be placed on such support. Nonexpendable grants, gifts, and bequests may be restricted for endowment or loan, permanently or temporarily.

ENCUMBRANCES

Encumbrances are an element of budget accountability. Encumbrances are commitments for unfilled contracts for goods and services (e.g., purchase orders). The purpose of an encumbrance is to prevent further expenditure of funds because of commitments already made. At year-end, *open* encumbrances are treated as reservations of fund balance.

EXAMPLE 6.4
On January 5, 19X2, a purchase order (or contract) is entered into for $10,000. The entry is:

Encumbrances	10,000	
Reserve for Encumbrances		10,000

On December 16, 19X2, the amount actually incurred is recorded. The entries are:

Reserve for Encumbrances	10,000	
Encumbrances		10,000
Expenditures	10,000	
Vouchers Payable		10,000

FUND RAISING

Fund raising is essential. Are contributions being received as expected? Actual contributions are compared to expected contributions. Compare budgeted time and cost to obtain contributions to actual time and cost for contributions received for variance determination and analysis purposes. Budget revisions may be required. Are fund-raising costs in line with amounts obtained? If not, why? Is a cost control program needed? Do fund-raising efforts have to be improved?

BUDGET CALENDAR

The budget calendar may be different from that of the overall organization, because the grantor may have a different time period and the contract may have stipulated due dates. A budget calendar sets forth the time table in the budget process. Each step should be completed by the due date. Individual programs may also have their own budget calendar.

An illustrative budget calendar follows.

Activity	Date	Responsible Party
Make preliminary budget request.	Aug. 1	Department manager
Prepare draft budget.	Sept. 1	Department manager
Review budget.	Oct. 1	Controller
Prepare final budget.	Dec. 1	Controller
Review budget.	Jan. 1	Budget committee
Make final budget.	Feb. 1	Budget committee
Make budget revisions.	March 1	Department manager
Present final budget.	May 1	Chief executive

BUDGETING FOR SPECIFIC NPOs

Hospitals

The budget for a hospital may be expressed in dollars (such as for income and expenses) or in nondollar terms (such as the number of hours of operations and the number of patients served).

Higher value and importance are associated with crucial health care, such as emergency room, trauma, and intensive care. The highest-quality care is sought. Prices may therefore be increased for such services, especially if competitive health care providers have poor reputations.

The revenue budget is based on prior-year figures, incorporating changes for the present environment (such as reductions in Medicare and Medicaid reimbursements, or increasing demand for services). The revenue budget considers the doctors' caseload and the patient mix. Revenue sources include patient service revenues, donations, research grants, membership fees, tuition from education programs, rental income, royalties, gift shop, investment income, cafeteria income, and parking fees.

Budgeted costs include hospital supplies, salaries, fringe benefits, rent, insurance (e.g., malpractice), utilities, and bad debts. Health care costs consider average age of patients and extent of illness.

Labor standards aid administrators in forecasting staffing requirements for physicians, nurses, custodians, and other staff members. Doctors' salaries are a semivariable cost, because the salaries are fixed and the doctors also receive a percentage of patient revenues. The fixed salaries are easy to budget because they are contractual, but the variable portion is harder to predict because it is based on estimated patients to be served.

The supplies budget is typically estimated based on previous experience at expected service levels.

The overhead rate depends on the expected activity level.

There are several methods hospitals may use to cost their services. A common approach is the ratio of cost to charges (RCC). It is a top-down scheme where the ratio of departmental costs to charges is first projected. The ratio is then applied to individual medical procedures. RCC may not represent the actual cost of the procedures, since data are based on aggregate information and the percentage relationship is not always constant. The RCC pricing approach may give a distorted result of the actual cost of the procedure.

Other methods of costing services are actual total cost, relative value units (RVUs), standard cost, diagnosis costing, and activity-based costing.

Actual costing tracks material, labor, and overhead at the procedure levels.

Under RVUs, two steps exist. First, labor costs are computed for a departmental service. Second, the department labor costs are assigned to components needed to conduct a particular procedure. The labor costs are collected in total and then assigned to a specific service. The drawback to RVU is that only labor cost is measured, while material and overhead are excluded.

Standard costing allocates material, labor, and overhead based on what costs should be. Standards are set for resource allocation, output levels, and quality. Variance analysis compares actual performance to standard performance.

Some hospitals use diagnosis standards to price their services. This is a type of job order costing using a fixed predetermined allocation of funds based on the diagnosis. This approach does not furnish data on individual operating efficiency. Therefore, an in-house system should be formulated to appraise performance.

Activity-based-costing (ABC) traces costs to activities, and assigns them to services by using a cost/effect relationship such as in the hospitals' admissions and records departments. Medical records can be traced to patients through a cost driver such as how long the patient is hospitalized. ABC allows for the evaluation of costs by doctor, patient, or payment plan.

Libraries

The library budget should meet the mission of the library. The budget should limit excessive spending and efficiently utilize funds. Standards may be established, such as for cataloging.

The library director prepares a budget after receiving input from library department coordinators, librarians, and academic department chairpersons.

Library budgets are set about one year before the actual expenditure of money. In the interim, changes in revenue and expenses may occur from projected amounts. Periodic revision of budget amounts may be needed.

The library budget may be broken down by responsibility center. Library responsibility centers include library instruction, database search services, and technical services. For example, in a college, a librarian may be assigned to one or more academic departments, each having its own budget.

A budget may be by subdivision of the library by activity, including cataloging, requisitioning, and processing publications; handling exhibitions; database services; library tours; collection; and training. A library information service budget may be allocated based on the aged, the handicapped, and in-library users. Funds may be allocated based on a predetermined standard, such as student enrollment, number of faculty, number of courses, and library circulation.

Budgeted revenue includes grants, contracts, donor contributions, fee and service revenue, rentals of cassettes, late fee fines, rental of room space, photocopy fees, and sale of old books. Budgeted costs include those for books, periodicals and monographs, microfilms, supplies, librarians' salaries, bindery, supplies, equipment (e.g., computers), exhibitions, insurance, utilities, cleaning, security, videos, and such subscriptions as those to on-line services.

A school library's main purpose is to support curriculum of the school with information resources. A secondary purpose is to support academic research by faculty. Books and periodicals are bought to support instruction, to furnish access to the resources, and to offer reference and instructional services. The library may be segregated into reference, reserve, circulation, periodicals, and so on.

Funds may have to be transferred between categories. For example, funds for new books and periodicals may be transferred from the Accounting Department to the Economics Department for political reasons or because of emphasis on one of a college's scholarship activities. Funds may be transferred because of donor limitations, changes in laws, or changes in personnel and facilities.

One problem in a library budget is the inability to put a dollar figure on intellectual services such as research.

Cost cutting may be undertaken by canceling periodicals and reference services.

Leisure Activities Clubs

The estimated revenue includes membership dues, initiation fees, special assessments, outdoor sports (swimming, tennis, golf), hotel or clubhouse facilities (room charges, restaurant, health spa, athletic facilities), gift shop, hair salon, parking, and investment income. Expenses are budgeted by program and by function. Program services include expenses associated with outdoor sports, hotel or clubhouse, gift shop, and so on. Expenses for supporting services include those for general and administrative, maintenance of facilities, and entertainment.

Labor Unions

Estimated revenue includes union dues, agency fees, administrative charges, and sales of union materials. Budgeted expenses are by program and function, and are segregated between program services and supporting services. Program services include dues to affiliated locals, negotiation, grievance, organizational, and strike fund.

Social Services

Budgeted revenue includes public support and indirect support. Public support includes contributions, special events, and bequests and legacies. Indirect support includes government and foundation grants. Expenses are budgeted by program and function. Program services include mental health, family advisement, and drug and alcohol treatment. Supporting service expenses include general and administrative, and fund raising.

CHAPTER 7

Zero Base Budgeting and Program Budgeting

This chapter deals with two major budgeting methods, zero base budgeting and program budgeting.

ZERO BASE BUDGETING

Unlike a traditional budget, zero base budgeting (ZBB) starts anew each period without considering what happened in the previous periods. ZBB is like "cleaning house" and getting rid of the "deadwood." A current service (previously undertaken) that is inefficient or not needed will be discontinued. Zero base budgeting was first applied by Texas Instruments in 1969 and is used today by some nonprofit organizations. It may be done for the entire organization or just selected areas of activity. ZBB deals mostly with ongoing programs but also covers new activities. It usually has a one-year focus.

Under ZBB, you must be open-minded and must evaluate proposed alternatives. Nothing is taken for granted. Managers must justify each budget line item. Is a particular activity no longer needed or useful? Programs should be supported at other than 100 percent (from zero upward). This allows for better management of the organization.

ZBB is priority-based. It analyzes services, activities, operations, projects, and programs in order to find ways of enhancing efficiency at lower cost. Alternative ways of achieving the final objective are reviewed, considering time and cost. Input-output relationships are considered. The proper funding level is decided upon. Performance and effectiveness are evaluated.

ZBB requires detailed information on the costs and benefits of alternative programs. Dollars should be assigned to benefits to be achieved. ZBB may allow for the elimination of duplicate and overlapping programs. However, what are the consequences of not approving a package?

Budget amounts for an activity start at zero or a stated percentage of the current year's amount (e.g., 60 percent). ZBB is a means of review of existing and prospective programs to reallocate resources to result in more effectiveness and efficiency. ZBB should be modified as circumstances dictate.

An integration of objectives at lower levels to higher levels should exist. Goal congruence should exist within the organization at each responsibility center. Subgoals should be consistent with overall goals.

Decision packages are interrelated. For example, funding for one package may cause a change in the funding for another package.

Alternative options in ZBB include:

- Keeping the service as is.
- Ceasing the activity.
- Curtailing the program.
- Expanding the function.
- Decentralizing the operation.
- Centralizing the program.
- Integrating functions.

ZBB may uncover redundancies and duplication of efforts, may focus on dollars required for programs rather than percentages, may allocate limited resources in the most efficient and the most effective way, may permit comparison among responsibility units, set forth priorities within and among responsibility units, and may allow a performance audit to determine efficiency of operations.

In looking at a service, the following questions should be asked:

- What is the purpose of the activity?
- Are objectives being measured properly?
- Are objectives being achieved?
- What is the negative effect of not funding the activity?
- Will an alternative way of performing the function reduce quality?
- How will the alternative impact cost and time to achieve?
- What is the risk involved?

Zero Base Budgeting Procedures

ZBB is a continual process. Each manager must justify his or her budget request in detail from a zero base. There should be an appraisal of the output for each activity, service, operation, or function of a cost/responsibility center. The consequences of turning down a proposed service or activity should also be considered.

The process begins with determining objectives and assumptions. Assumptions include growth rate in wages and fringe benefits. It is recommended that an organization test ZBB in one responsibility unit before employing it throughout the entire organization. ZBB should be phased-in gradually. For example, initially only 10 percent of the budget may be based on ZBB before proceeding further, so as to gain experience. Flexibility should exist for adjusting to new information, new assumptions, and new limitations.

The activities or services of the unit are expressed in decision packages that are to be reviewed and ranked in priority order throughout different levels in the organization. Funds should be allocated based on those activities achieving the best results.

One approach in ZBB is for administrators to identify different effort levels to conduct each activity. A minimum spending amount is used, say 60 percent of the current operating level. Then, administrators should stipulate separate decision packages and the costs and benefits of additional spending levels for that activity. This evaluation forces administrators to take into account and evaluate a spending level lower than the current operating level. This provides management with an alternative of terminating an activity or choosing from several effort levels. This provides tradeoffs and shifts in expenditure levels among units.

A program is not funded unless justifiable. Procedures and policies are evaluated on whether they still accomplish goals. For example, some library programs are added or dropped depending on how good or bad they are. Funding levels may be revised.

The ZBB process is outlined in Figure 7.1.

Activity Units

The basic cost element of ZBB is the *activity unit,* representing the lowest unit for which a budget applies. The objectives of an activity unit should be clearly stated and specific. An activity unit may be an operation, a function, a program activity, an organizational unit, or a line item. A manager

F I G U R E 7.1

ZBB Process

Planning assumptions
Priority ranking
Evaluation and control
Budget preparation
Identification of decision units
Appraisal of decision units

is responsible for a unit. The unit must achieve its designated purposes. Examples of decision units are data processing, quality control, research and development, and legal services. Priority is given to services required by law, government dictate, or other limitations. Those responsible for an activity must also have the control over it.

Decision units of comparable size in terms of dollars, quantity, staff, and so on should be compared.

Evaluation of Decision Units

After the decision unit's purpose has been stated, financial and physical resources are specified. This includes dollar allocations, number and category of employees, and equipment. A description should be provided of the operations to be performed, the priority importance of activities, and the workflow. Measures should be specified to gauge productivity and effectiveness. Performance standards and workload should be established. Ways to measure performance include:

- Comparison of actual results to budget yardsticks.
- Input (cost and time) / output (income, quality) relationship.
- Quality control including difficulties experienced.
- Net cash flow generated.
- Internal audit of each responsibility unit.

Decision Packages

Making a decision package is one of the first steps in ZBB. The decision package enumerates the way the manager recommends the activity to be performed in terms of both cost and time. Alternative ways to conduct the service in dollars and time are also specified. Costs may be lowered by decreasing quality, but this may not be in the best interest of the nonprofit entity. If completion time is accelerated, this may increase costs because of overtime.

Decision packages may take the following forms:

- A package for new operations or services.
- A package leaving the activity "as is" (status quo).
- A package at a base amount plus additional amounts of activity for ongoing programs.

Alternatives are specified in each package.

Decision packages should be specific and focused, and should have realistic goals. A decision package should not lump together many aspects, because this would make it "cloudy." For example, difficulty exists when a project covers differing functional or organizational lines. The decision package should contain a narrative of why the activity is needed, the reasons for the cost and time specified, alternative ways of achieving objectives, and cost / benefit analysis.

A detailed, standardized listing of the decision packages should be provided for review. The information contained in a decision package includes:

- A description of the proposed program.
- The costs and time of each alternative option.
- The risk and uncertainty associated with the activity.
- The financial and nonfinancial resources required.
- A plan for achieving the objective.
- Priority specification.
- A list of the individuals responsible for the operation or service.
- Input and outcome measures, including numerical and qualitative.
- The consequences of not engaging in an activity.
- Technological and operational factors.
- Benefits to be achieved.
- Legal considerations.
- Support and staff requirements, including particular expertises.

A decision package may be mutually exclusive or incremental. If mutually exclusive, the acceptance of one alternative precludes the acceptance of another. If incremental, different effort levels exist. For example, one package may need 200 workhours per week while another may require 250 workhours per week.

The interrelationship between decision packages may cause ranking problems.

Questions to be answered include:

- Will the proposed activity generate immediate and tangible results?
- Can a function be undertaken at a lower activity level without sacrificing productivity?
- Are resources matched with objectives?
- What is the time period covered (short-term, long-term)?

Ranking Packages

Each activity is ranked to determine whether it meets the nonprofit organization's mission. The ranking is done in decreasing order by importance to the organization. Ranking should consider the advantages and disadvantages of the decision package.

Prioritization of decision packages includes consideration of legal requirements, operating needs, time, risk, and staff requirements. All relevant quantitative and qualitative factors should be considered. Cost / benefit analysis should be conducted for each decision unit.

Highest priority is given to the minimum increment of service representing the amount of service the organization must conduct so as to perform useful service. Further, service increments are provided in priority order.

Final ranking is done by senior administrators after receiving input from managers. Initial ranking is done at lower management levels, where the packages are first developed. Intermediate rankings are done by middle management after reviewing lower management recommendations. If lower-level management recommendations are rejected, the reasons should be provided.

To avoid overwhelming upper managerial levels with too much detail, the ranked decision packages may be combined into major candidates for review and ranking.

There should be a cutoff for operations and services at each of the approved levels. For instance, a 70 percent cutoff may be set for middle management, but a 90 percent cutoff may be set for upper management. The 70 percent middle-management cutoff line would necessitate that the manager remove the highest-ranked package until the expenditure represented for the removed packages equaled 70 percent of the previous year's budget. These packages would then be reviewed for appropriateness. The balance of the decision packages would then be closely appraised.

There should be a ranking table for decision packages by responsibility unit so as to aid in their review of matters such as meeting financial and nonfinancial criteria. Even nonfunded projects should be ranked in the event unexpected funding (e.g., a sudden donation) becomes available. Further, what is low priority today may be high priority tomorrow. An example might be new government regulations making a program (e.g., environmental protection, affirmative action) legally required. Modifications may be made to the priority listing based on changing circumstances.

Different ranking approaches are possible, such as single standard, voting, and major category.

A single standard is most suitable for similar packages. All packages are appraised based on just one feature (e.g., return on investment, net present value, profit, cash savings, or cost / benefit ratio). This approach is not appropriate for dissimilar packages because a vital activity (e.g., safety or health) may be absent.

The voting approach involves action by a voting committee. The majority vote determines the ranking. Of course, a legally required program is funded. Special consideration is given to projects involving minimum organizational requirements.

Under the major category system, decision packages are segregated. The decision packages in each category are then ranked. Some categories are more important than others. Budgets for each category are different. For instance, a category with significant growth expectation may be funded five times as much as one with doubtful prospects. The emphasis is on "key" categories. Once the allocations are made, budgets are detailed.

EXAMPLE 7.1

A manager completes a decision package for each activity to be conducted in a unit. If there are 25 possible services (existing and new), 25 decision packages will be prepared.

A typical decision package for activity X to be carried out in Unit A appears as follows:

Decision Package for Activity X

	Cost	Time
_____ Alternative 1		
_____ Recommended approach		
_____ Alternative 2		

Each of the decision packages for all 25 activities is then submitted to upper management. Upper management then evaluates the decision packages from all the units, including unit A. A budget ceiling puts a dollar cutoff on how many activities will be supported. The packages are ranked in priority order. Those exceeding the budget cutoff are funded fully or partly. If partly funded, the activity might be done by an alternative, cheaper (or less time-consuming) way than that recommended.

Conclusion

The ZBB approach budgets funds for activities and operations at the *minimum* funding level. The survival level is the one at which lower funding would eliminate the unit. Any funding above the minimum level must be supported and justified to a reasonable degree. All activities, whether existing or new, must be justified. Why is service B needed? What is the justification? What is the cost / benefit? How does the service achieve the overall objectives of the organization? If the service, activity, program, or operation cannot be justified, it should be terminated.

ZBB may result in greater effectiveness, efficiency, and cost control. Resources are identified and controlled. Service levels may be matched to available resources. Planning and communication are achieved between lower, middle, and upper management. Participative management is fostered, and all managers are part of the process. Creativity should be encouraged along with subordinate involvement, because of on-the-job experience.

Activities may have to be reorganized to achieve better results. The specification of alternatives may result in innovative and better ways to perform.

ZBB is a time-consuming process and may best be implemented to decision units on a rotating basis over a longer-term time period (e.g., every five years). Yearly ZBB is probably not cost-effective, considering the cost and time.

PROGRAM BUDGETING

Program budgets aid in planning, allocating, and controlling resources. After a goal is established, the program to achieve it is formed. An attempt is made to maximize a program's output subject to budget constraints. The budget ceiling considers prior growth rates, competitive factors, and costs.

Program budgeting is done by program rather than by organizational unit. It provides better cost control over programs. It allows for more realistic pricing of products and services, so that realistic fees and reimbursements may be achieved.

Outputs are compared to inputs for each program, to gauge success. Outputs are the results and performance achieved. Some examples of program activities include research and development, training, public relations, new college curriculum, new service line, and government contract.

Program budgeting is a management approach to identify objectives, to formulate alternative ways to accomplish the objectives, to allocate resources (e.g., staff, equipment, supplies) to achieve those objectives, to specify service levels, to estimate program costs, and to specify measures of accomplishment by program. Programs are ranked, and those having the highest ratio of benefits to costs are selected first. Only productive programs satisfying organizational goals will continue. What are the consequences of eliminating a program?

Program budgeting is a multiperiod focus. Program budgets are established for projects or programs of a one-time, long-term nature involving significant cash outlays. Possible problems and difficulties should be anticipated. Responsibility should be assigned for specific operations and activities. Are project costs logical? Any modifications should be made to make the plan even better.

Each program must be justified yearly. Programs should be prioritized. Consideration should be given to the interrelationship of programs.

Programs may be considered either direct or support. Direct programs directly apply to an NPO's objectives (e.g., teaching, research). Support programs service one or more other programs (e.g., a computer center).

What programs will be undertaken in keeping with the NPO's mission, how much of the resources will be allocated to each program, and what will be the sources of funds for financing each program?

The Program Budgeting Process

The steps in program budgeting follow:

- Define the problem.
- Establish program priorities.
- Allocate costs to programs.
- Appraise the cost effectiveness of programs.
- Select the most cost-effective program.

The emphasis is on programs. The manager must set forth for each program projected costs at various levels of effort. Direct costs are attributable to a specific program. Indirect costs must be allocated to programs,

T A B L E 7.1

Program Budget by Item

Program	Wages	Rent	Insurance	Utilities	Total
A	$ 30,500	$10,000	$ 6,800	$1,000	$ 48,300
B	28,000	12,200	5,900	1,200	47,300
C	32,400	11,600	4,100	1,500	49,600
D	41,000	13,000	7,600	1,300	62,900
Total	$131,900	$46,800	$24,400	$5,000	$208,100

projects, and services. This is accomplished by assigning an identification number by both project and employee. This will track who gets charged for such costs as travel, wages, supplies, and telephone. The highest cost is usually salaries of staff assigned to programs. The government (federal, state, and local) may define what costs are acceptable to be charged to a particular program or service in connection with government contracts and grants.

An NPO having many programs should segregate its total budget into subbudgets, including budgets for each activity within each program or function, and a budget for each program or service area. Each function will have its own detailed budget and the NPO's entire budget will be a composite of the individual functional budgets.

A project should be broken down by major activity or task, and then further segregated into subactivities. The program budget looks at the tasks to be performed, the type of employees needed, the required workhours, and the time frame.

Financial Aspects

Some programs are basically only revenue centers, such as fund raising, while others are just cost centers, such as an entitlement program (e.g., welfare). Program analysis should also be performed for control purposes such as revenue per unit, cost per unit, cost per service hour, and trend in revenue or cost.

Table 7.1 shows a program budget by item.

This table allows the NPO's management to determine how much is spent on each program (cost objective), as well as the cost distribution by item.

A program may have multiple goals. If the objectives are clearly defined, each may be specified within the budget or in narrative form.

The revenue, support, and cost for each program must be considered. A detailed program budget appears in Table 7.2.

T A B L E 7.2

Program Budget

Program Budget			
Revenue and Support:			
Contributions		$530,000	
Grants		260,000	
Membership fees		110,000	
Contracts		315,000	
Special events		66,000	
Sale of merchandise		35,000	
Legacies and bequests		71,000	
Investment income		14,000	
Miscellaneous income		3,000	
Total Revenue and Support			$1,404,000
Expenses:			
Salaries			
Program Director	$100,000		
Event Coordinator	25,000		
Other	45,000	170,000	
Fringe benefits		40,000	
Payroll taxes		11,000	
Rent		120,000	
Supplies		210,000	
Insurance		60,000	
Telephone		20,000	
Electric		15,000	
Promotion		78,000	
Depreciation		34,000	
Postage		12,000	
Legal		83,000	
Accounting		56,000	
Entertainment		121,000	
Travel		137,000	
Conference fees		5,000	
Awards		4,000	
Miscellaneous		2,000	
Total Expenses			$1,178,000
Excess (Deficit) of Total			
Revenue and Support over Expenses			$ 226,000

Table 7.3 presents an illustrative program expense budget by service center.

T A B L E   7.3

Program Expense Budget by Service Center

	Recreation Services	Day-Care Services	Community Services	General	Total
Salaries	$100,000	$ 60,000	$ 80,000	$ 50,000	$290,000
Fringe benefits*	20,000	12,000	16,000	10,000	58,000
Payroll taxes*	5,000	3,000	4,000	2,500	14,500
Total compensation	$125,000	$ 75,000	$100,000	$ 62,500	$362,500
Professional fees	55,000	40,000	38,000	24,000	157,000
Rent	30,000	20,000	25,000	15,000	90,000
Utilities	14,000	12,000	8,000	5,000	39,000
Supplies	28,000	39,000	41,000	21,000	129,000
Postage	6,000	5,000	4,000	3,000	18,000
Total Expenses	$258,000	$191,000	$2l6,000	$130,500	$795,500

*For budget purposes, fringe benefits and payroll taxes may be based on a specified percentage of salaries. In this case, it is assumed to be 20% and 5%, respectively.

Timing Considerations

A time sheet is needed for project activities comparing projected time, actual time, new completion dates (if any), and reasons for delay. If a project is completed too early, were corners cut? A bar chart may show activity and service times. The quality of the program should be checked at important stages during the process to identify possible problems and correct them.

Conclusion

Program budgeting should be integrated into the financial and managerial systems. Programs may be budgeted by department, by segment, and by responsibility unit. The program budget is the estimated cost of performing an operation, a service, or an activity. Programming is structuring the approach to accomplish a desired objective. For example, a program budget may allocate financial and human resources to a particular activity or function such as feeding the homeless, treating patients, servicing student needs, and crime prevention.

A program budget has a detailed plan. It specifies the mix of resources needed to achieve the objective such as capital, facilities, and labor. Alternatives are appraised. The emphasis is output-driven rather than input-generated. It is future-oriented, examining the impact on the future of present decisions and choices.

CHAPTER 8

Analysis of Cost Behavior and Flexible Budgeting

"But in Colorado's less frugal nonprofits, as much as 40 cents of every donated dollar can go toward paying salaries, renting office space and covering expense accounts. When almost half of every dollar is earmarked for operating costs, eyebrows rise, but how much is too much? It shouldn't go much higher than 30 cents.

Colorado Association of Nonprofit Organizations
Denver Business Journal
December 2, 1994

Not all costs behave the same way. There are certain costs that vary in proportion to changes in volume or activity, such as repairs and maintenance. There are other costs that do not change even though volume changes, such as rent and insurance. An understanding of cost behavior is helpful:

1. For break-even and cost-volume-profit analysis.
2. To appraise divisional performance.
3. For flexible budgeting.
4. To make short-term choice decisions.
5. For pricing of services and products.
6. Establishing bid prices on contracts and proposals.

ANALYSIS OF COST BEHAVIOR

For planning, control, and decision-making purposes, mixed costs need to be separated into variable and fixed components. Since the mixed costs contain both fixed and variable elements, the analysis takes the following mathematical form, which is called a cost-volume formula (flexible budget formula or cost function):

Total Expenses = Fixed Expenses + Variable Expenses

or, in an equation form,

$$Y = a + bX$$

where Y = Total Expenses
$\quad X$ = Activity Level
$\quad a$ = Fixed Expenses
$\quad b$ = Variable Expenses per Unit of X

Separating the mixed cost into its fixed and variable components is the same thing as estimating the parameter values a and b in the cost-volume formula. There are several methods available to be used for this purpose, including the high-low method and regression analysis (discussed in Chapter 5). They are illustrated below.

THE HIGH-LOW METHOD

The high-low method, as the name indicates, uses two extreme data points to determine the values of a (the fixed cost portion) and b (the variable rate) in the equation $Y = a + bX$. The extreme data points are the highest representative XY pair and the lowest representative x-y pair. The activity-level X, rather than the mixed-cost item Y, governs their selection.

The high-low method is explained, step by step, as follows:

Step 1. Select the highest pair and the lowest pair.

Step 2. Compute the variable rate, b, using the formula:

$$\text{Variable rate} = \frac{\text{Difference in Cost } Y}{\text{Difference in Activity} X}$$

Step 3. Compute the fixed-cost portion as:

Fixed Cost Portion = Total Mixed Cost − Variable Cost

EXAMPLE 8.1
XYZ Community Health Clinic decided to relate labor and personnel costs to patient-days to develop a cost-volume formula in the form $Y = a + bX$. Eight monthly observations were collected. They are given on the top of page 181.

Month	Patient-Days (X)	Labor Costs (Y)
1	550	$14,400
2	575	14,700
3	425	12,300
4	400	12,150
5	350	11,250
6	200	8,400
7	400	11,700
8	450	12,750

The high-low points selected from the monthly observations are:

	Y	X
High	$14,700	575
Low	8,400	200
Difference	$ 6,300	375

Thus

$$\text{Variable rate } b = \frac{\text{Difference in } Y}{\text{Difference in } X} = \frac{\$6,300}{375 \text{ days}} = \$16.80 \text{ per day}$$

The fixed-cost portion then is:

$$\$14,700 - (\$16.80)(575 \text{ days}) = \$5,040$$

Therefore, the cost-volume formula for labor costs is:

$$\$5,040 \text{ Fixed} + \$16.80 \text{ per Patient-Day}$$

The high-low method is simple and easy to use. It has the disadvantage, however, of using two extreme data points, which may not be representative of normal conditions. The method may yield unreliable estimates of a and b in our formula. In such a case, it would be wise to drop them and choose two other points that are more representative of normal situations. Be sure to check the scatter diagram for this possibility.

REGRESSION ANALYSIS

Unlike the high-low method, in an effort to estimate the variable rate and the fixed cost portion, the regression method includes all the observed data and attempts to find a line of best fit.

EXAMPLE 8.2

To illustrate the computations of b and a, we will refer to the data in Table 8.1 (presented later in this chapter, on page 184). The Excel regression result is presented below.

Summary Output

Regression Statistics

Multiple R	0.9967077
R squared	0.9934263
Adjusted R Square	0.9923307
Standard Error	171.98425
Observations	8

Anova

	df	SS	MS	F	Significance F
Regression	1	26819716	26819716	906.7275	8.9E-08
Residual	6	177471.4984	29578.58		
Total	7		26997187.5		

	Coefficients	Standard Error	t Statistic	P Value	Lower 95%	Upper 95%	Lower 95%	Upper 95%
Intercept	5204.8046	240.3333769	21.6566	6.33E-07	4616.73	5792.88	4616.72	5792.87
X variable 1	16.71987	0.555257565	30.11192	8.9E-08	15.3612	18.07854	15.3612	18.0785

The cost-volume formula then is

$$Y = \$5,204.81 + \$16.72X, \qquad R^2 = 99.34\%$$
$$(0.55)$$

or

$$\$5,204.81 \text{ fixed, plus } \$16.72 \text{ per patient-day}$$

Note a high R squared and a low standard error of the variable rate b.

EXAMPLE 8.3

Assume that 500 patient-days are to be expended next month. The projected labor costs will be computed as follows:

$$Y = \$5,204.81 + \$16.72X = \$5,204.81 + \$16.72(500) = \$13,564.81$$

FLEXIBLE BUDGETING AND COST CONTROL

A flexible budget is a tool that is extremely useful in cost control. In contrast to a static budget, which was discussed in Chapter 6, the flexible budget is characterized as follows:

1. It is geared toward a range of activity rather than a single level of activity.

2. It is dynamic in nature, rather than static. By using the cost-volume formula (or the flexible budget formula), a series of budgets can be easily developed for various levels of activity.

The static (fixed) budget is geared for only one level of activity and has problems in cost control. Flexible budgeting distinguishes between fixed and variable costs, thus allowing for a budget which can be automatically adjusted (via changes in variable cost totals) to the particular level of activity actually attained. Thus, variances between actual costs and budgeted costs are adjusted for volume ups and downs before differences due to price and quantity factors are computed.

The primary use of the flexible budget is to accurately measure performance by comparing actual costs for a given output with the budgeted costs for the same level of output.

Flexible budgeting is used to determine the impact of planned activities on cash flow and the financial statements. Overall activity will fluctuate depending upon the demand for services by the customers. Even if the fixed budget is prepared, the budget ultimately used as a comparison with actual results should be based on the actual, not the anticipated level of activity. You don't want to compare apples and oranges. The preparation of the budget based on actual activity is possible, because the flexible budgeting approach can be expressed in terms of the cost-volume formula.

EXAMPLE 8.4

This example illustrates the problem that a hospital unit can face with a static (or fixed) budget in evaluating its performance and how the problem can be corrected with a flexible budget.

Table 8.1 (page 184) which shows a fixed budget, clearly indicates that responsibility center managers are liable to be rewarded or penalized for reasons beyond their control. For example, the x-ray unit may show low profits due to reduced numbers of patients utilizing the facility, which is outside managers' control. Also, cost variances are useless, in that they are comparing oranges with apples. The problem is that the budget costs are based on an activity level of 2,000 patients, whereas the actual costs were

T A B L E   8.1

X-RAY UNIT: MEDICAL SERVICE CORPORATION *Performance Report—Static Budget (May 1996)*			
	Master budget	**Actual**	**Variance**
Units	2,000	1,200	800
Sales revenue	$60,000	$36,000	$24,000[a]
Variable costs:			
Film	16,000	11,500	4,500[b]
Other material	4,000	3,000	1,000[b]
Technician	3,000	2,500	500[b]
Other labor	900	600	300[b]
Other variable	2,400	2,000	400[b]
Total variable	$26,300	$19,600	$ 6,700[b]
Contribution margin	$33,700	$16,400	$17,300[a]
Fixed costs:			
Rent	$800	800	0
Depreciation	400	400	0
Supervison	2,000	2,000	0
Other fixed	3,500	3,300	200[b]
Total fixed	$ 6,700	$6,500	$ 200[b]
Operating income	$27,000	$9,900	$17,100[a]

[a] Unfavorable.

[b] Favorable.

incurred at an activity level below this (1,200 patients). From a control standpoint, it makes no sense to try to compare costs at one activity level with costs at a different activity level. Such comparisons would make the manager look good as long as the actual service level was less than the budgeted level.

The flexible budget is designed to overcome this deficiency. Table 8.2 illustrates the underlying concept. In this budget, costs are separated into variable and fixed costs, using the cost-volume formula. The budget is based on the 1,200 actual number of patients. The variable cost that changes with the level of output is subtracted from the revenue to arrive at the *contribution margin* realized at each level of activity. Operating income for each specified level of output is then obtained by deducting fixed costs from each budgeted contribution margin. The unit manager is thus freed from forces beyond his or her control, in this example the number of patients

T A B L E   8.2

	X-RAY UNIT: MEDICAL SERVICE CORPORATION *Flexible Budget (May 1996)*					
		Number of x-rays per month				
	Budgeted per Unit	**$1,000**	**$1,200**	**$1,400**	**$1,800**	**$2,000**
Sales revenue	$30.00	$30,000	$36,000	$42,000	$54,000	$60,000
Variable costs:						
Film	8.00	8,000	9,600	11,200	14,400	16,000
Other material	2.00	2,000	2,400	2,800	3,600	4,000
Technician	1.50	1,500	1,800	2,100	2,700	3,000
Other labor	0.45	450	540	630	810	900
Other variable	1.20	1,200	1,440	1,680	2,160	2,400
Total variable	$13.15	$13,150	$15,780	$18,410	$23,670	$26,300
Contribution margin	$16.85	$16,850	$20,220	$23,590	$30,330	$33,700
Fixed costs:						
Rent		$800	$800	$800	$800	$800
Depreciation		400	400	400	400	400
Supervision		2,000	2,000	2,000	2,000	2,000
Other fixed		3,500	3,500	3,500	3,500	3,500
Total fixed		$ 6,700	$ 6,700	$ 6,700	$ 6,700	$ 6,700
Operating Income		$10,150	$13,520	$16,890	$23,630	$27,000

served. The manager is held accountable only for profits that are attainable with the number of patients actually served, not the expected number. Table 8.3 presents the performance report using a flexible budgeting system. Virtually all cost variances are unfavorable, which calls for management's attention and need to be investigated.

A flexible budget, unlike a fixed (or static) budget, is not considered a form of appropriations, but rather serves as an approved plan that can facilitate budgetary control and operational evaluations. It seeks only to judge the manager on actual performance and does not reward or penalize him or her for influences upon which he or she has no control.

When a flexible budget system is used, integrating it into the hospital's accounting system is not appropriate. However, if a fixed budget is used due to preference or a legal requirement, it may be effective to consolidate the budgetary accounts into the accounting system. The basis of accounting used to prepare a budget for the hospital should be accrual, the same as the basis used to record the organization's actual transactions.

T A B L E   8.3

X-RAY UNIT: MEDICAL SERVICE CORPORATION *Performance Report—Flexible Budget (May 1996)*			
Units	Costs incurred	Flexible budget	Variance explanation
Units	1,200	1,200	0
Sales revenue	$36,000	$36,000	0
Variable costs:			
Film	11,500	9,600	$1,900[a]
Other material	3,000	2,400	600[a]
Technician	2,500	1,800	700[a]
Other labor	600	540	60[a]
Other variable	2,000	1,440	560[a]
Total variable	$19,600	$15,780	$3,820[a]
Contribution margin	$16,400	$20,220	$3,820[a]
Fixed costs:			
Rent	800	800	0
Depreciation	400	400	0
Supervision	2,000	2,000	0
Other fixed	3,300	3,500	200[b]
Total fixed	$ 6,500	$ 6,700	$ 200[b]
Operation income	$ 9,900	$13,520	$3,620[a]

[a] Unfavorable
[b] Favorable

EXAMPLE 8.5

Tables 8.4 and 8.5 illustrate another hospital's flexible budget and variance analysis.

STANDARD COSTS AND VARIANCE ANALYSIS

One of the most important phases of responsibility accounting is establishing standard costs and evaluating performance by comparing actual costs with the standard costs. *Standard costs* are costs that are established in advance based on quantitative and qualitative measurements, to serve, initially,

T A B L E 8.4

JOHN JAY HOSPITAL Flexible Budget for Department 1				
Level of (Related to)	70%	85%	90%	100%
Direct	$262,500	$318,750	$337,500	$375,000
Direct	100,000	100,000	100,000	100,000
Allocated	80,000	80,000	80,000	80,000
Allocated:				
Dept. 5	100,000	100,000	100,000	100,000
Dept. 6	20,000	20,000	20,000	20,000
Dept. 7	55,000	62,500	65,000	70,000
Total	$617,500	$681,250	$702,500	$745,000
Billing	$ 57,750	$ 70,125	$ 74,250	$ 82,500
Cost per Unit of Service	$ 10.69	$ 9.71	$ 9.46	$ 9.03

T A B L E 8.5

JOHN JAY HOSPITAL Flexible Budget for Department 1			
Level of (Related to)	Actual Expenses, 85%	Flexible Budget, 85%	Variances
Direct	$320,000	$318,750	($1,250)
Direct	101,000	100,000	(1,000)
Allocated	78,000	80,000	2,000 Favorable
Allocated:			
Dept. 5	100,500	100,000	(500)
Dept. 6	22,500	20,000	(2,500)
Dept. 7	64,000	62,500	(1,500)
Total	$686,000	$681,250	($4,750)

Notes: 1. Direct variable expense variance probably resulted in the department's lack of ability to control variable costs.
2. Direct fixed expense variance suggests that the departmental supervisor "overspent" his allocated fixed expenses.
3. Departments 5 and 6 variances probably caused by inadequate methods of cost control.
4. Department 7 variance could have been caused by having too many employees or the inability to control costs.
5. In all unfavorable cases, all individual expense items should be reviewed with departmental supervisors.

as targets to be met and, after the fact, to determine how well those targets were actually met. The standard cost is based on physical and dollar measures: it is determined by multiplying the standard quantity of an input by its standard price.

The difference between the actual costs and the standard costs, called the "variance," is calculated for individual cost centers.

GENERAL MODEL FOR VARIANCE ANALYSIS

Two general types of variances can be calculated for most cost items: a price/rate variance and a usage/efficiency variance.

The price variance is calculated as follows:

$$\text{Price Variance} = \text{Actual Quantity} * (\text{Actual Price} - \text{Standard Price})$$
$$= AQ * (AP - SP)$$
$$= \underset{(1)}{(AQ * AP)} - \underset{(2)}{(AQ * SP)}$$

The quantity variance is calculated as follows:

$$\underset{\text{Variance}}{\text{Quantity}} = (\text{Actual Quantity} - \text{Standard Quantity}) * \text{Standard Price}$$
$$= (AQ - SQ) * SP$$
$$= \underset{(2)}{(AQ * SP)} - \underset{(3)}{(SQ * SP)}$$

Figure 8.1 shows a general model (a 3-column model) for variance analysis that incorporates items (1), (2), and (3) from the above equations.

It is important to note three things:

1. A price variance and a quantity variance can be calculated for materials and labor. The variance is not called by the same name, however. For example, a price variance is called a "materials price variance" in the case of materials, but a "wage rate variance" in the case of labor.

2. A cost variance is unfavorable (U) if the actual price AP or the actual quantity AQ exceeds the standard price SP or the standard quantity SQ; a variance is favorable (F) if the actual price or actual quantity is less than the standard price or standard quantity.

3. The standard quantity allowed for output—item (3)—is the key concept in variance analysis. This is the standard quantity that should have been used to produce actual output. It is computed by multiplying the actual output by the number of input units allowed.

F I G U R E 8.1

A General Model for Variance Analysis

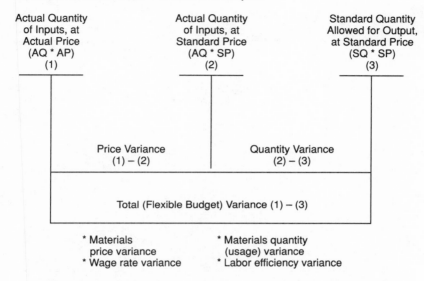

Actual Quantity of Inputs, at Actual Price (AQ * AP) (1)	Actual Quantity of Inputs, at Standard Price (AQ * SP) (2)	Standard Quantity Allowed for Output, at Standard Price (SQ * SP) (3)
Price Variance (1) – (2)	Quantity Variance (2) – (3)	
Total (Flexible Budget) Variance (1) – (3)		

```
* Materials              * Materials quantity
  price variance           (usage) variance
* Wage rate variance     * Labor efficiency variance
```

We will now illustrate the variance analysis for materials and labor cost items.

Materials Variances

A materials purchase price variance is isolated at the time of purchase of the material. The purchasing department is responsible for any materials price variance that might occur. The materials quantity (usage) variance is computed based on the actual quantity used. The mission center is responsible for any materials quantity variance.

Unfavorable price variances may be caused by inaccurate standard prices, inflationary cost increases, scarcity in raw material supplies resulting in higher prices, or purchasing inefficiencies. Unfavorable material quantity variances may be explained by poorly trained workers, by improperly adjusted machines, or by outright waste.

EXAMPLE 8.6

An association uses a standard cost system. The standard (budgeted) costs for its services are as follows:

- Materials: 2 reams at $3 per ream for its newsletter.
- Labor: 1 hour at $5 per hour.

F I G U R E   8.2

Materials Variances

Actual Quantity of Inputs, at Actual Price (AQ * AP) (1)	Actual Quantity of Inputs, at Standard Price (AQ * SP) (2)	Standard Quantity Allowed for Output, at Standard Price (SQ * SP) (3)
25,000 reams * $2.99 = $74,750	25,000 reams * $3.00 = $75,000	20,000 reams~ * $3.00 = $60,000

Price Variance
$250 (F)

20,750 reams * $3.00
= $62,250

Quantity Variance
$2,250 (U)

~ 10,000 units actually produced * 2 reams allowed per unit = 20,000 reams.

During March, 25,000 reams of paper were purchased for $74,750, and 20,750 reams of paper were used in producing 10,000 units of service. Direct labor costs incurred were $49,896 (10,080 direct labor-hours).

Using the general model (3-column model), the materials variances are shown in Figure 8.2.

It is important to note that the amount of materials purchased (25,000 reams) differs from the amount of materials used in production (20,750 reams). The materials purchase price variance was computed using 25,000 reams purchased, whereas the materials quantity (usage) variance was computed using the 20,750 reams used in production. A total variance cannot be computed because of the difference.

Alternatively, we can compute the materials variances as follows:

$$\text{Materials price variance} = AQ(AP - SP)$$
$$= (AQ * AP) - (AQ * SP)$$
$$= (25,000 \text{ reams})(\$2.99 - \$3.00)$$
$$= \$74,750 - \$75,000$$
$$= \$250(F)$$

Materials quantity (usage) variance $= (AQ - SQ)SP$

$$= (20,750 \text{ reams} - 20,000 \text{ reams})(\$3.00)$$
$$= \$62,250 - \$60,000$$
$$= \$2,250(U)$$

Labor Variances

Labor variances are computed in a manner similar to the materials variances, except that in the three-column model the terms "efficiency" and "rate" are used in place of the terms "quantity" and "price." The department manager or program manager is responsible for both the prices paid for labor services and the quantity of labor services used. Therefore, the department must explain why any labor variances occur.

Unfavorable rate variances may be explained by an increase in wages, or by the use of labor commanding higher wage rates than contemplated. Unfavorable efficiency variances may be explained by poor supervision, poor-quality workers, poor quality of materials requiring more labor time, or employee unrest.

EXAMPLE 8.7

Using the same data as given in Example 8.6, the labor variances can be calculated as shown in Table 8.6.

T A B L E 8.6

Labor Variances

Actual Hours of Inputs, at Actual Rate (*AH* * *AR*)	Actual Hours of Inputs, at Standard Rate (*AH* * *SR*)	Standard Hours Allowed for Output, at Standard Rate (*SH* * *SR*)
(1)	(2)	(3)
10,080 *h* * $4.95 = $49,896	10,080 *h* * 5.00 = $50,400	10,000 *h~* * $5.00 = $50,000
Rate		Efficiency
Variance		Variance
(1) – (2)		(2) – (3)
$504 (*F*)		$400 (*U*)
	(1) – (3) Total Variance $104 (*F*)	

Notes: * = 1 hour (h) allowed per unit = 10.000 hours. ~ 10.000 = units actually produced.

Note: The symbols AQ, SQ, AP, and SP have been changed to AH, SH, AR, and SR to reflect the terms "hour" and "rate."

Alternatively, we can calculate the labor variances as follows:

$$\text{Wage rate variance} = AH(AR - SR)$$
$$= (AH * AR) - (AR * SR)$$
$$= (10,080 \text{ Hours})(\$4.95 - \$5.00)$$
$$= \$49,896 - \$50,400$$
$$= \$504 \ (F)$$
$$\text{Labor efficiency variance} = (AH - SH)SR$$
$$= (10,080 \text{ Hours} - 10,000 \text{ Hours}) * \$5.00$$
$$= \$50,400 - \$50,000$$
$$= \$400(U)$$

More detailed variance computations such as revenue variances are covered in Chapter 6.

Variance analysis is a key tool for measuring performance of a cost center. Variances may be related, so a favorable variance in one responsibility area may result in an unfavorable one in other segments of the nonprofit entity. Variances may be as detailed as necessary, considering the cost/benefit relationship. Variances may be evaluated daily, weekly, monthly, quarterly, or yearly, depending on the importance of identifying a problem quickly.

Further, variance determination and analysis aids in decision making, pricing formulation, and cost control; in ensuring goal congruence and in establishing goals; in identifying trouble spots; in enhancing employee motivation, operational efficiency, and productivity; and in fostering communication.

A *performance report* based on the analysis of variances must be prepared for each department, cost center program, or activity, addressing the following questions:

1. Is the variance favorable or unfavorable?
2. If it is unfavorable, is it significant enough for further investigation?
3. If it is significant, is it controllable?
4. Who is responsible for what portion of the total variance?
5. What are the causes of an unfavorable variance?
6. What is the remedial action to take?

The report is useful in two ways: (1) in focusing attention on situations in need of management action and (2) in increasing the precision of planning and control of costs. The report should be produced as part of the overall standard costing and responsibility accounting system.

Improving Managerial and Departmental Performance

For a nonprofit's executive director, who doesn't understand what being a business means, it can be scary. But for a nonprofit that's been delivering services in different ways . . . the knowledge about their market, service, and costs are all in place. All that is usually lacking is a pricing mechanism and a specific business plan.

Richard Crimmins
Entrepreneurial Management Center
Vermont Business, *May, 1986*

Managerial and departmental control in the private sector is predicated on the general goal of shareholder wealth maximization. Shareholder wealth generally translates into return on investment (ROI) or residual income (RI) measures. In the public sector, however, there are no consensus performance measures for managerial control. The reason arises from the basic role of nonprofit organizations. This chapter begins by discussing the concept of responsibility accounting, briefly reviews private sector measures of ROI and RI, and presents alternative performance measures that are pertinent to nonprofit organizations.

THE LONG AND THE SHORT OF RESPONSIBILITY ACCOUNTING

Responsibility accounting is the system for collecting and reporting revenue and cost information by areas of responsibility. It operates on the premise that managers should be held responsible for their performance, the performance of their subordinates, and all activities within their responsibility center. Responsibility accounting, also called activity accounting, has the following advantages:

1. It facilitates delegation of decision making.
2. It helps management promote the concept of management by objective. In management by objective, managers agree on a set of goals. The manager's performance is then evaluated based on his or her attainment of these goals.
3. It provides a guide to the evaluation of performance and helps to establish standards of performance which are then used for comparison purposes.
4. It permits effective use of the concept of management by exception, which means that the manager's attention is concentrated on the important deviations from standards and budgets.

RESPONSIBILITY ACCOUNTING AND RESPONSIBILITY CENTER

For an effective responsibility accounting system, the following three basic conditions are necessary:

1. The organization structure must be well defined. Management responsibility and authority must go hand in hand at all levels, and must be clearly established and understood.
2. Standards of performance in revenues and costs must be properly determined and well defined.
3. The responsibility accounting reports (or performance reports) should include only items that are controllable by the manager of the responsibility center. Also, they should highlight items calling for managerial attention.

A well-designed responsibility accounting system establishes responsibility centers within the organization. A *responsibility center* is defined as a unit in the organization which has control over costs, revenues, and/or both. Responsibility centers can be one of the following types.

Cost (Expense) Center.   A cost center is the unit within the organization which is responsible only for costs. Examples would be nursing services in a hospital or support units such as library services and laundry services. *Variance analysis* based on standard costs and flexible budgets would be a typical performance measure of a cost center. These topics were covered in Chapters 6 and 8.

Profit Center   A profit center is the unit which is held responsible for the revenues earned and costs incurred in that center. In contrast with a cost center, in which management attention is focused on cost control, in a profit center the manager is encouraged to be concerned with both costs and with providing a sufficient quantity and quality of services to generate adequate revenues. Examples might include departments in a hospital or program managers in many nonprofit organizations. *The contribution approach to cost allocation* is widely used to measure the performance of a profit center. This approach will be discussed later in the chapter.

MISSION CENTERS AND SERVICE CENTERS

Irrespective of type, responsibility centers of NPOs can be viewed as either mission centers or service centers. Mission centers are directly related to the objectives or missions of the NPO. They may also be called "direct services," "program centers," or "line programs." Service centers, which are non-revenue-producing, administrative, or support centers, provide support to both mission centers and other service centers. Mission centers are often called revenue-producing centers, since they charge clients for their services, while service centers do not. Table 9.1 presents some examples of mission and service centers for NPOs.

THE PRIVATE SECTOR MEASURES

There are two popular measures for evaluating responsibility centers in the private sector: return on investment (ROI) and residual income (RI). They are discussed briefly below.

ROI relates operating income to operating assets. Specifically,

$$\text{ROI} = \frac{\text{Operating Income}}{\text{Operating Asets}}$$

EXAMPLE 9.1
Consider the following financial data for a division:

Operating assets	$100,000
Operating income	$ 18,000

$$\text{ROI} = \frac{\$18,000}{\$100,000} = 18\%$$

T A B L E 9.1

NPO Mission and Service Centers

	Mission Centers	Service Centers
Hospitals	Pediatrics	Housekeeping
	Obstetrics	Plant maintenance
	Surgical	Dietary
	Inpatient care	Medical records
	Laboratory	Administration
	Radiology	
	Routine care	
	Outpatient care	
Children's Care Center	Foster home care	Accounting
	Psychological testing	Building and grounds
	Social work counseling	Laundry
	Psychotherapy	Social service
	Alcohol rehabilitation	Marketing
	Community outreach	
Museum	Curatorial	Accounting and finance
	Education	Personnel
	Research center	Switchboard
	Art School	Purchasing and printing
	Drama School	Grounds maintenance
		Heating plant
		Service building
		Security
		Administration
College	Educational departments	Administration
	Housing	Library
	Dining	

The ROI can be expressed as a product of these two factors, as shown below.

$$\text{ROI} = \frac{\text{Operating Income}}{\text{Operating Assets}} = \frac{\text{Operating Income}}{\text{Revenue}} \times \frac{\text{Revenue}}{\text{Operating Assets}}$$

$$= \text{Margin} \times \text{Asset Turnover}$$

What this formula implies is that, knowing the interrelationships among revenue, investment, and expenses, the private sector management can evaluate decisions and performance in each of these areas in light of their potential impact on ROI.

EXAMPLE 9.2

Assume the same data as in Example 9.1. Also assume revenue of $200,000. Then,

$$\text{ROI} = \frac{\text{Operating Income}}{\text{Operating Assets}} = \frac{\$18,000}{\$100,000} = 18\%$$

Alternatively,

$$\text{Margin} = \frac{\text{Operating Income}}{\text{Revenue}} = \frac{\$18,000}{\$200,000} = 9\%$$

$$\text{Turnover} = \frac{\text{Revenue}}{\text{Operating Assets}} = \frac{\$200,000}{\$100,000} = 2 \text{ times}$$

Therefore,

$$\text{ROI} = \text{Margin} \times \text{Turnover} = 9\% \times 2 \text{ Times}$$

Another approach to measuring performance is residual income. RI is the operating income which a division is able to earn above some minimum rate of return on its operating assets. RI, unlike ROI, is an absolute amount of income rather than a specific rate of return. When RI is used to evaluate divisional performance, the objective is to maximize the total amount of residual income, not to maximize the overall ROI figure.

$$\text{RI} = \text{Operating Income} -$$
$$(\text{Minimum Required Rate of Return} \times \text{Operating Assets})$$

EXAMPLE 9.3

In Example 9.1, assume the minimum required rate of return is 13 percent. Then the residual income of the division is:

$$\$18,000 - (13\% \times \$100,000) = \$18,000 - \$13,000 = \$5,000$$

In the nonprofit sector there are no performance measures that are readily available, widely acceptable, and homogeneous, such as ROI and RI.

SEGMENTAL REPORTING FOR MISSION CENTERS

Segmental reporting is the process of reporting activities of mission centers such as divisions, programs, or service territories. The *contribution approach* is valuable for segmented reporting because it emphasizes the cost behavior patterns and the controllability of costs that are generally useful for contribution analysis of various segments of an organization.

The contribution approach attempts to measure the performance of segments of an organization. It classifies costs as being either direct (traceable) or common to the segments. Only those costs that are directly identified with the segments are allocated; costs that are not direct to the segments are treated as common costs and are not allocated.

Under the contribution approach, we deduct variable costs from revenue to arrive at a contribution margin. The direct fixed costs are then deducted from the contribution margin, yielding a segment margin. The segment margin is a measure of a segment success that is also useful for long-term planning and mix decision making.

The contribution approach is based on the thesis that:

1. Fixed costs are much less controllable than variable costs.

2. *Direct* fixed costs and *common* fixed costs must be clearly distinguished. Direct fixed costs can be identified directly with a particular segment of an organization, whereas common fixed costs are those costs which cannot be identified directly with the segment.

3. Common fixed costs should be clearly identified as unallocated in the contribution income statement by segments. Any attempt to allocate these types of costs, on some arbitrary basis, to the segments of the organization can destroy the value of responsibility accounting. It would lead to unfair evaluation of performance and misleading managerial decisions.

The following concepts are highlighted in the contribution approach:

1. *Contribution margin.* Revenues minus variable costs.

2. *Segment margin.* Contribution margin minus direct (traceable) fixed costs. Direct fixed costs include discretionary fixed costs (such as certain advertising, R&D, promotion, and engineering) and traceable and committed fixed costs (such as depreciation, insurance, and the segment managers' salaries).

3. *Surplus.* Segment margin less unallocated common fixed costs.

Segmental reporting can be made by:

- Division.
- Programs.
- Activities.
- Service territory.
- Service center.

T A B L E 9.2

Segmental Income Statement

1. Segments Defined as Divisions

	Segments		
	Total Organization	Division 1	Division 2
Revenue	$150,000	$90,000	$60,000
Less: Variable costs	60,000	44,000	16,000
Contribution margin	$ 90,000	$46,000	$44,000
Less: Direct fixed costs	70,000	43,000	27,000
Divisional segment margin	$ 20,000	$ 3,000	$17,000
Less: Unallocated common fixed costs	$ 10,000		
Surplus	$ 10,000		

2. Segments Defined as Programs of Division 2

	Segments		
	Division 2	Program 1	Program 2
Revenue	$60,000	$20,000	$40,000
Less: Variable costs	16,000	7,000	9,000
Contribution margin	$44,000	$13,000	$31,000
Less: Direct fixed costs	26,500	9,500	17,000
Program margin	$17,500	$ 3,500	$14,000
Less: Unallocated common fixed costs	$ 500		
Divisional segment margin	$17,000		

EXAMPLE 9.4

Table 9.2 illustrates two levels of segmental reporting:

1. By segments defined as divisions.
2. By segments defined as programs of a division.

The segment margin is the best measure of the contribution of a segment. Unallocated fixed costs are common to the segments being evaluated and should be left unallocated in order not to distort the performance results of segments.

PERFORMANCE MEASURES FOR MANAGERIAL CONTROL

At all organizational levels basic financial performance measures are essential, such as achievement of budget objectives and/or variances from budget or standard. There are alternative measures for performance and managerial control. They are in fact control surrogates designed to serve as reliable signals to guide performance evaluation and resource allocation decisions at all levels for nonprofit organizations. They include such measures as schedule attainment percentage and the proportion of personnel retained during a period. Many of them are nonfinancial measures of the social benefits provided by nonprofits. Table 9.3 summarizes illustrative control surrogates for some selected nonprofit organizations.

The output of many individual activities in NPOs can be measured as easily as can that of corresponding activities in for-profit ones (e.g, clerical work, vehicle maintenance, food service). The problem of measuring performance in nonfinancial terms is not unique to NPOs. The same problem exists for for-profit organizations where discretionary costs predominate (e.g., personnel, research, law).

T A B L E 9.3

Control Surrogates for Nonprofits

Nonprofits	Output Indicators or Control Surrogates
University/college	Quality education, number of degrees granted, number of faculty publications, number of patents obtained, percentage of graduates obtaining immediate employment or admission to higher degree programs, job placement
Health care organization	Percent of successful treatment, mortality rate, increase in life years, number of malpractice lawsuits, percentage decrease in pain, percentage returning to work
Welfare agency/rehabilitation	Percent of successful treatment, finding a job, better child care, rate of recidivism
Cultural organization	Number of admissions, number of membership, number of honors and awards
Foundation	Dollar amount of money raised, yield on invested money, costs/funds received ratio
College professors	Peer review, student evaluation
Physicians	Peer review

Recently, the Government Accounting Standards Board (GASB) has developed service effort and accomplishment (SEA) measures for public health agencies, as shown in Table 9.4.

Note that the GASB distinguishes among inputs, outputs, and outcomes. *Inputs* are expenditures; *outputs* are essentially process measures, such as number of visits per month in a clinic or number of student-days in a school; and *outcomes* are results measures, such as infant mortality rates in a clinic or academic test scores in a school. Further, the GASB has developed efficiency measures as a cost per unit (for example, cost per immunization in a clinic and average cost per student-day in a school). Efficiency measures are computed for both outputs and inputs.[1]

T A B L E 9.4

Recommended SEA Measures for Public Health Agencies

Indicator	Rationale for Selecting Indicator
Maternal and Child Health (MCH) Care	
Inputs:	
Expenditures (may be broken out by program or activity) in current and constant dollars.	Measure of resources used to provide services.
Output:	
Number of clients admitted to Maternal and Child Health (MCH) program.	
Number of clinic visits per month.	Widely reported measure that provide an indication of Maternal and Child Health (MCH) program outputs.
Number of prenatal and postnatal mothers contacted.	
Outcome:	
Infant mortality rate.	
Low-birth-weight rates.	
Teenage pregnancy rate.	Widely accepted measures used by public health officials to measure Maternal and Child Health (MCH) program outcomes.
Rate of lead poisoning cases.	
Reported cases of preventable diseases in children.	
Number of clients authorized to be served and actually served by Women, Infants, and Child (WIC) program.	

T A B L E 9.4—*Continued*

Recommended SEA Measures for Public Health Agencies

Percentage of low-birth-weight babies in target population.	Widely reported measures by Maternal and Child Health (MCH) program to provide indicators of the accomplishment of short-term Maternal and Child Health (MCH) program objectives.
Projected low-birth-weight births prevented.	
Projected infant deaths prevented.	
Cases of measles prevented.	
Efficiency:	
Cost per immunication.	Indication of the agency's efficiency in purchasing immunizations.
Cost of Women, Infants, and Child (WIC) supplements per unit.	Indication of the agency's efficiency in purchasing Women, Infants, and Child (WIC) supplements.
Number of premature births/number of patients.	Indication of the agency's efficiency in reducing premature births.
Projected health care costs saved through routine checkups/costs of routine checkups.	Indication of the agency's efficiency in reducing future health care costs.

Source: Governmental Accounting Standards Board.

ENDNOTE

1. For more details, refer to Vivian L. Carpenter, "Improving Accountability: Evaluating the Performance of Public Health Agencies," *Association of Government Accountants Journal*, Fall 1990.

C H A P T E R   10*

Short-Term and Long-Term Financing

A determination must be made by the nonprofit organization (NPO) as to what type of financing is needed and why. The wrong type of financing may have disastrous effects. There are many factors involved in selecting the appropriate kind of financing, including cost; use of funds, maturity, and collateral requirements; stability of operations; relationships; restrictive provisions; diversity and flexibility; and amount, timing, and predictability of sources for repayment. The financing strategy may need to be adjusted as events change.

It is essential that the NPO be able to continue to raise money from external sources. The NPO's survival depends on fund raising. Typically, profits generated from operations is a secondary source of funds.

A mix of financing may be used. Financing sources include fund raising, grants, contracts, loans, revenue bonds, leasing, trade credit, royalties and licenses, internally generated funds, sales of merchandise, and joint ventures.

Capital refers to the NPO's long-term debt and fund balance. Debt financing involves repayment of principal and interest. Repayment restrictions may require reserves to be held. Interest rates increase as the maturity period of the debt increases because of greater risk.

It is generally better to borrow short-term when receipts to repay borrowing are assured in the near term. It is recommended to borrow long-term for long-lived assets such as a new building, or for permanent increases in current assets such as classroom supplies. Long-term debt would be suitable

---

*This chapter was coauthored by Robert Fonfeder, Ph.D., CPA, a professor at Hofstra University, and a financial consultant.

in such a case, to match the life of the related fixed asset. Long-term debt may be paid from such sources as other debt, gifts, grants, accumulated surplus of cash receipts over cash expenditures, and funds generated from operations. Intermediate-term debt may be used to fund asset purchases until a mortgage or bond may be issued or until a major fund-raising campaign is completed.

SEED CAPITAL

Seed capital is the money used to start an NPO, before working capital is even raised. Seed funds may be used to buy assets, to perform a feasibility analysis, or to engage in test marketing. A high interest rate or restrictions may be placed because of the higher risk, since the proposed NPO may not materalize. The NPO is not yet a viable entity, and all money invested or lent may be lost.

JOINT VENTURES

An NPO may join with a commercial business in a program. The commercial business partner should preferably share the NPO's values. Both partners or only one may contribute staff, money, physical resources, product development, marketing and distribution, and political contacts. Often, the commercial business provides significant funds to support the NPO's activities. The joint venture partners may be able to obtain more favorable financing terms.

INTERNALLY GENERATED FUNDS

The best source of funds is current, unrestricted operations, because these are internally generated and do not involve costs or limitations. This source shows good operating performance. Hard money is revenue that can be relied on with high certainty, such as college tuition for a university. Soft money is revenue that has some uncertainty of being received, such as gifts and grants. Revenue may be obtained from many sources, including membership fees, contributions, contracts, fees from admission to special events, royalties, investment income, sales of books, journals, newsletters, advertising space, and educational programs.

ANNUAL MEMBERSHIP DUES

Membership dues may be used to pay operating and fund-raising costs. To stimulate membership, perks should be offered, such as a health and dental plan, credit cards, purchase discounts, membership certificates, and personal items (e.g., pins, hats).

SALES OF MERCHANDISE

Sales of merchandise may raise funds and are usually used by small NPOs having a "narrow" appeal and a lack of volunteers. Funds from such sales are typically used to support operating expenses. A ready market for the merchandise should exist. Two approaches are to have a place of business or to have volunteers going to neighbors (e.g., Girl Scout cookies). It involves selecting what to sell, its price, the inventory level, and volunteer time availability. It is important to have an agreement with the manufacturer to return unsold merchandise. Costs are high because of the cost of the product and low productivity.

TRADE CREDIT

Trade credit is accounts payable representing unpaid bills to suppliers (who are anxious to sell their products). The NPO may stretch accounts payable if it is short of cash. If the NPO pays within the credit period, there is no interest charged representing free financing. For these reasons, it is the best external financing source.

Short-term credit is often used to finance temporary or seasonal expansion of current assets. It is a form of short-term loan. Trade credit is automatic and recurring. Its a spontaneous financing source tied to the NPO's activity level.

A volume (quantity) discount is a reduction in the price the NPO pays if a large quantity of items is ordered. A larger order usually provides a higher discount. Although a quantity discount reduces the cost of buying supplies, it can increase the carrying cost of holding a greater amount of supplies.

EXAMPLE 10.1
The NPO buys 100,000 items instead of 75,000. It will receive a 2 percent discount off the purchase cost of $2 each. However, holding the higher level of supplies will increase carrying costs by $3,000. The larger order is justified as indicated below.

Savings due to discount ($100,000 × $2 × 0.02)	$4,000
Less: Increase in carrying cost	3,000
Net advantage	$1,000

Many suppliers establish credit terms that authorize cash discounts in exchange for early payment of the amount bought. If the NPO takes advantage of the cash discount, it will reduce the purchase cost.

An opportunity cost is the net revenue the NPO loses by rejecting an alternative action. It should typically take advantgage of a discount offered by a creditor because of the high opportuntity cost. If the NPO is short of funds to pay the supplier early, the NPO should borrow the money when the interest rate of the loan is below the annual rate of the discount. For example, if the terms of sale are 2/10, net/30, the NPO has 30 days to pay the bill but will get a 2 percent discount if it pays in 10 days.

The following formula is used to compute the opportunity cost percentage on an annual basis:

$$\text{Opportunity Cost} = \frac{\text{Discount Percent}}{100 - \text{Discount Percent}} \times \frac{360}{N}$$

where N is the number of days payment can be delayed by forgoing the cash discount. This equals the number of days credit is outstanding less the discount period.

The numerator of the first term (discount percent) is the cost per dollar of credit, whereas the denominator (100 − discount percent) represents the money available by forgoing the cash discount. The second term represents the number of times this cost is incurred in a year.

If the NPO elects not to pay within the discount period, it should hold on to the money as long as possible. For example, if the terms are 2/10, net/60, it should not pay for 60 days.

EXAMPLE 10.2

The opportunity cost of not taking a discount when the terms are 3/15, net/60, is computed as follows:

$$\text{Opportunity Cost} = \frac{3}{100 - 3} \times \frac{360}{60 - 15} = \frac{3}{97} \times \frac{360}{45} = 24.7\%$$

Table 10.1 presents the opportunity cost associated with failing to pay within the discount period specified.

T A B L E   10.1

Credit Terms and Opportunity Costs

Credit Terms	Opportunity Cost
2/10, net 30	36.7%
2/10, net 45	21.0
2/10, net 60	14.7
2/10, net 90	9.2

A trade discount is a discount offered to a particular class of customer, such as a religious educational center.

FUND RAISING

Fund raising is needed by an NPO for success or even continued existence. Fund raising has the objective of acquiring, retaining, and maximizing donors. Charitable contributions are relied upon as a major revenue source. More than $350 billion is donated to more than one million nonprofits recognized by the Internal Revenue Service (IRS). Fund-raising methods are often combined. Funds may be obtained from individuals, corporations, foundations, and other funding agencies. However, most funds (about 85 percent) are obtained directly from individuals. Corporate giving is only about 5 percent of total philanthropy, and corporate gifts are obtained only through personal relationships with top executives. "Cold letters" do not work with corporate executives. Foundations usually account for only about 6 percent of total giving. Ask for more with the expectation you will get less. Think big not small!

Contributions may be unrestricted (for general support of basic activities) or restricted (to be spent only as stipulated by the donor).

In deciding on the amount of funds to raise, ask: Why is the money needed? How will the money be spent? How long will the money be needed? Who will benefit? Will the donor receive publicity (e.g., in a newsletter, or through media exposure)? How will the community and social needs be served? What programs will be implemented?

Development is the planned promotion of the NPO and its objectives to obtain public financial support and participation. Fund development should be coordinated and cooperative. Fund raising requires clear and realistic goals, specific plans, and strategies. An inventory of human and physical resources should be taken. The "right" person should be used for raising funds from selected sources.

Successful fund raising may be achieved in the following ways: by a stimulating and "moving" solicitation letter; in response to a professional and detailed proposal; through personal contacts and, relationships; through auctions; by developing sound ideas; via mass mailings, telemarketing, and rallies, and in response to radio and television ads. Determine whether the costs associated with a fund-raising campaign would justify the funds expected to be obtained.

The fund-raising method chosen should be appropriate and flexible under the circumstances, considering the audience, the cost, and the need.

Fund raising is an ideal source of funding because there is no principal or interest repayment required. Future earnings and reserves are not tied up.

A detailed fund-raising plan is needed. Alternative strategies must be set forth to accomplish the specified goal.

There is a learning curve in fund raising, meaning that as more experience is gained, the time and cost required to obtain gifts go down.

Gifts may be monetary (cash) or nonmonetary (e.g., securities, real property, personal property, royalties, and insurance policies with the NPO as beneficiary).

Goal Specification

An identifiable and quantitative purpose must be specified. What specifically is the money to be used for? Is it for an existing or a new program? What benefit will the program offer and to whom? The purpose must match the donor's preferences. The program must satisfy a need and be salable to prospective donors. Creative ideas are most attractive. Enthusiasm must be fostered.

The proposed program must "fit" the overall organizational objectives. Otherwise, the entity's credibility may suffer. Organizational priorities must be enumerated and stuck to for consistency.

Financial Aspects

Record keeping and processing of information is essential. Monies received should be accurately accounted for and donor restrictions on the money specified. Expenditures should be properly documented, approved, and accounted for.

Cost estimates for alternative strategies should be set forth. Fund-raising costs may be decreased by using internal resources such as staff, volunteers, mailing lists, office space, and computer facilities.

According to Jim Greenfield,[1] the national average is $0.20 in fund-raising costs per $1 donated. A reasonable and maximum relationship of cost to revenue should be specified not only in total but for each cost item. An example follows.

Cost Item	Cost per $1 Donated			
	Reasonable	Maximum	Actual	Reason
Direct mail renewal	$0.15	$0.25	$0.18	
Capital campaign	0.08	0.12	0.15	
Cost of benefit event	0.40	0.50	0.65	

The excess of (1) actual over reasonable and (2) actual over maximum should be explained. Reasons justifying actual being higher than expected should be provided.

The expected donor contributions should be determined based on the last three years', or the last five years', contributions. An average for a long time period levels out variability. A simple average may be determined as shown in the following example.

EXAMPLE 10.3

An NPO has accumulated the donations received over the last five years. It wants to estimate the donations for the current year based on a simple average of the last five years. The following information is presented:

Year	Donation
19X9	$120,000
19X8	100,000
19X7	110,000
19X6	90,000
19X5	115,000
Total	$535,000

The simple average is:

$$\frac{\text{Total}}{\text{Years}} = \frac{\$535,000}{5} = \$107,000$$

Therefore, the expected contribution for the current year is $107,000.

A weighted average may be more realistic than a simple average. Because it gives more weight to the most recent years, reflecting higher current donations and recent fund-raising experience. If a five-year weighted average is used, the last year is given a weight of 5 while the first year is assigned a weight of 1. The computation follows using the same information as in example 10.3.

Year	Donation	×	Weight	=	Total
19X9	$120,000	×	5	=	$ 600,000
19X8	100,000	×	4	=	400,000
19X7	110,000	×	3	=	330,000
19X6	90,000	×	2	=	180,000
19X5	115,000	×	1	=	115,000
Total			15		$1,625,000

T A B L E 10.2

Condensed Statement of Income and Expenses

Income:		
Contracts	$100,000	
Grants	300,000	
Contributions	500,000	
Legacies	30,000	
Investment income	50,000	
Gain on sale of investments	20,000	
Total income		$1,000,000
Expenses:		
Client services	$200,000	
Administration	160,000	
Research	140,000	
Total expenses		500,000
Excess of income over expenses		$ 500,000
Excess restricted by donors	$200,000	
Unrestricted	300,000	
Total		$ 500,000

The weighted-average donation for the five-year period will be:

$$\frac{\$1,625,000}{15} = \$108,333$$

Other methods, such as the moving average, are discussed in Chapter 5.

Often, for fund-raising purposes, an NPO will distribute summary financial data. It is best *not* to show a significant excess of income over costs because this might discourage fund raising. A condensed statement including donor restrictions is presented in Table 10.2.

Legal Considerations

Laws related to fund raising must be adhered to, so an attorney specializing in the area of fund raising must be retained. Further, a donor restriction is legally binding.

The NPO must comply with applicable tax laws and public reporting requirements. For example, if gifted property is sold within two years after receipt, IRS Form 8282 must be filed.

Budget

The written fund-raising proposal should have supporting documentation including project description and budget.

T A B L E 10.3

Fund-Raising Event Income and Costs

Income		
Registration fees	$ 20,000	
Sales of plaques, pins, clothing, etc.	6,000	
Ads taken out	5,000	
Sponsorship	15,000	
Donations: general and specific	<u>120,000</u>	
Total Income		$166,000
Costs		
Accounting	$ 12,000	
Legal	14,000	
Video production costs	6,000	
Printing and xeroxing	15,000	
Hotel costs (e.g., rooms)	38,000	
Food and liquor	11,000	
Telephone	3,000	
Postage	1,000	
Consulting fees (e.g., public relations)	2,000	
Data processing	500	
Supplies	<u>1,500</u>	
Total Expenses		<u>104,000</u>
Excess of income over expenses		$ 62,000

The budget helps to determine the amount of money required to accomplish the goal. Obtain cost estimates from vendors, forecast payroll costs, estimate operating expenses (e.g., rent and telephone), and undertake cost/benefit analysis.

Prepare a budget breaking down fixed, variable, and semivariable (or mixed) costs. Fixed costs such as rent, data processing, and insurance remain constant. Variable costs such as supplies, marketing brochures, labor, printing, and postage vary with the activity. Semivariable costs such as telephone and utilities are both fixed and variable. The costs incurred should justify the amount expected to be raised from contributions. Determine a reasonable expense/revenue relationship. Try not to exceed the maximum percentage (e.g., 30 percent).

A *flexible budget* may be used which is based on variable costs and fixed costs, and on the cost-volume formula.

An illustrative budget for a fund-raising event is shown in Table 10.3, showing projected revenue and costs.

F I G U R E 10.1

Fund-Raising Worksheet

Description:_____   Priority Level: _____
Identification Number: _____   Target Dates: _____
Number of Prospective Donors:_____
Profile of Donors: _____
Dollar Goal: _____
Estimated Contributions: _____
Goals: _____
Objectives: _____
Needs: _____
Benefits: _____
Problems: _____
Main Competition for Funds: _____
Costs by Category:
   Postage _____
   Travel _____
   Telephone _____
   Etc. _____
Total Cost: _____
Estimated Profit: _____
Responsible Individuals:

Activities	Name	Due Date
_____	_____	_____
_____	_____	_____
_____	_____	_____

Worksheet

A worksheet for fund raising should be prepared, such as that presented in Figure 10.1.

Special Events

A fund-raising event may be held either to obtain money directly or to recognize donors. Respected and well-known people in the field should be invited, so as to attract more participation and possible media attention. A lot of planning, time, and execution are involved. Examples are dances, fashion shows, movies, and dinners. Volunteers should be encouraged. The cost of the event should not be more than one-half the amount raised. Cost/benefit analysis for the event should be undertaken. Responsibility should be placed for control purposes, as in "Mr. X is in charge of follow-up telephone calls."

Solicitation

An annual giving program strives for unrestricted, recurring gifts. The campaign may occur several times yearly or only at one time. There is a yearly solicitation program for short-term needs. The objective is to receive funds to support current operations and to retain donors to support future programs. A support constituency is needed, including individuals, foundations, companies, associations and societies, and government. About 80 to 85 percent of gifts are made by individuals, so efforts should be concentrated on them. Because annual giving is based on *relationships*, donor relations programs must be emphasized. Solicitation may be by mail, personal visit, or telephone call.

A determination must be made of what form of solicitation is best for a particular donor. For example, a foundation requires a proposal, an individual (small gift) may need direct mail, and an individual (large gift) requires personal visit.

Let us consider direct mail. Donor renewal may be better done at least cost through direct mail than telemarketing. If repeated mail solicitation gets no response, it may be followed up by telemarketing.

Direct mail is sent to past and potential donors to solicit money and/or time. The solicitation letter should be persuasive with a clear description of the need for and the nature of the request, along with supporting documentation, goals to be achieved, amount solicited, and reason for funds. A reply envelope should be provided. The more dollars you ask for, the lower the response rate will be.

Direct mail is very costly, especially in the starting phase. The smaller the average gift, the higher the percentage cost. A direct mail program requires costs of mailing, printing of a letter and brochure, designing, and compilation. A mailing list may need to be bought such as from a professional organization. Some mailing lists are free, such as from community residents. "Inactive" donors who have not given for some time or those who never respond may be deleted from the list.

Direct mail cost can be minimized through third class or bulk rate. First class should be used only if a timely response is required. Mailing information, such as ways to expedite delivery via bar codes and costs, may be obtained by contacting the Superintendent of Documents, Government Printing Office, Washington, DC 20402-9371. The U.S. Postage Service Domestic Mail Manual provides current regulations and procedures regarding direct mail.

Each large donor should receive a personal telephone call or a visit. Personal solicitation, especially if the person asking for the funds is already known to the donor, work best. It is harder to turn down a colleague, a friend, or someone trustworthy you know.

Advertising solicitation is usually for a special purpose. Advertising should be placed in the media to reach the target audience, and it should have an emotional appeal. The graphics should be carefully designed, with an imporant message. A coupon should be included. Advertising has a high cost.

Planned Giving

In planned giving, which is for substantial gifts and must be structured in legal and accounting terms, people assign a percentage of their estates to the NPO upon death or during life, as stipulated in the will or the living trust. Deferred giving is usually for endowment purposes. The deferred gift is usually over a number of years. For example, a trust may pay income to the donor and/or the beneficiaries over life. When the last trust beneficiary dies, the sum in the trust passes to the charity.

Capital Campaign

This represents large donations (typically restricted) from major donors to build or to modernize a facility (e.g., a child-care center, a library, a dorm, or a hospital wing). Face-to-face solicitation is usually required. Preferably, each member of the campaign should be asked for a donation before seeking donations from others. The capital gift is usually paid in installments over several years. Target dates must be set forth.

Collections

Collections may be in the form of canisters at cash registers, passing around a basket (e.g., religious institution), and door-to-door volunteer solicitation. Small amounts are received from many contributors. A very limited amount of funds is raised, but the cost is low because of volunteer efforts.

Employee Giving

Employees may give their time, or may donate money through payroll deductions.

Donor Relations

A database should consist of current and prospective donors and personal information about them that might assist in fund raising. The personal information may consist of education, experience, interests, and so on. Prepare a list of donors by possible amount.

Potential donors include foundations, trade associations, professional organizations, government agencies, and individuals. Make sure you contact those who share your goals and concerns. What are the donor's interests? What has the donor given in the past? To whom? Do the prospective donor's resources, interests, and objectives match that of the NPO? What is unique or important about your request? How will the donor benefit (e.g., public relations, press release, plaque, company name on building or laboratory, favorable write-ups in local papers, endowed chair, award or citation, framed certificate)? Conduct oral and written surveys of donors to obtain their views. Be sensitive to their requests.

Provide options for donor support or participation. Flexibility is needed to obtain funding or time, because donors may place certain conditions before giving money or services. Try to get follow-up pledges. Further, communicate the NPO's tax-exempt status so the donor knows the contribution will be tax-deductible.

In attempting to upgrade a donor to a higher gift level, a personal telephone call or a visit may be appropriate. Try to obtain multiple gifts from the same donor yearly. Establish donor clubs and membership drives. Recognize and reward donors. The strategy used should be based on what would most motivate the donor.

The publication of a monthly newsletter may enhance fund raising and strengthen donor relations. For example, a newsletter may be used to notify the public of the donor's contribution. Acknowledge receipt of donations through official correspondence including thank-you letters or cards, and personal telephone calls.

Some companies favor supporting community activities in their geographic area. Companies also tend to donate money to NPOs related to corporate activities. An example is a pharmaceutical company giving to a health care facility.

Professional Management

Fund-raising consultants may be hired. Fund raisers may be paid a specified fee, a percentage of funds raised, or some combination. Expense reimbursement is separately paid. You get what you pay for in a professional fund raiser. In general, professionally managed fund-raising programs usually cost less, per dollar raised, than homemade campaigns. They also result in faster funds.

Committees

An advisory committee should be established, including membership of accountants, auditors, and attorneys, to assure that financial and legal aspects have been addressed. The Board of Directors/Trustees sets forth priorities and objectives. The marketing committee promotes the fund-raising efforts to obtain donors. The fund-raising committee consists of those with contracts and personal relationships.

Trade and Professional Associations

A trade or professional association dealing with your same NPO's activities may be contacted. For example, the American Institute of Certified Public Accounts (AICPA) may provide support for an accounting professorship or a controversial but important accounting area being researched.

Foundations

Foundations may be public or private. A foundation may be formed by companies or by individuals. References for fund-raising procedures and sources are *The Foundation Directory and Supplement* and *The National Directory of Corporate Giving*.

References

Refer to industry information and publications in your field, such as journals, magazines, and newsletters. An example is publications in the health services field.

Potential donors' names may be found in membership lists of other organizations, publications related to the NPO's activities, real estate records, grant lists, volunteer rosters, personnel rosters of foundations, reference books, and media references to donors.

Fund raisers should review business publications for possible donors including *Forbes*, *Business Week*, *Money*, *Fortune*, *Harvard Business Review*, and *The Wall Street Journal*. For legal matters, refer to Bruce Hopkins's book, *The Law of Fund Raising*.[2]

Sources of information on obtaining corporate donations follow:

- Local Chambers of Commerce.
- *Giving USA*, the annual report of information and trends on American philanthropy published by the American Association of Fund-Raising Counsel.
- The Taft Group, 12300 Twinbrook Parkway, Suite 450, Rockville, Maryland 20852.
- *Who's Who in Business and Industry*, Marquis Who's Who, 200 East Ohio Street, Chicago, Illinois 60611.
- Standard and Poor's *Register of Corporations*.
- Directors and executives.
- Moody's *Industrial Manual*.
- Dun and Bradstreet's *Million Dollar Directory*.

Resources

The use of external resources may aid fund-raising efforts. These resources include federal and local government reports that cite statistical information, on-line databases, and professional association data. Resources for fund raising include:

- Society for Nonprofit Organizations, 6314 Odana Road, Suite 1, Madison, WI 53719; (608) 247-9777.
- The Grantsmanship Center, P.O. Box 17220, Los Angeles, CA 90017; (310) 482-9860.
- American Society of Association Executives, 1575 I Street, N.W., Washington, DC 20005; (202) 626-2723.
- *The Chronicle of Philanthropy*, 1255 23rd St., N.W., Suite 775, Washington, DC 20037; (202) 466-1032.
- American Association of Fundraising Counsel Trust for Philanthropy, 25 West 43rd Street, New York, NY 10036.
- National Society for Fund Raising Executives, 1101 King St., Suite 700, Alexandria, VA 22314; (703) 684-0410.
- National Center for Nonprofit Boards, 2000 L Street, Washington, DC 20036.
- Association for Healthcare Philanthropy, 313 Park Avenue, Suite 400, Falls Church, VA 22046; (703) 532-6243.

Software

Fund-raising software may be used, such as:

- *Fundraising Toolbox*, 2221 East Lamar Boulevard, Suite 360, Arlington, TX 76006; (800) 458-4392.
- *Fundware Systems*, 3114 Thompson Avenue, Des Moines, IA 50317; (515) 263-0817.

ADVANCES

Short-term financing may be achieved by receiving an advance (retainer) against a contract or grant. However, if the NPO decides at a later date it no longer wants the contract or grant, or in fact unsatisfactorily performs, it may have to return the advance.

GRANTS AND CONTRACTS

Grants may be received from companies, federal or local government, foundations, and other grant-giving organizations. Grants are difficult to get, and costly, and are time-consuming to apply for. Community foundations offer

F I G U R E   10.2

Grant Proposal Format

Summary
Introduction
Statement of the Problem
Need
Objectives
Methods
Appraisal
Funding Request
Budget

the best opportunities to obtain a major grant for local or regional organizations. Applying should not be attempted unless the chance of obtaining a grant is above average.

What are the restrictions, if any, on grant funds? Grants are typically given for specific projects or programs. An example is a grant for a new show by a performing arts group. Another example is a medical research program undertaken by a hospital through grant funds.

A thorough feasibility study should be undertaken before proceeding with a grant proposal. A decision on acceptance usually takes a long time. Government grants are a volatile means of financing and cannot be relied on consistently as a source of financing programs or projects. Government funds usually involve restrictions and involve a lot of paperwork. Contact the U.S. Office of Grants and Contracts for filing information. It may be easier in some cases to obtain corporate grants. Examples of corporate foundations include Ford Motor, Exxon, and General Electric. A listing of foundations is found in the "Cumulative List of Organizations Described" in IRS publications. Also refer to the Foundation Center, *The National Data Book* for a list of foundations. (The Foundation Center is located at 79 Fifth Avenue, New York, NY. The telephone number is (212) 620-4230.)

A grant proposal includes a budget, narrative information, and a budget summary. The narrative explains the budget figures. Itemization is made of the major costs. The grant proposal budget includes: personnel and fringe benefits, travel, equipment (e.g., computers), supplies, consulting fees, construction costs, indirect costs, telephone, insurance, licenses, and miscellaneous costs.

The format for a proposal to obtain a grant appears in Figure 10.2.

F I G U R E 10.3

Illustrative Budget for a Grant Proposal

1. Personnel
   A. Salaries and Wages
      Full-Time
         Director
         Counselors
         Clerks
      Volunteers
         Social Work
   B. Fringe Benefits
      Health Care
      Life Insurance
   C. Consultants and Contract Services
      Per-Day Honorarium
         Accounting
         Legal
         Public Relations
2. Nonpersonnel
   A. Rent
      Office Space
      Computer Equipment
   B. Utilities
   C. Maintenance Services
   D. Renovations
   E. Office Supplies
   F. Xeroxing
   G. Travel
      Local
      Out of Town
   H. Telephones
   I. Postage
   J. Insurance
   K. Professional Dues
   L. Subscriptions
   M. Publications
   N. Other
Total

Grant budget requests must be more detailed for government than foundations. An illustrative budget appears in Figure 10.3.

An itemization is typically provided of major budgeted costs in sup-plementary schedules. For example, the breakdown of salaries and wages would include number of employees, title, monthly salary or hourly rate, and percentage of time by project.

ROYALTIES AND LICENSES

The NPO may receive funding by licensing its product (e.g., education television program) or through sales of its books (e.g., Bibles).

GOVERNMENT LOANS

Loans that may be available from government agencies are at low interest rates relative to market rates, and are secured.

BANK LOANS

Bank loans may be short-term, intermediate-term, or long-term. The length of a bank loan depends on many factors, including expected future interest rates, loan restrictions, risk, and anticipated cash flows.

Short-Term Loans

Short-term loans are for one year or less. The NPO may take out such a loan to make current payments (e.g., for supplies or payroll). The loan im-proves the NPO's liquidity and cash flow. Repayment may be from funds generated from operations.

In a seasonal line of credit, inventory or receivables are financed in one season of the year and repaid in another season, when inventory is sold or receivables collected. The risk to the NPO is that it will not generate ad-equate cash to pay the short-term debt when due.

The NPO, in obtaining short-term loans, often relies to some extent on cash flows from fund-raising activities to pay those loans.

Interest

It should be determined whether the interest applies to the beginning or the average loan balance. What works best for the NPO depends on the pattern of borrowing and repayment.

Interest on a loan may be paid either at maturity (ordinary interest) or in advance (discounting the loan). When interest is paid in advance, the loan proceeds are reduced and the effective (true) interest cost is increased.

EXAMPLE 10.4

An NPO borrows $100,000 at 8 percent interest per annum and repays the loan one year later.

$$\text{Interest} = \$100,000 \times 0.08 = \underline{\$8,000}$$

The effective interest rate remains at 8 percent. If the loan were discounted, the proceeds of the loan would be smaller.

$$\text{Proceeds} = \text{Principal} - \text{Interest}$$
$$\$92,000 = \$100,000 - \$8,000$$

In this case, the effective interest rate would be higher:

$$\text{Effective Interest Rate} = \frac{\text{Interest}}{\text{Proceeds}} = \frac{\$8,000}{\$92,000} = 8.7\%$$

Compensating Balance

When an NPO borrows under a credit line, it may need to keep a deposit with the bank that does not earn interest. The deposit is referred to as a *compensating balance* and is expressed as a percentage of the loan. The compensating balance in effect increases the cost of the loan. A compensating balance may also apply on the unusued portion of the credit line.

EXAMPLE 10.5

Assume the same information as the prior example, except there is a 10 percent compensating balance requirement.

$$\text{Compensating Balance} = 100,000 \times 0.10 = \$10,000$$
$$\text{Proceeds} = \text{Principal} - \text{Interest} - \text{Compensating Balance}$$
$$\$82,000 = \$100,000 - \$8,000 - \$10,000$$
$$\text{Effective Interest Rate} = \frac{\text{Interest}}{\text{Proceeds}} = \frac{\$8,000}{\$82,000} = 9.8\%$$

EXAMPLE 10.6

An NPO borrows $400,000 and must keep a 12 percent compensating balance. It also has an unused credit line of $200,000, for which a 10 percent compensating balance is required. The minimum balance the NPO must maintain is:

$$(\$400,000 \times 0.12) + (\$200,000 \times 0.10) = \text{Minimum Balance}$$
$$\$48,000 + \$20,000 = \underline{\$68,000}$$

Interest rates and compensating balance requirements increase as the risk of the borrower increases.

The amount of borrowing needed may be computed using the following formula:

Amount of Loan Needed =

$$\frac{\text{Peak Credit Need} - \text{Average Operational Need for Cash}}{1 - \text{Compensating Balance Percentage}}$$

EXAMPLE 10.7

After preparing a cash budget, an NPO decides its seasonal borrowing need will be a peak of $100,000 during a year. The compensating balance requirement is 10 percent. The normal cash need is $40,000.

The amount of loan needed to satisfy the peak credit need is:

$$\frac{\$100,000 - \$40,000}{1 - 0.10} = \frac{\$60,000}{0.90} = \underline{\$66,667}$$

Pledges Receivable as Security

An NPO can use pledges receivable as collateral for a short-term borrowing. Pledges from corporate donors are of higher quality than those from individuals, because the former are more likely to fulfill their promise due to greater financial standing. Pledges must be *written* to serve as collateral. Oral pledges are not acceptable security.

In general, banks will lend up to 75 percent of *quality* pledges used as collateral. Because of the greater uncertainty with pledges, the interest rate charged by the bank is usually about 3 percentage points above the prime interest rate. Also, there is usually an administrative fee of about 1 percent of the loan for pledged amounts.

Intermediate-Term Loans

Intermediate-term (or term) loans generally require collateral and are paid over a number of years (usually over one year but less than five years).

Will a financially strong member, a community group, or another organization cosign a bank loan to the NPO?

Intermediate-term loans are typically repaid in periodic payments. The NPO should work out an installment repayment schedule it is comfortable with, whether constant or irregular. There may also be a balloon payment, meaning the last payment is significantly more than the others.

Lenders will usually include restrictive loan provisions such as prohibiting the NPO from pledging certain assets to another lender (referred to as a "negative pledge clause"), preventing the selling off of certain assets, or keeping a minimum working capital (current assets less current liabilities). These restrictions are designed to protect the lender but may tie the hands of the NPO's management.

Intermediate-term bank loans may be obtained under a line of credit, through revolving credit, or on a transaction basis.

In a line of credit, the bank allows for a maximum amount of credit to be extended to the NPO over a specified time period (usually for one-year renewal periods). The credit line may be on a seasonal basis. The maxium credit line should be the NPO's expected "peak" need.

The line of credit may require a "clean-up period" during which all borrowings must be repaid. Lines of credit are often issued for one-year periods and must be renewed. They may not be appropriate for nonseasonal working capital purposes when cash inflow will be available only over an extended time period. A line of credit may be secured against the income from a grant or contract.

A commitment fee may be charged by the bank on the unused portion of the credit line. This increases the effective financing cost.

EXAMPLE 10.8
If the committment fee is 0.25 percent and the unused credit line is $1,000,000, the annual charge is $2,500.

A revolving credit places a "ceiling" on the credit limit. The NPO borrows, repays, and reborrows as needed. The agreement is usually for more than one year. In fact, it may run for many years, provided both parties live up to their arrangement. It is best used if the NPO is seasonal or experiences asset growth.

A revolving credit agreement may be financially suitable for an NPO that engages in a few large projects yearly. For example, a relief center may borrow under a revolving credit to pay for urgently needed relief supplies when a disaster occurs, and may repay the loan from anticipated donations. An example might be what occurred in the Oklahoma City bombing.

Loans may be taken out on a transaction basis for a specific purpose. An example is borrowing for funds to remodel the NPO's facilities. The loan may be paid back from increased membership fees due to the remodeling effort.

Long-Term Loans

Long-term loans (usually for more than five years) are used to finance long-term assets (e.g., buildings) and the permanent growth of working capital assets. They are usually collateralized against the property financed.

The NPO should never borrow long-term funds at short-term interest rates (if these are higher). Short-term rates have built in higher administrative costs.

The NPO may benefit from a long loan repayment period with small annual payments. The NPO should stipulate the right to pay off the loan early without penalty. This may be advisable when interest rates have decreased and the NPO can substitute low-interest debt for its high-interest loan.

The repayment schedule should take into account the NPO's cash-flow ability, stability, ability to obtain attractive financing, future spending needs, interest rate charged, and loan restrictive provisions.

The NPO may need to prepare a business plan and documentation to obtain the loan.

BRIDGE FINANCING

A bridge loan is to be refinanced by another loan in the future. It is temporary financing that precedes permanent financing. For example, an NPO may need to buy land before constructing a new building, and may take out a short-term loan to do so with the certain expectation of receiving a 25-year mortgage from the bank.

EQUIPMENT FINANCING

Equipment may be the collateral for a loan; computers, for example, may be bought with bank financing. The loan may be repaid with money generated from operations. However, cash flows may be uncertain. There is a risk that the market value of the equipment may decline because of obsolescence and use. The value would be even lower in a forced-sale situation.

CONSTRUCTION FINANCING

The construction loan is repaid usually from refinancing with a mortgage. Such financing has project risk to the NPO in that the funds may be insufficient; the building may not be completed on time, resulting in higher interest expense; construction costs may be higher than expected;

construction specifications may not have been met; or expected permanent financing may not be available.

LONG-TERM DEBT: MORTGAGES AND BONDS PAYABLE

Long-term debt is permanent financing. It is typically payable in installments over a long time period. The two types of long-term debt are mortgage payable and corporate bonds (for larger NPOs).

Mortgages

A mortgage is permanent, long-term financing used to buy real property (e.g., a building). The mortgage may be paid from rental income. The ability to repay depends on the occupancy rate of the premises. If mortgage payments are not made, the property may be foreclosed on.

In a *blanket mortgage*, the lender has a lien on all the NPO's real assets. In *after acquired clause*, real property acquired after the issuance of the mortgage represents additional collateral for the loan.

Bonds Payable

A bond is a written promise to repay a loan on a specified date. The costs of a bond include accounting and legal fees, brokerage fees, interest, printing costs, and insurance. Bonds issued by NPOs have tax-exempt interest, so their interest rate may be lower than on conventional loans. Bonds are only issued by large NPOs (e.g., hospitals, universities).

The *indenture* describes the features of the bond issue (e.g., payment dates, call provisions, and restrictions). A bond may be secured (with collateral) or unsecured.

Bonds usually come in $1,000 denominations. Many bonds have maturities of 10 to 30 years.

EXAMPLE 10.9
An NPO issues a $100,000, 8 percent, 10-year bond. The semiannual interest payment is $4,000 ($100,000 × 8% × 6/12).

A bond issued at face value is said to be sold at 100 percent. If a bond is sold below its face value (less than 100%), it is issued at a *discount*. If a bond is issued above face value (more than 100 percent), it is issued at a *premium*.

Why would an NPO's bond be issued at a discount or a premium? A bond may be issued at a discount when the interest rate on the bond is below the prevailing market interest rate for that type of security. It may also be issued at a discount if the NPO is risky, or there is a very long maturity period. A bond is issued at a premium when the opposite market conditions exist.

Revenue bonds are secured *only* against the income generated from the project financed. Examples are hospital buildings, low-income housing, and dormitories. The revenue generated is expected to pay principal and interest in a timely fashion. Revenue bonds have a lower interest rate and are issued on the capital markets.

Bonds may be refunded before maturity through the exercise of a call privilege (if one exists). A call feature in a bond enables the NPO to retire it before the expiration date.

When future interest rates are expected to drop, a call provision is recommended. Such a provision enables the NPO to buy back the higher-interest bond and issue a lower-interest one.

SOCIAL LENDERS

Social lenders include community organizations, foundations, and other socially conscious groups (e.g., environmentalists) that share similar views with the NPO. These are referred to as soft loans. The terms for such loans are usually more favorable than conventional loans, including lower interest rates, less collateral requirements, and payment deferrals. However, social lenders may place greater restrictions on fund use because they are concerned with fulfilling a socially conscious cause. For example, a social lender providing construction financing for an educational center may restrict the education programs by excluding those dealing with remedial work.

FRIENDS AND FOUNDATIONS

Friends may provide funding or may cosign loans for the NPO, particularly at the initial stages. They are usually understanding, flexible, patient, and willing to take on greater risk for a cause. For example, concerned citizens may be receptive to providing noninterest loans to an NPO dealing with handicapped children. Wealthy individuals and foundations may also give attractive short-term loans.

TRUSTEES AND OFFICERS

Loans may be received from trustees and officers. The NPO must be careful not to give the appearance of a lack of independence or favorable treatment so full documentation is needed. Such loans should be a last resort because they are viewed with suspicion.

NATIONAL OFFICES

A low-cost loan on favorable terms may be available from the national office to which the NPO is associated. An example might be a religious institution.

INSURANCE COMPANY LOANS

Insurance companies typically provide longer-term loans than banks and are a good source of mortgage financing.

The cash value of life insurance may be donated to the NPO. Borrowings can be made against these policies. The insurance contract is, in effect, the collateral for the loan. Advantages include a lower interest rate, and such loans do not have to be repaid. Upon the death of the insured, the principal and interest owed reduce the face value of the policy's proceeds.

LEASING

The NPO may lease property instead of buying it. Leasing is an alternative to long-term debt. Leasing is generally better for larger NPOs such as hospitals and universities. The NPO should shop around for the best deal.

Advantages of leasing are:

- The lessor's expert service is available.
- An immediate cash outlay is not required.
- Usually there is a purchase option allowing the lessee to obtain the property at a bargain price at the lease expiration date.
- Fewer restrictions exist on a lease than on a loan (e.g., minimum cash balance).
- Lessee minimizes obsolescence risk of property, since the lessor gets back the obsolete property at the end of the lease.

Disadvantages of leasing are:

- Higher cost in the long-term than if the asset were purchased.
- The interest cost on a lease is usually more than the interest rate on a loan.
- The lessee may have to keep outdated property no longer needed (e.g., a computer system).

RISK ANALYSIS

Risk considerations associated with financing may include the reason for the loan, the repayment source, the nature of the collateral, and the time period. Risk is greater, with the more uncertainty associated with repayment sources, longer maturity of assets being financed, and illiquidity of the security. The wrong type of financing may be disastrous to the NPO. What impact will the financing have on the NPO's operations and its ability to repay? Will the NPO lose some control to the lender? Will important assets have to be sold to make repayment? Will the lender require a change in management?

Figure 10.4 presents risk analysis for funding requirements and sources.

SOFTWARE

Software programs exist to track donors, create budgets and fund reports, perform data management functions, donor profiles, recordkeeping, preparation of reports, and donor giving analysis. For computerized grant software refer to the *Directory of Computer and High Technology Grants* (published by Research Grant Guides, P.O. Box 1214, Loxahatchee, FL 33470).

COST OF FINANCING

Lower cost of capital may be achieved by:

- Pooling pension funds from many nonprofit employees to buy an NPO's bonds.
- Pooling a bond issue of several NPOs to share issuance costs. The issue proceeds are allocated proportionately.

FIGURE 10.4

Matching Funding Sources to Funding Requirements

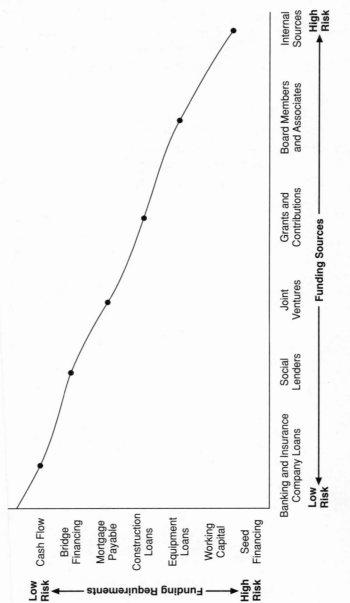

Notes: In terms of funding requirements, low risk is when there exists a predictable repayment source. High risk is when the repayment source is highly unpredictable.

In terms of funding sources, low risk is in regard to low risk tolerance. High risk is a high tolerance.

TIMING OF FINANCING

Financing should be obtained at the right times. Is cash needed to pay expenses until the expected revenue is forthcoming? Is temporary financing needed to complete a grant request or contract that is highly probable? Can the loan be repaid from a predictable source? A comparison should be made between the schedule of debt payment and the timing of cash inflows.

ENDNOTES

1. Jim Greenfield, *Fund Raising Management: Evaluating and Managing the Fund Development Process* (New York: John Wiley, 1991).

2. Bruce Hopkins, *The Law of Fund Raising* (New York: John Wiley, 1994).

Management of Financial Resources and Investment

A nonprofit has got to manage limited resources well in order to provide resources to those in need of them, so they have to make their dollars go as far as they can, whether it's to provide hot meals or health services.

Jo G. Pritchard, United Way of the Capital Area,
Sponsor of the fourth annual Mississippi Management Seminar for Nonprofits,
Mississippi Business Journal, *July 25, 1994*

In nonprofit organizations, management is often preoccupied with its welfare objectives and ignores the operation's efficiency and operating cost controls. An operations planning and control framework is required. NPOs need to integrate available operations management planning tools, such as time series forecasting, aggregate production planning, ABC analysis, and material requirements planning, to facilitate better demand and resource management. The model's purpose is to provide management with better resource planning and a base of performance evaluation.

EFFECTIVE MANAGEMENT OF WORKING CAPITAL

Effective management of working capital improves cash flows and minimizes the risk that the NPO will run short of cash. By optimally managing cash, accounts receivable, pledges receivables, and inventory, an NPO can minimize its liquidity risk. The amount invested in each current asset may change daily and should be monitored carefully to ensure that funds are used in the most productive way possible. Cash refers to currency and demand deposits; excess funds may be invested in marketable securities. Cash management involves accelerating cash inflow and delaying cash outflow. Pledges and other receivables management involves soliciting donors with good financial standing and speeding up collections. Inventory management involves having the optimal order size at the right time.

CASH MANAGEMENT

The goal of cash management is to invest excess cash for a return and at the same time to have adequate liquidity. A proper cash balance, neither excessive nor deficient, should exist; for example, nonprofit agencies with many bank accounts may be accumulating excessive balances. Proper cash forecasting is particularly crucial in a recession and is required to determine (1) the optimal time to receive or pay funds and (2) the amount to transfer daily between accounts. A daily computerized listing of cash balances and transaction reporting can let you know the up-to-date cash balance so you can decide how best to use the funds. You should also assess the costs you are paying for banking services, looking at each account's cost.

When cash receipts and cash payments are highly synchronized and predictable, your nonprofit entity may keep a smaller cash balance; if quick liquidity is needed, it can invest in marketable securities. Any additional cash should be invested in income producing securities with maturities structured to provide the necessary liquidity.

At a minimum, an agency should hold in cash the greater of (1) compensating balances (deposits held by a bank to compensate it for providing services) or (2) precautionary balances (money held for emergency purposes) plus transaction balances (money to cover checks outstanding). It must also hold enough cash to meet its daily requirements.

A number of factors go into the decision on how much cash to hold, including the organization's liquid assets, business risk, maturity dates, ability to borrow on short notice and on favorable terms, and rate of return; economic conditions; and the possibility of unexpected problems, such as donor defaults.

Acceleration of Cash Inflow

To improve cash inflow, you should evaluate the causes of and take corrective action for delays in having cash receipts deposited. Ascertain the origin of cash receipts, how they are delivered, and how cash is transferred

F I G U R E 11.1

Float on a Check Issued and Mailed by Payer to Payee

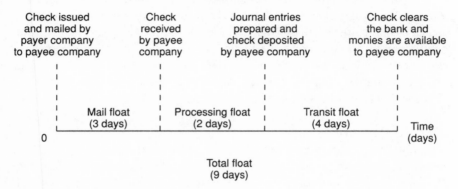

from outlying accounts to the main account. Also investigate banking policy regarding availability of funds and the length of the time lag between when a check is received and when it is deposited.

The types of delays in processing checks are (1) "mail float," the time required for a check to move from payer to payee; (2) "processing float," the time needed for the payee to enter the payment; and (3) "deposit collection float," the time it takes for a check to clear.

Figure 11.1 depicts the total float of a check.

You should try out all possible ways to accelerate cash receipts including the use of lockboxes, return envelopes, preauthorized debits (PADs), wire transfers, and depository transfer checks.

Lockbox

A lockbox represents a way to place the optimum collection point near payers. Payments are mailed to strategic post office boxes geographically situated to reduce mailing and depositing time. Banks make collections from these boxes several times a day and deposit the funds to the agency's account. They then prepare a computer listing of payments received by account and a daily total, which is forwarded to the NPO.

To determine the effectiveness of using a lockbox, you should determine the average face value of checks received, the cost of operations eliminated, reducible processing overhead, and the reduction in "mail float" days. Because per-item processing costs for lockboxes are typically significant, it makes the most sense to use one for low-volume, high-dollar collections.

However, NPOs with high-volume, low-dollar receipts are using them more and more as technological advances lower their per-item cost.

Wholesale lockboxes are used for checks received from other organizations. As a rule, the average dollar cash receipts are large, and the number of cash receipts is small. Many wholesale lockboxes result in mail time reductions of no more than one business day and check-clearing time reductions of only a few tenths of one day. They are therefore most useful for NPOs that have gross revenues of at least several million dollars and that receive large checks from distant constituents.

Return Envelopes

Providing return envelopes can accelerate payer remissions. On the return envelope, you can use bar codes, nine-digit code numbers, or post office box numbers. Another option is Accelerated Reply Mail (ARM), in which a unique "truncating" ZIP code is assigned to payments such as lockbox receivables. The coded remittances are removed from the postal system and processed by banks or third parties.

Electronic Wire Transfers

To accelerate cash flow, you may transfer funds between banks by wire transfers through computer terminal and telephone. Such transfers should be used only for significant dollar amounts, because wire transfer fees are assessed by both the originating and the receiving banks. Wire transfers are best for intraorganization transfers, such as transfers to and from investments, deposits to an account made the day checks are expected to clear, and deposits made to any other account that requires immediate availability of funds. They may also be used to fund other types of checking accounts, such as payroll accounts. In order to avoid unnecessarily large balances in an account, you may fund it on a staggered basis. However, to prevent an overdraft, you should make sure a balance is maintained in another account at the bank.

There are two types of wire transfers—preformatted (recurring) and free-form (nonrepetitive). Recurring transfers do *not* involve extensive authorization and are suitable for ordinary transfers in which the NPO designates issuing and receiving banks and provides its account number. Nonrecurring transfers require greater control, including written confirmations instead of telephone or computer terminal confirmations.

Depository Transfer Checks (DTCs)

Paper or paperless depository checks may be used to transfer funds between the NPO's bank accounts. They do not require a signature, since the check is payable to the bank for credit to the NPO's account. DTCs typically clear in one day. *Manual* DTCs are preprinted checks that include all information except the amount and date; *automated* DTCs are printed, as needed. It is usually best to use the bank's printer since it is not cost-effective for the NPO to purchase a printer. Automatic check preparation is advisable only for NPOs that must prepare a large number of transfer checks daily.

EXAMPLE 11.1

ABC Agency obtains average cash receipts of $200,000 per day. It usually takes five days from the time a check is mailed until the funds are available for use. The amount tied up by the delay is:

$$5 \text{ Days} \times \$200,000 = \$1,000,000$$

You can also calculate the return earned on the average cash balance.

EXAMPLE 11.2

An NPO's weekly average cash balances are as follows:

Week	Average Cash Balance
1	$12,000
2	17,000
3	10,000
4	15,000
Total	$54,000

The monthly average cash balance is:

$$\frac{\$54,000}{4} = \$13,500$$

If the annual interest rate is approximately 12 percent, the monthly return earned on the average cash balance is:

$$\$13,500 \times \frac{0.12}{12} = \underline{\$135}$$

If you are thinking of establishing a lockbox to accelerate cash inflow, you will need to determine the maximum monthly charge you will incur for the service.

EXAMPLE 11.3

It takes XYZ NPO about seven days to receive and deposit payments from clients. Therefore, XYZ is considering establishing a lockbox system. It expects the system to reduce the float time to five days. Average daily collections are $500,000. The rate of return is 12 percent.

The reduction in outstanding cash balances arising from implementing the lockbox system is:

$$2 \text{ Days} \times \$500,000 = \$1,000,000$$

The return that could be earned on these funds in a year is:

$$\$1,000,000 \times 0.12 = \$120,000$$

The maximum monthly charge the NPO should pay for this lockbox arrangement is therefore:

$$\frac{\$120,000}{12} = \$10,000$$

You should compare the return earned on freed cash to the cost of the lockbox arrangement to determine whether using the lockbox is financially advantageous.

EXAMPLE 11.4

An NPO's financial officer is determining whether to initiate a lockbox arrangement that will cost $150,000 annually. The daily average collections are $700,000. Using a lockbox will reduce mailing and processing time by two days. The rate of return is 14 percent.

Annual return on freed cash (14% × 2 × $700,000)	$196,000
Annual cost	$150,000
Net advantage of lockbox system	$ 46,000

Sometimes you need to determine whether to switch banks in order to lower the overall costs associated with a lockbox arrangement.

EXAMPLE 11.5

You now have a lockbox arrangement in which bank A handles $5 million a day in return for an $800,000 compensating balance. You are thinking of canceling this arrangement and further dividing your western region by entering into contracts with two other banks. Bank B will handle $3 million a day in collections with a compensating balance of $700,000, and bank C will handle $2 million a day with a compensating balance of $600,000. Collections will be half a day quicker than they are now. Your return rate is 12 percent.

Accelerated cash receipts	
($5 million per day × 0.5 day)	$2,500,000
Increased compensating balance	500,000
Improved cash flow	$2,000,000
Rate of return	× 0.12
Net annual savings	$ 240,000

Delay of Cash Outlay

Delaying cash payments can help your company earn a greater return and have more cash available. You should evaluate the payees and determine to what extent you can reasonably stretch time limits without incurring finance charges or impairing your credit rating.

There are many ways to delay cash payments, including centralizing payables, having zero balance accounts, and paying by draft.

Centralize Payables

You should centralize your NPO's payable operation—that is, make one center responsible for making all payments—so that debt may be paid at the most profitable time and so that the amount of disbursement float in the system may be ascertained.

Zero Balance Account (ZBA)

Cash payments may be delayed by maintaining zero balance accounts in one bank in which you maintain zero balances for all the NPO's disbursing units with funds being transferred in from a master account as needed. The advantages of ZBAs are that they allow better control over cash payments and reduced excess cash balances in regional banks. Use of ZBAs is an aggressive strategy that requires the NPO to put funds into its payroll and payables checking accounts only when it expects checks to clear. However, watch out for overdrafts and service charges.

Drafts

Payment drafts are another strategy for delaying disbursements. With a draft, payment is made when the draft is presented for collection to the bank, which in turn goes to the issuer for acceptance. When the draft is approved, the NPO deposits the funds to the payee's account. Because of this delay, you can maintain a lower checking balance. Banks usually impose a charge for drafts, and you must endure the inconveniences of formally approving them before payment. Drafts can provide a measure of protection against fraud and theft because they must be presented for inspection before payment.

Delay Mail

You can delay cash payment by drawing checks on remote banks (e.g., a New York NPO might use a Texas bank), thus ensuring that checks take longer to clear. You may also mail checks from post offices that offer limited service or at which mail must go through numerous handling points.

If you utilize the mail float properly, you can maintain higher actual bank balances than book balances. For instance, if you write checks averaging $200,000 per day and they take three days to clear, you will have $600,000 ($200,000 × 3) in your checking account for those three days, even though the money has been deducted in your records.

Check Clearing

You can use probability analysis to determine the expected date for checks to clear. Probability is defined as the degree of likelihood that something will happen and is expressed as a percentage from 0 to 100. For example, it's likely that not all payroll checks are cashed on the payroll date, so you can deposit some funds later and earn a return until the last minute.

Delay Payment to Employees

You can reduce the frequency of payments to employees (e.g., expense account reimbursements, payrolls); for example, you can institute a monthly payroll rather than a weekly one. In this way, you have the use of the cash for a greater time period. You can also disburse commissions on funds raised when the pledges are collected rather than when the pledges are made. Finally, you can utilize noncash compensation and remuneration methods (e.g., distribute souvenirs instead of bonuses).

Other ways exist to delay cash payments. Instead of making full payment on an invoice, you can make partial payments. You can also delay payment by requesting additional information about an invoice from the vendor before paying it. Another strategy is to use a charge account to lengthen the time between when you buy items and when you pay for them. In any event, never pay a bill before its due date.

EXAMPLE 11.6

Every two weeks the NPO disburses checks that average $500,000 and take three days to clear. You want to find out how much money can be saved annually if the transfer of funds is delayed from an interest-bearing account that pays 0.0384 percent per day (annual rate of 14 percent) for those three days.

$$\$500,000 \times (0.000384 \times 3) = \underline{\$576}$$

The savings per year is $576 × 26 (yearly payrolls) = $14,976.

A cash management system is shown in Table 11.1.

T A B L E 11.1

_____

Cash Management System

Acceleration of Cash Receipts	Delay of Cash Payments
Use a lockbox.	Delay frequency of paying employees.
Use concentration banking.	Pay by draft.
Use preauthorized checks.	Requisition more frequently.
Use preaddressed stamped envelopes.	Use a disbursing float.
Obtain deposits on large orders.	Use charge accounts.
Charge interest on overdue receivables.	Use a lockbox system.

CASH MODELS

A number of mathematical models have been developed to assist the financial manager in distributing an agency so that they provide a maximum return to the agency. A model developed by William Baumol can determine the optimum amount of cash for an entity to hold under conditions of certainty. The objective is to minimize the sum of the fixed costs of transactions and the opportunity cost (return forgone) of holding cash balances that do not yield a return. These costs are expressed as

$$F \times \frac{(T)}{C} + i\frac{(C)}{2}$$

where F = the fixed cost of a transaction
T = the total cash needed for the time period involved
i = the interest rate on marketable securities
C = cash balance (or transaction size)
C^* = optimal level of cash

The optimal level of cash is determined using the following formula:

$$C^* = \sqrt{\frac{2FT}{i}}$$

EXAMPLE 11.7
The United Way estimates a cash need for $4 million over a one-month period, during which the cash account is expected to be disbursed at a constant rate. The opportunity interest rate is 6 percent per annum, or 0.5 percent for a one-month period. The transaction cost each time you borrow or withdraw is $100.

According to the Baumol model, the optimal transaction size (the optimal borrowing or withdrawal lot size) and the number of transactions you should make during the month follow:

$$C* = \sqrt{\frac{2FT}{i}} = \sqrt{\frac{2(100)(4,000,000)}{0.0005}} = \$400,000$$

The optimal transaction size is $400,000. The average cash balance is:

$$\frac{C*}{2} = \frac{\$400,000}{2} = \underline{\$200,000}$$

The number of transactions required is:

$$\frac{\$4,000,000}{\$400,000} = 10 \text{ transactions during the month}$$

There is also a model for cash management when cash payments are uncertain. The Miller-Orr model places upper and lower limits on cash balances. When the upper limit is reached, a transfer of cash to marketable securities is made; when the lower limit is reached, a transfer from securities to cash occurs. No transaction occurs as long as the cash balance stays within the limits.

Factors taken into account in the Miller-Orr model are the fixed costs of a securities transaction (F), assumed to be the same for buying as well as selling; the daily interest rate on marketable securities (i); and the variance of daily net cash flows $(\sigma^2; \sigma$ is a Greek sigma). The objective is to meet cash requirements at the lowest possible cost. A major assumption of this model is the randomness of cash flows. The control limits in the Miller-Orr model are d dollars as an upper limit and zero dollars at the lower limit. When the cash balance reaches the upper level, d less z dollars (optimal cash balance) of securities are bought, and the new balance becomes z dollars. When the cash balance equals zero, z dollars of securities are sold and the new balance again reaches z. Of course, in practice the minimum cash balance is established at an amount greater than zero because of delays in transfer; the higher minimum in effect acts as a safety buffer.

The optimal cash balance z is computed as follows:

$$Z = 3\sqrt{\frac{3F\sigma^2}{4i}}$$

The optimal value for d is computed as $3z$.
The average cash balance approximates $(z + d)/3$.

EXAMPLE 11.8

You wish to use the Miller-Orr model. The following information is supplied:

Fixed cost of a securities transaction	$10
Variance of daily net cash flows	$50
Daily interest rate on securities (10%/360)	0.0003

The optimal cash balance, the upper limit of cash needed, and the average cash balance follow:

$$z = \sqrt[3]{\frac{3(10)(50)}{4(0.0003)}} = \sqrt[3]{\frac{3(10)(50)}{0.0012}} = \sqrt[3]{\frac{1,500}{0.0012}} = \sqrt[3]{1,2500,000}$$

$$= \underline{\$102}$$

The optimal cash balance is $102; the upper limit is $306($102 × 3). The average cash balance is $136[($102 + $306)/3].

When the upper limit of $306 is reached, $204 of securities ($306 − $102) will be purchased to bring the account to the optimal cash balance of $102. When the lower limit of zero dollars is reached, $102 of securities will be sold to again bring it to the optimal cash balance of $102.

TAKING ADVANTAGE OF A CASH DISCOUNT

Many suppliers typically offer lower unit prices if payment is made within a specified period. The agency should generally take advantage of a cash discount offered for early payment, because failing to do so results in a high opportunity cost. The cost of not taking a discount equals

$$\frac{\text{Discount Lost}}{\substack{\text{Dollar Proceeds You Have} \\ \text{Use of by Not Taking the} \\ \text{Discount}}} \times \frac{360}{\substack{\text{Number of Days You Have} \\ \text{Use of the Money by Not} \\ \text{Taking the Discount}}}$$

EXAMPLE 11.9

Assume a $1,000 invoice with credit terms of 2/10, net/30. You fail to take the discount and pay the bill on the thirtieth day. The cost of the discount is:

$$\frac{\$20}{\$980} = \frac{360}{20} = 36.7\%$$

Thus you would be better off taking the discount even if you needed to borrow the money from the bank, since the opportunity cost is 36.7 percent. The interest rate on a bank loan would be far less.

BANKING RELATIONSHIPS

Before establishing a relationship with a bank, you should appraise its financial soundness by checking the ratings compiled by financial advisory services such as Moody's and Standard and Poor's (S&P). Your NPO may want to limit its total deposits at any one bank to no more than the amount insured by the Federal Deposit Insurance Corporation (FDIC), especially if the bank is having difficulties. You should check for additional interest earnings from improved yield, resulting in overall increase in amount available for investment.

You may also decide to use different banks for different services. In selecting a bank, consider location (which affects lockboxes and disbursement points), type and cost of services, and availability of funds.

You may undertake a bank account analysis by comparing the value of the NPO balance maintained at the bank to the service charges imposed or compensating balances. Banks will provide such analyses for you, if you wish, but you should scrutinize a bank's analysis closely to be sure it is accurate. Also check out additional services provided for the same amount of bank charges.

Most checks clear in one business day; a clearing time of three or more business days is rare. Try to arrange for the financial institution to give same-day credit on deposits received prior to a specified cutoff time. If the deposit is made over the counter, the funds may not be immediately available; if the deposit is made early enough, especially through a lockbox, they may be.

MANAGEMENT OF PLEDGES AND OTHER RECEIVABLES

Many NPOs have uncollected pledges sitting on their books. Knowing how to secure and collect on pledges is a difficult task, but is a major source of cash. Managing pledges by donors and speeding effort is essential. Grants receivable are similar to pledges, even though they may be little more collectible than pledges than individuals, because they tend to stem from a formalized route. Receivables due from insiders, notes, and loan receivables also need to be carefully scrutinized.

INVENTORY MANAGEMENT

The purpose of inventory management is to develop policies that will achieve an optimal inventory investment. Successful inventory management minimizes inventory and lowers cost. It is important to create a sound inventory control system. The first step in this effort is to decide what to stock. Decisions should be based on importance of demand, rate of use, cost, and availability. For instance, a high-value, slow-moving item that can be readily acquired should not be stocked unless it has a high demand. On the other hand, a low-value, fast-moving, high-demand, or easily available item should be stocked. The second step is to know how much to order and when to reorder.

Investment in Inventory

You should consider the average investment in inventory, which equals the average inventory balance times the per unit cost.

EXAMPLE 11.10

An NPO places an order for 5,000 units at the beginning of the year. Each unit costs $10. The average investment is:

Average inventory[a]	2,500 units
Unit cost	$\times \$10$
Average investment	$\underline{\$25,000}$

[a] $\frac{\text{Quantity}(Q)}{2} = \frac{5,000}{2}$

   To get an average, add the beginning balance and the ending balance and then divide by 2. This gives the midvalue.

   The more frequently an NPO places an order, the lower the average investment.

Determining Carrying and Ordering Costs

You want to determine the costs for planning, financing, record keeping, and control associated with inventory. Once inventory costs are known, you can compute the amount of timeliness of financing.

   Inventory carrying costs include warehousing, handling, insurance, and the opportunity cost of holding inventory. A provisional cost for spoilage and obsolescence should also be included in the analysis. The more the inventory held, the greater the carrying cost. Carrying cost is computed as follows:

$$\text{Carrying Cost} = \frac{Q}{2} \times C$$

where $\frac{Q}{2}$ = average quantity

   C = carrying cost per unit

A knowledge of inventory carrying costs will help you determine which items are worth storing. Inventory ordering costs are the costs of placing an order and receiving the merchandise. They include freight and the clerical costs incurred in placing the order. To minimize ordering you should enter the fewest number of orders possible. In the case of produced items, ordering cost also includes scheduling cost. Ordering cost is as follows:

$$\text{Ordering Cost} = \frac{S}{Q} \times P$$

where S = total usage
Q = quantity per order
P = cost of placing an order

The total inventory cost (carrying cost + ordering cost) is therefore:

$$\frac{QC}{2} + \frac{SP}{Q}$$

A knowledge of ordering costs helps you decide how many orders you should place during the period to suit your needs. A tradeoff exists between ordering and carrying costs. A large order quantity increases carrying costs but lowers ordering cost.

Economic Order Quantity

The economic order quantity (EOQ) is the optimum amount of goods to order each time to minimize total inventory costs. EOQ analysis should be applied to every product that represents a significant proportion of sales.

$$\text{EOQ} = \sqrt{\frac{2SP}{C}}$$

The EOQ model assumes:

- Demand is constant and known with certainty.
- Depletion of stock is linear and constant.
- No discount is allowed for quantity purchases.
- Lead time, the time interval between placing an order and receiving delivery, is a constant (that is, stockouts are not possible).

The number of orders for a period is the usage (S) divided by the EOQ. Figure 11.2 graphically shows the EOQ point.

F I G U R E   11.2

The EOQ Point

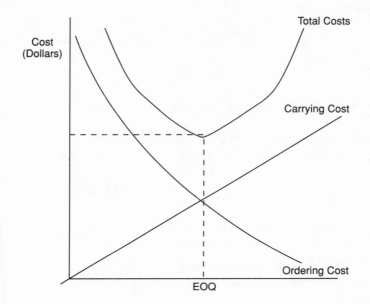

In the next two examples, we compute for a product the EOQ, the number of orders, and the number of days that should elapse before the next order is placed.

EXAMPLE 11.11

A charity uses 1,600 oil filters yearly for its moving trucks. The cost of placing an order is $5.00, the unit cost is $3.50, the carrying cost is 20 percent, and the carrying cost per unit is $0.70 (20% × $3.50). Assume 255 working days in a year. The charity wants to know how frequently to place orders to lower its costs. Note:

S = 1,600 filters per year
P = $5.00 per order
C = $0.70 per unit

$$\text{EOQ} = \sqrt{\frac{2SP}{C}} = \sqrt{\frac{2(1600)(5)}{0.7}} = \sqrt{22857} = 151 \text{ Filters}$$

The number of orders each year is:

$$\frac{S}{\text{EOQ}} = \frac{1600}{151} = 10.60$$

Therefore, an order should be placed almost every month (255/10.60 = 24 days)

Reorder Point

The reorder point (ROP) is a signal that tells you when to place an order. Calculating the reorder point requires a knowledge of the lead time between order and receipt of merchandise. It may be influenced by the months of supply, the total dollar ceilings on inventory to be held, or the inventory to be ordered.

Reorder point is computed as follows:

$$\text{ROP} = \text{Lead Time} \times \text{Average Usage per Unit of Time} = L \times \frac{S}{\text{Working Days}}$$

This reveals the inventory level at which a new order should be placed. If a safety stock is needed, add to the ROP as follows:

$$\text{ROP} = L \times \frac{S}{\text{Working Days}} + (M - A)$$

where M = most used during lead time period
A = average used during lead time period

You have to know at what inventory level you should place an order to reduce inventory costs and have an adequate stock of goods with which to satisfy client or patron orders.

EXAMPLE 11.12

In Example 11.11, we assumed 255 working days in a year. Assume that each order requires three working days of lead time. What is the reorder point? The reorder point is:

$$3 \text{ Days} \times \frac{1600}{255 \text{ Working Days}} = 3 \times 6.27 = 19 \text{ Filters}$$

When the inventory level drops to 19 units, a new order should be placed.

EXAMPLE 11.13

The most oil filters used during any three-day order periods was 30. The average or expected rate of use is 18 filters (6×3). What is the reorder point? The reorder point is:

$$3 \text{ Days} \times \frac{1600}{255 \text{ Days}} + (30 - 18) = 3 \times 6.27 + 12 = 31 \text{ Filters}$$

Quantity Discount

You may be entitled to a quantity discount when purchasing large orders. The discount reduces the cost of materials.

EXAMPLE 11.14

An NPO purchases 1,000 units of an item having a list price of $10 each. The quantity discount is 5 percent. The net cost of the item is:

Acquisition cost (1,000 × $10)	$10,000
Less: Discount (0.05 × $10,000)	500
Net cost	$ 9,500

INVESTING SURPLUS FUNDS AND INVESTMENT STRATEGIES

NPOs must place an increasing emphasis on ensuring that long-range plans are in place. As a part of strategic planning and after extensive financial analysis, they should establish investment strategies for surplus funds. For example, an investment plan may put funds in growth investments rather than in fixed-income vehicles, to keep up with inflation and operating needs over a longer period.

You do not want to be in the situation many in the nonprofit (sector) face when they use up their resources. It is critical to be proactive, rather than waiting for something negative to happen in the future.

This section covers how to manage a NPO's surplus liquidity funds. An organization's surplus funds or idle cash are usually considered to be of only a temporary nature. The funds should be made available to cover a shortfall in cash flow or working capital, or to serve as a reservoir for capital spending and acquisition. Most CFOs of NPOs should be conservative (not speculative) when considering investing idle cash in financial securities, since the money should be on hand without loss in value of the funds when needed.

How Is Surplus Cash Used?

Generally, there are three choices:

1. Investing in marketable securities.
2. Reducing outstanding debt.
3. Increasing compensating balances at banks.

What Are the Factors to Consider in Investment Decisions?

Consideration should be given to safety of principal, yield, and risk; stability of income; marketability and liquidity; and maturity.

Security of Principal

The key factor here is the degree of risk involved in a particular investment. The agency will not want to lose part or all of the initial investment. Security is usually given the highest priority for nonprofit organizations.

Yield and Risk

The primary purpose of investing is to earn a return on invested money in the form of interest, dividends, and capital appreciation. Many nonprofits have increased their efforts to monitor cash balances to ensure that surplus cash is invested immediately. However, increasing total returns would entail greater investment risks. Thus, yield and degree of risk are directly related. Greater risk also means sacrificing security of principal. CFOs of nonprofits generally rank yield as the least important of all the criteria in selecting an investment vehicle.

Stability of Income

When steady income is the most important consideration, money market investments should be emphasized. U.S. Treasury bills (T-bills) are considered the most stable of all money market instruments, mainly because they are backed by the full faith and credit of the federal government.

Marketability and Liquidity

The ability to find a ready market, when needed, to dispose of the investment at the right price is of great importance. Marketability and liquidity vary among money market instruments, depending not only on the stability of the instrument, but on the extent to which the active secondary market is available. T-bills, for example, are practically free from risk and enjoy an active market.

Maturity

One way to get around the liquidity/marketability problem while trying to obtain a higher yield is to time maturities so that securities mature at time when cash is needed. In other words, the maturity dates and the dates when funds are desired need to be synchronized. For example, part of the investment holdings may be earmarked for capital projects, and part for anticipated operating expenses. It is not too difficult to time maturities, since securities come in different maturity periods, such as one month, three months, one year, and five years.

What Are the Questions to Ask in Formulating Investment Strategies?

In developing the agency's investment strategy, it will be advisable to ask the following questions:

• How much excess money will be available to invest and for how long? Cash-flow projections should be made on a conservative basis in order to determine available funds for investment. A cash budget should produce an estimate of an NPO's needs for cash disbursement by months or weeks. Such an estimate would allow the CFO to determine what portion of the cash balances can be invested and how long.

• What proportions of funds does the NPO want safe and liquid? Nonprofit CFOs cannot afford to risk their funds. Is there a portion of money available for more aggressive investing? When the timing for cash needs is uncertain, funds must be held in short-term and liquid securities. Investment with longer maturities tend to offer higher yields but less liquidity. Nonprofit charters may place restrictions and limitations on their investment policy.

• What should be the mix of investments for diversification? Diversification can be in terms of the number of vehicles as well as their maturities. Different investments can be timed to mature when the funds are needed for operating expenses. In formulating an investment strategy, the CFO should investigate the investment vehicles available in the market, should determine their relative yields for maturities required, and should assess the differences in risk associated with them. On the basis of an overall assessment, a policy should be established and submitted to an investment committee for review and approval.

What Are the Types of Securities?

Securities cover a broad range of investment instruments, including common stocks, preferred stocks, bonds, and options. There are two broad categories of securities available to investors: equity securities, which represent ownership of an organization, and debt (or fixed-income) securities, which represent a loan from the investor to an organization or a government. Fixed-income securities generally stress current fixed income and offer little or no opportunity for appreciation in value. They are usually liquid and bear less market risk than other types of investments. This type of investment performs well during stable economic conditions and lower inflation. Examples of fixed-income securities include: corporate bonds,

T A B L E   11.2

Investment Vehicles as to Liquidity and Yield

	Degree of Liquidity		Degree of Risk
Cash	Overnight repurchase agreements	Risk-free	State investment pools
	State investment pools		Bank deposits (up to $100,000)
	Treasury bills		U.S. Treasury bills, notes and bonds
	Other treasuries		U.S. government agencies
	U.S. government agencies		U.S. Treasury repos
	Banker's acceptances		Banker's acceptances
	Negotiable CDs		Collateralized bank CDs
	Commercial paper		Commercial paper
	Nonnegotiable bank CDs	Higher-risk	Bank CDs (uninsured/uncollateralized)
	Long-term government bonds		
Illiquid	U.S. agency bonds		

Source: Adapted from Girard Miller, *Investing Public Funds* (Chicago: Government Finance Officers Association, 1986), pp. 119–29.

government securities, mortgage-backed securities, preferred stocks, and money market (short-term debt) securities. Nonprofit financial managers must be knowledgeable about each investment instrument with respect to its liquidity, risk, and yield. Table 11.2 ranks the investment options according to their relative liquidity and risk. Which investment vehicle you decide to use will depend upon the agency's investment policy, its tolerance for risk, and the amount of cash available for investment.

Each type of security has not only distinct characteristics, but also advantages and disadvantages which vary by an investor. This section focuses on investing in money market securities and government securities, since they are the most popular and secure investment instruments available to nonprofit organizations.

How about Mortgage-Backed Securities?

A mortgage-backed security is a share in an organized pool of residential mortgages. Some are pass-through securities; the principal and interest payments on them are passed through to holders, usually monthly. There are several kinds of mortgage-backed securities. They include:

1. *Government National Mortgage Association (GNMA—Ginnie Mae) securities.* GNMA primarily issues pass-through securities. These securities pass through all payments of interest and principal received on a pool of federally insured mortgage loans. GNMA guarantees that all payments of principal and interest will be made on the mortgages on a timely basis. Since many mortgages are repaid before maturity, investors in GNMA pools usually recover most of their principal investment well ahead of schedule. Ginnie Mae is considered an excellent investment. The higher yields, coupled with the U.S. government guarantee, provide a competitive edge over other intermediate-term to long-term securities issued by the U.S. government and other agencies.

2. *Federal Home Loan Mortgage Corporation (FHLMC—Freddie Mac) securities.* Freddie Mac was established to provide a secondary market for conventional mortgages. It can purchase conventional mortgages for its own portfolio. Freddie Mac also issues pass-through securities—called participation certificates (PCs)—and guaranteed mortgage certificates (GMCs) that resemble bonds. Freddie Mac securities do not carry direct government guarantees and are subject to state and federal income tax.

3. *Federal National Mortgage Association (FNMA—Fannie Mae) securities.* The FNMA is a publicly held corporation whose goal is to provide a secondary market for government-guaranteed mortgages. It does so by financing its purchase by selling debentures (with maturities of several years) and short-term discount notes (from 30 to 360 days) to private investors. The FNMA securities are not government-guaranteed and are an unsecured obligation of the issuer. For this reason, they often provide considerably higher yields than Treasury securities.

4. *Collateralized mortgage obligations (CMOs).* CMOs are mortgage-backed securities that separate mortgage pools into short-, medium-, and long-term portions. Investors can choose between short-term pools (such as five-year pools) and long-term pools (such as 20-year pools).

Mortgage-backed securities enjoy liquidity and a high degree of safety since they are either government-sponsored or otherwise insured. These are important features for NPO investors.

Other Money-Market (Short-Term Fixed Income) Securities

Besides bonds and mortgage-backed securities, there are other significant forms of debt instruments from which NPO investors may choose, and they are primarily short-term in nature.

Certificates of Deposit (CDs)

These safe instruments are issued by commercial banks and thrift institutions and have traditionally been in amounts of $10,000 or $100,000 (jumbo CDs). CDs have fixed maturity periods varying from several months to many years. There is a penalty for cashing in a certificate prior to the maturity date.

Repurchase Agreements (Repos)

A repurchase agreement is a form of loan in which the borrower sells securities (such as government securities and other marketable securities) to the lender, but simultaneously contracts to repurchase the same securities either on call or on a specified date at a price that will produce an agreed yield. For example, an investment officer agrees to buy a 90-day Treasury bill from a bank at a price to yield 7 percent with a contract to buy the bill back one day later. Repos are attractive to NPO investors because, unlike demand deposits, repos pay explicit interest, and it may be difficult to locate a one-day-maturity government security. Although repos can be a sound investment, it will cost to buy them (such as bank safekeeping fees, legal fees, and fees for paperwork).

Banker's Acceptances (BAs)

A banker's acceptance is a draft drawn on a bank by a corporation to pay for merchandise. The draft promises payment of a certain sum of money to its holder at some future date. What makes BAs unique is that by prearrangement a bank accepts them, thereby guaranteeing their payment at the stated time. Most BAs arise in foreign trade transactions. The most common maturity for BAs is three months, although they can have maturities of up to 270 days. Their typical denominations are $500,000 and $1 million. BAs offer the following advantages as an investment vehicle:

- Safety.
- Negotiability.
- Liquidity, since an active secondary market for instruments of $1 million or more exists.
- Several basis points higher yield spread than those of T-bills.
- Comparatively small investment amounts, producing a yield similar to that of CDs with comparable face value.

Commercial Paper

Commercial paper, issued by large corporations to the public, usually comes in minimum denominations of $25,000. It represents an unsecured promissory note, and usually carries a higher yield than a small CD. Its maturity is usually 30, 60, and 90 days. The degree of risk depends on the NPO's credit rating.

Treasury Bills

Treasury bills have a maximum maturity of one year and common maturities of 91 and 182 days. They trade in minimum units of $10,000. They do not pay interest in the traditional sense; they are sold at a discount, and redeemed when the maturity date comes around, at face value. T-bills are extremely liquid, in that there is an active secondary or resale market for these securities. T-bills have an extremely low risk because they are backed by the U.S. government. Table 11.3 summarizes the money market, short-term instruments most widely used by NPOs against the characteristics described above. Understanding the unique features of each type of security available to NPOs is critical to the formulation of prudent investment strategies.

HOW TO COMPUTE THE YIELD ON SECURITIES

Nonprofit financial managers should know how to compute key investment-related statistics such as the yield on various securities. For example, some instruments are bought on a premium or a discount basis.

Yields on discount securities such as T-bills are calculated using the formula:

$$\frac{P1 - P0}{P0} \times \frac{360}{n}$$

where $P1$ = redemption price
$P0$ = purchase price
n = maturity in days

Money Market Investments Used by NPOs

Investment Instrument	Obligation Issuer	Denomination	Maturities	Marketability	Yield Basis	Comments/Restrictions
U.S. Treasury bills	U.S. government obligations	$10,000 to $1 million	3, 6, 9, and 12 months	Excellent secondary market	Discounted on 365-day basis. Also offered as tax anticipation bills through special auctions.	Popular investment. Can be purchased in secondary market for varying maturities.
Repurchase agreements	Commercial banks	$100,000 minimum	Overnight minimum; 1–21 days common	No secondary market	Established as part of purchase agreement. Yield generally close to prevailing federal rates.	Open: can liquidate at any time. Fixed: maturity set for specific period.
Negotiable certificates of deposit	Commercial banks	$500,000 to $1 million	Unlimited; 30-day minimum	Active secondary market	Interest maturity on 360-day basis.	Backed by credit of the issuing bank.
Nonnegotiable certificates of deposit	Commercial banks and savings and loan associations	$1,000 minimum (usually $100,000)	30-day minimum	Limited secondary market	Interest maturity on 365-day basis.	Lower interest rates for amounts under $100,000; 90-day interest penalty for early withdrawal.
Commercial paper	Promissory notes of finance companies	$100,000 to $5 million	5–270 days	No secondary market	Either discounted or interest-bearing on a 360-day basis.	Dealers will often negotiate "buy-back" agreements at a lower rate prior to maturity.
Banker's acceptances	Commercial banks	$25,000 to $1 million	Up to 6 months	Good secondary market	Discounted on a 360-day basis.	Backed by credit of issuing bank with specific collateral.
U.S. agency securities	Various federal agencies	$1,000 to $25,000	30 days, 270 days, and 1 year	Good secondary market	Discounted on a 360-day basis.	Not a legal obligation of or guaranteed by the federal government.

Source: Alan Walter Skiss, *Financial Management in Public Organizations* (Pacific Grove, CA: Brooks/Cole, 1989), p. 108.

EXAMPLE 11.15

Assume that:

$P1 = \$10,000$
$P0 = \$9,800$
$\quad n = 91$ days

Then the T-bill yield is:

$$\frac{\$10,000 - \$9,800}{\$9,800} \times \frac{360}{91} = \frac{\$200}{\$9,800} \times 3.956 = 0.0807 = 8.07\%$$

You can either hold T-bills to maturity or sell them in open markets. Moreover, you can buy already-issued securities in the so-called secondary market. Trading in the secondary market occurs any time during normal business hours. Newspapers routinely report what is bid, what is asked, and the yield. You can calculate the purchase price of a T-bill in the secondary market on a discount basis, as follows:

$$d = \frac{n}{360} \times db \qquad P0 = \$100 - d$$

where d = full discount per \$100 maturity value
$\quad\quad n$ = days to maturity
$\quad db$ = discount basis (%)
$\quad P0$ = purchase price

EXAMPLE 11.16

An agency buys a T-bill due in 250 days on an 8.7% discount basis. What is the purchase price?

$$d = \frac{n}{360} \times db = \frac{250}{360} \times 8.7\% = 6.04\% = \$6.04 \text{ per } \$100 \text{ maturity value}$$

$P0 = \$100 - d = \$100 - \$6.04 = \$93.96$ per \$100 price

What if an agency sells T-bills prior to maturity at discount rates different from the original discount basis? Then the holding period return (HPR), better known as annualized bond equivalent yield (BEY), can be calculated using the formula:

$$\text{BEY} = \frac{S - P}{P} \times \frac{365}{N} \times 100$$

where S = price at sale
$\quad\quad P$ = price at purchase
$\quad\quad N$ = number of days held (holding period)

EXAMPLE 11.17

A 250-day bill was purchased at an 8.7% discount and sold at 8.6% discount after a 30-day holding period. What is the BEY?

We know $N = 30$ days and P (the purchase price) = \$93.96 (from Example 11.16). First, we must compute S, which is the price of a 220-day T-bill (250 days – 30 days) at 8.6% discount.

$$d = \frac{n}{360} \times db = \frac{220}{360} \times 8.6\% = 5.26\% = \$5.26 \text{ per } \$100 \text{ Maturity Value}$$

$$S = P0 = \$100 - d = \$100 - \$5.26 = \$94.74 \text{ per } \$100 \text{ Price.}$$

In other words, the 220-day T-bill sold at 8.6% discount is priced at \$94.74.

$$\text{BEY} = \frac{\$94.74 - \$93.96}{\$93.96} \times \frac{365}{30} \times 100 = 10.01\%$$

HOW DO YOU CHOOSE MONEY MARKET FUNDS?

A money market fund is a special form of mutual fund. The investor can own a portfolio of high-yielding CDs, T-bills, and other similar securities of short-term nature by investing a small amount. There is a great deal of liquidity and flexibility in withdrawing funds through check-writing privileges. Money market funds are considered very conservative, because most of the securities purchased by the funds are quite safe. They are perfectly suitable for NPOs.

Money market mutual funds invest in short-term government securities, commercial paper, and certificates of deposit. They provide more safety of principal than other mutual funds since net asset value never fluctuates. Each share has a net asset value of \$1.

The yield, however, fluctuates daily. The advantages are:

• Money market funds are no-load.
• There may be a low deposit in these funds.
• The fund is a form of checking account.

The disadvantage is that the deposits in these funds are not insured, as it would be in a money market account or other federally insured deposit in a bank.

Refer back to Table 11.3 for a summary of the money market instruments available to nonprofit CFOs, and their main characteristics. Understanding the unique features of each type of security is critical to the formulation of prudent investment strategies.

A CAVEAT ABOUT DERIVATIVES

The three fundamental priorities of every investment policy are safety of principal first, liquidity second, and yield last. For our former Treasurer of Orange County, California it was yield first, second, and third.

John Moorlach, Orange County Treasurer–Tax Collector, after the Orange County bankruptcy.

Derivatives are defined as financial contracts whose values are designed to track the return on stocks, bonds, currencies, and so on. Derivatives may also be contracts derived from an indicator such as an interest rate, a stock, or a bond index. The value of the derivative is directly tied to the underlying investment instrument. A leveraged investment is bought on credit and has a lot of risk.

The quote above quite eloquently testifies how a potentially serious consequence can be created through risky and aggressive investment policy for the organization. The use of derivative investments and other aggressive financial strategies to enhance returns needs to be under intensive scrutiny by nonprofit organizations. With leveraged derivatives, when you win, you win big. But when you lose, you lose big. The Orange County debacle put a $2 billion loss in the hands of the county government and its agencies. Derivatives and leveraged investment vehicles are interest-sensitive. For example, if interest rates go up, the value of a derivative or of a bond, for that matter) goes down.

C H A P T E R 12

Cost Accounting and Cost Analysis for Pricing

NPOs should integrate several operations management planning tools, such as time series forecasting, aggregate production planning, ABC analysis, and material requirements planning, to facilitate better demand and resource management.

Chwen Sheu and John G. Wacker, "A Planning and Control Framework for Non-Profit Humanitarian Organizations," International Journal of Operations and Production, *vol. 14, issue 4 , 1994, pp. 64–78*

Even though there is no profit incentive in NPOs, cost accounting is vital. The uses of cost information are to measure effectiveness and to find out whether predetermined goals have been attained, as follows:

1. For expense control.
2. For preparation of operating budgets.
3. For establishing prices for services rendered.

It is important to be able to measure the quality of service provided in units of service—a difficult measurement, to say the least. Even after such measurement has been accomplished, the organization's ultimate effect on society is even more difficult to quantify.

Nonprofit organizations have tended to lag behind profit-oriented ones in the development of cost accounting systems, primarily due to the absence of an inventoriable product. Job order, process, and estimated cost accumulation systems are rarely encountered because nonprofit entities are service-oriented. Services cannot, in most instances, be stored and later distributed. Service organizations are generally highly labor-intensive.

COST ANALYSIS FOR PRICING

Various funding practices are found in NPOs. Some rely heavily on contributions, donations, or grants to provide free services to the clients. Others charge users for services rendered at a rate close to the full cost of such services; full costs include all program-specific costs, as well as a fair share of common or indirect fixed costs. Still others depend on contributions, donations, and grants to finance the bulk of their expenses, and cover the rest of the expenses through service fees collected from users, or clients.

The extent of pricing and the actual pricing practice used by an NPO are the result of a policy decided upon after deliberate consideration of costs, revenues, and external support. This policy is often affected by the need to negotiate cost reimbursement contracts with government agencies or with private insurers. In some programs only program-specific variable costs are reimbursable. Frequently, only a program's direct fixed costs as well as variable costs are reimbursable. In many programs, however, the full costs are reimbursable.

COST FINDING AND PRICING

The big questions for NPOs are:

- How much does it cost to provide our services?
- How much should we charge for our services?

Nonprofit cost accounting systems must address these questions. They should provide nonprofit managers with information that is designed to (1) distinguish between direct and indirect costs, (2) allocate certain support costs to cost objects (e.g., department, programs, or services), and (3) determine a full-cost per unit of service.

There are two basic types of responsibility centers or cost centers in an NPO: mission centers and service centers. A mission center (such as the curatorial department in a museum) is where the revenue production activities take place. It is frequently called a revenue-producing center. A service center (such as the finance department of a museum) provides support to both mission centers and other service centers. For the purpose of measuring the full cost of mission centers, the costs of a service center should be allocated to the appropriate mission centers.

The main objective of cost accounting in nonprofit organizations is to match costs incurred with the various services rendered. This assignment of costs may be accomplished for certain direct costs. However, indirect costs may require some type of allocation. The process of allocation of costs to mission centers (revenue-producing) is common to nonprofit entities and is called *cost finding*. This process is similar to full absorption costing in a normal manufacturing company, where overheads are assigned to direct costs of products. Cost finding and cost allocation are also essential for establishing prices for services rendered. For example, hospital patient charges must cover the direct costs of providing care, a fair share of service center (support department) costs, and a portion of the discounts and allowances due to free care (Medicaid and Medicare). The total cost of care is used to determine the patient charge in the same manner as a manufacturing firm determines the selling price per unit of product.

The cost-finding procedure may be summarized as follows:

- Direct costs associated to a revenue center are appropriately recorded. An example of a direct cost would be a nurse's salary in an emergency room of a hospital.
- Unassociated or indirect costs are recorded in general operating accounts. An example of an indirect cost would be a janitor's salary in the same hospital.
- Operating statistics are developed as a basis for prorating indirect costs to mission centers. Support department costs are allocated to patient service departments (revenue centers) and to each other as well.
- Indirect costs are prorated or allocated by using the appropriate operating statistics.
- The cost-finding procedure is only acceptable for a cost center structure and when adequate statistical information for allocating costs are available.

ALLOCATION OF SERVICE CENTER COSTS TO MISSION CENTERS

Some service center costs are direct. Examples are the salaries of the workers in the center. Other service center costs are indirect—that is, they are incurred jointly with some other center. An example is depreciation of building. These indirect costs must be allocated on some arbitrary basis. The problem is one of selecting appropriate bases for assigning the indirect costs of service centers to other centers. Service center costs should be allocated on a basis that reflects the type of activity in which the service center is engaged. The ideal basis should be logical, should have a high cause-and-effect relationship between the service provided and the costs of providing it, and should be easy to implement. For example, kitchen expenses are caused by the preparation of meals; the allocation base should be meals served.

The basis selected may be supported by physical observation, by correlation analysis, or logical analysis of the relationships between the centers. A list of some service centers and possible bases for allocation is given below.

Service Centers	Allocation Basis
Laundry services	Pounds processed
Housekeeping	Number of square cubic feet
Dietary	Number of meals served
Supplies	Number of requisitions
Nurse supervisors	Number of beds supervised
Personnel	Number of employees
Waste disposal	Number of rooms serviced
Power	Kilowatt-hours used
Buildings and grounds	Number of square or cubic feet
Maintenance and repairs	Machine hours or number of calls
Personnel	Number of employees
Cafeteria	Number of employees
Purchasing	Number of orders

PROCEDURE OF SERVICE CENTER COST ALLOCATION

Once the service center costs are known, the next step is to allocate the service center costs to the mission centers. This may be accomplished by one of the following procedures:

1. Direct method.
2. Step-down (two-stage) method.
3. Reciprocal method.

Direct Method

The direct method is a method of allocating the costs of each service center directly to mission centers, with no intermediate allocation to other service centers. That is, no consideration is given to services performed by one service center for another. This is perhaps the most widely used method because of its simplicity and ease of use.

EXAMPLE 12.1

Assume the following data for Cleanup Air USA:

	Service Cost Centers		Mission Cost Centers	
	Housekeeping (HK)	Fund Raising (FR)	A Recycling	B Public Education
Overhead costs before allocation	$20,000	$10,000	$30,000	$40,000
Square feet by housekeeping	15,000	20,000	60,000	40,000
Labor-hours by fund-raising	5,000	4,000	50,000	30,000
Total units of service			100 days	150 seminars

Using the direct method yields:

The Direct Method

	Service Cost Centers		Mission Cost Centers	
	Housekeeping (HK)	Fund Raising (FR)	A Recycling	B Public Education
Overhead costs	$20,000	$10,000	$30,000	$40,000
Reallocation:				
HK (60%, 40%)[a]	($20,000)		12,000	8,000
FR(5/8, 3/8)[b]		($10,000)	6,250	3,750
Full cost			$48,250	$51,750
Total units of service			100 days	150 seminars
Unit cost			$ 483 per day	$345 per seminar

[a]Base is (60,000 + 40,000 = 100,000); 60,000/100,000 = 0.6; 40,000/100,000 = 0.4.
[b]Base is (50,000 + 30,000 = 80,000); 50,000/80,000 = 5/8; 30,000/80,000 = 3/8.

Step-Down (Two-Stage) Method

This is a method of allocating services rendered by service centers to other service centers using a sequence of allocation; also called the "two-stage method," the "pyramiding process," or the "sequential method." The sequence normally begins with the center that renders service to the greatest number of other service centers; the sequence continues in step-by-step fashion and ends with the allocation of costs of service centers that provide the least amount of service. After a given service center's costs have once been allocated, it will not receive any charges from the other service centers. Using the same data, the step-down method yields:

The Step Method

	Service Cost Centers		Mission Cost Centers	
	Housekeeping (HK)	Fund Raising (FR)	A Recycling	B Public Education
Overhead costs	$20,000	$10,000	$30,000	$40,000
Reallocation:				
HK (1/6, 1/2, 1/3)[a]	($20,000)	3,333	10,000	6,667
FR (5/8, 3/8)[b]		($13,333)	8,333	5,000
Full cost			$48,333	$51,667
Total units of service			100 days	150 seminars
Unit cost			$ 483 per day	$344 per seminar

[a]Base is (20,000 + 60,000 + 40,000 = 120,000); 20,000/120,000 =1/6; 60,000/120,000 =1/2; 40,000/120,000 = 1/3.
[b]Base is (50,000 + 30,000 = 80,000); 50,000/80,000 = 5/8; 30,000/80,000 = 3/8.

Reciprocal Method

The reciprocal method, also known as the "reciprocal service method," the "matrix method," the "double-distribution method," and the "simultaneous allocation method," is more refined than the step-down approach. It too acknowledges that non-revenue-producing departments provide service to each other; however, it also allows a second round of allocations. After the initial round of allocations, a cost center is still eligible to receive allocations (unlike the step-down technique). Then, the second allocation is identical to the step-down method. The method sets up simultaneous equations to determine the allocable cost of each service center.

Using the same data, we set up the following equations:

$$HK = \$20,000 + 50/85 \; FR$$
$$FR = \$10,000 + 1/6 \; HK$$

Substituting FR from the second equation into the first:

$$HK = \$20,000 + 50/85 \; (\$10,000 + 1/6 \; HK)$$

Solving for HK gives HK = $28,695. Substituting HK = $28,695 into the second equation and solving for FR gives FR = $14,782.

Using these solved values, the reciprocal method yields:

The Reciprocal Method

	Service Cost Centers		Mission Cost Centers	
	Housekeeping (HK)	Fund Raising (FR)	A Recycling	B Public Education
Overhead costs	$20,000	$10,000	$30,000	$40,000
Reallocation:				
HK (1/6, 1/2, 1/3)	(28,695)	4,782	14,348	9,565
FR (50/85, 30/85, 5/8)	8,695	(14,782)	5,217	870
Full cost			$49,565	$50,435
Total units of service			100 days	150 seminars
Unit cost			$ 496 per day	$336 per seminar

In the next section, a cost-finding worksheet for hospitals is illustrated, using the step-down and reciprocal methods.

Table 12.1 illustrates the step-down approach. It lists cost centers to which costs are to be allocated in the left-hand column, and cost centers from which costs are to be allocated across the top. The adjusted balances from the ledger accounts of a hospital are in the first column; and columns 2 through 15 are used to allocate costs. The final totals in column 16 represent the fully allocated costs of the revenue-producing centers. Statistics are the basis for the cost allocation; and in this particular example, such statistics are shown in Table 12.2.

The reciprocal method is illustrated in Table 12.3. It can be noted that a second round of allocations takes place for laundry, records, and pharmacy.

Under both the step-down and the reciprocal methods, care must be taken in determining which cost centers provide the most service to other departments. Those departments providing the least service to other non-revenue cost centers should be closed out last.

Cost-Finding Worksheet: Step-Down Method

	1	2	3	4	5	6	7
	Adjusted Balances	Depreciation	Employee Benefits	Subtotals	Fiscal and Administrative Services	Plant Operation and Maintenance	Housekeeping
Depreciation	$ 50,000	$50,000					
Employee benefits	48,240	$ 900	$48,240				
Fiscal and administrative services	97,000	2,500	$ 7,920	$105,820	$105,820		
Plant operation and maintenance	63,000	200	2,250	67,750	$ 9,993	$77,743	
Housekeeping	31,000	1,400	2,070	33,270	4,907	$ 334	$38,511
Laundry	24,000	1,400	1,530	26,930	3,972	2,335	$ 1,162
Dietary	86,000	4,200	4,140	94,340	13,915	7,006	3,486
Nursing service—administrative office	9,000	200	720	9,920	1,463	334	166
Central supply	19,000	1,600	900	21,500	3,171	2,669	1,328
Pharmacy	25,000	500	1,260	26,760	3,947	834	415
Medical records	10,000	400	720	11,120	1,640	667	332
Cost of meals sold							
Operating rooms	18,000	3,000	1,080	22,080	3,257	5,004	2,490
Laboratory	30,000	800	1,800	32,600	4,808	1,334	664
Radiology	40,000	1,400	2,520	43,920	6,478	2,335	1,162
Cost of drugs sold							
Nursing units—adult and pediatric	218,000	29,000	17,640	264,640	39,037	48,386	24,069
Newborn nursery	27,000	1,400	2,160	30,560	4,508	2,335	1,162
Outpatient clinic	15,000	1,500	810	17,310	2,553	2,502	1,245
Emergency rooms	13,000	1,000	720	14,720	2,171	1,668	830
Cafeteria sales	(17,000)			(17,000)			
Total	$806,240	$50,000	$48,240	$806,240	$105,820	$77,743	$38,511

	8 Laundry	9 Dietary	10 Nursing Administrative Office	11 Central Supply	12 Pharmacy	13 Medical Records	14 Subtotals	15 Net Cost of Meals Sold	16 Total Costs
Depreciation									
Employee benefits									
Fiscal and administrative services									
Plant operation and maintenance									
Housekeeping									
Laundry	$34,399								
Dietary	$ 200	$118,947							
Nursing service—administrative office	40		$11,923						
Central supply	6,000		$ 720	$35,388					
Pharmacy	30				$31,986				
Medical records	20					$13,779			
Cost of meals sold		$27,000					$ 27,000	$27,000	
Operating rooms	6,500		896	$ 4,320	$ 2,668		47,215	$ 609	$ 47,824
Laboratory	70				552		40,028	516	49,544
Radiology	400				644		54,939	709	55,648
Cost of drugs sold					18,400		18,400		18,400
Nursing units—adult and pediatric	16,739	91,947	9,211	29,493	7,422	$10,610	541,554	6,952	$548,506
Newborn nursery	2,200		440	405	460	1,102	43,172	557	43,729
Outpatient clinic	800		304	180	734	1,378	27,008	348	27,356
Emergency rooms	1,400		352	990	1,104	689	23,924	309	24,233
Cafeteria sales							(17,000)	17,000	
Total	$34,399	$118,947	$11,923	$35,388	$31,986	$13,779	$806,240	$27,000	$806,240

T A B L E 12.2

Cost-Finding Statistics Supporting Cost-Finding Worksheet

Allocation Bases	1 Depreciation (square ft)	2 Employee Benefits (Payroll dollars)	3 Fiscal and Administrative Services (Accumulated Expenses)	4 Plant Operation and Maintenance (square ft)	5 Housekeeping (square ft)	6 Laundry (lb)
Fiscal and administrative services	900	$ 88,000				
Plant operation and maintenance	2,500	25,000	$ 67,750			
Housekeeping	200	23,000	33,270	200		
Laundry	1,400	17,000	26,930	1,400	1,400	
Dietary	4,200	46,000	94,340	4,200	4,200	2,000
Nursing services—administrative office	200	8,000	9,920	200	200	400
Central supply	1,600	10,000	21,500	1,600	1,600	60,000
Pharmacy	500	14,000	26,760	500	500	300
Medical records	400	8,000	11,120	400	400	200
Cost of meals sold						
Operating rooms	3,000	12,000	22,080	3,000	3,000	65,000
Laboratory	800	20,000	32,600	800	800	700
Radiology	1,400	28,000	43,920	1,400	1,400	4,000
Cost of drugs sold						
Nursing units—adults and pediatric	29,000	196,000	264,640	29,000	29,000	167,400
Newborn nursery	1,400	24,000	30,560	1,400	1,400	22,000
Outpatient clinic	1,500	9,000	17,310	1,500	1,500	8,000
Emergency rooms:	1,000	8,000	14,720	1,000	1,000	14,000
(1) Totals	50,000	$536,000	$717,420	46,600	46,400	344,000
(2) Accumulated expenses per Table 12.1	$50,000	$ 48,240	$105,820	$77,743	$38,511	$ 34,399
Unit cost multiplier (line 2/line 1)	1.00	.09	.1475	1.668	.83	.10
Table 12.1 column number	2	3	5	6	7	8

Allocation Bases	7 Dietary (Meals Served)	8 Nursing Administrative Office (Hours)	9 Central Supply (Priced Requisitions)	10 Pharmacy (Priced Requisitions)	11 Medical Records (Estimated Time)	12 Net Cost of Meals Sold (Accumulated Expenses)
Fiscal and administrative services						
Plant operation and maintenance						
Housekeeping						
Laundry						
Dietary		9,000				
Nursing services—administrative office						
Central supply						
Pharmacy						
Medical records						
Cost of meals sold	18,000					
Operating rooms		11,200	$ 9,600	$ 2,900		$ 47,215
Laboratory				600		40,028
Radiology				700		54,939
Cost of drugs sold				20,000		
Nursing units—adult and pediatric	61,300	115,137	65,540	8,067	77%	541,554
Newborn nursery		5,500	900	500	8	43,172
Outpatient clinic		3,800	400	800	10	27,008
Emergency rooms:		4,400	2,200	1,200	5	23,924
(1) Totals	79,300	149,037	$78,640	$34,767	100%	$777,840
(2) Accumulated expenses per Table 12.1	$118,947	$ 11,923	$35,388	$31,986	$13,779	$ 10,000
Unit cost multiplier (line 2/line 1)	1.50	.08	.45	.92		.0129
Table 12.1 column number	9	10	11	12	13	15

T A B L E 12.3

Cost-Finding Worksheet: Reciprocal (Double-Distribution) Method

	1	2	3	4	5	6	7	
	Unassigned Expenses	Non-Revenue-Producing Departments			Revenue-Producing Departments			Total
		Dept. 1	Dept. 2	Dept. 3	Dept. A	Dept. B	Dept. C	
Trial balance, December 31, 1997	$80,000	$100,000	$60,000	$40,000	$200,000	$250,000	$150,000	$880,000
Allocation of unassigned expenses	−80,000	+10,000	+6,000	+4,000	+20,000	+25,000	+15,000	−0−
Subtotal	$ −0−	110,000	66,000	44,000	220,000	275,000	165,000	880,000
Initial allocation of Dept. 1		−110,000	+27,500	+16,500	+33,000	+22,000	+11,000	−0−
Subtotal		−0−	93,500	60,500	253,000	297,000	176,000	880,000
Initial allocation of Dept. 2		+9,350	−93,500	+18,700	+37,400	−0−	+28,050	−0−
Subtotal		9,350	−0−	79,200	290,400	297,000	204,050	880,000
Initial allocation of Dept. 3		−0−	+15,840	−79,200	+27,720	+35,640	−0−	−0−
Subtotal		9,350	15,840	−0−	318,120	332,640	204,050	880,000
Final allocation of Dept. 1		−9,350	+2,337	+1,403	+2,805	+1,870	+935	−0−
Subtotal		$ −0−	18,177	1,403	320,925	334,510	204,985	880,000
Final allocation of Dept. 2			−18,177	+4,039	+8,079	−0−	+6,059	−0−
Subtotal			$ −0−	5,442	329,004	334,510	211,044	880,000
Final allocation of Dept. 3				−5,442	+2,381	+3,061	−0−	−0−
Full-cost total				−0−	$331,385	$337,571	$211,044	$880,000

ORGANIZATIONAL CONSIDERATIONS IN COST CONTROL

A nonprofit organization should be organized in segments, depending on the type of service rendered (i.e., each segment should be built around the type of service provided). This type of structure permits a matching of the revenue gathering activity with expense incurrence by individual responsibility. In fact, traditional responsibility accounting systems are desirable because this type of reporting structure requires a sound organization and clearly assigned responsibilities. Nonprofit organizations tend to be governed from the top by some type of board. Examples include the hospital boards, school boards, club boards, and church boards. As a general rule, these boards are composed of either professional people (usually relative to the organization's services provided) or concerned citizens with minimal administrative expertise. Unfortunately, the lack of profit as a motivation and the majority of emphasis being placed on the providing of service results in financial control being given insufficient attention at the board level. As a matter of fact, the chief administrator and his or her assistant administrators are often professionals or technicians who tend to lack leadership and managerial skills. However, these situations have become less prevalent in recent years.

Because most NPO boards are not management oriented, the controller has administrative responsibility. The controller usually has responsibility for all aspects of the management and financial control system. In large organizations, the controller maintains a technical staff of accountants, auditors, an electronic data processing (EDP) staff, and similarly trained persons.

Two control systems should be designed to accumulate financial data for two different purposes:

- One control system should be structured in terms of programs or services.
- The other control system should be structured in terms of organizational responsibilities.

As expenditures are incurred, they are recorded simultaneously to both areas, resulting in summarizations to reflect the cost of service elements, service subcategories, service categories, and at the same time budgetary or fiscal performance in each responsibility area.

ACTIVITY-BASED COSTING

An activity-based cost (ABC) system is one which first traces costs to activities and then to products or services. Traditional product costing also involves two stages, but in the first stage, costs are traced to departments, not to activities. In both traditional and activity-based costing, the second stage consists of tracing costs to the product or the service. The principal difference between the two methods is the number of cost drivers used. Activity-based costing uses a larger number of cost drivers than the one or two volume-based cost drivers typical in a conventional system. In fact, the approach separates indirect costs into cost pools, where each cost pool is associated with a different cost driver. Then a predetermined overhead rate is computed for each cost pool and each cost driver. In consequence, this method has enhanced accuracy.

First-Stage Procedure

In the first stage of activity-based costing, indirect costs are divided into homogeneous cost pools. A *homogeneous* cost pool is a collection of indirect costs for which cost variations can be explained by a single cost driver. Overhead activities are homogeneous whenever they have the same consumption ratios for all products or services.

Once a cost pool is defined, the cost per unit of the cost driver is computed for that pool. This is referred to as the *pool rate*. Computation of the pool rate completes the first stage. Thus, the first stage produces two outcomes: (1) a set of homogeneous cost pools and (2) a pool rate.

Second-Stage Procedure

In the second stage, the costs of each pool are traced to products or services. This is done using the pool rate computed in the first stage and the measure of the amount of resources consumed by each service. This measure is simply the quantity of the cost driver used by each service. Thus, the indirect cost assigned from each cost pool to each service is computed as follows:

Applied Indirect Cost = Pool Rate × Cost Driver Units Used

The total indirect cost per unit of service is obtained by first tracing the indirect costs from the pools to the individual services. This total is then divided by the number of units served. The result is the unit indirect cost. Adding the per-unit indirect cost to the per-unit direct costs yields the total full costs per unit of service.

EXAMPLE 12.2

Suppose that an NPO has costs on a consulting engagement, and the direct costs are: professional labor at $50,000 and travel costs at $14,000. It has established the following overhead cost pools and cost drivers for its service:

Overhead Cost Pool	Budgeted Overhead Cost	Cost Driver	Predicted Level for Cost Driver	Predetermined Overhead Rate
Telephone calls	$ 10,000	Number of calls	1,000	$10 per call
Computer time	125,000	Amount of computer time (hours)	1,000	$125 per hour
Fringe benefits	80,000	Direct labor dollars	$200,000	40% of direct labor dollar
Other overhead costs	$150,000	Direct labor-hours	10,000	$15 per hour
Total	$365,000			

Program 107 has the following requirements:

Telephone calls	50 calls
Computer time	100 hours
Fringe benefits	$50,000
Other overhead costs	500 labor-hours

The overhead assigned to Program 107 is computed below:

Overhead Costs Pool	Predetermined Overhead Rate	Level of Cost Driver	Assigned Overhead Cost
Telephone calls	$10 per call	50 calls	$ 500
Computer time	$125 per hour	100 hours	12,500
Fringe benefits	40%	$50,000	20,000
Other overhead costs	$15 per labor-hour	500 labor-hours	7,500
Total			$40,500

The total overhead cost assigned to Program 107 is $40,500. Thus, the total full cost of the program is $104,500 ($50,000 direct professional labor + $14,000 travel costs + $40,500 applied overhead) .

Compare this with the overhead cost that is assigned to the program if the NPO uses a single predetermined overhead rate based on direct labor-hours:

$$\frac{\text{Total Budgeted Overhead Cost}}{\text{Total Predicted Machine-Hours}} = \frac{\$365,000}{10,000}$$

$$= \$36.50 \text{ per direct Labor-Hour}$$

Under this approach, the total overhead cost assigned to Program 107 is $18,250 ($36.50 per labor-hour × 500 labor-hours). Thus, the total full cost of the program is $82,250 ($50,000 direct professional labor + $14,000 travel costs + $18,250 applied overhead).

The reason for this wide discrepancy is that this program requires a relatively large amount of computer time, varying labor rates, and fringe benefits. Thus, the program is relatively costly in terms of driving overhead costs. Use of a single predetermined overhead rate obscures that fact.

Inaccurately calculating the overhead cost per unit to the extent illustrated above can have serious adverse consequences for an NPO. For example, it can lead to poor decisions about pricing, program, or contract bidding.

MORE ON WHY TO USE ACTIVITY-BASED COSTING

Using a single, companywide rate for applying support department costs would result in overcosting some services and undercosting others. The needs of revenue centers for support activities depend on the services rendered. Therefore, departmental cost pools will provide more accurate cost information.

Activity-based costing, unlike the traditional product costing method, attempts to identify why an overhead item exists. The reasons for its existence are referred to as *cost drivers,* because they drive the costs. Traditional costing does not consider differences between jobs that affect the cost generators. The use of cost drivers provides improved costing data. ABC is an accounting system that identifies the various activities performed in an organization and collects costs on the basis of the underlying nature and extent of those activities. This approach recognizes that costs originate from, and are driven up or down by, factors other than volume and direct labor.[1] For example, hospital administrators can go beyond average costing techniques to study the basic factors affecting hospital costs and the controlling forces behind these factrors.[2]

The benefits of an ABC system are numerous from the standpoint of planning, control, and decision making. They include:

1. Cost reduction by eliminating the activities that do not add value.
2. Improved product or service cost data.
3. Improved decisions about pricing, service mixes, and product strategies based on more accurate cost information.
4. Greater control of costs because of a focus on the behavior of costs at their origination, both short-term and long-term.
5. More accurate evaluation of performance by programs and responsibility centers.

Value-Added and Non-Value-Added Activities and Costs

Under ABC, costs can be subdivided into value-added cost and non-value-added cost. Value-added costs contribute to meeting department objectives. Non-value-added costs do not contribute to the accomplishment of the department's mission statement. In using ABC, the department managers are devoted to reducing the costs of activities that do not directly help to accomplish the organization's mission objectives. The non-value-added costs are the costs that the managers should focus their attention on and should try to avoid as much as possible.

The ability to divide the cost into value-added and non-value-added is one advantage of the activity-based cost accounting system. Under traditional accounting, we are not able to divide overhead into these details, and managers are not able to recognize which costs are not contributing to the department's mission objective.

Take a library, for example. Each library has its own mission objective. The primary service objectives of a specific library will vary. Therefore, differences will exist in the definition of value-added activities. Examples of non-value-added activities are reporting, moving library materials, sorting, storing, counting, recording, and checking. The costs of these activities generate non-value-added costs. They reduce the service level to the patrons of the library because, with an increase in these costs, less time and fewer resources are available for patron services. Other examples of non-value-added activities are the time spent for departmental parties, jury duty, docked time not reported, activities involving promotion or tenure process, university-wide committee meetings, recruiting, compiling workload statistical summaries, performance by administrative personnel of tasks that should be assigned to lower-level personnel, preparing budgets or strategic plans that are later rejected, and wasted idle time during holiday periods when library use decreases. These and a number of other activities performed within a library may add no value to the patron-oriented objectives of the various departments. Activity-based accounting concentrates its efforts on reducing these costs first when cost curtailment is required. Under traditional accounting methods, the costs associated with these activities are part of the general overhead and are not separately reported, making it harder to control them or understand how they are interrelated.[3]

Given the examples of non-value-added costs, we can go on to see the value-added costs. Value-added costs are easy. If a cost incurred contributes to the goal of the department, the cost can be considered a value-added cost. Take the circulation department, for example; its mission objective is to maximize the availability of library materials to patrons. All costs incurred to help achieve this goal may be considered value-added costs.

The benefit of separating non-value-added costs from value-added costs are obvious. The separation of these costs allows the department manager to concentrate on reducing non-value-added costs. Under traditional accounting, it would take the manager a long time to figure out what costs should be cut.

In addition, when activities are the focus of a cost report rather than the object of expenditure reporting and overhead, identification of the specific factors causing cost incurrence is easier. The cost incurrence activities are called "cost drivers." They are the activities that create the cost. In traditional cost reports, it is difficult to isolate the specific activities that cause increases in cost. Under ABC, cost cutting can be achieved by reducing non-value-added activities that will leave patron services intact. Efforts should be made to reduce activities listed under the non-value-added column when cost curtailment becomes necessary.

Product Costing Less Distorted

Using single pools of indirect costs and overhead application bases such as direct labor-hours or direct labor dollars is no longer considered good enough. The costs resulting from such broad averages are often misleading because they fail to capture cause-and-effect relationships. In ABC, unlike traditional costing, overhead costs are allocated by tracing costs to activities and then allocating the activities and their costs to products or services. With a minimum of detail, there are three steps for product costing in ABC:

1. Identify the major cost elements in an organization and separate them into cost pools.

2. Identify the drivers of the most significant costs (i.e., the activities that drive the costs).

3. Calculate the rate for each cost pool by determining the volume of each driver.

The following is a list of cost drivers for various activities.

Activity Pool	Cost Driver
1. General administration and MIS	Direct labor dollars
2. Marketing and member services	Number of members
3. Recruiting personnel	Number of hires
4. Ordering	Number of purchase orders
5. Accounts payable/receivable	Number of vendor invoices
6. Data processing	Number of reports requested; transactions processed; programming hours; program change requests
7. Accounting	Number of reports requested; dollars expended
8. Record storage	Number of move notices; number of treatments
9. Xeroxing	Number of copies
10. Quality control	Number of inspection hours spent; samples analyzed
11. Centralized appointment center	Number of appointments made
12. Employee insurance	Number of claims filed
13. Account receivable	Number of client invoices
14. Payroll and mail delivery	Number of employees
15. Supervision costs	Hours of treatment received; number of patient-days as percentage of direct cost
16. Respiratory therapy	Number of hookups
17. Laboratory	Number of lab test orders
18. Claims payment	Number of claims processed
19. Utilization review	Number of authorization forms processed
20. Pharmacy	Number of prescriptions filled
21. Radiology	Number of x-rays

Improving Performance

One of the major advantages of ABC is that it shows the connections between performance of certain activities and the demands those activities make on an organization's resources. As a result, ABC gives management a clearer picture of how programs, services, regions, or facilities not only generate revenues but also consume resources. The contribution analysis provided by ABC can assist managers by focusing their attention and energy on improving activities that will have the biggest impact on the bottom line.

ABC activities within various departments may be compared, or may be combined with activities within other departments. For example, the total cost of maintaining quality would encompass many costs. It would be the sum of the inspection costs in the purchasing department, the inspection costs in the service departments, and the customer service costs in the marketing department. Only if detailed costs are kept by activities can total NPO costs or quality (or any other aspect of the NPO's activities, such as acquiring, storing, and handling materials) be obtained.

Cost management is defined here as the performance by executives and others in the cost implications of their short-run and long-run planning and control functions. Cost accounting systems exist to provide information to help executives in performing their cost management duties. More than ever, managers' primary cost management focus is on underlying activities and services, not products. If the activities are managed well, costs will fall and the resulting services will be more competitive. If massive changes are made in activities and operations, managers want their accounting systems to change accordingly.

Existing cost accounting systems often fail to highlight interrelationships among activities in different departments or functional areas. Developments in information-gathering technology—including bar coding, numerically controlled equipment, and hand-held computers—has made practical the gathering and processing of more detailed information demanded by ABC.

ENDNOTES

1. Mark E. Beischel, "Improving Production with Process Value Analysis," *Journal of Accountancy,* September 1990, p. 53.

2. Medhat A. Helmi and Murat N. Tanju, "Activity-Based Costing May Reduce Costs, Aid Planning," *Healthcare Financial Management,* November 1991, p. 95.

3. G. Stevenson Smith, *Managerial Accounting for Library and Non-profit Organizations* (New York: American Library Association, 1991).

Analysis for Nonroutine Decisions and Financial Modeling for Program Analysis

They need financial-management systems, word-processing systems and database systems and so on.

David Bresnick
Executive Director of Nonprofit Computer Services (NCS),
a nonprofit computer consulting firm in New York,
PC Week, April 15, 1986.

Nonprofit financial management is constantly faced with the problem of choosing between alternative courses of action in performing various functions. Typical decisions to be tackled include:

1. Whether to make or buy.
2. Adding and deleting programs.
3. Pricing a service.
4. Decentralizing service delivery services.
5. Adopting a major change in treatment methods.
6. Investing in long-term facilities.

All such decisions typically involve substantial changes in the existing cost and/or revenue structure. In a short-term situation, fixed costs are generally irrelevant to the decision at hand. Nonprofit financial managers must recognize, as a major decision tool, an important concept: *relevant costs* and *relevant revenues*. Relevant costs and revenues are defined as all changes in future cash outflows and inflows of the entity that are expected to result from adopting a given proposal.

MAKE OR BUY DECISION

The decision whether to perform a service internally or to outsource it is called a "make-or-buy decision." This decision involves both quantitative and qualitative factors. The qualitative factors include ensuring service quality and the necessity for long-run business relationships with the supplier. The quantitative factors deal with cost. The quantitative effects of the make-or-buy decision are best seen through the relevant cost approach.

EXAMPLE 13.1

Eldorado Junior High School is considering various proposals to reduce costs and eliminate its operating deficits. The school currently employs its own janitorial staff, incurring the following costs:

Labor	$200,000
Supplies	80,000
Overhead (indirect)	260,000
	$540,000

Overhead includes depreciation of $40,000, allocated administrative and other fixed costs of $200,000, and variable indirect costs of $20,000. The employees' union is demanding a general increase in wages. Management estimates that wages will go up by 20 percent. An independent contractor has offered to provide the janitorial services at an annual fee of $400,000. Should Eldorado accept the contractor's offer?

The key to the decision lies in the investigation of those relevant costs that change between the make-or-buy alternatives. Assuming that the service capacity will be idle if not used to perform the service, the analysis takes the following form:

	Perform Internally	Outsource
Purchase price		$400,000
Labor	$240,000	
Supplies	80,000	
Overhead that can be avoided by outsourcing	20,000	
Total relevant costs	$340,000	$400,000
Difference in favor of performing internally	$60,000	

Note that (1) depreciation of $40,000 is a sunk cost and therefore is irrelevant, and (2) allocated fixed costs cannot be saved by going outside and hence are irrelevant.

The make-or-buy decision must be investigated, along with the broader perspective of considering how best to utilize available facilities. The alternatives are:

1. Leaving facilities idle.
2. Outsourcing and renting out idle facilities.
3. Outsourcing and using idle facilities for other services.

EVALUATING A PROPOSAL TO DISCONTINUE A PROGRAM

The decision to drop an old program or add a new one must take into account both qualitative and quantitative aspects. Attention must be paid to the relevancy of fixed costs common to programs. After all, any final decision should be based primarily on the impact the decision will have on contribution margin.

EXAMPLE 13.2

ABC Agency reports a deficit of $10,050 for the month of January, as shown below. The report is made under three cost categories: variable, direct (program-specific) fixed, and common fixed. The agency is considering the decision to drop program B because the statement shows it is losing money.

REVENUE AND COST REPORT, JANUARY 19X7

	Program A		Program B		TOTAL
	3250		750		
	Total	Per Unit	Total	Per unit	
Variable revenues	$ 6,500	$ 2	$22,500	$30	$ 29,000
Costs	32,500	10	18,750	25	51,250
Margin	$(26,000)	$(8)	$ 3,750	$ 5	$(22,250)
Direct (program-specific) fixed revenues	$ 72,500		$ 6,000		$ 78,500
Costs:					
Salaries	12,500		11,000		23,500
Employee benefits, etc.	1,200		1,000		2,200
Depreciation	200		100		300
Total costs	$ 13,900		$12,100		$ 26,000
Margin	$ 58,600		(6,100)		$ 52,500

	Total	Per Unit	Total	Per Unit	TOTAL
Total program specific margin	$32,600		$ (2,350)		$ 30,250
Common fixed revenues					$ 32,200
Costs:					
Salaries					37,500
Employee benefits					3,400
Office					15,000
Travel					6,300
Rent					6,700
Utilities					1,200
Depreciation					2,100
Others					300
Total costs					$ 72,500
Margin					$(40,300)
Total excess (deficit)					$(10,050)

Note that program A is highly subsidized, since the agency spends $8 more of variable costs over variable revenues for every unit of service. However, program A contributes $32,600 toward the agency's common fixed costs because of various revenue sources such as grants, contributions, and public support. This is not the case for program B. Should program B be discontinued? Assume the following additional information that is pertinent to program B:

1. Depreciation of $100 in program B relates to a piece of equipment having no alternative use and no disposal value.
2. Some donors are opposed to dropping program B. As a result, revenues, now classified under common fixed, are expected to go down by $800.
3. There is no need to renew the lease on one building currently rented for $4,000.
4. One program B employee cannot be terminated due to her age and past service. Her monthly salary of $1,000 will continue.

The analysis of the nonroutine proposal to drop program B can be analyzed using "incremental reasoning." It shows a projected savings of $4,450 for the agency instead of a savings of $2,350 as might be inferred from routine revenue and cost reports.

Deficit avoided	$2,350
Depreciation avoided	−100
Common fixed revenues forgone	−800
Savings in rental	4,000
Salaries not avoided	−1,000
Net savings from dropping program B	$4,450

CAPITAL BUDGETING

Many nonroutine decisions facing nonprofit organizations are ones of capital budgeting. Capital budgeting is the process of making long-term planning decisions for alternative investment opportunities. There are many investment decisions that the organization may have to make in order to provide further service and grow. Examples of capital budgeting applications are whether to purchase a computer, whether to keep or sell a segment, whether to lease or buy, what asset to invest in, and what services to provide.

What Are the Types of Investment Projects?

There are typically two types of long-term investment decisions:

1. *Selection decisions* in terms of obtaining new facilities or expanding existing ones. Examples include:
   a. Investments in property and equipment as well as other types of assets.
   b. Resource commitments in the form of new service development, expansion or introduction of a computer or network, refunding of long-term debt, and so on.
   c. Mergers and acquisitions in the form of buying another NPO to add a new service line.
2. *Replacement decisions* in terms of replacing existing facilities with new ones. Examples include replacing an old computer system with a high-tech one.

What Are the Features of Investment Projects?

Long-term investments have two important features:

1. They typically involve a large amount of initial cash outlays which tend to have a long-term impact on the agency's future viability. Therefore, this initial cash outlay needs to be justified on a cost-benefit basis.
2. There are expected recurring cash inflows (increased revenues, savings in cash operating expenses, etc.) over the life of the investment project. This frequently requires considering the *time value of money*.

UNDERSTANDING THE CONCEPT OF TIME VALUE OF MONEY

A dollar now is worth more than a dollar to be received later. This statement sums up an important principle: Money has a time value. The truth of this principle is not that inflation might make the dollar received at a later time worth less in buying power. The reason is that you could invest the dollar now and have more than a dollar at the specified later date.

Time value of money is a critical consideration in evaluating investment proposals. For example, compound interest calculations are needed to determine future sums of money resulting from an investment. Discounting, or the calculation of present value, which is inversely related to compounding, is used to evaluate the future cash flow associated with capital budgeting projects.

How Do You Calculate Future Values?

A dollar in hand today is worth more than a dollar to be received tomorrow because of the interest it could earn if it were put into a savings account or an investment account. Compounding interest means that interest earns interest. For the discussion of the concepts of compounding and time value, let us define:

F_n = future value: the amount of money at the end of year n
P = principal
i = annual interest rate
n = number of years

Then,

F_1 = the amount of money at the end of year 1
   = principal and interest = $P + iP = P(1+i)$
F_2 = the amount of money at the end of year 2
   = $F_1(1+i) = P(1+i)(1+i) = P(1+i)^2$

The future value of an investment compounded annually at rate i for n years is:

$$F_n = P(1+i)^n$$

What Is Present Value?

Present value is the present worth of future sums of money. The process of calculating present values, or discounting, is actually the opposite of finding the compounded future value. By reversing the computations in the previous section, we can compute the present value of future cash flows.

Recall that:

$$F_n = P(1+i)^n$$

Therefore,

$$P = \frac{F_n}{(1+i)^n} = F_n \frac{1}{(1+i)^n} = F_n \cdot T1(i,n)$$

where $T1(i,n)$ represents the present value of $1 (see Table E.1 in Appendix E).

In connection with present value calculations, the interest rate i is called the *discount rate*. We use the cost of capital (or minimum required of return) as the discount rate.

EXAMPLE 13.3

You have been given an opportunity to receive $20,000 on a date 6 years from now. If you can earn 10 percent on your investments, what is the most you should pay for this opportunity? To answer this question, you must compute the present value of $20,000 to be received 6 years from now at a 10 percent rate of discount. F_6 is $20,000, i is 10 percent, and n is 6 years. $T1(10\%,6)$ from Table E.1 is 0.564.

$$P = \$20,000\frac{1}{(1+0.1)^6} = \$20,000 T1(10\%,6) = \$20,000(0.564) = \$11,280$$

This means that you can earn 10 percent on your investment, and you would be indifferent to receiving $11,280 now or $20,000 on a date 6 years from today, since the amounts are time-equivalent. In other words, you could invest $11,280 today at 10 percent and have $20,000 in 6 years.

Present Value of Mixed Streams of Cash Flows

The present value of a series of mixed cash flows is the sum of the present value of each individual cash flow. We know that the present value of each individual amount is the amount times the appropriate $T1$ value.

EXAMPLE 13.4

An investment of $32,000 now is expected to generate cash flow savings of $10,000, $20,000, and $5,000 at the end of each of the following three years. The applicable discount rate is 10%, the rate at which investment funds can be generated. Is the investment financially desirable? The present value of this series of mixed streams of cash inflows is calculated as follows:

Year	Cash inflows	×	T1(10%, n)	Present Value
1	$10,000		0.909	$ 9,090
2	$20,000		0.826	$16,520
3	$ 5,000		0.751	$ 3,755
				$29,365

Since the present value of future cash benefits amounts to only $29,365, the $32,000 investment is not desirable.

Present Value of an Annuity

Interest received from bonds, pension funds, and insurance obligations all involve annuities. To compare these financial instruments, we need to know the present value of each. The present value of an annuity (P_n) can be found by using the following equation:

$$P = A \cdot \frac{1}{(1+i)^1} + A \cdot \frac{1}{(1+i)^2} + \ldots + A \cdot \frac{1}{(1+i)^n} = A \cdot T_2(i,n)$$

where $T2(i,n)$ represents the present value of an annuity of $1 discounted at i percent for n years (see Table E.2 in Appendix E)

EXAMPLE 13.5
If cash inflows form an annuity of $10,000 for 3 years, the present value is:

$P = A \cdot T2(i,n)$
$P = \$10,000 \, T2(10\%, 3 \text{ years}) = \$10,000 \, (2.487) = \$24,870$

Use of Financial Calculators and Spreadsheet Programs

There are many financial calculators that contain preprogrammed formulas to perform many present value and future applications. They include the Hewlett-Packard 10B, the Sharpe EL733, and the Texas Instrument BA35. Furthermore, spreadsheet software such as Microsoft's Excel has built-in financial functions to perform many such applications.

HOW DO YOU MEASURE INVESTMENT WORTH?

Several methods of evaluating investment projects are as follows:

1. Payback period.
2. Net present value (NPV).
3. Internal rate of return (IRR).
4. Benefit/cost (B/C) ratio.

The NPV method and the IRR method are called *discounted cash flow (DCF) methods*. Each of these methods is discussed below.

Payback Period

The payback period measures the length of time required to recover the amount of initial investment. It is computed by dividing the initial investment by the cash inflows through increased revenues or cost savings.

EXAMPLE 13.6

Assume:

Cost of investment	$18,000
Annual cash savings	$ 3,000

Then, the payback period is:

$$\text{Payback Period} = \frac{\text{Initial Investment}}{\text{Cost Savings}} = \frac{\$18,000}{\$3,000} = 6 \text{ Years}$$

Decision rule: Choose the project with the shorter payback period. The rationale behind this choice is: The shorter the payback period, the less risky the project, and the greater the liquidity.

EXAMPLE 13.7

Consider the two projects whose after-tax cash inflows are not even. Assume that each project costs $1,000.

	Cash Inflow	
Year	A ($)	B ($)
1	100	500
2	200	400
3	300	300
4	400	100
5	500	
6	600	

When cash inflows are not even, the payback period has to be found by trial and error. The payback period of project A is ($1,000= $100 + $200 + $300 + $400) 4 years. The payback period of project B is ($1,000 = $500 + $400 + $100/$300) 2 1/3 years.

$$2 \text{ Years} + \frac{\$100}{\$300} = 2 \ 1/3 \text{ Years}$$

Project B is the project of choice in this case, since it has the shorter payback period.

The advantages of using the payback period method of evaluating an investment project are that (1) it is simple to compute and easy to understand, and (2) it handles investment risk effectively. The shortcomings of this method are that (1) it does not recognize the time value of money, and (2) it ignores the impact of cash inflows received after the payback period; essentially, cash flows after the payback period determine profitability of an investment.

Net Present Value

Net present value (NPV) is the excess of the present value (P) of cash inflows generated by the project over the amount of the initial investment (I):

$$\text{NPV} = P - I$$

The present value of future cash flows is computed using the so-called cost of capital (or minimum required rate of return) as the discount rate. When cash inflows are uniform, the present value will be:

$$P = A \cdot T2 \ (i,n)$$

where A is the amount of the annuity. (The value of $T2$ is found in Table E.2 of Appendix E.)

Decision rule: If NPV is positive, accept the project. Otherwise, reject it.

EXAMPLE 13.8
Consider the following investment:

Initial investment	$37,910
Estimated life	5 years
Annual cash inflows	$10,000
Cost of capital (minimum required rate of return)	8%

Present value of the cash inflows is:

$$P = A \cdot T2(i,n)$$

$$= \$10,000 \cdot T2(8\%,5 \text{ years})$$

$= \$10,000(3.993)$	$39,930
Initial investment (I)	37,910
Net present value (NPV = $P - I$)	$ 2,020

Since the NPV of the investment is positive, the investment should be accepted.

The advantages of the NPV method are that it obviously recognizes the time value of money and that it is easy to compute whether the cash flows form an annuity or vary from period to period.

EXAMPLE 13.9

A university is considering the purchase of a computer at a cost of $140,000 in order to reduce data processing costs. The computer would have a salvage value of $20,000 at the end of four years. The annual cash flow savings in payroll costs, supplies, and utilities would amount to $48,000 during the next four years. Increase in annual repairs and maintenance expenses as a result of the new computer would be $2,500, $5,000, $7,500, and $10,000, respectively, during the next four years. The cost of the computer would be depreciated at the rate of $30,000 each year. The university considers a 12 percent annual interest rate to be the relevant rate for discounting its future cash flows. Is this investment desirable?

		Years			
	0	1	2	3	4
Initial investment (I)	−140000				
Annual savings		48000	48000	48000	48000
Repairs and maintenance		−2500	−5000	−7500	−10000
Salvage value					20000
Annual cash flow	−140000	45500	43000	40500	58000
Present value of $1 (T1 at 12%)	1	0.8929	0.7972	0.7118	0.6355
Present value (P)	−140000	40626.95	34279.6	28827.9	36859

Net present value (NPV = $P - I$)	$593.45
NPV(rate, value1, value2,...)	$528.11
IRR(values, guess)	12.19%

Notes:
1. Depreciation is a noncash charge, and therefore irrelevant. It is also irrelevant due to the fact that nonprofits are not subject to income taxes.
2. The NPV of the project is $593.45, as shown above while using *Excel's* function.—NPV(rate,value1,value2)—yields $528.11, which is due to rounding errors.

Internal Rate of Return

Internal rate of return (IRR) is defined as the rate of interest that equates I with the P of future cash inflows. In other words, at IRR:

$$I = P \quad \text{or} \quad \text{NPV} = 0$$

Decision rule: Accept the project if the IRR exceeds the cost of capital. Otherwise, reject it.

EXAMPLE 13.10

Assume the same data given in Example 13.8, and set the following equality $(I = P)$:

$$\$39,710 = \$10,000 \cdot T2(i,5 \text{ years})$$

$$T2(i,5 \text{ years}) = \frac{\$37,910}{\$10,000} = 3.791$$

which stands at 10 percent in the five-year line of Table E.2 in Appendix E.

Since the IRR of the investment is greater than the cost of capital (8 percent), accept the project.

The advantage of using the IRR method is that it does consider the time value of money. The shortcomings of this method are that (1) it is time-consuming to compute, especially when the cash inflows are not even, although most financial calculators and PCs have a key to calculate IRR, and (2) it fails to recognize the varying sizes of investment in competing projects.

Can a Computer Help?

Spreadsheet programs can be used in making IRR calculations. For example, Lotus 1-2-3 has a function @IRR(guess, range). Lotus 1-2-3 considers negative numbers to be cash outflows (such as the initial investment) and positive numbers to be cash inflows. Many financial calculators have similar features. As in Example 3.10, suppose you want to calculate the IRR of a $37,910 investment (the value -37910 entered in cell A3) that is followed by 10 monthly cash inflows of $10,000 ($B3...K3$). Using a guess of 8% (the value of .08, which is in effect the cost of capital), your formula would be @IRR(0.12,$A3...K3$) and Lotus 1-2-3 would return 10. Microsoft's Excel has the IRR function command.

EXAMPLE 13.11

In Example 13.9, using Excel's function IRR(values,guess) yields the IRR of 12.19 percent, which is greater than the cost of capital of 12 percent. So the project is financially desirable.

Benefit/Cost Ratio

The benefit/cost (B/C) ratio, commonly called the "present value index," is the ratio of the total present value of future cash inflows to the initial investment, that is, P/I. This ratio is used as a means of ranking projects in descending order of attractiveness.

Decision rule: If the B/C ratio is greater than 1, accept the project.

EXAMPLE 13.12

Using the data in Example 13.8, the benefit/cost ratio is

$$\frac{P}{I} = \frac{\$39,930}{\$37,910} = 1.05$$

Since this project generates $1.05 for each dollar invested (i.e., its B/C ratio is greater than 1), accept the project.

The ratio has the advantage of putting all projects on the same relative basis regardless of size.

HOW TO SELECT THE BEST MIX OF PROJECTS WITH A LIMITED BUDGET

Many NPOs specify a limit on the overall budget for capital spending. Capital rationing is concerned with the problem of selecting the mix of acceptable projects that provides the highest overall NPV. The benefit/cost ratio is used widely in ranking projects competing for limited funds.

EXAMPLE 13.13

The Westmont Agency has a fixed budget of $250,000. Data for initial cash outlay and the present value of benefits for six projects are given below. The agency needs to select a mix of acceptable projects from the following:

Projects	I ($)	P ($)	NPV ($)	Benefit/Cost Ratio	Ranking
A	70,000	112,000	42,000	1.6	1
B	100,000	145,000	45,000	1.45	2
C	110,000	126,500	16,500	1.15	5
D	60,000	79,000	19,000	1.32	3
E	40,000	38,000	−2,000	0.95	6
F	80,000	95,000	15,000	1.19	4

The ranking resulting from the profitability index shows that the NPO should select projects A, B, and D.

	I	P
A	$ 70,000	$112,000
B	100,000	145,000
D	60,000	79,000
	$230,000	$336,000

Therefore,

$$NPV = \$336,000 - \$230,000 = \$106,000$$

THE CHOICE OF THE DISCOUNT RATE AND THE COST OF CAPITAL

Project managers must know the cost of capital, often called *the minimum required rate of return*, that is used either as a discount rate under the NPV method or as a hurdle rate under the IRR method. For this reason, the choice of the discount rate may make the difference between acceptance and rejection of a project. Unfortunately, no straightforward guidelines are available for choosing a proper discount rate for nonprofit investments. At least in theory, the cost of capital is defined as the rate of return that is necessary to maintain the value of the agency. Two common bases are: (1) the cost of borrowing the money necessary to finance a project and (2) the return that could be realized if a comparable investment were invested for the same period of time. In case more than one source is used for funding, the cost of capital is computed as a weighted average of the various capital components.

Cost of Long-Term Debt

The cost of long-term debt is the interest rate charged on the funds.

Cost of Grants and Contributions

The cost of grants and contributions is generally considered free.

Measuring the Overall Cost of Capital

The NPO's overall cost of capital is the weighted average of the individual capital costs, with the weights being the proportions of each type of financing used.

The computation of overall cost of capital is illustrated in the following example.

EXAMPLE 13.14

Assume that the capital structure at the latest statement date is indicative of the proportions of financing that the NPO intends to use over time. The computation is illustrated below.

Source of Funds	Specific Cost of Capital	Proportion of Weighted Average	
		Financing	Cost of Capital
Long-term debt	10%	3/4	7.5%
Grants and contributions	0	1/4	0
Weighted-average cost of capital			7.5%

The overall cost of capital is 7.5%

LEASE VERSUS PURCHASE

When confronted with the need to make large capital expenditures, NPOs often consider lease-purchasing equipment or facilities rather than paying outright. A major advantage of leasing is that costly one-time cash outlays, which can disrupt the budget, are avoided.

EXAMPLE 13.15

An agency can either purchase a minicomputer for $61,000 or lease it at an annual $13,000 payment and own it after five years. The anticipated discount rate will be 8 percent. Is it more economical to lease or to purchase? The present value of $15,000 a year for five years at 8% is:

$$\$13,000 \; T2(8\%, 5 \text{ Years}) = \$13,000 \; (3.993) = \$51,909$$

Since the purchase price is higher than $51,909, it would be more economical to lease.

PROGRAM ANALYSIS THROUGH FINANCIAL MODELING

More NPOs are increasingly using financial modeling to develop their budgets and making program choices and analyses. This section introduces financial modeling. A financial model is a system of mathematical equations, logic, and data, which describes the relationships among financial and operating variables. A financial model can be viewed as a subset of broadly defined planning models or, as a stand-alone functional system that attempts to answer a certain financial planning problem.

A Financial Model

A financial model is one in which:

1. One or more financial and operating variables appear (expenses, revenues, cash flow, etc.).
2. The model user can manipulate (set and alter) the value of one or more variables.
3. The purpose of the model is to influence strategic decisions by revealing to the decision maker the implications of alternative values of these financial variables.

Financial models fall into two types: simulations better known as "what-if" models and optimization models. "What-if" models attempt to simulate the effects of alternative management policies and assumptions about the NPO's external environment. They are basically a tool for management's laboratory. Optimization models are the ones in which the goal is to maximize or minimize an objective such as volume or cost. Multiobjective techniques such as goal programming are being experimented.

Models can be deterministic or probabilistic. Deterministic models do not include random or probabilistic variables whereas probabilistic models incorporate random numbers and/or one or more probability distributions for variables such as costs. Financial models can be solved and manipulated computationally to derive current and projected future implications and consequences. Due to technological advances in computers (such as spreadsheets, financial modeling languages, graphics, database management systems, and networking), more companies are using modeling.

Budgeting and Financial Modeling

Basically, a financial model is used to build a comprehensive budget (that is, projected financial statements such as the surplus/deficit, the balance sheet, and the cash-flow statement). Such a model can be called a budgeting model, since we are essentially developing a master budget with such a model. Applications and uses of the model, however, go beyond developing a budget. They include:

- Financial forecasting and analysis.
- Capital expenditure analysis.
- Analysis for mergers and acquisitions.
- Labor contract negotiations.

- Cost-volume-profit analysis.
- Lease/purchase evaluation.
- Appraisal of performance by segments.
- Market analysis.
- New service analysis.
- Development of long-term strategy.
- Planning of financial requirements.
- Risk analysis.
- Cash-flow analysis.
- Cost and price projections.

Use Of Financial Modeling in Practice

The use of financial modeling, especially a computer-based financial modeling system is rapidly growing. The reason is quite simple: the growing need for improved and quicker support for management decisions as a decision support system (DSS) and wide and easy availability of computer hardware and software.

Some of the functions served by financial models are:

- Projecting financial results under a given set of assumptions; to evaluate the financial impact of various assumptions and alternative strategies; and to prepare long range financial forecasts.
- Providing answers to insights into "what-if" questions.
- Projecting operating results and various financing needs.
- Generating performance reports of various cost centers.
- Projecting financial implications of capital investment programs.
- Showing the effects of various service and activity levels on budget and cash flow.
- Forecasting revenues and costs by division, by month.
- Evaluate alternatives of leasing or buying computer equipment.
- Generating activity statements, cash flow, present value, and discounted rate of return for potential ventures, based on revenue and cash flow forecasts.

Supported by the expanded capabilities provided by models, NPOs are able to include long-term strategic considerations in their plans, thus enabling them to investigate the possible impact of their current decisions on the long term welfare of the NPO.

Developing Financial Models

Development of financial models essentially involves two steps: (1) definition of variables and input parameters and (2) model specification. Generally speaking, the model consists of three important ingredients:

- Variables.
- Input parameter values.
- Definitional and/or functional relationships.

Definition of Variables

Fundamental to the specification of a financial model is the definition of the variables to be included in the model. There are basically three types of variables: policy variables, external variables, and performance variables. The policy variables (often called "control variables") are variables over which management can exert some degree of control. Examples of policy variables are cash management, working capital, debt management, merger-acquisition decisions, and the size of cash balances and the liquid asset position. The external variables are the environmental variables that are external to the NPO—generally speaking, donations and pledges influenced by overall general economic conditions. The performance variables, often called "output variables", measure the NPO's performance, which are usually endogenous. The output variables of a financial model would be the line items of the balance sheet, cash budget, surplus/deficit statement, or statement of cash flow.

Input Parameter Values

The model includes various input parameter values. For example, in order to generate the balance sheet, the model needs to input beginning balances of various asset, liability, and fund balance accounts. These input and parameter values are supplied by management.

Model Specification

Once we define various variables and input parameters for our financial model, we must then specify a set of mathematical and logical relationships linking the input variables to the performance variables. The relationships usually fall into two types of equations: definition equations and behavioral equations. Definitional equations take the form of accounting identities. Behavioral equations involve theories or hypotheses about the behavior of certain economic and financial events. They must be empirically tested and validated before they are incorporated into the financial model.

Definitional Equations

Definitional equations are exactly what the term refers to—mathematical or accounting definitions. Definitional equations are fundamental definitions in accounting for the balance sheet and statement of activities, respectively. For example,

$$\text{Surplus} = \text{Revenues} - \text{Expenses}$$
$$\text{Cash} = \text{Cash}(-1) + \text{CR} + \text{Debt} - \text{CD} - \text{LP}$$

which is a typical cash equation in a financial model. It states that ending cash balance (Cash) is equal to the beginning cash balance (Cash(−1)) plus cash receipts (CR) plus borrowings (Debt) minus cash disbursements (CD) minus loan payments (LP).

Behavioral Equations

Behavioral equations describe the behavior of the NPO regarding the specific activities that are subject to empirical testing and validation. For example, donations and contributions (DC) may be a function of such variables as gross domestic product (GDP), promotional efforts (PE), interest rates (I), competition (C), community support (CS), and number of volunteers (NV). Symbolically,

$$DC = f\,(\text{GDP}, PE, I, C, CS, NV, \text{etc.})$$

Assuming linear relationship among these variables, we can specify the model as follows:

$$DC = a + b\text{GDP} + cPE + dI + eC + fCS + gNV$$

With the data on DC, GDP, PE, I, C, CS, and NV, we will be able to estimate parameter values a, b, c, d, e, and f, using linear regression. We can test the statistical significance of each of the parameter estimates and evaluate the overall explanatory power of the model, measured by the t statistic and R squared, respectively.

This way we will be able to identify most influential factors that affect the donation and contribution for an NPO. With the best model chosen, nonprofit managers can simulate the effects of alternative promotional strategies on donations and contributions. We can also experiment with alternative assumptions regarding the external economic factors such as GDP and competition.

A "What-If" Model for College Planning

The following example shows a simple financial model for the instructional program for a college.

EXAMPLE 13.16[1]

This model puts together the relationships of important instructional variables for a college. The equations are developed in accordance with the college's policies regarding section sizes, faculty salaries and workloads, the number of nonteaching faculty, and other expenses. Two "what-if" scenarios are addressed:

    1. How much tuition and fees should the college charge for it to break even? The spreadsheet simulation, shown below, indicates that the college should charge $8,891, at which amount the revenues available for instruction equal the costs of instruction.

A "What-If" Model for College Planning

Name and Symbol	Initial Value
Tuition and fees per student (TF)	?
Number of students (NS)	1,550
Other revenue available for instruction such as endowment (OR)	$ 400,000
Instruction cost other than faculty compensation (IC)	$7,993,000
Number of courses per student per semester (NC)	5
Average number of students per section (ANS)	24.3
Number of sections offered (NSO)	323
Number of FTE teaching faculty (NF)	107.8
Number of FTE nonteaching faculty such as sabbaticals and leave (NFN)	12.3
Average compensation per faculty (AC)	$ 51,525
Number of sections per teaching faculty (NSF)	3

Planning Model	Results
$NSO = (NS \times NC)/ANS$	318.93
$NF = NSO/NSF$	107.7
$TE = AC \times (NF + NFN) + IC$	$14,181,152.50

Decision Analysis	Results
1. $TF = (TE - OR)/NS$	8891

2. Assuming that tuition is set at \$8,250 by the trustees, what is the number of enrollments required for the college to break even? The spreadsheet simulation below indicates 1,670 students.

Name and Symbol	Initial Value
Tuition and fees per student (TF)	\$ 8,250
Number of students (NS)	1572
Other revenue available for instruction such as endowment (OR)	\$ 400,000
Instruction cost other than faculty compensation (IC)	\$7,993,000
Number of courses per student per semester (NC)	5
Average number of students per section (ANS)	24.3
Number of sections offered (NSO)	323
Number of FTE teaching faculty (NF)	107.8
Number of FTE nonteaching faculty such as sabbaticals and leave (NFN)	12.3
Average compensation per faculty (AC)	\$ 51,525
Number of sections per teaching faculty (NSF)	3
Total expenses (TE)	?

Planning Model	Results
$NSO = (NS \times NC)/ANS$	323.46
$NF = NSO/NSF$	107.67
$TE = AC \times (NF + NFN) + IC$	\$14,181,152.50

Decision Analysis	Results
2. $NS = (TE - OR)/TF$	1670

A model such as this could be used to answer a variety of "what-if" scenarios by changing the parameters in the model or by changing the college's policy regarding faculty workloads, salaries, section sizes, or any combination of these. Examples include:

1. If we increase the course offerings, by how much would tuition have to be increased?

2. What would happen if we increase the number of students by 15 percent?

3. What would happen to average faculty compensation if we reduced (a) the number of sections by, say, 10 percent; (b) the number of nonteaching faculty by 10 percent, or; (c) nonfaculty instruction costs by 10 percent?

Financial models can be complicated and detailed enough to quantify the NPO's policy decisions and require policymakers to determine which variables are policy-driven and which can be formula- or equation-driven. Computer-based models for a variety of NPOs are being developed and spreadsheet packages can be utilized to tailor the NPO's management and policy needs.

HOFPLAN for Hospitals

Some hospitals use a model called "HOFPLAN." This model is capable to compute:

1. Fees by class of patient.
2. Direct costs and charges by cost center.
3. Reimbursements by financial class.
4. Financial statements.

Based on specific assumptions such as the type of patient, the length of stay, unit variable costs, total fixed costs, units of service for each cost center, the allocation method, growth rates, seasonal patterns, the endowment revenue, bad debts, and depreciation, hospitals can quickly see the "bottom-line impact" of varying any of these assumptions.

ENDNOTE

1. This example is largely based on Robert N. Anthony, and David W. Yound, *Management Control in Nonprofit Organizations* (Burr Ridge, IL: Irwin, 1994), pp. 447–49.

Glossary of Nonprofit Financial Management Terms

ACCRUAL METHOD OF ACCOUNTING   The recognition of revenue when earned and expenses when incurred.

ACTIVITY-BASED COSTING (ABC)   A costing system which traces costs first to activities and then to services. It separates overhead costs into overhead cost pools, where each cost pool is associated with a different cost driver. Then a predetermined overhead rate is computed for each cost pool and each cost driver. In consequence, this method has enhanced service costing accuracy.

ADMINISTRATIVE BUDGET   A formal and comprehensive financial plan through which management of an NPO may control day to day affairs and activities.

AGENCY FUND   The assets held in a fund under an agency relationship for another entity. For example, it consists of resources retained by ABC NPO as an agent for DEF NPO governmental unit.

ALLOTMENT   The part of an appropriation that may be encumbered or expended during an allotment period, which is usually a period of time less than one fiscal year. Bimonthly and quarterly allotment periods are most common.

ANALYSIS OF VARIANCES   The analysis and investigation of causes for variances between standard costs and actual costs; also called "variance analysis." A variance is considered favorable if actual costs are less than standard costs; it is unfavorable if actual costs exceed standard costs. Unfavorable variances are the ones that need further investigation for their causes. Analyses of variances reveal the causes of these deviations. This feedback aids in planning future goals, controlling costs, evaluating performance, and taking corrective action. Management by exception is based on the analysis of variances and attention is given to only the variances that require remedial actions.

ANNUAL BUDGET   A budget prepared for a calendar or fiscal year. See also *Long-Range Budget*.

APPORTIONMENT   The allocation of state or federal aid, district taxes, or other monies among NPOs.

APPROPRIATION   The authorization of a governmental unit to spend money within specified restrictions such as amount, time period, and objective.There must be prior approval for such expenditure through agreements or legislation.

ASSESSED VALUATION   The value placed upon personal or real property by a governmental unit for taxation purposes.

BALANCED BUDGET   A budget in which total expenditures equal total revenue. An entity has a budget surplus if expenditures are less than tax revenues. It has a budget deficit if expenditures are greater than tax revenues.

BANKRUPTCY   A situation in which an entity's liabilities exceed the fair value of its assets.

BENEFIT/COST ANALYSIS   See *Cost/Benefit Analysis*.

301

BEQUEST   A conditional pledge based on some uncertain future event that must occur.

BOND FUND   A fund established for the receipt and distribution of monies received from the issuance of a bond.

BONDED DEBT SERVICE   The expenses incurred for interest and redemption of bonds.

BREAK-EVEN ANALYSIS   A branch of cost-volume-revenue (CVR) analysis that determines the break-even revenues, which is the level of activity where total costs equal total revenue. See also *Cost-Volume-Revenue Analysis.*

BUDGET   A quantitative plan of financial operation consisting of an estimate of proposed revenue and expenditures for a specified time period and purpose. The budget expresses the organizational goals in terms of specific financial and operating objectives. Advantages of budget preparation are planning, communicating entitywide goals to subunits, fostering cooperation between departments, exerting control by evaluating actual figures to budget figures, and revealing the interrelationship of one function to another. See also *Master Budget.*

BUDGET CONTROL   The budgetary actions carried out according to a budget plan. Through the use of a budget as a standard, an organization ensures that managers are implementing its plans and objectives and their activities are appraised by comparing their actual performance against budgeted performance. Budgets are used as a basis for rewarding or punishing them, or perhaps for modifying future budgets and plans.

BUDGET VARIANCE   Any difference between a budgeted figure and an actual figure.

BUDGETARY ACCOUNTABILITY   The process of recording budgetary amounts in the accounts of a fund. Recording the balances has a dual effect. The control aspect of the budgetary function is stressed and recognition is given to the legal foundations of the budget.

BUDGETING MODELS   Mathematical models that generate a surplus planning budget. The models help budget analysts answer a variety of "what-if" questions. The resultant calculations provide a basis for choice among alternatives under conditions of uncertainty. Budgeting models are usually quantitative and computer-based. There are primarily two approaches to modeling: simulation and optimization. See also *Financial Models; Simulation Models.*

CAPITAL BUDGET   A budget or plan of proposed acquisitions and replacements of long-term assets and their financing. A capital budget is developed using a variety of capital budgeting techniques such as the payback method, the net present value (NPV) method, or the internal rate of return (IRR) method. See also *Capital Budgeting.*

CAPITAL BUDGETING   The process of making long-term planning decisions for capital investments. There are typically two types of investment decisions: (1) Selecting new facilities or expanding existing facilities. Examples include: (*a*) investments in long-term assets such as property and equipment; and (*b*) resource commitments in the form of new service development, market research, refunding of long-term debt, or introduction of a computer network. (2) Replacing existing facilities with new facilities. An example is replacing obsolete office equipment with new equipment.

CAPITAL CAMPAIGN   Large donations usually restricted by major donors to construct a facility (e.g., a hospital wing).

CAPITAL EXPENDITURE BUDGET   A budget plan prepared for individual capital expenditure projects. The time span of this budget depends upon the project. Capital expenditures to be budgeted include replacement, acquisition, or construction of facilities and major equipment. See also *Capital Budgeting*.

CAPITAL PROJECTS FUND   A fund that accounts for financial resources to be used for the acquisition or construction of facilities.

CAPITAL RATIONING   A problem of selecting the mix of acceptable projects that provides the highest overall net present value (NPV) where an entity has a limit on the budget for capital spending. The profitability index is used widely in ranking projects competing for limited funds.

CARRYING COSTS   The costs incurred in maintaining an inventory, including storage and handling costs.

CASH BUDGET   A budget for cash planning and control presenting expected cash inflow and outflow for a designated time period. The cash budget helps management keep cash balances in reasonable relationship to its needs. It aids in avoiding idle cash and possible cash shortages.

CASH FLOW   (1) Cash receipts minus cash disbursements from a given operation or asset for a given period. "Cash flow" and "cash inflow" are often used interchangeably. (2) The monetary value of the expected benefits and costs of a project. It may be in the form of cash savings in operating costs or the difference between additional dollars received and additional dollars paid out for a given period.

CASH-FLOW STATEMENT   A statement showing what sources of cash have come into the NPO and what the cash has been spent on. Cash flow is broken down into operating, investing, and financing activities.

CHIEF FINANCIAL OFFICER (CFO)   The number one financial officer of an NPO. He or she is a vice president of finance.

COEFFICIENT OF DETERMINATION   A statistical measure of how good the estimated regression equation is. Simply put, it is a measure of "goodness of fit" in the regression.

COLA   An acronym for "cost of living allowance."

COLLECTION PERIOD   The number of days it takes to collect receivables; 365 days divided by the receivables turnover.

COLLEGE FUNDS   The funds set up for college and university accounting, consisting of current funds, loan funds, endowment funds, annuity and life funds, agency funds, and plant funds.

COMMON COSTS   A cost shared by different departments, programs, or activities. Also called "joint costs" or "indirect costs."

COMPREHENSIVE BUDGET   See *Master Budget*.

CONTINUOUS BUDGET   An annual budget which continues to the earliest one month or period and adds the most recent one month or period, so that a twelve-month or other periodic forecast is always available.

CONTRIBUTION   The price per unit less variable cost per unit.

CONTRIBUTION MARGIN (CM)   The difference between revenue and the variable costs of the project or service, also called marginal income. The amount of money available to cover fixed cost to generate surplus.

CONTROL CONCEPT   A concept that ensures that actions are carried out or implemented according to a plan or goal.

COST/BENEFIT ANALYSIS   An analysis to determine whether the favorable results of an alternative are sufficient to justify the cost of taking that alternative. This analysis is widely used in connecting with capital expenditure projects.

COST-VOLUME FORMULA   The cost function in the form of $Y = a + bX$, where $Y =$ semivariable (or mixed) costs to be broken up, $X =$ any given measure of activity such as volume and labor hours, $a =$ fixed cost component, and $b =$ variable rate per unit of X. The formula is used for cost prediction and flexible budgeting purposes.

COST-VOLUME-REVENUE (CVR) ANALYSIS   An analysis that deals with how revenue and costs change with a change in volume. More specifically, it looks at the effects on surplus or deficit of changes in such factors as variable costs, fixed costs, fees, volume, and mix of services rendered. By studying the relationships of costs, revenue, and activity, an NPO is better able to cope with many planning decisions.

COST CENTER   The unit within the organization in which the manager is responsible only for costs. A cost center has no control over the generating of revenue.

COST CONTROL   The steps taken by management to assure that the cost objectives set down in the planning stage are attained, and to assure that all segments of the organization function in a manner consistent with its policies. For effective cost control, most organizations use standard cost systems, in which the actual costs are compared against standard costs for performance evaluation and the deviations are investigated for remedial actions. Cost control is also concerned with feedback that might change any or all of the future plans, the method of delivery services, or both.

COST DRIVER   A factor that causes a cost item to be incurred (e.g., labor-hours, number of patient-days, or number of inspections).

COST-EFFECTIVE PROGRAM   Among decision alternatives, the one whose cost is lower than its benefit. The most cost-effective program is the one whose cost/benefit ratio is the lowest among various programs competing for a given amount of funds. See also *Cost/Benefit Analysis.*

COST MANAGEMENT   A system that measures the cost of significant activities, recognizes non-value-added costs, and identifies activities that will improve overall performance.

COST POOL   A group of related costs that are assigned together to a set of cost objectives (such as services, programs, or activities).

CURRENT RATIO   Current assets divided by current liabilities.

DECISION SUPPORT SYSTEM (DSS)   A branch of the broadly defined management information system (MIS). An information system that provides answers to problems and integrates the decision maker into the system as a component. The system utilizes such quantitative techniques as regression and financial planning modeling. DSS software furnishes support to the managers in the decision-making process.

DEFICIT   The excess of liabilities over assets.

DEFICIT SPENDING   The excess of actual expenditures over actual revenue, also called an "operating deficit."

DISCOUNTED CASH-FLOW (DCF) TECHNIQUES   Methods of selecting and ranking investment proposals, such as the net present value (NPV) and internal rate of return (IRR) methods where time value of money is taken into account.

DISCRETIONARY (FIXED) COSTS   The fixed costs that change because of managerial decisions; also called "management (fixed) costs" or "programmed (fixed) costs." Examples of this type of fixed costs are advertising outlays, training costs, and research and development costs.

DOUBTFUL PLEDGES   Pledges made but not likely to be received.

DSS   See *Decision Support System.*

ECONOMIC ORDER QUANTITY (EOQ)   The order size that should be ordered at one time to minimize the sum of carrying and ordering costs. At the EOQ amount, total ordering cost equals total carrying cost.

ENCUMBRANCES   The obligations in the form of purchase orders, contracts, and other commitments reserved for a specific purpose.

ENDOWMENT   Donated funds to be spent for a general or specific purpose.

ENDOWMENT FUNDS   Funds established to preserve the various goals (e.g., educational, charitable, cultural, and/or scientific) of the nonprofit entity.

EOQ   See *Economic Order Quantity.*

EXPENDITURES   The amounts paid or liabilities incurred for all purposes.

EXPONENTIAL SMOOTHING   A forecasting method of continually revising a forecast in the light of more recent experience.

FAVORABLE VARIANCE   The excess of standard (or budgeted) costs over actual costs. See also *Variance.*

FEE FOR SERVICE   A method of pricing nonprofit services. The price is agreed in advance, such as college tuition and Medicaid.

FINANCIAL MODELS   The functional branch of a general corporate planning model. It is essentially used to generate pro forma financial statements and financial ratios. A financial model is a mathematical model describing the interrelationships among financial variables of the entity. It is the basic tool for budgeting and budget planning. Also, it is used for risk analysis and "what-if" experiments. Many financial models are built using special modeling languages such as IFPS/Plus or spreadsheet programs such as Excel.

FINANCIAL PROJECTION   The essential element of planning that is the basis for budgeting activities and estimating future financing needs of an NPO. Financial projections (forecasts) begin with forecasting sales and their related expenses.

FIXED BUDGET   See *Static Budget.*

FLASH REPORT   A report that provides the highlights of key information promptly to the responsible managers. An example is an exception report such as performance reports that highlight favorable or unfavorable variances. A flash report allows managers to take corrective action for an unfavorable variance.

FLEXIBLE (VARIABLE) BUDGET   A budget based on different levels of activity; an extremely useful tool for comparing the actual cost incurred to the cost allowable for the activity level achieved. It is dynamic in nature rather than static.

FLEXIBLE BUDGET FORMULA   See *Cost-Volume Formula*.

FORECAST   (1) A projection or an estimate of revenue, surplus, or costs. (2) A projection of future financial position and operating results of an organization. See also *Financial Projection*.

FORM 990   A U.S. IRS tax form (Return of Organization Exempt from Income Tax) to be filed by nonprofits under section 501(C) of the IRS Code.

FORM 990-EZ   A simplified U.S. IRS form 990 for use by an NPO with gross receipts less than $100,000 for the year and total assets less than $250,000 at the end of the year.

FORM 990-T   An exempt organization business income tax return. U.S. IRS form.

FORM 990-W   A U.S. IRS form for reporting estimated tax on unrelated business taxable income, for tax-exempt organizations.

FORM 1041   A U.S. IRS income tax return to be filed by estates and trusts.

FULL-TIME EQUIVALENT (FTE)   One person working full time for 52 weeks. It is computed to measure personnel expenditures uniformly.

FUND   A fiscal and accounting entity with a self-balancing set of accounts recording cash and other financial resources, together with related liabilities and residual balances, and changes therein.

FUND ACCOUNTING   A system used by nonprofit organizations. Since there is no profit motive, accountability is measured instead of profitability.

FUND BALANCES   See *Net Assets*.

GENERAL FUND   A primary operating fund of a governmental unit.

GOAL SEEKING   A situation in which a manager wishes to determine what change would have to take place in the value of a specified variable in a specified time period to achieve a specified value for another variable.

GOVERNMENT ACCOUNTING STANDARD BOARD (GASB)   An organization that formulates accounting and budgeting standards for governmental units.

ILLIQUID   (1) Lacking enough liquid assets, like cash and marketable securities, to cover short-term obligations. (2) Having current liabilities exceed current assets.

INCOME   Revenue and nonrevenue receipts.

INCREMENTAL BUDGET   A budget in which next year's budget will differ little from this year's budget and line item adjustments are made on a straight percentage basis.

INDIRECT PUBLIC SUPPORT   Contributions received indirectly from the public conducted by federated fund-raising agencies and similar fund raising organizations such as the United Way.

INSOLVENCY   The failure of an entity to meet its obligations as they become due. An analysis of insolvency concentrates on the operating and capital structure of the agency. The proportion of long-term debt in the financing structure must also be considered.

INTERNAL CONTROL   The segregation of duties; the safeguarding of assets and of the accuracy of accounting records.

INTERNAL RATE OF RETURN (IRR)   The rate earned on a proposal. The rate of interest that equates the initial investment (I) with the present value (PV) of future cash inflows.

INVENTORY TURNOVER   The number of times inventory is sold during the year. It equals cost of goods sold divided by the average dollar balance. Average inventory equals the beginning and ending balances divided by two.

INVESTMENT CENTER   A responsibility center within an organization that has control over revenue, cost, and investment funds. A profit center whose performance is evaluated on the basis of the return earned on invested capital.

JUDGMENTAL FORECAST   A forecasting method that brings together in an organized way personal judgments about the process being analyzed.

JUST-IN-TIME (JIT) SYSTEM   A demand-pull system where demand for customer output (not plans for using input resources) triggers production. Production activities are "pulled," not "pushed," into action. JIT, in its purest sense, is buying and producing in very small quantities just in time for use.

LEAD TIME   The time (usually measured in days) required for inventory to arrive after an order is placed.

LEAST-SQUARED METHOD   A method of fitting a trend line which minimizes the sum of the squares of the errors between the estimated points on the trend line and the actual observed points that were used to fit the line.

LINE ITEM BUDGET   A budget typically used by NPOs in which budgeted financial statement elements are grouped by administrative entities and object. These budget item groups are usually presented in an incremental fashion that is in comparison to previous periods.

LIQUIDITY   The ability of current assets to meet current liabilities when due.

LONG-RANGE BUDGET   The projections that cover more than one fiscal year; also called "strategic budgeting." The five-year budget plan is the most commonly used in practice. See also *Annual Budget*.

MANAGEMENT BY EXCEPTION   The management concept or policy by which management devotes its time to investigating only those situations in which actual results differ significantly from planned results. The idea is that management should spend its valuable time concentrating on the more important items (such as the shaping of the entity's future strategic course).

MANAGEMENT BY OBJECTIVES (MBO)   A system of performance appraisal having the following characteristics: (1) It is a formal system in that each manager is required to take certain prescribed actions and to complete certain written documents. (2) The manager and subordinates discuss the subordinate's job description, agree to short-term performance targets, discuss the progress made toward meeting these targets, and periodically evaluate the performance and provide the feedback.

MANAGEMENT CONTROL SYSTEM A system under which managers assure that resources are obtained and used effectively and efficiently in the accomplishment of the organization's goals.

MANAGEMENT INFORMATION SYSTEM (MIS) A computer-based system which transforms data into information useful in the support of decision making.

MASTER (COMPREHENSIVE) BUDGET A plan of activities expressed in monetary terms of the assets, fund balance, revenues, and costs which will be involved in carrying out the plans. Simply put, a master budget is a set of projected or planned financial statements.

MISSION CENTER A responsibility center in an NPO that contributes directly to the objectives of the NPO. An example is the curatorial department in a museum.

MIXED COSTS The costs that vary with changes in volume but, unlike variable costs, do not vary in direct proportion; also called "semivariable costs." Examples are telephone and electric bills.

MODEL A mathematical abstract of a real-life system.

MOVING AVERAGE An average that is updated as new information becomes available.

MULTIPLE REGRESSION ANALYSIS A statistical procedure that attempts to assess the relationship between the dependent variable and two or more independent variables. For example, funds raised are related to such explanatory factors as the number of prospective donors, advertising, and fund-raising events.

NAIVE MODELS A group of forecasting techniques that assume that recent periods are the best predictors of the future.

NEGATIVE CASH FLOW A situation in which cash inflows are less than cash outflows. This is an unfavorable situation because it may result in liquidity problems.

NET ASSETS Total assets minus total liabilities; also called "fund balances."

NET PRESENT VALUE (NPV) The difference between the present value (PV) of cash inflows generated by the project and the amount of the initial investment (I).

NET PRESENT VALUE METHOD A method widely used for evaluating investment projects. Under the net present value method, the present value (PV) of all cash inflows from the project is compared against the initial investment (I).

NONCASH CONTRIBUTIONS Contributions made other than in cash, including donations of equipment, real estate, securities, and services.

NONDUES REVENUE Revenue other than membership dues, such as grants and gifts.

NONREVENUE RECEIPTS The receipts of money in exchange for property of the entity or for which the entity incurs an obligation.

NPO An abbreviation for "nonprofit organization."

OBJECT As used in an expenditure classification, a term that applies to the item purchased or the service obtained.

OPPORTUNITY COST The net benefit forgone by rejecting an alternative. There is always an opportunity cost involved in making a choice decision. It is a cost incurred relative to the alternative given up.

ORDERING COSTS   The costs of getting an item into the inventory; these costs are incurred each time an order is placed. An example is the cost of processing an order.

OUT-OF-POCKET COSTS   The actual cash outlays made during the period for payroll, advertising, and other operating expenses. Depreciation is not an out-of-pocket cost, since it involves no current cash expenditure.

PAYBACK PERIOD   The number of years it takes to recover your initial investment. The payback period equals the initial investment divided by the annual cash inflow.

PERFORMANCE BUDGET   A medium- to short-range budget used by NPOs. It is typical of the type incorporated by a program planning budgeting system (PPBS) but without reference to long-range goals.

PLANNED GIVING   Gifts to be made to nonprofit organizations in the form of wills and bequests and as a beneficiary of the donor's life insurance policy.

PLANNING   The selection of short- and long-term objectives and the drawing up of tactical and strategic plans to achieve those objectives. In planning, managers outline the steps to be taken in moving the organization toward its objectives. After deciding on a set of strategies to be followed, the organization needs more specific plans, such as locations, methods of financing, hours of operations, and so on. As these plans are made, they will be communicated throughout the organization. When implemented, the plans will serve to coordinate, or meld together, the efforts of all parts of the organization toward the entity's objectives.

PRESENT VALUE   The current worth of future sums of money.

PROFITABILITY INDEX   The ratio of the total present value of future cash inflows to the initial investment.

PROGRAM   A group of related activities that consists of a unique combination of objects that operate together to achieve common goals.

PROGRAM SERVICE   A major (usually ongoing) objective of an organization such as adoptions, recreation for the elderly, rehabilitation, or publication of journals or newsletters. It can also include the entity's unrelated trade or business activities whose income is taxable.

PROGRAM SERVICE REVENUE   Revenue from services that form the basis of an organization's exemption from tax; also called "exempt function income." Examples are tuition received by a school, and revenue from admissions to a concert or another performing arts event.

PROGRAM-PLANNING-BUDGETING SYSTEM (PPBS)   A planning-oriented approach to developing a program budget. A program budget is a budget wherein expenditures are based primarily on programs of work and secondarily on character and object. It is a transitional type of budget between the traditional character and object budget, on the one hand, and the performance budget on the other. The major contribution of PPBS lies in the planning process, that is, the process of making program policy decisions that lead to a specific budget and specific multi-year plans.

PROGRAM-RELATED INVESTMENT INCOME   Income generated from investments made to accomplish an exempt purpose of the investing entity rather than to produce income. Examples are scholarship loans, low-interest loans to charitable organizations, and aid to victims of a disaster.

PROJECTED (BUDGETED) FUND STATEMENT   A schedule for expected assets, liabilities, and fund balance. It projects an entity's financial position as of the end of the budgeting year. Reasons for preparing a budgeted balance sheet are that it (1) discloses unfavorable financial conditions that management may want to avoid, (2) serves as a final check on the mathematical accuracy of all other budgets, and (3) highlights future resources and obligations.

PROJECTED (BUDGETED) STATEMENT OF INCOME AND EXPENDITURES   A summary of various component projections of income and expenditures for the budget period. It indicates the expected surplus or deficit for the period.

RATE OF RETURN ON INVESTMENT (ROI)   (1) For the agency as a whole, net surplus after taxes divided by invested capital. (2) For the segment of an organization, net operating surplus divided by operating assets. (3) For capital budgeting purposes (also called "simple," "accounting," or "unadjusted rate of return"), expected future net surplus divided by initial (or average) investment.

REGRESSION ANALYSIS   A statistical procedure for mathematically estimating the average relationship between the dependent variable (revenue, for example) and one or more independent variables (price and advertising, for example).

RELEVANT COSTS   Expected future costs, which will differ between the alternatives being considered.

REORDER POINT   The inventory level at which it is appropriate to replenish stock.

RESIDUAL   The difference between an actual value and its forecast value, also called an "error" or a "deviation."

RESPONSIBILITY ACCOUNTING   The collection, summarization, and reporting of financial information about various decision centers (responsibility centers) throughout an organization; also called "activity accounting."

RESPONSIBILITY CENTER   A unit in the organization that has control over costs, revenues, or investment funds. For accounting purposes, responsibility centers are classified as cost centers, revenue centers, profit centers, and investment centers, depending on what each center is responsible for.

RESTRICTED REVENUE   Monies that are received with some strings attached.

REVENUE   An addition to assets for which no obligations are incurred. Income derived from rendering services or selling a product.

REVENUE BUDGET   An operating plan for a period expressed in terms of activity volume and fees for each class of service. The preparation of a revenue budget is the starting point in budgeting since revenue influences nearly all other items.

REVENUE FORECASTING   The projection or prediction of future revenue. The foundation for the quantification of the entire business plan and a master budget. Revenue forecasts serve as a basis for planning.

SECTION 501(C)   The IRS Code under which nonprofit organizations are organized. Section 501(C) entities are exempt from federal and usually from state income taxes.

SEGMENTED REPORTING   The process of reporting activities of various segments of an organization such as divisions, departments, service lines, or service territories.

SENSITIVITY ANALYSIS   A form of simulation that enables decision makers to experiment with decision alternatives using a "what-if" approach. The manager might wish to evaluate alternative policies and assumptions about the external environment by asking a series of "what-if" questions. See also *Simulation*.

SERVICE CENTER   A responsibility center in an NPO that contributes to the work of other responsibility centers. An example is the personnel department in a museum.

SIMPLE REGRESSION   A regression analysis which involves one independent variable. For example, total factory overhead is related to one activity variable (either direct labor-hours or machine-hours).

SIMULATION   An attempt to represent a real-life system via a model, to determine how a change in one or more variables affects the rest of the system; also called "what-if" analysis. See also *Financial Models; Simulation Models*.

SIMULATION MODELS   "What-if" models that attempt to simulate the effects of alternative management policies and assumptions about the entity's external environment. They are basically a tool for management's laboratory.

SITE-ORIENTED BUDGETING   A budgeting method in which emphasis is placed on differences among sites, such as schools, rather than on differences among programs.

STATEMENT OF FUNCTIONAL EXPENSES   A statement of an organization's expenses designated by object classifications (e.g., legal fees, salaries, and supplies). These expenses are allocated into three functions: program services, management and general, and fund raising.

STATEMENT OF REVENUE, EXPENSES, AND CHANGES IN NET ASSETS, OR FUND BALANCES   A required financial statement of NPOs showing operating performance.

STATIC (FIXED) BUDGET   A budget based on one level of activity (e.g., one particular volume of sales or production).

STEP METHOD   The method of support cost allocation that allows for partial recognition of services rendered by support departments to other support departments.

STEP-DOWN ALLOCATION METHOD   See *Step Method*.

STRATEGIC PLANNING   The implementation of an organization's objectives. Strategic planning decisions will have long-term impacts on the organization, while operational decisions are day-to-day in nature.

SURPLUS-VOLUME CHART   A chart that determines how surpluses vary with changes in volume.

SYNERGY   A merger of comparable NPOs resulting in operational efficiencies and cost reduction such as by eliminating duplication. Synergy is the idea that "two plus two is greater than four."

TIME VALUE OF MONEY   The value of money at different time periods. As a rule, $1 today is worth more than $1 tomorrow. The time value of money is a critical consideration in financial decisions.

TOTAL QUALITY CONTROL (TQC)   A quality program in which the goal is complete elimination of service deficiencies.

TOTAL QUALITY MANAGEMENT (TQM)   The application of quality principles and concepts to all the organization's efforts to satisfy customers.

TRANSFER   The interfund payments or receipts not chargeable to expenditures or credited to income.

TREND   The movement and direction of an item over time.

TREND LINE   A line fitted to sets of data points, which describes the relationship between time and the dependent variable.

TURNOVER   The number of times an asset, such as inventory or receivables, turns over during an accounting period.

UNAPPROPRIATED FUND BALANCE   The portion of a fund balance not segregated for specific purposes.

UNENCUMBERED BALANCE   The portion of an appropriation or allotment not yet expended or obligated.

UNRELATED BUSINESS INCOME TAX (UBIT)   Tax imposed under section 1.511 of the IRS regulation on revenues from a trade or business, which a nonprofit entity constantly carries on and which is unrelated to the tax-exempt purposes of the entity.

UNRESTRICTED REVENUE   Monies on which the grantor has tied no strings on how the money may be spent.

VARIABLE BUDGET   See *Flexible Budget*.

VARIANCE   The difference of revenues, costs, and surplus from planned amounts. One of the most important phases of responsibility accounting is establishing standards in costs, revenues, and surplus and establishing performance by comparing actual amounts with the standard amounts. The differences (variances) are calculated for each responsibility center, and analyzed. Unfavorable variances are investigated for possible remedial action.

VOLUME-BASED COST DRIVER   A cost driver that is based on service volume, such as labor-hours or units of service.

WEIGHTED AVERAGE   An average of revenue, costs, and net assets giving more weight to the most recent years.

"WHAT-IF" ANALYSIS   See *Simulation*.

ZERO-BASE BUDGETING   A planning and budgeting tool that uses cost/benefit analysis of projects and functions to improve resource allocation in an organization. Traditional budgeting tends to concentrate on the incremental change from the previous year. It assumes that the previous year's activities and programs are essential and must be continued. Under zero-base budgeting, however, cost and benefit estimates are built up from scratch, from the zero level, and must be justified.

Tax Return Requirements and Filing

A nonprofit organization (NPO) does not typically pay income tax or property tax. However, it must file information returns with the IRS and the applicable state tax agency. With a few exceptions, all exempt organizations (except private foundations) must prepare Form 990. Estimated taxes may have to be paid quarterly.

IRS FORM 990

IRS Form 990 (Return of Organization Exempt from Income Tax) must be filed yearly. (However, smaller NPOs may omit certain sections.) It is due the fifteenth day of the fifth month following the year-end. An extension of time to file may be made with IRS Form 2758. If not filed on time, a penalty will be assessed.

IRS Form 990 includes the following information:

- List of officers, directors, and trustees.
- Balance at beginning and end of year.
- Itemization of revenue and expenses by major activity and/or program such as by fund raising.
- Description of activities.

Table B.1 presents IRS Form 990.

Schedule A to Form 990 must also be filed for all 501(c)(3) publicly supported NPOs. Schedule A appears in Table B.2. Form 990-EZ is a short form to be filed by NPOs with gross receipts less than $100,000 and total assets less than $250,000 at year-end. Table B.3 presents Form 990-EZ.

Form 990-PF must be filed by private foundations. A copy appears in Table B.4. Most NPOs having "unrelated business" income must file Form 990-T (Exempt Organization Business Income Tax Return). Table B.5 presents this form. College fraternities are nonprofit entities under IRS guidelines but must pay tax on income earned and not contributed over 15 percent. They cannot receive more than 35 percent of their income from nonmembers (e.g., renters, summer boarders).

TABLE B.1

Form **990**	**Return of Organization Exempt From Income Tax**	OMB No. 1545-0047
Department of the Treasury	Under section 501(c) of the Internal Revenue Code (except black lung benefit trust or private foundation) or section 4947(a)(1) nonexempt charitable trust	**19 94**
Internal Revenue Service	Note: *The organization may have to use a copy of this return to satisfy state reporting requirements.*	This Form is Open to Public Inspection

A For the 1994 calendar year, OR tax year period beginning _____ , 1994, and ending _____ , 19___

B Check if: ☐ Change of address ☐ Initial return ☐ Final return ☐ Amended return (required also for State reporting)	Please use IRS label or print or type. See Specific Instructions.	C Name of organization	D Employer identification number
		Number and street (or P.O. box if mail is not delivered to street address) Room/suite	E State registration number
		City, town, or post office, state, and ZIP code	F Check ▶ ☐ if exemption application is pending

G Type of organization—▶ ☐ Exempt under section 501(c)( ) ◀ (insert number) OR ▶ ☐ section 4947(a)(1) nonexempt charitable trust

Note: *Section 501(c)(3) exempt organizations and 4947(a)(1) nonexempt charitable trusts MUST attach a completed Schedule A (Form 990).*

H(a) Is this a group return filed for affiliates? . . . . ☐ Yes ☐ No

(b) If "Yes," enter the number of affiliates for which this return is filed:. . ▶ _____

(c) Is this a separate return filed by an organization covered by a group ruling? ☐ Yes ☐ No

I If either box in H is checked "Yes," enter four-digit group exemption number (GEN) ▶ ....

J Accounting method: ☐ Cash ☐ Accrual ☐ Other (specify) ▶ _____

K Check here ▶ ☐ if the organization's gross receipts are normally not more than $25,000. The organization need not file a return with the IRS; but if it received a Form 990 Package in the mail, it should file a return without financial data. **Some states require a complete return.**

Note: *Form 990-EZ may be used by organizations with gross receipts less than $100,000 and total assets less than $250,000 at end of year.*

Part I   Statement of Revenue, Expenses, and Changes in Net Assets or Fund Balances

1	Contributions, gifts, grants, and similar amounts received:					
a	Direct public support		1a			
b	Indirect public support		1b			
c	Government contributions (grants)		1c			
d	**Total** (add lines 1a through 1c) (attach schedule—see instructions) (cash $ _____ noncash $ _____)				1d	
2	Program service revenue including government fees and contracts (from Part VII, line 93)				2	
3	Membership dues and assessments (see instructions)				3	
4	Interest on savings and temporary cash investments				4	
5	Dividends and interest from securities				5	
6a	Gross rents		6a			
b	Less: rental expenses		6b			
c	Net rental income or (loss) (subtract line 6b from line 6a)				6c	
7	Other investment income (describe ▶)				7	
8a	Gross amount from sale of assets other than inventory	(A) Securities	8a	(B) Other		
b	Less: cost or other basis and sales expenses.		8b			
c	Gain or (loss) (attach schedule)		8c			
d	Net gain or (loss) (combine line 8c, columns (A) and (B))				8d	
9	Special events and activities (attach schedule—see instructions):					
a	Gross revenue (not including $ _____ of contributions reported on line 1a)		9a			
b	Less: direct expenses other than fundraising expenses .		9b			
c	Net income or (loss) from special events (subtract line 9b from line 9a)				9c	
10a	Gross sales of inventory, less returns and allowances . .		10a			
b	Less: cost of goods sold		10b			
c	Gross profit or (loss) from sales of inventory (attach schedule) (subtract line 10b from line 10a) .				10c	
11	Other revenue (from Part VII, line 103)				11	
12	**Total revenue** (add lines 1d, 2, 3, 4, 5, 6c, 7, 8d, 9c, 10c, and 11)				12	
13	Program services (from line 44, column (B)—see instructions)				13	
14	Management and general (from line 44, column (C)—see instructions)				14	
15	Fundraising (from line 44, column (D)—see instructions)				15	
16	Payments to affiliates (attach schedule—see instructions)				16	
17	**Total expenses** (add lines 16 and 44, column (A))				17	
18	Excess or (deficit) for the year (subtract line 17 from line 12)				18	
19	Net assets or fund balances at beginning of year (from line 74, column (A))				19	
20	Other changes in net assets or fund balances (attach explanation)				20	
21	Net assets or fund balances at end of year (combine lines 18, 19, and 20)				21	

For Paperwork Reduction Act Notice, see page 1 of the separate instructions. Cat. No. 11282Y Form **990** (1994)

T A B L E B.1—*Continued*

Form 990 (1994)   Page **2**

Part II Statement of | All organizations must complete column (A). Columns (B), (C), and (D) are required for section 501(c)(3) and (4)
            Functional Expenses | organizations and section 4947(a)(1) nonexempt charitable trusts but optional for others. (See instructions.)

Do not include amounts reported on line 6b, 8b, 9b, 10b, or 16 of Part I.		(A) Total	(B) Program services	(C) Management and general	(D) Fundraising
22	Grants and allocations (attach schedule) . . (cash $ _____ noncash $ _____)	22			
23	Specific assistance to individuals (attach schedule)	23			
24	Benefits paid to or for members (attach schedule).	24			
25	Compensation of officers, directors, etc. . .	25			
26	Other salaries and wages	26			
27	Pension plan contributions	27			
28	Other employee benefits	28			
29	Payroll taxes	29			
30	Professional fundraising fees	30			
31	Accounting fees	31			
32	Legal fees	32			
33	Supplies	33			
34	Telephone	34			
35	Postage and shipping	35			
36	Occupancy	36			
37	Equipment rental and maintenance	37			
38	Printing and publications	38			
39	Travel	39			
40	Conferences, conventions, and meetings . .	40			
41	Interest	41			
42	Depreciation, depletion, etc. (attach schedule)	42			
43	Other expenses (itemize): a	43a			
b	....	43b			
c	....	43c			
d	....	43d			
e	....	43e			
44	Total functional expenses (add lines 22 through 43) *Organizations completing columns (B)-(D), carry these totals to lines 13-15* .	44			

Reporting of Joint Costs.—Did you report in column (B) (Program services) any joint costs from a combined
educational campaign and fundraising solicitation?   . . . . ▶ ☐ Yes   ☐ No
If "Yes," enter **(i)** the aggregate amount of these joint costs $_____; **(ii)** the amount allocated to Program services $_____;
(iii) the amount allocated to Management and general $_____; and **(iv)** the amount allocated to Fundraising $_____

Part III Statement of Program Service Accomplishments (See instructions.)

		Program Service Expenses' (Required for 501(c)(3) and (4) orgs., and 4947(a)(1) trusts; but optional for others.)
	What is the organization's primary exempt purpose? ▶... All organizations must describe their exempt purpose achievements. State the number of clients served, publications issued, etc. Discuss achievements that are not measurable. (Section 501(c)(3) and (4) organizations and 4947(a)(1) nonexempt charitable trusts must also enter the amount of grants and allocations to others.)	
a	....(Grants and allocations $)	
b	....(Grants and allocations $)	
c	....(Grants and allocations $)	
d	....(Grants and allocations $)	
e	Other program services (attach schedule) (Grants and allocations $)	
f	**Total of Program Service Expenses** (should equal line 44, column (B), Program services). . . . . . ▶	

T A B L E B.1—*Continued*

Form 990 (1994)   Page **3**

Part IV. Balance Sheets

Note: *Where required, attached schedules and amounts within the description column should be for end-of-year amounts only.*

	(A) Beginning of year		(B) End of year
Assets			
45 Cash—non-interest-bearing		45	
46 Savings and temporary cash investments		46	
47a Accounts receivable 47a			
b Less: allowance for doubtful accounts 47b		47c	
48a Pledges receivable 48a			
b Less: allowance for doubtful accounts 48b		48c	
49 Grants receivable		49	
50 Receivables due from officers, directors, trustees, and key employees (attach schedule)		50	
51a Other notes and loans receivable (attach schedule) 51a			
b Less: allowance for doubtful accounts 51b		51c	
52 Inventories for sale or use		52	
53 Prepaid expenses and deferred charges		53	
54 Investments—securities (attach schedule)		54	
55a Investments—land, buildings, and equipment: basis 55a			
b Less: accumulated depreciation (attach schedule) 55b		55c	
56 Investments—other (attach schedule)		56	
57a Land, buildings, and equipment: basis 57a			
b Less: accumulated depreciation (attach schedule) 57b		57c	
58 Other assets (describe ▶ _____)		58	
59 Total assets (add lines 45 through 58) (must equal line 75)		59	
Liabilities			
60 Accounts payable and accrued expenses		60	
61 Grants payable		61	
62 Support and revenue designated for future periods (attach schedule)		62	
63 Loans from officers, directors, trustees, and key employees (attach schedule)		63	
64a Tax-exempt bond liabilities (attach schedule)		64a	
b Mortgages and other notes payable (attach schedule)		64b	
65 Other liabilities (describe ▶ _____)		65	
66 Total liabilities (add lines 60 through 65)		66	
Fund Balances or Net Assets			
Organizations that use fund accounting, check here ▶ ☐ and complete lines 67 through 70 and lines 74 and 75 (see instructions).			
67a Current unrestricted fund		67a	
b Current restricted fund		67b	
68 Land, buildings, and equipment fund		68	
69 Endowment fund		69	
70 Other funds (describe ▶ _____)		70	
Organizations that do not use fund accounting, check here ▶ ☐ and complete lines 71 through 75 (see instructions).			
71 Capital stock or trust principal		71	
72 Paid-in or capital surplus		72	
73 Retained earnings or accumulated income		73	
74 Total fund balances or net assets (add lines 67a through 70 OR lines 71 through 73; column (A) must equal line 19 and column (B) must equal line 21)		74	
75 Total liabilities and fund balances/net assets (add lines 66 and 74)		75	

Form 990 is available for public inspection and, for some people, serves as the primary or sole source of information about a particular organization. How the public perceives an organization in such cases may be determined by the information presented on its return. Therefore, please make sure the return is complete and accurate and fully describes the organization's programs and accomplishments.

T A B L E B.1—*Continued*

Part V List of Officers, Directors, Trustees, and Key Employees (List each one even if not compensated; see instructions.)

(A) Name and address	(B) Title and average hours per week devoted to position	(C) Compensation (if not paid, enter -0-)	(D) Contributions to employee benefit plans & deferred compensation	(E) Expense account and other allowances

Did any officer, director, trustee, or key employee receive aggregate compensation of more than $100,000 from your organization and all related organizations, of which more than $10,000 was provided by the related organizations?. ▶ ☐ Yes ☐ No
If "Yes," attach schedule—see instructions.

Part VI Other Information		Yes	No
76	Did the organization engage in any activity not previously reported to the IRS? If "Yes," attach a detailed description of each activity.	76	
77	Were any changes made in the organizing or governing documents, but not reported to the IRS? . . .	77	
	If "Yes," attach a conformed copy of the changes.		
78a	Did the organization have unrelated business gross income of $1,000 or more during the year covered by this return?	78a	
b	If "Yes," has it filed a tax return on Form 990-T, Exempt Organization Business Income Tax Return, for this year?	78b	
79	Was there a liquidation, dissolution, termination, or substantial contraction during the year? If "Yes," attach a statement; see instructions.	79	
80a	Is the organization related (other than by association with a statewide or nationwide organization) through common membership, governing bodies, trustees, officers, etc., to any other exempt or nonexempt organization? (See instructions.)	80a	
b	If "Yes," enter the name of the organization ▶ .... and check whether it is ☐ exempt OR ☐ nonexempt.		
81a	Enter the amount of political expenditures, direct or indirect, as described in the instructions . |81a|		
b	Did the organization file Form 1120-POL, U.S. Income Tax Return for Certain Political Organizations, for this year? .	81b	
82a	Did the organization receive donated services or the use of materials, equipment, or facilities at no charge or at substantially less than fair rental value?	82a	
b	If "Yes," you may indicate the value of these items here. Do not include this amount as revenue in Part I or as an expense in Part II. (See instructions for reporting in Part III.) . |82b|		
83	Did the organization comply with the public inspection requirements for returns and exemption applications?	83	
84a	Did the organization solicit any contributions or gifts that were not tax deductible?	84a	
b	If "Yes," did the organization include with every solicitation an express statement that such contributions or gifts were not tax deductible? (See General Instruction M.)	84b	
85	Section 501(c)(4), (5), or (6) organizations.—a Were substantially all dues nondeductible by members?	85a	
b	Did the organization make only in-house lobbying expenditures of $2,000 or less?	85b	
	If "Yes" to either 85a or 85b, do not complete 85c through 85h below unless the organization received a waiver for proxy tax owed for the prior year.		
c	Dues, assessments, and similar amounts from members . . . . |85c|		
d	Section 162(e) lobbying and political expenditures . . . . |85d|		
e	Aggregate nondeductible amount of section 6033(e)(1)(A) dues notices . . . . . |85e|		
f	Taxable amount of lobbying and political expenditures (line 85d less 85e; see instructions) . |85f|		
g	Does the organization elect to pay the section 6033(e) tax on the amount in 85f?	85g	
h	If section 6033(e)(1)(A) dues notices were sent, does the organization agree to add the amount in 85f to its reasonable estimate of dues allocable to nondeductible lobbying and political expenditures for the following tax year? . . .	85h	
86	Section 501(c)(7) organizations.—Enter:		
a	Initiation fees and capital contributions included on line 12 . . . . |86a|		
b	Gross receipts, included on line 12, for public use of club facilities (See instructions.) |86b|		
87	Section 501(c)(12) organizations.—Enter: a Gross income from members or shareholders |87a|		
b	Gross income from other sources. (Do not net amounts due or paid to other sources against amounts due or received from them.) . . . . |87b|		
88	At any time during the year, did the organization own a 50% or greater interest in a taxable corporation or partnership? If "Yes," complete Part IX	88	
89	Public interest law firms.—Attach information described in the instructions.		
90	List the states with which a copy of this return is filed ▶		
91	The books are in care of ▶ ....Telephone no. ▶ (.........)........................... Located at ▶ .... ZIP code ▶		
92	Section 4947(a)(1) nonexempt charitable trusts filing Form 990 in lieu of Form 1041, U.S. Income Tax Return for Estates and Trusts, check here ▶ ☐ and enter the amount of tax-exempt interest received or accrued during the tax year . . ▶	92		

T A B L E   B.1—*Continued*

Form 990 (1994)   Page 5

Part VII   Analysis of Income-Producing Activities

Enter gross amounts unless otherwise indicated.	Unrelated business income		Excluded by section 512, 513, or 514		(E) Related or exempt function income (See instructions.)
	(A) Business code	(B) Amount	(C) Exclusion code	(D) Amount	
93 Program service revenue:					
a _____					
b _____					
c _____					
d _____					
e _____					
f _____					
g Fees and contracts from government agencies					
94 Membership dues and assessments . . .					
95 Interest on savings and temporary cash investments					
96 Dividends and interest from securities . . .					
97 Net rental income or (loss) from real estate:					
a debt-financed property					
b not debt-financed property					
98 Net rental income or (loss) from personal property					
99 Other investment income					
100 Gain or (loss) from sales of assets other than inventory					
101 Net income or (loss) from special events . .					
102 Gross profit or (loss) from sales of inventory .					
103 Other revenue: a _____					
b _____					
c _____					
d _____					
e _____					
104 Subtotal (add columns (B), (D), and (E)) . . .					

105 Total (add line 104, columns (B), (D), and (E)) . . . . ▶ _____

Note: *(Line 105 plus line 1d, Part I, should equal the amount on line 12, Part I.)*

Part VIII   Relationship of Activities to the Accomplishment of Exempt Purposes

Line No. ▼	Explain how each activity for which income is reported in column (E) of Part VII contributed importantly to the accomplishment of the organization's exempt purposes (other than by providing funds for such purposes). (See instructions.)

Part IX   Information Regarding Taxable Subsidiaries (Complete this Part if the "Yes" box on line 88 is checked.)

Name, address, and employer identification number of corporation or partnership	Percentage of ownership interest	Nature of business activities	Total income	End-of-year assets
	%			
	%			
	%			
	%			

Please Sign Here

Under penalties of perjury, I declare that I have examined this return, including accompanying schedules and statements, and to the best of my knowledge and belief, it is true, correct, and complete. Declaration of preparer (other than officer) is based on all information of which preparer has any knowledge.

▶ Signature of officer	Date	▶ Title

Paid Preparer's Use Only

Preparer's signature ▶	Date	Check if self-employed ▶ ☐	Preparer's social security no.
Firm's name (or yours if self-employed) and address ▶		E.I. No. ▶	
		ZIP code ▶	

T A B L E B.2

SCHEDULE A (Form 990) Department of the Treasury Internal Revenue Service	**Organization Exempt Under Section 501(c)(3)** (Except Private Foundation), and Section 501(e), 501(f), 501(k), or Section 4947(a)(1) Nonexempt Charitable Trust **Supplementary Information** ▶ Must be completed by the above organizations and attached to their Form 990 (or 990-EZ).	OMB No. 1545-0047 1994

Name of the organization	Employer identification number
Family Service Agency of Utopia, Inc.	12 ⁞ 3456789

Part I Compensation of the Five Highest Paid Employees Other Than Officers, Directors, and Trustees
(See instructions.) (List each one. If there are none, enter "None.")

(a) Name and address of each employee paid more than $50,000	(b) Title and average hours per week devoted to position	(c) Compensation	(d) Contributions to employee benefit plans & deferred compensation	(e) Expense account and other allowances
Roshan Contractor, M.S.W. 41 Allegro Way, Utopia, PA	Dep. to the Director 45 hrs./wk.	$56,000	$1,634	-0-
Mehroo Aziz 50 Mountain View, Utopia, PA	Ch. Counseling Services 45 hrs./wk.	52,000	1,490	-0-

Total number of other employees paid over $50,000 . . . . ▶	-0-		

Part II Compensation of the Five Highest Paid Independent Contractors for Professional Services
(See instructions.) (List each one (whether individuals or firms.) (If there are none, enter "None.")

(a) Name and address of each independent contractor paid more than $50,000	(b) Type of service	(c) Compensation
None		

Total number of others receiving over $50,000 for professional services . . . . ▶		

Part III Statements About Activities

		Yes	No
1	During the year, has the organization attempted to influence national, state, or local legislation, including any attempt to influence public opinion on a legislative matter or referendum? . . . . If "Yes," enter the total expenses paid or incurred in connection with the lobbying activities. ▶ $ _____ Organizations that made an election under section 501(h) by filing Form 5768 must complete Part VI-A. Other organizations checking "Yes," must complete Part VI-B AND attach a statement giving a detailed description of the lobbying activities.	1		X
2	During the year, has the organization, either directly or indirectly, engaged in any of the following acts with any of its trustees, directors, officers, creators, key employees, or members of their families, or with any taxable organization with which any such person is affiliated as an officer, director, trustee, majority owner, or principal beneficiary:			
a	Sale, exchange, or leasing of property?	2a		X
b	Lending of money or other extension of credit?	2b		X
c	Furnishing of goods, services, or facilities?	2c		X
d	Payment of compensation (or payment or reimbursement of expenses if more than $1,000)? See Part V,	2d	X	
e	Transfer of any part of its income or assets? . . . . ▹ . . . Form 990 . .	2e		X
	If the answer to any question is "Yes," attach a detailed statement explaining the transactions.			
3	Does the organization make grants for scholarships, fellowships, student loans, etc.?	3		X
4	Attach a statement explaining how the organization determines that individuals or organizations receiving grants or loans from it in furtherance of its charitable programs qualify to receive payments. (See instructions.)			

For Paperwork Reduction Act Notice, see page 1 of the Instructions to Form 990 (or Form 990-EZ).   Cat. No. 11285F   Schedule A (Form 990) 1994

T A B L E B.2—*Continued*

Schedule A (Form 990) 1994   Page **2**

Part IV   Reason for Non-Private Foundation Status (See instructions for definitions.)

The organization is not a private foundation because it is (please check only **ONE** applicable box):

5   ☐ A church, convention of churches, or association of churches. Section 170(b)(1)(A)(i).

6   ☐ A school. Section 170(b)(1)(A)(ii). (Also complete Part V, page 3.)

7   ☐ A hospital or a cooperative hospital service organization. Section 170(b)(1)(A)(iii).

8   ☐ A Federal, state, or local government or governmental unit. Section 170(b)(1)(A)(v).

9   ☐ A medical research organization operated in conjunction with a hospital. Section 170(b)(1)(A)(iii). **Enter the hospital's name, city, and state ▶** ....

10   ☐ An organization operated for the benefit of a college or university owned or operated by a governmental unit. Section 170(b)(1)(A)(iv). (Also complete the **Support Schedule** below.)

11a ☒ An organization that normally receives a substantial part of its support from a governmental unit or from the general public. Section 170(b)(1)(A)(vi). (Also complete the **Support Schedule** below.)

11b ☐ A community trust. Section 170(b)(1)(A)(vi). (Also complete the **Support Schedule** below.)

12   ☐ An organization that normally receives: **(a) no more than 33⅓%** of its support from gross investment income and unrelated business taxable income (less section 511 tax) from businesses acquired by the organization after June 30, 1975, and **(b) more than 33⅓%** of its support from contributions, membership fees, and gross receipts from activities related to its charitable, etc., functions—subject to certain exceptions. See section 509(a)(2). (Also complete the **Support Schedule** below.)

13   ☐ An organization that is not controlled by any disqualified persons (other than foundation managers) and supports organizations described in: **(1)** lines 5 through 12 above; or **(2)** section 501(c)(4), (5), or (6), if they meet the test of section 509(a)(2). (See section 509(a)(3).)

Provide the following information about the supported organizations. (See instructions for Part IV, line 13.)

(a) Name(s) of supported organization(s)	(b) Line number from above

14   ☐ An organization organized and operated to test for public safety. Section 509(a)(4). (See instructions.)

Support Schedule (Complete only if you checked a box on line 10, 11, or 12 above.) *Use cash method of accounting.*

Note: *You may use the worksheet in the instructions for converting from the accrual to the cash method of accounting.*

Calendar year (or fiscal year beginning in) . ▶	(a) 1993	(b) 1992	(c) 1991	(d) 1990	(e) Total
15 Gifts, grants, and contributions received. (Do not include unusual grants. See line 28.). .	$742,300	$696,800	$640,600	$594,300	$2,674,000
16 Membership fees received	1,100	1,500	1,500	1,400	5,500
17 Gross receipts from admissions, merchandise sold or services performed, or furnishing of facilities in any activity that is not a business unrelated to the organization's charitable, etc., purpose	31,200	26,400	30,600	24,900	113,100
18 Gross income from interest, dividends, amounts received from payments on securities loans (section 512(a)(5)), rents, royalties, and unrelated business taxable income (less section 511 taxes) from businesses acquired by the organization after June 30, 1975. . . .	26,000	27,700	22,100	20,400	96,200
19 Net income from unrelated business activities not included in line 18 .					
20 Tax revenues levied for the organization's benefit and either paid to it or expended on its behalf .					
21 The value of services or facilities furnished to the organization by a governmental unit without charge. Do not include the value of services or facilities generally furnished to the public without charge . .					
22 Other income. Attach a schedule. Do not include gain or (loss) from sale of capital assets					
23 Total of lines 15 through 22.	$800,600	$752,400	$694,800	$641,000	$2,888,800
24 Line 23 minus line 17.	$769,400	$726,000	$664,200	$616,100	$2,775,700
25 Enter 1% of line 23	$ 8,006	$ 7,524	$ 6,948	$ 6,410	

26   Organizations described in lines 10 or 11:

a Enter 2% of amount in column (e), line 24 . . . . $ 55,514

b Attach a list (which is not open to public inspection) showing the name of and amount contributed by each person (other than a governmental unit or publicly supported organization) whose total gifts for 1990 through 1993 exceeded the amount shown in line 26a. Enter the sum of all these excess amounts here . . . . ▶ -0-

(Support Schedule continued on page 3)

T A B L E B.2—*Continued*

Schedule A (Form 990) 1994   Page 3

Part IV   Support Schedule (continued) (Complete only if you checked a box on line 10, 11, or 12.)

27   Organizations described on line 12:   N/A

a   Attach a list, for amounts shown on lines 15, 16, and 17, to show the name of, and total amounts received in each year from, each "disqualified person." Enter the sum of such amounts for each year:

   (1993) .... (1992) .... (1991) .... (1990) ....

b   Attach a list to show, for 1990 through 1993, the name of, and amount included in line 17 for, each person (other than a "disqualified person") from whom the organization received, during that year, an amount that was more than the larger of (1) the amount on line 25 for the year or (2) $5,000. Include organizations described in lines 5 through 11, as well as individuals. After computing the difference between the amount received and the larger amount described in (1) or (2), enter the sum of all these differences (the excess amounts) for each year:

   (1993) .... (1992) .... (1991) .... (1990) ....

28   For an organization described in line 10, 11, or 12, that received any unusual grants during 1990 through 1993, attach a list (which is not open to public inspection) for each year showing the name of the contributor, the date and amount of the grant, and a brief description of the nature of the grant. Do not include these grants in line 15. (See instructions.)   N/A

Part V   Private School Questionnaire
             (To be completed ONLY by schools that checked the box on line 6 in Part IV)   N/A

		Yes	No
29	Does the organization have a racially nondiscriminatory policy toward students by statement in its charter, bylaws, other governing instrument, or in a resolution of its governing body?	29	
30	Does the organization include a statement of its racially nondiscriminatory policy toward students in all its brochures, catalogues, and other written communications with the public dealing with student admissions, programs, and scholarships?	30	
31	Has the organization publicized its racially nondiscriminatory policy through newspaper or broadcast media during the period of solicitation for students, or during the registration period if it has no solicitation program, in a way that makes the policy known to all parts of the general community it serves?.	31	

If "Yes," please describe; if "No," please explain. (If you need more space, attach a separate statement.)

....
....
....
....

32	Does the organization maintain the following:		
a	Records indicating the racial composition of the student body, faculty, and administrative staff?	32a	
b	Records documenting that scholarships and other financial assistance are awarded on a racially nondiscriminatory basis?	32b	
c	Copies of all catalogues, brochures, announcements, and other written communications to the public dealing with student admissions, programs, and scholarships?	32c	
d	Copies of all material used by the organization or on its behalf to solicit contributions?	32d	

If you answered "No" to any of the above, please explain. (If you need more space, attach a separate statement.)

....
....

33	Does the organization discriminate by race in any way with respect to:		
a	Students' rights or privileges?.	33a	
b	Admissions policies?	33b	
c	Employment of faculty or administrative staff?	33c	
d	Scholarships or other financial assistance? (See instructions.)	33d	
e	Educational policies?	33e	
f	Use of facilities?	33f	
g	Athletic programs?	33g	
h	Other extracurricular activities?	33h	

If you answered "Yes" to any of the above, please explain. (If you need more space, attach a separate statement.)

....
....
....

| 34a | Does the organization receive any financial aid or assistance from a governmental agency? . . . . . . | 34a | |
| b | Has the organization's right to such aid ever been revoked or suspended? . . . . | 34b | |

If you answered "Yes" to either 34a or b, please explain using an attached statement.

| 35 | Does the organization certify that it has complied with the applicable requirements of sections 4.01 through 4.05 of Rev. Proc. 75-50, 1975-2 C.B. 587, covering racial nondiscrimination? If "No," attach an explanation. (See instructions for Part V.) . . | 35 | |

T A B L E B.2—*Continued*

Schedule A (Form 990) 1994   Page **4**

Part VI-A   Lobbying Expenditures by Electing Public Charities (See instructions.)
(To be completed **ONLY** by an eligible organization that filed Form 5768)

Check here ▶   a   ☐ If the organization belongs to an affiliated group (see instructions).

Check here ▶   b   ☐ If you checked **a** and "limited control" provisions apply (see instructions).   **N/A**

	Limits on Lobbying Expenditures (The term "expenditures" means amounts paid or incurred)		(a) Affiliated group totals	(b) To be completed for ALL electing organizations
36	Total lobbying expenditures to influence public opinion (grassroots lobbying)	36		
37	Total lobbying expenditures to influence a legislative body (direct lobbying)	37		
38	Total lobbying expenditures (add lines 36 and 37)	38		
39	Other exempt purpose expenditures (see Part VI-A instructions)	39		
40	Total exempt purpose expenditures (add lines 38 and 39) (see instructions)	40		
41	Lobbying nontaxable amount. Enter the amount from the following table—			
	If the amount on line 40 is— The lobbying nontaxable amount is—			
	Not over $500,000 . . . . 20% of the amount on line 40			
	Over $500,000 but not over $1,000,000 . . $100,000 plus 15% of the excess over $500,000			
	Over $1,000,000 but not over $1,500,000 . $175,000 plus 10% of the excess over $1,000,000	41		
	Over $1,500,000 but not over $17,000,000 . $225,000 plus 5% of the excess over $1,500,000			
	Over $17,000,000 . . . . $1,000,000 .			
42	Grassroots nontaxable amount (enter 25% of line 41)	42		
43	Subtract line 42 from line 36. Enter -0- if line 42 is more than line 36	43		
44	Subtract line 41 from line 38. Enter -0- if line 41 is more than line 38	44		

Caution: *File Form 4720 if there is an amount on either line 43 or line 44.*

4-Year Averaging Period Under Section 501(h)
(Some organizations that made a section 501(h) election do not have to complete all of the five columns below.
 See the instructions for lines 45 through 50.)

	Calendar year (or fiscal year beginning in) ▶	Lobbying Expenditures During 4-Year Averaging Period				
		(a) 1994	(b) 1993	(c) 1992	(d) 1991	(e) Total
45	Lobbying nontaxable amount (see instructions)					
46	Lobbying ceiling amount (150% of line 45(e))					
47	Total lobbying expenditures (see instructions)					
48	Grassroots nontaxable amount (see instructions)					
49	Grassroots ceiling amount (150% of line 48(e))					
50	Grassroots lobbying expenditures (see instructions)					

Part VI-B   Lobbying Activity by Nonelecting Public Charities
(For reporting by organizations that did not complete Part VI-A)   **N/A**

During the year, did the organization attempt to influence national, state or local legislation, including any attempt to influence public opinion on a legislative matter or referendum, through the use of:	Yes	No	Amount
a Volunteers			
b Paid staff or management (include compensation in expenses reported on lines c through h) . . .			
c Media advertisements			
d Mailings to members, legislators, or the public			
e Publications, or published or broadcast statements			
f Grants to other organizations for lobbying purposes			
g Direct contact with legislators, their staffs, government officials, or a legislative body. . . .			
h Rallies, demonstrations, seminars, conventions, speeches, lectures, or any other means			
i Total lobbying expenditures (add lines c through h)			

If "Yes" to any of the above, also attach a statement giving a detailed description of the lobbying activities.

T A B L E B.2—*Continued*

Schedule A (Form 990) 1994

Page 5

Part VII   Information Regarding Transfers To and Transactions and Relationships With Noncharitable Exempt Organizations

51 Did the reporting organization directly or indirectly engage in any of the following with any other organization described in section 501(c) of the Code (other than section 501(c)(3) organizations) or in section 527, relating to political organizations?

		Yes	No
a Transfers from the reporting organization to a noncharitable exempt organization of:			
(i) Cash	51a(i)		X
(ii) Other assets	a(ii)		X
b Other transactions:			
(i) Sales of assets to a noncharitable exempt organization	b(i)		X
(ii) Purchases of assets from a noncharitable exempt organization	b(ii)		X
(iii) Rental of facilities or equipment	b(iii)	X	
(iv) Reimbursement arrangements	b(iv)		X
(v) Loans or loan guarantees	b(v)		X
(vi) Performance of services or membership or fundraising solicitations	b(vi)		X
c Sharing of facilities, equipment, mailing lists, other assets, or paid employees	c		X

d If the answer to any of the above is "Yes," complete the following schedule. Column (b) should always show the fair market value of the goods, other assets, or services given by the reporting organization. If the organization received less than fair market value in any transaction or sharing arrangement, show in column (d) the value of the goods, other assets, or services received.

(a) Line no.	(b) Amount involved	(c) Name of noncharitable exempt organization	(d) Description of transfers, transactions, and sharing arrangements
b(iii)	$800	Fraternal Society of Utopia	Rental of hall, kitchen, dining room equipment and supplies for the agency's annual dinner/dance.

52a Is the organization directly or indirectly affiliated with, or related to, one or more tax-exempt organizations described in section 501(c) of the Code (other than section 501(c)(3)) or in section 527? ☐ Yes ☒ No
b If "Yes," complete the following schedule.

(a) Name of organization	(b) Type of organization	(c) Description of relationship
None		

T A B L E B.2—*Continued*

FAMILY SERVICE AGENCY OF UTOPIA, INC.
EIN: 12-3456789
Form 990 (1994) Schedule Attachment

Part I, line 1d: Contributions, gifts, grants, etc.

> No single contributor gave $5,000 or more during the year.

Part I, line 8c: Sale of assets other than inventory

Proceeds from sales of:
Publicly traded securities	$24,200
Cost and sales expenses	23,700
Gain	$ 500

Part I, line 9: Special events and activities

	Dinner/ dance	Celebrity auction	Raffle	Total
Gross revenue	$14,500	$9,200	$4,700	$28,400
Less:				
Direct expenses	11,200	3,700	3,100	18,000
Net income	$ 3,300	$5,500	$1,600	$10,400

Part I, line 10: Sales

Proceeds from sale of educational publications	$1,400
Cost of publications sold	$1,000
Gross profit	$ 400

Part I, line 16:

Payments to affiliates	$12,400

> Two percent (2%) of unrestricted contributions collected were paid to the National Association of Family Service Agencies for its general operations, as required by our affiliation agreement with that organization.

Part II, line 22: Grants and allocations

Family Counseling:
National Association of Family Service Agencies Milwaukee, Wisconsin 53226	$ 3,000

Adoption Services:
National Association of Family Service Agencies	$10,000
Utopia Adolescent Center Utopia, Pennsylvania 11111	5,000
Utopia Children's Services Utopia, Pennsylvania 11111	6,000
Total	$21,000

Foster Home Care:
Utopia Children's Services	$ 5,000
Utopia Adolescent Center	6,900
Total	$11,900

T A B L E   B.2—*Continued*

FAMILY SERVICE AGENCY OF UTOPIA, INC.
EIN: 12-3456789
Form 990 (1994) Schedule Attachment

Part II, line 23: Specific assistance to individuals

Adoption assistance to low-income families	$20,400
Reimbursement of out-of-pocket expenses for foster home care	25,400
Total	$45,800

Part II, line 42: Depreciation AND Part IV, line 57 -- Land, buildings, equipment

Asset	Date acquired	Cost	Prior years' depreciation	Method	Useful life	Current depreciation
Land	1992	$ 45,500	--	--	--	--
Office equip.	1987	3,000	$2,450	S.L.	8 years	$ 350
Office equip.	1994	11,500	--	S.L.	8 years	1,150
Building	1992	128,000	5,550	S.L.	30 years	3,700
Total		$188,000	$8,000			$5,200

Part IV, line 54: Investments - securities (end of year)

Common stock	Number of shares	Book value (cost)
A Corporation	4,000	$ 98,000
B Corporation	1,600	17,400
C Corporation	1,000	22,100
D Corporation	1,200	58,200
E Corporation	800	43,700
F Corporation	2,000	109,200
G Corporation	1,000	62,400
H Corporation	600	16,500
I Corporation	900	46,900
Total		$474,400

Part IV, line 62: Support and revenue designated for future periods

	Designated for Year			
	1994	1995	1996	Total
Received prior to 1994	$20,000	$20,800	$20,800	$61,600
Received in 1994		9,000	9,000	18,000
Expended (earned) in 1994	(20,000)			(20,000)
Balance at end of 1994	$ -0-	$29,800	$29,800	$59,600

All of the above represent grants designated by contributors to support adoption services in future periods.

T A B L E B.2—*Continued*

FAMILY SERVICE AGENCY OF UTOPIA, INC.
EIN: 12-3456789
Form 990 (1994) Schedule Attachment

Part IV, line 64b: Mortgages and other notes payable

> Mortgage payable to State Bank of Utopia
> @6% per annum $3,200

Part V: List of Officers, Directors, Trustees, and Key Employees (Continued)

(A)	(B)	(C)	(D)	(E)
Name & address	Title & avg. hrs. per week devoted to position	Compensation	Cont. to employee benefit plans & deferred compensation	Expense account & other allowances
Zenobia Boyce 23 Wonderful Way Utopia, PA 11111	Secretary 3 hrs./wk.	-0-	-0-	-0-

FAMILY SERVICE AGENCY OF UTOPIA, INC.
EIN: 12-3456789
Attachment for Schedule A (Form 990) (1994)

Part III, Item 4

> Organizations receiving grants are required to furnish:
>
> 1. A copy of their section 501(c)(3) determination letter from the IRS.
>
> 2. Audited financial statements for the 2 preceding years.
>
> 3. Evidence of service quality and effectiveness in reaching poverty level population.
>
> 4. Quarterly report of services delivered.

✩ U.S. GOVERNMENT PRINTING OFFICE: 1994—375–041

T A B L E B.3

Form **990-EZ**	**Short Form** **Return of Organization Exempt From Income Tax** Under section 501(c) of the Internal Revenue Code (except black lung benefit trust or private foundation) or section 4947(a)(1) nonexempt charitable trust ► For organizations with gross receipts less than $100,000 and total assets less than $250,000 at the end of the year. ► *The organization may have to use a copy of this return to satisfy state reporting requirements.*	OMB No. 1545-1150 **1994** This Form is Open to Public Inspection

Department of the Treasury
Internal Revenue Service

A For the 1994 calendar year, OR tax year beginning _____ , 1994, and ending _____ , 19 ___

B Check if: ☐ Change of address ☐ Initial return ☐ Final return ☐ Amended return (required also for State reporting)	Please use IRS label or print or type. See Specific Instruc- tions.	**C** Name of organization Number and street (or P.O. box, if mail is not delivered to street address) Room/suite City, town or post office, state, and ZIP code	**D** Employer identification number **E** State registration number **F** Check ► ☐ if exemption application is pending

G Accounting method: ☐ Cash   ☐ Accrual   ☐ Other (specify) ►

H Enter four-digit group exemption number (GEN)

I Type of organization— ► ☐ Exempt under section 501(c)(   ) ◄ (insert number) OR ► ☐ section 4947(a)(1) nonexempt charitable trust

Note: *Section 501(c)(3) organizations and section 4947(a)(1) nonexempt charitable trusts MUST attach a completed Schedule A (Form 990).*

J Check ► ☐ if the organization's gross receipts are normally not more than $25,000. The organization need not file a return with the IRS; but if the organization received a Form 990 Package in the mail, the organization should file a return without financial data. **Some states require a complete return.**

K Enter the organization's 1994 gross receipts (add back lines 5b, 6b, and 7b, to line 9) .   .   .   .   ► $ _____
If $100,000 or more, the organization must file **Form 990** instead of Form 990-EZ.

Part I   Statement of Revenue, Expenses, and Changes in Net Assets or Fund Balances

Revenue	**1** Contributions, gifts, grants, and similar amounts received (attach schedule—see instructions) .	**1**	
	2 Program service revenue including government fees and contracts	**2**	
	3 Membership dues and assessments (see instructions)	**3**	
	4 Investment income	**4**	
	5a Gross amount from sale of assets other than inventory **5a**		
	b Less: cost or other basis and sales expenses **5b**		
	c Gain or (loss) from sale of assets other than inventory (line 5a less line 5b) (attach schedule) .	**5c**	
	6 Special events and activities (attach schedule—see instructions):		
	a Gross revenue (not including $ _____ of contributions reported on line 1) **6a**		
	b Less: direct expenses other than fundraising expenses **6b**		
	c Net income or (loss) from special events and activities (line 6a less line 6b)	**6c**	
	7a Gross sales of inventory, less returns and allowances. **7a**		
	b Less: cost of goods sold **7b**		
	c Gross profit or (loss) from sales of inventory (line 7a less line 7b)	**7c**	
	8 Other revenue (describe ► _____)	**8**	
	9 **Total revenue** (add lines 1, 2, 3, 4, 5c, 6c, 7c, and 8) . . . . . . ►	**9**	
Expenses	**10** Grants and similar amounts paid (attach schedule)	**10**	
	11 Benefits paid to or for members.	**11**	
	12 Salaries, other compensation, and employee benefits	**12**	
	13 Professional fees and other payments to independent contractors	**13**	
	14 Occupancy, rent, utilities, and maintenance	**14**	
	15 Printing, publications, postage, and shipping	**15**	
	16 Other expenses (describe ► _____)	**16**	
	17 **Total expenses** (add lines 10 through 16) . . . . ►	**17**	
Net Assets	**18** Excess or (deficit) for the year (line 9 less line 17)	**18**	
	19 Net assets or fund balances at beginning of year (from line 27, column (A)) (must agree with end-of-year figure reported on prior year's return)	**19**	
	20 Other changes in net assets or fund balances (attach explanation)	**20**	
	21 Net assets or fund balances at end of year (combine lines 18 through 20) . . ►	**21**	

Part II   Balance Sheets—If Total assets on line 25, column (B) are $250,000 or more, Form 990 must be filed instead of Form 990-EZ.

	(A) Beginning of year		(B) End of year
22 Cash, savings, and investments		**22**	
23 Land and buildings		**23**	
24 Other assets (describe ► _____)		**24**	
25 Total assets		**25**	
26 Total liabilities (describe ► _____)		**26**	
27 Net assets or fund balances (line 27 of column (B) must agree with line 21) . .		**27**	

For Paperwork Reduction Act Notice, see page 1 of the separate instructions.   Cat. No. 10642I   Form **990-EZ** (1994)

T A B L E   B.3—*Continued*

Form 990-EZ (1994)   Page **2**

Part III Statement of Program Service Accomplishments—(see instructions)		**Expenses**
What is the organization's primary exempt purpose? _____ Describe what was achieved in carrying out the organization's exempt purposes. Fully describe the services provided, the number of persons benefited, or other relevant information for each program title.		(Required for 501(c)(3) and (4) organizations and 4947(a)(1) trusts; optional for others.)

28 ....

....

.... (Grants $) | **28a** |

29 ....

....

.... (Grants $) | **29a** |

30 ....

....

.... (Grants $) | **30a** |

31 Other program services (attach schedule) . . . . (Grants $) | **31a** |

32 Total program service expenses (add lines 28a through 31a) . . . . ▶ | **32** |

Part IV. List of Officers, Directors, Trustees, and Key Employees (List each one even if not compensated. See instructions.)				
(A) Name and address	(B) Title and average hours per week devoted to position	(C) Compensation (If not paid, enter -0-.)	(D) Contributions to employee benefit plans & deferred compensation	(E) Expense account and other allowances
....				
....				
....				
....				
....				

Part V Other Information	Yes	No

33   Did the organization engage in any activity not previously reported to the IRS? If "Yes," attach a detailed description of each activity . .

34   Were any changes made to the organizing or governing documents but not reported to the IRS? . . . .
    If "Yes," attach a conformed copy of the changes.

35   *If the organization had income from business activities, such as those reported on lines 2, 6, and 7 (among others), but NOT reported on Form 990-T, attach a statement explaining your reason for not reporting the income on Form 990-T.*

  a   During the year covered by this return, did the organization have unrelated business gross income of $1,000 or more or incur liability for the section 6033(e) tax on lobbying and political expenditures? . . . .

  b   If "Yes," has it filed a tax return on **Form 990-T**, Exempt Organization Business Income Tax Return, for this year? .

36   Was there a liquidation, dissolution, termination, or substantial contraction during the year? (If "Yes," attach a statement; see instructions.) .

37a   Enter amount of political expenditures, direct or indirect, as described in the instructions. ▶ | **37a** |

  b   Did the organization file **Form 1120-POL**, U.S. Income Tax Return for Certain Political Organizations, for this year? .

38a   Did the organization borrow from, or make any loans to, any officer, director, trustee, or key employee OR were any such loans made in a prior year and still unpaid at the start of the period covered by this return? . . . .

  b   If "Yes," attach the schedule specified in the instructions and enter the amount involved . . | **38b** |

39   *Section 501(c)(7) organizations.*—Enter:

  a   Initiation fees and capital contributions included on line 9 . . . . | **39a** |

  b   Gross receipts, included on line 9, for public use of club facilities (see instructions). . . | **39b** |

  c   Does the club's governing instrument or any written policy statement provide for discrimination against any person because of race, color, or religion? (If "Yes," attach statement; see instructions.). . . . .

40   List the states with which a copy of this return is filed. ▶ ....

41   The books are in care of ▶ .... Telephone no. ▶ (......) ....
    Located at ▶ .... ZIP code ▶ ....

42   *Section 4947(a)(1) nonexempt charitable trusts filing Form 990-EZ in lieu of Form 1041, U.S. Income Tax Return for Estates and Trusts.*—Check here ▶ ☐
    and enter the amount of tax-exempt interest received or accrued during the tax year . . . ▶ | 42 |

Please Sign Here	Under penalties of perjury, I declare that I have examined this return, including accompanying schedules and statements, and to the best of my knowledge and belief, it is true, correct, and complete. Declaration of preparer (other than officer) is based on all information of which preparer has any knowledge.		
	▶ Signature of officer Date	▶ Title	

Paid Preparer's Use Only	Preparer's signature ▶	Date	Check if self-employed ▶ ☐	Preparer's social security no.
	Firm's name (or yours if self-employed) and address ▶		E.I. No. ▶	
			ZIP code ▶	

T A B L E B.4

Form **990-PF**	**Return of Private Foundation**	OMB No. 1545-0052
Department of the Treasury Internal Revenue Service	or Section 4947(a)(1) Nonexempt Charitable Trust Treated as a Private Foundation	19**93**
	Note: The organization may be able to use a copy of this return to satisfy state reporting requirements	

For calendar year 1993, or tax year beginning _____ , 1993, and ending _____ , 19___

Use the IRS label. Otherwise, please print or type. See Specific Instructions.	Name of organization **The Christiansen Foundation**			A Employer identification number 13 : 5326271
	Number and street (or P.O. box number if mail is not delivered to street address) **60 Broad Street**	Room/suite		B State registration number (see instruction F)
	City or town, state, and ZIP code **New York, NY 10017**			C If exemption application is pending, check here ▶ ☐

H Check type of organization: ☒ Section 501(c)(3) exempt private foundation
☐ Section 4947(a)(1) nonexempt charitable trust   ☐ Other taxable private foundation

D 1. Foreign organizations, check here   ▶ ☐
2. Organizations meeting the 85% test, check here and attach computation.   ▶ ☐
E If private foundation status was terminated under section 507(b)(1)(A), check here ▶ ☐

I Fair market value of all assets at end of year (from Part II, col. (c), line 16) ① 2,900,461
J Accounting method: ☐ Cash ☒ Accrual ☐ Other (specify) _____
(Part I, column (d) must be on cash basis.)

F If the foundation is in a 60-month termination under section 507(b)(1)(B), check here ▶ ☐
G If address changed, check here ▶ ☐

Part I — Analysis of Revenue and Expenses (The total of amounts in columns (b),(c), and (d) may not necessarily equal the amounts in column (a) (see instructions).) ②

		(a) Revenue and expenses per books ③	(b) Net investment income ⑥	(c) Adjusted net income ⑧	(d) Disbursements for charitable purposes (cash basis only) ⑨
Revenue	1 Contributions, gifts, grants, etc., received (attach schedule)				
	2 Contributions from split-interest trusts				
	3 Interest on savings and temporary cash investments	8,330	8,330		
	4 Dividends and interest from securities	226,483	226,483		
	5a Gross rents	0	0		
	b (Net rental income or (loss) 0)				
	6 Net gain or (loss) from sale of assets not on line 10 ④	20,000			
	7 Capital gain net income (from Part IV, line 2) ⑦		2,274		
	8 Net short-term capital gain			0	
	9 Income modifications				
	10a Gross sales less returns and allowances 0				
	b Less: Cost of goods sold 0				
	c Gross profit or (loss) (attach schedule)	0			
	11 Other income (attach schedule)	0			
	12 Total (add lines 1 through 11)	254,813	237,087	0	
Operating and Administrative Expenses	13 Compensation of officers, directors, trustees, etc.	20,395	4,046		16,349
	14 Other employee salaries and wages	13,211	0		13,211
	15 Pension plans, employee benefits	966	0		966
	16a Legal fees (attach schedule)	0	0		0
	b Accounting fees (attach schedule)	0	0		0
	c Other professional fees (attach schedule)	19,138	6,363		12,775
	17 Interest	0	0		0
	18 Taxes (attach schedule) (see instructions)	4,519	0		0
	19 Depreciation (attach schedule) and depletion	0	0		
	20 Occupancy	10,507	722		9,785
	21 Travel, conferences, and meetings				
	22 Printing and publications				
	23 Other expenses (attach schedule)	11,340	0		11,340
	24 Total operating and administrative expenses (add lines 13 through 23)	80,076	11,131	0	64,426
	25 Contributions, gifts, grants paid	790,059			790,059
	26 Total expenses and disbursements (add lines 24 and 25)	870,135	11,131	0	854,485 ⑩
	27a Excess of revenue over expenses and disbursements (line 12 minus line 26) ⑤	(615,322)			
	b Net investment income (if negative, enter "-0-")		225,956		
	c Adjusted net income (if negative, enter "-0-")			0	

For Paperwork Reduction Act Notice, see page 1 of the instructions.   84-1126480   Form **990-PF** (1993)

CHRISFDN X93

T A B L E B.4—*Continued*

EIN 13-5326271

Form 990-PF (1993)   Page 2

Part II **Balance Sheets** Attached schedules and amounts in the description column should be for end-of-year amounts only. (See instructions.)	Beginning of year (a) Book Value	End of year (b) Book Value	End of year (c) Fair Market Value
1 Cash—non-interest-bearing . . . . ⑪ .	4,021	5,087	5,087
2 Savings and temporary cash investments	39,400	227,000	227,000
3 Accounts receivable ▶ _____			
Less: allowance for doubtful accounts ▶ _____	47,438	0	
4 Pledges receivable ▶ _____			
Less: allowance for doubtful accounts ▶ _____	0	0	
5 Grants receivable			
6 Receivables due from officers, directors, trustees, and other disqualified persons (attach schedule) (see instructions) . . .			
7 Other notes and loans receivable (attach schedule) ▶ _____			
Less: allowance for doubtful accounts ▶ _____	0	0	
8 Inventories for sale or use			
9 Prepaid expenses and deferred charges			
10a Investments—U.S. and state government obligations (attach schedule)	3,554,409	2,668,374	2,668,374
b Investments—corporate stock (attach schedule) . .			
c Investments—corporate bonds (attach schedule) . . .			
11 Investments—land, buildings, and equipment: basis ▶ _____			
Less: accumulated depreciation (attach schedule) ▶ _____	0	0	
12 Investments—mortgage loans			
13 Investments—other (attach schedule)			
14 Land, buildings, and equipment: basis ▶ _____			
Less: accumulated depreciation (attach schedule) ▶ _____	0	0	
15 Other assets (describe ▶ _____)			
16 Total assets (to be completed by all filers—see instructions)	3,645,268	2,900,461	2,900,461
17 Accounts payable and accrued expenses	33,691	7,175	
18 Grants payable			
19 Support and revenue designated for future periods (attach schedule)			
20 Loans from officers, directors, trustees, and other disqualified persons			
21 Mortgages and other notes payable (attach schedule)			
22 Other liabilities (describe ▶ Taxes Payable _____)	10,926	4,519	
23 Total liabilities (add lines 17 through 22)	44,617	11,694	
Organizations that use fund accounting, check here ▶ ☒ and complete lines 24 through 27 and lines 31 and 32.			
24a Current unrestricted fund	1,520,029	808,145	
b Current restricted fund			
25 Land, buildings, and equipment fund			
26 Endowment fund	2,080,622	2,080,622	
27 Other funds (describe ▶ _____)			
Organizations not using fund accounting, check here ▶ ☐ and complete lines 28 through 32.			
28 Capital stock or trust principal			
29 Paid-in capital or capital surplus			
30 Retained earnings or accumulated income			
31 Total net assets or fund balances (see instructions)	3,600,651	2,888,767	
32 Total liabilities and net assets/fund balances (see instructions)	3,645,268	2,900,461	

(left margin labels: Assets, Liabilities, Net Assets or Fund Balances)

Part III **Analysis of Changes in Net Assets or Fund Balances**		
1 Total net assets or fund balances at beginning of year—Part II, column (a), line 31	**1**	3,600,651
(must agree with end-of-year figure reported on prior year's return)		
2 Enter amount from Part I, line 27a . . . . ⑫	**2**	(615,322)
3 Other increases not included in line 2 (itemize) ▶ _____	**3**	
4 Add lines 1, 2, and 3	**4**	2,985,329
5 Decreases not included in line 2 (itemize) ▶ Change in market value of securities _____	**5**	96,562
6 Total net assets or fund balances at end of year (line 4 minus line 5)—Part II, column (b), line 31 . .	**6**	2,888,767

CHRISFON X93

T A B L E B.4—*Continued*

Form 990-PF (1993)   Page 3

Part IV   Capital Gains and Losses for Tax on Investment Income

(a) List and describe the kind(s) of property sold, e.g., real estate, 2-story brick warehouse; or common stock, 200 shs. MLC Co.		(b) How acquired P—Purchase D—Donation	(c) Date acquired (mo., day, yr.)	(d) Date sold (mo., day, yr.)
1	100 shares AT&T	P	11/01/58	12/11/93
	1200 shares Xerox ⑬	D	7/11/67	12/01/93
	7500 shares ITT	D	6/01/53	6/01/93
	2000 shares GM	P	8/03/71	5/27/93

(e) Gross sales price minus expense of sale	(f) Depreciation allowed (or allowable)	(g) Cost or other basis ⑭	(h) Gain or (loss) (e) plus (f) minus (g)
46,000		22,000	24,000
144,000	—	176,000	(32,000)
350,000		300,000	50,000
135,000		117,000	18,000

Complete only for assets showing gain in column (h) and owned by the foundation on 12/31/69

(i) F.M.V. as of 12/31/69	(j) Adjusted basis as of 12/31/69	(k) Excess of col. (i) over col. (j), if any	(l) Losses (from col. (h)) Gains (excess of col. (h) gain over col. (k), but not less than "-0-")
29,726	22,000	7,726	16,274
		⑮	(32,000)
365,000	300,000	65,000	0
			18,000

2 Capital gain net income or (net capital loss). { If gain, also enter in Part I, line 7 } { If (loss), enter "-0-" in Part I, line 7 } | 2 | ⑯ | 2,274

3 Net short-term capital gain or (loss) as defined in sections 1222(5) and (6):
   If gain, also enter in Part I, line 8, column (c) (see instructions). If (loss), enter "-0-"
   in Part I, line 8 . . . . | 3 | | 0

Part V   Qualification Under Section 4940(e) for Reduced Tax on Net Investment Income

(For optional use by domestic private foundations subject to the section 4940(a) tax on net investment income.)

If section 4940(d)(2) applies, leave this part blank.
                                                                          ⑰
Was the organization liable for the section 4942 tax on the distributable amount of any year in the base period? . . ☐ Yes ☐ No
If "Yes," the organization does not qualify under section 4940(e). Do not complete this part.

1 Enter the appropriate amount in each column for each year; see instructions before making any entries.

(a) Base period years Calendar year (or tax year beginning in)	(b) Adjusted qualifying distributions	(c) Net value of noncharitable-use assets	(d) Distribution ratio (col. (b) divided by col. (c))
1992			
1991			
1990			
1989			
1988			

2 Total of line 1, column (d) . . . . | 2 |

3 Average distribution ratio for the 5-year base period—divide the total on line 2 by 5, or by
   the number of years the foundation has been in existence if less than 5 years . . . . | 3 |

4 Enter the net value of noncharitable-use assets for 1993 from Part X, line 5 . . . . . . | 4 |

5 Multiply line 4 by line 3 . . . . | 5 |

6 Enter 1% of net investment income (1% of Part I, line 27b) . . . . | 6 |

7 Add lines 5 and 6 . . . . | 7 |

8 Enter qualifying distributions from Part XII, line 4 . . . . | 8 |

If line 8 is equal to or greater than line 7, check the box in Part VI, line 1b, and complete that part using a 1% tax rate. See
the Part VI instructions.

CHRISFON X83

T A B L E B.4—Continued

Form 990-PF (1993)   Page 4

Part VI Excise Tax on Investment Income (Section 4940(a), 4940(b), 4940(e), or 4948—see instructions)

1a Exempt operating foundations described in section 4940(d)(2), check here ☐ and enter "N/A" on line 1.		
Date of ruling letter: _____ (attach copy of ruling letter if necessary—see instructions)		
b Domestic organizations that meet the section 4940(e) requirements in Part V, check here ☐ and enter 1% of Part I, line 27b . . . . (⑱) . .	1	4,519
c All other domestic organizations enter 2% of line 27b. Exempt foreign organizations enter 4% of line 27b		
2 Tax under section 511 (domestic section 4947(a)(1) trusts and taxable foundations only. Others enter "-0-")	2	0
3 Add lines 1 and 2	3	4,519
4 Tax under subtitle A (domestic section 4947(a)(1) trusts and taxable foundations only. Others enter "-0-")	4	0
5 Tax on investment income (line 3 minus line 4 (but not less than "-0-"))	5	4,519
6 Credits/Payments:		
a 1993 estimated tax payments and 1992 overpayment credited to 1993 6a (⑲) 5,000		
b Exempt foreign organizations—tax withheld at source 6b		
c Tax paid with application for extension of time to file (Form 2758) . . . 6c		
d Backup withholding erroneously withheld 6d		
7 Total credits and payments (add lines 6a through d)	7	5,000
8 Enter any PENALTY for underpayment of estimated tax. Check here ☐ if Form 2220 is attached . .	8	0
9 TAX DUE. If the total of lines 5 and 8 is more than line 7, enter AMOUNT OWED . . . . ▶	9	0
10 OVERPAYMENT. If line 7 is more than the total of lines 5 and 8, enter the AMOUNT OVERPAID . . ▶	10	481
11 Enter the amount of line 10 to be: Credited to 1994 estimated tax ▶ 481	Refunded ▶	11	0

Part VII Statements Regarding Activities (㉑)

File Form 4720 if the answer is "No" to question 10b, 11b, or 14b or "Yes" to question 10c, 12b, 13a, 13b, or 14a(2), unless an exception applies.		Yes	No
1a During the tax year, did the organization attempt to influence any national, state, or local legislation or did it participate or intervene in any political campaign?	1a		X
b Did it spend more than $100 during the year (either directly or indirectly) for political purposes (see instructions for definition)?	1b		X
If the answer is "Yes" to 1a or 1b, attach a detailed description of the activities and copies of any materials published or distributed by the organization in connection with the activities.			
c Did the organization file Form 1120-POL, U.S. Income Tax Return for Certain Political Organizations, for this year?	1c		X
2 Has the organization engaged in any activities that have not previously been reported to the IRS?	2		X
If "Yes," attach a detailed description of the activities.			
3 Has the organization made any changes, not previously reported to the IRS, in its governing instrument, articles of incorporation, or bylaws, or other similar instruments? If "Yes," attach a conformed copy of the changes	3		X
4a Did the organization have unrelated business gross income of $1,000 or more during the year?	4a		X
b If "Yes," has it filed a tax return on Form 990-T, Exempt Organization Business Income Tax Return, for this year?	4b	N/A	
5 Was there a liquidation, termination, dissolution, or substantial contraction during the year? . . . . (㉒)	5		X
If "Yes," attach the statement required by General Instruction T.			
6 Are the requirements of section 508(e) (relating to sections 4941 through 4945) satisfied either:			
• By language written into the governing instrument, or (㉒)			
• By state legislation that effectively amends the governing instrument so that no mandatory directions that conflict with the state law remain in the governing instrument?	6	X	
7 Did the organization have at least $5,000 in assets at any time during the year?	7	X	
If "Yes," complete Part II, column (c), and Part XV.			
8a Enter the states to which the foundation reports or with which it is registered (see instructions) ▶ New York (㉓)			
_____			
b If the answer is "Yes" to line 7, has the organization furnished a copy of Form 990-PF to the Attorney General (or his or her designate) of each state as required by General Instruction G? If "No," attach explanation . . .	8b	X	
9 Is the organization claiming status as a private operating foundation within the meaning of section 4942(j)(3) or 4942(j)(5) for calendar year 1993 or taxable year beginning in 1993 (see instructions for Part XIV)? If "Yes," complete Part XIV (㉔)	9		X
10 Self-Dealing (section 4941):			
a During the year did the organization (either directly or indirectly):			
(1) Engage in the sale or exchange, or leasing of property with a disqualified person? (㉕)	10a(1)		X
(2) Borrow money from, lend money to, or otherwise extend credit to (or accept it from) a disqualified person?	10a(2)		X
(3) Furnish goods, services, or facilities to (or accept them from) a disqualified person?	10a(3)		X
(4) Pay compensation to or pay or reimburse the expenses of a disqualified person? (㉖)	10a(4)	X	
(5) Transfer any income or assets to a disqualified person (or make any of either available for the benefit or use of a disqualified person)?	10a(5)		X
(6) Agree to pay money or property to a government official? (Exception: Check "No" if the organization agreed to make a grant to or to employ the official for a period after he or she terminates government service, if he or she is terminating within 90 days.)	10a(6)		X

CHRISFDN.X93

T A B L E B.4—*Continued*

Form 990-PF (1993)   Page 5

Part VII   Statements Regarding Activities (continued)

		Yes	No
10b	If the answer is "Yes" to any of questions 10a(1) through (6), were the acts engaged in excepted acts as described in Regulations sections 53.4941(d)-3 and 4, or Notice 93–41, 1993–27 I.R.B. 13? **10b**	X	
c	Did the organization engage in a prior year in any of the acts described in 10a, other than excepted acts, that were acts of self-dealing not corrected by the first day of the tax year beginning in 1993? **10c**		X
11	Taxes on failure to distribute income (section 4942) (does not apply for years the organization was a private operating foundation as defined in section 4942(j)(3) or 4942(j)(5)).		
a	At the end of tax year 1993, did the organization have any undistributed income (lines 6d and 6e, Part XIII) for tax year(s) beginning before 1993? If "Yes," list the years ▶ _____ ' _____ ' _____ **11a**		X
b	If 11a is "Yes," is the organization applying the provisions of section 4942(a)(2) (relating to incorrect valuation of assets) to the undistributed income for ALL such years? (If "Yes," attach statement—see instructions.) **11b**	N/A	
c	If the provisions of section 4942(a)(2) are being applied to ANY of the years listed in 11a, list the years here. ▶ _____ ' _____ ' _____		
12	Taxes on excess business holdings (section 4943):		
a	Did the organization hold more than a 2% direct or indirect interest in any business enterprise at any time during the year? **12a**		X
b	If "Yes," did it have excess business holdings in 1993 as a result of (1) any purchase by the organization or disqualified persons after May 26, 1969; (2) the lapse of the 5-year period (or longer period approved by the Commissioner under section 4943(c)(7)) to dispose of holdings acquired by gift or bequest; or (3) the lapse of the 10-, 15-, or 20-year first phase holding period? (Use Schedule C, Form 4720, to determine if the organization had excess business holdings in 1993.) **12b**	N/A	
13	Taxes on investments that jeopardize charitable purposes (section 4944) ⊘		
a	Did the organization invest during the year any amount in a manner that would jeopardize its charitable purposes? **13a**		X
b	Did the organization make any investment in a prior year (but after December 31, 1969) that could jeopardize its charitable purpose that had not been removed from jeopardy on the first day of the tax year beginning in 1993? **13b**		X
14	Taxes on taxable expenditures (section 4945) and political expenditures (section 4955):		
a	During the year did the organization pay or incur any amount to:		
(1)	Carry on propaganda, or otherwise attempt to influence legislation (section 4945(e))? **14a(1)**		X
(2)	Influence the outcome of any specific public election (see section 4955); or to carry on, directly or indirectly, any voter registration drive? **14a(2)**		X
(3)	Provide a grant to an individual for travel, study, or other similar purposes? **14a(3)**		X
(4)	Provide a grant to an organization, other than a charitable, etc., organization described in section 509(a)(1), (2), or (3), or section 4940(d)(2)? ⊘ **14a(4)**		X
(5)	Provide for any purpose other than religious, charitable, scientific, literary, or educational purposes, or for the prevention of cruelty to children or animals? **14a(5)**		X
b	If the answer is "Yes" to any of questions 14a(1) through (5), were all such transactions excepted transactions as described in Regulations section 53.4945 or Notice 93–41, 1993–27 I.R.B. 13? **14b**	N/A	
c	If the answer is "Yes" to question 14a(4), does the organization claim exemption from the tax because it maintained expenditure responsibility for the grant? **14c**	N/A	
	If "Yes," attach the statement required by Regulations section 53 4945–5(d).		
15	Did any persons become substantial contributors during the tax year? ⊘ **15**		X
	If "Yes," attach a schedule listing their names and addresses.		
16	During this tax year, did the organization maintain any part of its accounting/tax records on a computerized system? **16**	X	
17a	Did anyone request to see either the organization's annual return or its exemption application (or both)? ⊙ **17a**	X	
b	If "Yes," did the organization comply pursuant to the instructions? (See General Instruction Q.) **17b**	X	
18	The books are in care of ▶ The Foundation _____ Telephone no ▶ (212) 785-6423 Located at ▶ Address above _____ ZIP code ▶ _____		
19	Section 4947(a)(1) nonexempt charitable trusts filing Form 990-PF in lieu of Form 1041, U.S. Fiduciary Income Tax Return.—Check here ▶ ☐ and enter the amount of tax-exempt interest received or accrued during the year . . . . ▶	19	

Part VIII   Information About Officers, Directors, Trustees, Foundation Managers, Highly Paid Employees, and Contractors

1   List all officers, directors, trustees, foundation managers, and their compensation (see instructions):

(a) Name and address	(b) Title, and average hours per week devoted to position	(c) Contributions to employee benefit plans and deferred compensation	(d) Expense account, other allowances	(e) Compensation (If not paid, enter -0-)
Jane Cornell 60 Broad Street, New York, NY 10017	President 40 hours/wk	0	0	18,395
W.H. Larkin III 60 Broad Street, New York, NY 10017	Trustee 2 hours/week	0	0	1,000
Robert Perone 60 Broad Street, New York, NY 10017	Trustee 2 hours/week	0	0	1,000

CHRISFDN X93

T A B L E B.4—*Continued*

Form 990-PF (1993)　　　　　　　　　　　　　　　　　　　　　　　　　　Page 6

Part VIII　Information About Officers, Directors, Trustees, etc. (continued)

2　Compensation of five highest paid employees (other than those included on line 1—see instructions). If none, enter "NONE."

(a) Name and address of each employee paid more than $30,000	(b) Title and average hours per week devoted to position	(c) Contributions to employee benefit plans and deferred compensation	(d) Expense account, other allowances	(e) Compensation
NONE				

Total number of other employees paid over $30,000 . . . . ▶ | 0

3　Five highest paid persons for professional services—(see instructions). If none, enter "NONE."

(a) Name and address of each person paid more than $30,000	(b) Type of service	(c) Compensation
NONE		

Total number of others receiving over $30,000 for professional services . . . . ▶ | 0

Part IX-A　Summary of Direct Charitable Activities

List the foundation's four largest direct charitable activities during the tax year. Include relevant statistical information such as the number of organizations and other beneficiaries served, conferences convened, research papers produced, etc.	Expenses
1 Not Applicable	
2	
3	
4	

Part IX-B　Summary of Program-Related Investments (see instructions)

Describe any program-related investments made by the foundation during the tax year.	Amount
1 Not applicable	
2	
3	

CHRISFDN.X93

T A B L E B.4—*Continued*

Part X	**Minimum Investment Return (All domestic organizations must complete this part. Foreign foundations, see instructions.)**		
1	Fair market value of assets not used (or held for use) directly in carrying out charitable, etc., purposes:		
a	Average monthly fair market value of securities	1a	2,757,412
b	Average of monthly cash balances	1b	79,830
c	Fair market value of all other assets (see instructions)	1c	23,720
d	Total (add lines 1a, b, and c)	1d	2,860,962
e	Reduction claimed for blockage or other factors (attach detailed explanation) ▶ 1e 0		
2	Acquisition indebtedness applicable to line 1 assets	2	0
3	Line 1d minus line 2	3	2,860,962
4	Cash deemed held for charitable activities—Enter 1 1/2% of line 3 (for greater amount, see instructions)	4	42,914
5	Net value of noncharitable-use assets—Line 3 minus line 4 (Enter in Part V, line 4.)	5	2,818,048
6	Minimum investment return. (Enter 5% of line 5.)	6	140,902

Part XI	**Distributable Amount (see instructions)**	(Section 4942(j)(3) and (j)(5) private operating foundations and certain foreign organizations check here ▶ ☐ and do not complete this part.)		
1	Minimum investment return from Part X, line 6		1	140,902
2a	Tax on investment income for 1993 from Part VI, line 5	2a 4,519		
b	Income tax under subtitle A, for 1993	2b 0		
c	Line 2a plus line 2b		2c	4,519
3	Distributable amount before adjustments (line 1 minus line 2c)		3	136,383
4a	Recoveries of amounts treated as qualifying distributions	4a 0		
b	Income distributions from section 4947(a)(2) trusts	4b 0		
c	Line 4a plus line 4b		4c	0
5	Line 3 plus line 4c		5	136,383
6	Deduction from distributable amount (see instructions)		6	0
7	Distributable amount as adjusted (line 5 minus line 6). (Also enter in Part XIII, line 1.)		7	136,383

Part XII	**Qualifying Distributions (see instructions)**		
1	Amounts paid (including administrative expenses) to accomplish charitable, etc., purposes:		
a	Expenses, contributions, gifts, etc.—total from Part I, column (d), line 26	1a	854,485
b	Program-related investments—total of lines 1–3 of Part IX-B	1b	0
2	Amounts paid to acquire assets used (or held for use) directly in carrying out charitable, etc, purposes	2	
3	Amounts set aside for specific charitable projects that satisfy the:		
a	Suitability test (prior IRS approval required)	3a	
b	Cash distribution test (attach the required schedule)	3b	
4	Qualifying distributions (add lines 1a through 3b). (Enter in Part V, line 8, and Part XIII, line 4.)	4	854,485
5	Organizations that qualify under section 4940(e) for the reduced rate of tax on net investment income—enter 1% of Part I, line 27b (see instructions)	5	
6	Adjusted qualifying distributions (line 4 minus line 5)	6	854,485

Note: The amount on line 6 will be used in Part V, column (b), in subsequent years when calculating whether the foundation qualifies for the section 4940(e) reduction of tax in those years

T A B L E B.4—*Continued*

Form 990-PF (1993)   Page 8

Part XIII Undistributed Income (see instructions) (34)

		(a) Corpus	(b) Years prior to 1992	(c) 1992	(d) 1993
1	Distributable amount for 1993 from Part XI, line 7				136,383 (35)
2	Undistributed income, if any, as of the end of 1992:				
a	Enter amount for 1992 only				
b	Total for prior years: 19___,19___,19___				
3	Excess distributions carryover, if any, to 1993:				
a	From 1988	109,357			
b	From 1989	208,751			
c	From 1990 . (36)	(51,964)			
d	From 1991	79,147			
e	From 1992	101,101			
f	Total of lines 3a through e	446,392			
4	Qualifying distributions for 1993 from Part XII, line 4: $ 854,485 (37)				
a	Applied to 1992, but not more than line 2a .			0	
b	Applied to undistributed income of prior years (Election required—see instructions) . .		0		
c	Treated as distributions out of corpus (Election required—see instructions) . . .	0			
d	Applied to 1993 distributable amount . . .				136,383
e	Remaining amount distributed out of corpus	718,102			
5	Excess distributions carryover applied to 1993. (If an amount appears in column (d), the same amount must be shown in column (a).)	0			0
6	Enter the net total of each column as indicated below: (38)				
a	Corpus. Add lines 3f, 4c, and 4e. Subtract line 5.	1,164,494			
b	Prior years' undistributed income (line 2b minus line 4b).		0		
c	Enter the amount of prior years' undistributed income for which a notice of deficiency has been issued, or on which the section 4942(a) tax has been previously assessed.		0		
d	Subtract line 6c from line 6b. Taxable amount—see instructions		0		
e	Undistributed income for 1992 (line 2a minus line 4a). Taxable amount—see instructions . .			0	
f	Undistributed income for 1993 (line 1 minus lines 4d and 5). This amount must be distributed in 1994				0
7	Amounts treated as distributions out of corpus to satisfy requirements imposed by section 170(b)(1)(E) or 4942(g)(3) (see instructions) . .	0			
8	Excess distributions carryover from 1988 not applied on line 5 or line 7 (see instructions) . .	109,357			
9	Excess distributions carryover to 1994 (line 6a minus lines 7 and 8)	1,055,137			
10	Analysis of line 9:				
a	Excess from 1989	208,751			
b	Excess from 1990	(51,964)			
c	Excess from 1991	79,147			
d	Excess from 1992	101,101			
e	Excess from 1993	718,102			

CHRISFDN 793

T A B L E B.4—*Continued*

Form 990—PF (1993)   Page 9

Part XIV   Private Operating Foundations (see instructions and Part VII, question 9)

1a If the foundation has received a ruling or determination letter that it is a private operating foundation, and the ruling is effective for 1993, enter the date of the ruling . . . . ▶   ⑨

b Check box to indicate whether the organization is a private operating foundation described in section ☐ 4942(j)(3) or ☐ 4942(j)(5).

2a Enter the lesser of the adjusted net income from Part I or the minimum investment return from Part X (for 1991 through 1993; previously Part IX)	Tax year	Prior 3 years			
	(a) 1993	(b) 1992	(c) 1991	(d) 1990	(e) Total
b 85% of line 2a					
c Qualifying distributions from Part XII, line 4 (for 1991 through 1993, previously Part XIII, line 6)					
d Amounts included in line 2c not used directly for active conduct of exempt activities . .					
e Qualifying distributions made directly for active conduct of exempt activities (line 2c minus line 2d)					
3 Complete 3a, b, or c for the alternative test relied upon:					
a "Assets" alternative test—enter:					
(1) Value of all assets					
(2) Value of assets qualifying under section 4942(j)(3)(B)(i) . .					
b "Endowment" alternative test—Enter 2/3 of minimum investment return shown in Part X, line 6, (for 1991 through 1993; previously Part IX, line 6)					
c "Support" alternative test—enter:					
(1) Total support other than gross investment income (interest, dividends, rents, payments on securities loans (section 512(a)(5)), or royalties) . . .					
(2) Support from general public and 5 or more exempt organizations as provided in section 4942(j)(3)(B)(iii)					
(3) Largest amount of support from an exempt organization .					
(4) Gross investment income . . .					

Part XV   Supplementary Information (Complete this part only if the organization had $5,000 or more in assets at any time during the year—see instructions.)

1 Information Regarding Foundation Managers:

a List any managers of the foundation who have contributed more than 2% of the total contributions received by the foundation before the close of any tax year (but only if they have contributed more than $5,000). (See section 507(d)(2).)

NONE

b List any managers of the foundation who own 10% or more of the stock of a corporation (or an equally large portion of the ownership of a partnership or other entity) of which the foundation has a 10% or greater interest.

NONE

2 Information Regarding Contribution, Grant, Gift, Loan, Scholarship, etc., Programs:

Check here ▶ ☐ if the organization only makes contributions to preselected charitable organizations and does not accept unsolicited requests for funds. If the organization makes gifts, grants, etc., (see instructions) to individuals or organizations under other conditions, complete items 2a, b, c, and d.

a The name, address, and telephone number of the person to whom applications should be addressed:

Jane Cornell - 60 Broad Street, New York, NY 10017   212-678-6423

b The form in which applications should be submitted and information and materials they should include:

Letter describing activities/audited financial statements/Form 990

c Any submission deadlines:

NONE

d Any restrictions or limitations on awards, such as by geographical areas, charitable fields, kinds of institutions, or other factors:

NONE

CHRISFDN X93

T A B L E B.4—*Continued*

Form 990-PF (1993)				Page **10**

Part XV Supplementary Information (continued)

3   Grants and Contributions Paid During the Year or Approved for Future Payment

Recipient Name and address (home or business)	If recipient is an individual, show any relationship to any foundation manager or substantial contributor	Foundation status of recipient	Purpose of grant or contribution	Amount
a Paid during the year				
See attached schedule ④				
Total			▶ **3a**	0
b Approved for future payment See attached schedule				
Total			▶ **3b**	0

CHRISFDN X93

T A B L E B.4—*Continued*

Form 990-PF (1983)   Page 11

Part XVI-A Analysis of Income-Producing Activities ㊶

Enter gross amounts unless otherwise indicated.

1 Program service revenue:	Unrelated business income		Excluded by section 512, 513, or 514		(e) Related or exempt function income (See instructions.)
	(a) Business code	(b) Amount	(c) Exclusion code	(d) Amount	
a _____					
b _____					
c _____					
d _____					
e _____					
f _____					
g Fees and contracts from government agencies .					
2 Membership dues and assessments					
3 Interest on savings and temporary cash investments			14	8,330	
4 Dividends and interest from securities			14	226,483	
5 Net rental income or (loss) from real estate:					
a Debt-financed property.					
b Not debt-financed property					
6 Net rental income or (loss) from personal property . .					
7 Other investment income					
8 Gain or (loss) from sales of assets other than inventory			18	20,000	
9 Net income from special events					
10 Gross profit or (loss) from sales of inventory . . .					
11 Other revenue: a _____					
b _____					
c _____					
d _____					
e _____					
12 Subtotal (add columns (b), (d), and (e))		0		254,813	0

13 TOTAL (add line 12, columns (b), (d), and (e)) . . . . ▶ 13 ___ 254,813
(See worksheet for line 13 instructions to verify calculations.)

Part XVI-B Relationship of Activities to the Accomplishment of Exempt Purposes

Line No. ▼	Explain below how each activity for which income is reported in column (e) of Part XVI-A contributed importantly to the accomplishment of the organization's exempt purposes (other than by providing funds for such purposes). (See instructions.)
	N A

CHRISFDN X93

T A B L E B.4—*Continued*

Form 990-PF (1993)
Page 12

Part XVII Information Regarding Transfers To and Transactions and Relationships With Noncharitable Exempt Organizations

		Yes	No
1 Did the organization directly or indirectly engage in any of the following with any other organization described in section 501(c) of the Code (other than section 501(c)(3) organizations) or in section 527, relating to political organizations?			
a Transfers from the reporting organization to a noncharitable exempt organization of:			
(1) Cash	1a(1)		X
(2) Other assets	a(2)		X
b Other Transactions:			
(1) Sales of assets to a noncharitable exempt organization	b(1)		X
(2) Purchases of assets from a noncharitable exempt organization	b(2)		X
(3) Rental of facilities or equipment	b(3)		X
(4) Reimbursement arrangements	b(4)		X
(5) Loans or loan guarantees	b(5)		X
(6) Performance of services or membership or fundraising solicitations	b(6)		X
c Sharing of facilities, equipment, mailing lists, other assets, or paid employees	c		X

d If the answer to any of the above is "Yes," complete the following schedule. Column (b) should always show the fair market value of the goods, other assets, or services given by the reporting organization. If the organization received less than fair market value in any transaction or sharing arrangement, show in column (d) the value of the goods, other assets, or services received.

(a) Line no.	(b) Amount involved	(c) Name of noncharitable exempt organization	(d) Description of transfers, transactions, and sharing arrangements

2a Is the organization directly or indirectly affiliated with, or related to, one or more tax-exempt organizations described in section 501(c) of the Code (other than section 501(c)(3)) or in section 527? ☐ Yes ☒ No

b If "Yes," complete the following schedule

(a) Name of organization	(b) Type of organization	(c) Description of relationship

Part XVIII Public Inspection

1 Enter the date the notice of availability of the annual return appeared in a newspaper ► 5/09/94

2 Enter the name of the newspaper ► New York Times

3 Check here ► ☒ to indicate that you have attached a copy of the newspaper notice as required by the instructions. (If the notice is not attached, the return will be considered incomplete.)

Please Sign Here

Under penalties of perjury, I declare that I have examined this return, including accompanying schedules and statements, and to the best of my knowledge and belief, it is true, correct, and complete. Declaration of preparer (other than taxpayer or fiduciary) is based on all information of which preparer has any knowledge.

► Signature of officer or trustee   Date   ► Title

Paid Preparer's Use Only

Preparer's signature ►	Date	Check if self-employed ► ☐	Preparer's social security no
Firm's name (or yours if self-employed) and address ►		EI No. ►	
		ZIP code ►	

CHRISFDN 993

T A B L E   B.5

Form **990-T**	**Exempt Organization Business Income Tax Return** **(and proxy tax under section 6033(e))**	OMB No. 1545-0687
Department of the Treasury Internal Revenue Service	For calendar year 1994 or other tax year beginning ...., 1994, and ending ...., 19 .... ► See separate instructions.	**1994**

A ☐ Check box if address changed		Name of organization	D Employer identification number (Employees' trust, see instructions for Block D.)
B Exempt under section ☐ 501( )( ) or ☐ 408(e)	**Please Print or Type**	Number, street, and room or suite no. (If a P.O. box, see page 5 of instructions.)	
C Book value of all assets at end of year		City or town, state, and ZIP code	E Unrelated business activity codes (see instructions for Block E)

F   Group exemption number (see instructions for Block F) ►

G   Check type of organization. ► ☐ 501(c) Corporation   ☐ 501(c) Trust   ☐ Section 401(a) trust   ☐ Section 408(a) trust

H   Describe the organization's primary unrelated business activity. (See instructions for Block H.)

I   During the tax year, was the corporation a subsidiary in an affiliated group or a parent-subsidiary controlled group? . . ► ☐ Yes ☐No
If "Yes," enter the name and identifying number of the parent corporation. (See instructions for Block I.) ►

Part I Unrelated Trade or Business Income		(A) Income	(B) Expenses	(C) Net
1a Gross receipts or sales				
b Less returns and allowances _____ c Balance ►	1c			
2 Cost of goods sold (Schedule A, line 7)	2			
3 Gross profit (subtract line 2 from line 1c)	3			
4a Capital gain net income (attach Schedule D)	4a			
b Net gain (loss) (Form 4797, Part II, line 20) (attach Form 4797)	4b			
c Capital loss deduction for trusts	4c			
5 Income (loss) from partnerships (attach statement) . . .	5			
6 Rent income (Schedule C)	6			
7 Unrelated debt-financed income (Schedule E)	7			
8 Interest, annuities, royalties, and rents from controlled organizations (Schedule F)	8			
9 Investment income of a section 501(c)(7), (9), or (17) organization (Schedule G)	9			
10 Exploited exempt activity income (Schedule I).	10			
11 Advertising income (Schedule J)	11			
12 Other income (see instructions—attach schedule)	12			
13 TOTAL (combine lines 3 through 12)	13			

Part II Deductions Not Taken Elsewhere (See instructions for limitations on deductions.) (Except for contributions, deductions must be directly connected with the unrelated business income.)		
14 Compensation of officers, directors, and trustees (Schedule K)	14	
15 Salaries and wages	15	
16 Repairs and maintenance	16	
17 Bad debts	17	
18 Interest (attach schedule).	18	
19 Taxes and licenses.	19	
20 Charitable contributions (see instructions for limitation rules)	20	
21 Depreciation (attach Form 4562) . . . . [21]		
22 Less depreciation claimed on Schedule A and elsewhere on return . [22a]	22b	
23 Depletion	23	
24 Contributions to deferred compensation plans	24	
25 Employee benefit programs	25	
26 Excess exempt expenses (Schedule I)	26	
27 Excess readership costs (Schedule J)	27	
28 Other deductions (attach schedule)	28	
29 TOTAL DEDUCTIONS (add lines 14 through 28)	29	
30 Unrelated business taxable income before net operating loss deduction (subtract line 29 from line 13).	30	
31 Net operating loss deduction	31	
32 Unrelated business taxable income before specific deduction (subtract line 31 from line 30) . .	32	
33 Specific deduction	33	
34 Unrelated business taxable income (subtract line 33 from line 32). If line 33 is greater than line 32, enter the smaller of zero or line 32	34	

For Paperwork Reduction Act Notice, see page 1 of separate instructions.   Cat. No. 11291J   Form **990-T** (1994)

T A B L E B.5—*Continued*

Form 990-T (1994)   Page 2

Part III   Tax Computation

35 **Organizations Taxable as Corporations** (see instructions for tax computation)
Controlled group members (sections 1561 and 1563)—check here ☐ and:
a Enter your share of the $50,000, $25,000, and $9,925,000 taxable income brackets (in that order):
(1) |$ | (2) |$ | (3) |$ |
b Enter organization's share of: (1) additional 5% tax (not more than $11,750) |$ |
(2) additional 3% tax (not more than $100,000) . . . . |$ |
c Income tax on the amount on line 34 . . . . ▶ | 35c |

36 **Trusts Taxable at Trust Rates** (see instructions for tax computation) Income tax on the amount
on line 34 from: ☐ Tax rate schedule or ☐ Schedule D (Form 1041) . . . . ▶ | 36 |
37 Proxy tax (see instructions) . . . . ▶ | 37 |

Part IV   Tax and Payments

38a Foreign tax credit (corporations attach Form 1118; trusts attach Form 1116) . | 38a | |
b Other credits. (see instructions). . . . . | 38b | |
c General business credit—Check if from:
☐ Form 3800 or ☐ Form (specify) ▶ .... | 38c | |
d Credit for prior year minimum tax (attach Form 8801 or 8827) . . . | 38d | |
39 Total (add lines 38a through 38d) . . . . | 39 |
40 Subtract line 39 from the total of lines 35c and 37 **OR** the total of lines 36 and 37 . . . . | 40 |
41 Recapture taxes. Check if from: ☐ Form 4255 ☐ Form 8611 . . . . | 41 |
42a Alternative minimum tax |$ | **b** Environmental tax |$ | | 42c |
43 **Total tax** (add lines 40, 41, 42c) . . . . | 43 |
44 **Payments: a** 1993 overpayment credited to 1994 . . . . . . | 44a | |
b 1994 estimated tax payments . . . . | 44b | |
c Tax deposited with Form 7004 or Form 2758 . . . . | 44c | |
d Foreign organizations—Tax paid or withheld at source (see instructions) | 44d | |
e Other credits and payments (see instructions). . . . . | 44e | |
45 Total payments (add lines 44a through 44e) . . . . | 45 |
46 Estimated tax penalty (see the instructions on page 3). Check ▶ ☐ if Form 2220 is attached . | 46 |
47 **Tax due**—If line 45 is less than the total of lines 43 and 46, enter amount owed . . . . . ▶ | 47 |
48 **Overpayment**—If line 45 is larger than the total of lines 43 and 46, enter amount overpaid . . . ▶ | 48 |
49 Enter the amount of line 48 you want: **Credited to 1995 estimated tax** ▶ | Refunded ▶ | 49 |

Part V   Statements Regarding Certain Activities and Other Information (See instructions on page 11.)

		Yes	No
1	At any time during the 1994 calendar year, did the organization have an interest in or a signature or other authority over a financial account in a foreign country (such as a bank account, securities account, or other financial account)? If "Yes," the organization may have to file Form TD F 90-22.1. If "Yes," enter the name of the foreign country here ▶		
2	Was the organization the grantor of, or transferor to, a foreign trust that existed during the current tax year, whether or not the organization had any beneficial interest in it? . . . . If "Yes," the organization may have to file Forms 3520, 3520-A, or 926.		
3	Enter the amount of tax-exempt interest received or accrued during the tax year ▶ $		

SCHEDULE A—COST OF GOODS SOLD (See instructions on page 11.)
Method of inventory valuation (specify) ▶

1	Inventory at beginning of year	1		**6** Inventory at end of year. . . .	6	
2	Purchases.	2		**7** Cost of goods sold. Subtract line 6		
3	Cost of labor.	3		from line 5. (Enter here and on		
4a	Additional section 263A costs (attach schedule)	4a		line 2, Part I.)	7	
b	Other costs (attach schedule)	4b		**8** Do the rules of section 263A (with respect to	Yes	No
5	TOTAL—Add lines 1 through 4b	5		property produced or acquired for resale) apply to the organization?		

The books are in care of ▶	Telephone number ▶ ( )

Please Sign Here
Under penalties of perjury, I declare that I have examined this return, including accompanying schedules and statements, and to the best of my knowledge and belief, it is true, correct, and complete. Declaration of preparer (other than taxpayer) is based on all information of which preparer has any knowledge.

▶ _____ | _____ | ▶ _____
Signature of officer or fiduciary | Date | Title

Paid Preparer's Use Only

Preparer's signature ▶		Date	Check if self-employed ▶ ☐	Preparer's social security number
Firm's name (or yours, if self-employed) and address ▶			E.I. No. ▶	
			ZIP code ▶	

T A B L E B.5—*Continued*

Form 990-T (1994)   Page **3**

SCHEDULE C—RENT INCOME (FROM REAL PROPERTY AND PERSONAL PROPERTY LEASED WITH REAL PROPERTY)
(See instructions on page 12.)

1 Description of property

(1)

(2)

(3)

(4)

2 Rent received or accrued		**3 Deductions directly connected with the income in columns 2(a) and 2(b) (attach schedule)**
(a) From personal property (if the percentage of rent for personal property is more than 10% but not more than 50%)	**(b)** From real and personal property (if the percentage of rent for personal property exceeds 50% or if the rent is based on profit or income)	
(1)		
(2)		
(3)		
(4)		
Total	Total	Total deductions. Enter here and on line 6, column (B), Part I, page 1. ▶

Total Income (Add totals of columns 2(a) and 2(b). Enter here and on line 6, column (A), Part I, page 1.) . . ▶

SCHEDULE E—UNRELATED DEBT-FINANCED INCOME (See instructions on page 12.)

1 Description of debt-financed property	**2** Gross income from or allocable to debt-financed property	**3** Deductions directly connected with or allocable to debt-financed property	
		(a) Straight line depreciation (attach schedule)	**(b)** Other deductions (attach schedule)
(1)			
(2)			
(3)			
(4)			

4 Amount of average acquisition debt on or allocable to debt-financed property (attach schedule)	**5** Average adjusted basis of or allocable to debt-financed property (attach schedule)	**6** Column 4 divided by column 5	**7** Gross income reportable (column 2 × column 6)	**8** Allocable deductions (column 6 × total of columns 3(a) and 3(b))
(1)		%		
(2)		%		
(3)		%		
(4)		%		
			Enter here and on line 7, column (A), Part I, page 1.	Enter here and on line 7, column (B), Part I, page 1.

Totals . . . . ▶

Total dividends-received deductions included in column 8 . . . . ▶

SCHEDULE F—INTEREST, ANNUITIES, ROYALTIES, AND RENTS FROM CONTROLLED ORGANIZATIONS
(See instructions on page 13.)

1 Name and address of controlled organization(s)	**2** Gross income from controlled organization(s)	**3** Deductions of controlling organization directly connected with column 2 income (attach schedule)	**4** Exempt controlled organizations		
			(a) Unrelated business taxable income	**(b)** Taxable income computed as though not exempt under sec. 501(a), or the amount in col. (a), whichever is larger	**(c)** column (a) divided by column (b)
(1)					%
(2)					%
(3)					%
(4)					%

5 Nonexempt controlled organizations			**6** Gross income reportable (column 2 × column 4(c) or column 5(c))	**7** Allowable deductions (column 3 × column 4(c) or column 5(c))
(a) Excess taxable income	**(b)** Taxable income, or amount in column (a), whichever is larger	**(c)** Column (a) divided by Column (b)		
(1)		%		
(2)		%		
(3)		%		
(4)		%		
			Enter here and on line 8, column (A), Part I, page 1.	Enter here and on line 8, column (B), Part I, page 1.

Totals. . . . . ▶

T A B L E B.5—*Continued*

Form 990-T (1994)   Page **4**

SCHEDULE G—INVESTMENT INCOME OF A SECTION 501(c)(7), (9), OR (17) ORGANIZATION
(See instructions on page 13.)

1 Description of income	2 Amount of income	3 Deductions directly connected (attach schedule)	4 Set-asides (attach schedule)	5 Total deductions and set-asides (col. 3 plus col. 4)
(1)				
(2)				
(3)				
(4)				
Totals ▶	Enter here and on line 9, column (A), Part I, page 1.			Enter here and on line 9, column (B), Part I, page 1.

SCHEDULE I—EXPLOITED EXEMPT ACTIVITY INCOME, OTHER THAN ADVERTISING INCOME
(See instructions on page 14.)

1 Description of exploited activity	2 Gross unrelated business income from trade or business	3 Expenses directly connected with production of unrelated business income	4 Net income (loss) from unrelated trade or business (column 2 minus column 3). If a gain, compute cols. 5 through 7.	5 Gross income from activity that is not unrelated business income	6 Expenses attributable to column 5	7 Excess exempt expenses (column 6 minus column 5, but not more than column 4).
(1)						
(2)						
(3)						
(4)						
Column totals ▶	Enter here and on line 10, col. (A), Part I, page 1.	Enter here and on line 10, col. (B), Part I, page 1.				Enter here and on line 26, Part II, page 1.

SCHEDULE J—ADVERTISING INCOME (See instructions on page 14.)

Part I Income From Periodicals Reported on a Consolidated Basis

1 Name of periodical	2 Gross advertising income	3 Direct advertising costs	4 Advertising gain or (loss) (col. 2 minus col. 3). If a gain, compute cols. 5 through 7.	5 Circulation income	6 Readership costs	7 Excess readership costs (column 6 minus column 5, but not more than column 4).
(1)						
(2)						
(3)						
(4)						
Column totals (carry to Part II, line (5)) ▶						

Part II Income From Periodicals Reported on a Separate Basis (For each periodical listed in Part II, be sure to fill in columns 2 through 7 on a line-by-line basis.)

(1)						
(2)						
(3)						
(4)						
(5) Totals from Part I						
Column totals, Part II ▶	Enter here and on line 11, col. (A), Part I, page 1.	Enter here and on line 11, col. (B), Part I, page 1.				Enter here and on line 27, Part II, page 1.

SCHEDULE K—COMPENSATION OF OFFICERS, DIRECTORS, AND TRUSTEES (See instructions on page 14.)

1 Name	2 Title	3 Percent of time devoted to business	4 Compensation attributable to unrelated business
		%	
		%	
		%	
		%	
Total—Enter here and on line 14, Part II, page 1 . . . . ▶			

The nonprofit entity must make sure the donor's contribution will be tax-deductible. In this regard, certain rules must be followed, such as (1) the donor cannot maintain control over the donation, and (2) the donor may not receive any direct benefits from the donation. Donors must obtain a written acknowledgment for contributions of $250 or more to support a tax deduction. A canceled check is not sufficient to support a charitable deduction in excess of $250. If goods or services are provided by the NPO to the donor (e.g., dinner), only the excess donated over the fair market value of such goods or services is deductible as a charitable contribution.

STATE TAX FORMS

State reports are also required. Form CT-2, for example, is a periodic report filed in California. Table B.6 presents a copy of CT-2. New York State tax reporting includes Form ST-119.2 (Application for an Exempt Organization Certificate), shown in Table B.7, and Form CT-247 (Application for Exemption from Corporate Franchise Taxes by a Not-for-Profit Organization), presented in Table B.8.

T A B L E B.6

FORM **CT – 2** (REV. 7-94)

MAIL TO:
Registry of Charitable Trusts
P.O. Box 903447
Sacramento, CA 94203-4470
Telephone (916) 445-2021

PERIODIC REPORT

TO ATTORNEY GENERAL OF CALIFORNIA

Section 12586, California Government Code

Failure to file this report by the 15th day of the fifth month after the close of your accounting period may result in the loss of your tax exemption and the assessment of a minimum tax of $800 plus interest.

ACCOUNTING PERIOD — For the Year Beginning _____ , 19 ____ and Ending _____ , 19 ___

If address changed check here . . . ▶ ☐ and show changes below ▼
File Form with label. Otherwise, print or type address.

●Name of organization

Address (number and street)

City or town, State, and ZIP code

State Charity registration number CT | | | | | | |
(If unknown, leave blank)

Corporate or
Organization No._____

	Yes	No
A. Is the organization exempt from federal income tax?		

B. If "no", is this entity a split-interest trust?
If "no", affix Exhibit A to explain your federal tax status.

PART I   FILING REQUIREMENTS: CHECK ONE BOX AND ATTACH THE REQUIRED IRS FORMS

☐ This entity is **not** a private foundation. **We have attached** a completed copy of IRS Form 990 or 990EZ, and Schedule A (Form 990) and related attachments (even though we may not be required to file these uniform forms with the IRS). Omit Part III below.

☐ This entity is a private foundation. **We have attached** a completed copy of IRS Form 990-PF and related attachments. Complete all Parts below.

PART IA   ACTIVITIES: ENTER AMOUNTS AND CHECK BOX

	Yes	No

Gross receipts $_____   Total assets $_____
Are the program activities of this entity limited solely to grantmaking?. . . . .

PART II   STATEMENTS REGARDING THIS ORGANIZATION DURING THE PERIOD OF THIS REPORT   Yes | No

1 Was 50% or more of your total revenue from government agencies? (See line 1 instructions)   1
   If "yes", affix in sequence Exhibit 1. List the name, address or telephone number, grant amount, and purpose of grant for your two main granting agencies.

2 Were you audited by any government agency which resulted in audit exceptions in excess of $50,000 being taken?.   2
   If "yes", affix as Exhibit 2 a copy of the audit report. Enter here the total exceptions. . . . . 2a $_____

3 Did or will an independent public accountant issue a report on your financial statements?   3
   If "yes", enter here: Accountant's Name _____ Telephone ( )_____

4 Is any of your property held in the name of or commingled with the property of any other organization or person, other than pooled investment funds?   4
   If "yes", affix in sequence as Exhibit 4 a justification. Include a list and value of assets commingled if not provided in a prior year.

5 Were there any contracts, loans, leases or other financial transactions between the organization and any officer, director or trustee thereof either directly or with an entity in which any such officer, director or trustee had any financial interest?   5
   If "yes", affix in sequence as Exhibit 5 a full explanation. Enter here the amount involved. . . . . . . 5a $_____

6 Did you transfer or donate anything to an organization that is **not** tax-exempt under Section 501 (c) (3) or 501 (c) (4) of the IRC?   6
   If "yes", affix in sequence as Exhibit 6 a justification of why noncharitable entities receive your charitable property.
   Enter here the fair market value of the donations. . . . . 6a $_____

7 Did this organization regularly solicit salvage, sell salvage in a thrift store, or was it a party to a contract involving the solicitation or sale of salvage? If "yes", include amounts on Form 990, line 10.   7

8 Was there any theft, embezzlement or diversion of your charitable property; or, were you or any of your officers, directors or trustees a party to any court action in which it was alleged that any trust or fiduciary duty was breached?   8
   If "yes", affix in sequence as Exhibit 8 a full explanation. . . . .

9 Were any organization funds used to pay any penalty, fine or judgment?   9
   If "yes", affix as Exhibit 9 a full explanation. Enter here the total amount involved. . . . . 9a $_____

Under penalties of perjury, I declare that I have examined this report, including accompanying documents, schedules and statements, and to the best of my knowledge and belief, it is true, correct and complete.

Organization's area code and telephone number ( )_____-_____

Signature of authorized officer (See instructions)   Printed Name   Title   Date
PAGE 1, Duplicate—Retain for your records

T A B L E B.6—*Continued*

10 Did you receive $20,000 or more in direct public support (Form 990, line 1(a) or included in Form 990-PF, Part I, line 1)? 10
   If "yes", enter the following amounts that break down Form 990, line 1(a):
   (a) Support from the general public, contributions from individuals . . . . 10a _____
   (b) Foundation and trust grants, gifts, contributions . . . . 10b _____
   (c) Corporate and other business grants, gifts, contributions . . . . 10c _____
   (d) Bequests from wills and estates . . . . 10d _____
   (e) Total direct public support (add lines a through d. Should equal Form 990, line 1(a).) . . . . . 10e _____
11 Did you contract with or use the services of a fundraising consultant or commercial fundraiser?   11
   If "yes", complete Part IV (Form CT-2). . . . .
12 Did your invested assets total $50,000 or more? If "yes", complete Part V (Form CT-2) (See line 12 instructions) 12
13 Did you receive any income from any bingo game? 13
   If "yes", enter here and on Form 990, line 9a, the gross receipts provided by all bingo players before deductions for any
   costs or prizes, whether or not all gross receipts were received by your organization. . . . . 13a $_____
14 Enter the total annual compensation (salary plus all benefits) paid to the highest paid employee for:
   (a) The fiscal year* covered by this report . . . . 14a $_____
   (b) The fiscal year* covered by the prior report . . . . 14b $_____
              *(If a fiscal year report covers less than 12 months for any reason, annualize amounts to include a full year.)
   Employee compensation for the five highest paid employees:
   (c) Did any employee receive the benefit of a residence for personal use which was owned or leased by
        the organization? 14c
   (d) Did the organization lease, rent or purchase any equipment, property, or facility to or from an
        employee or any business entity in which the employee had any financial interest? 14d
        If "yes", enter here the total amount involved . . . . 14d $_____
   (e) Did the organization make any loans in excess of $5,000 to any employee? 14e

   If any of questions 14(c), (d), or (e) are answered "yes", affix in sequence as Exhibit 14 specific details to
   fully explain any "yes" response and fully complete Part I, Schedule A (Form 990).

15 Did you make payments totalling over $50,000 to any independent consultants or contractors other than for (a)
   fundraising, (b) accounting, (c) legal fees, (d) investment fees? 15
   If "yes", either fully complete Part II of Schedule A (Form 990) for the five highest paid regardless of the
   amounts; or, affix in sequence as Exhibit 15 a similar schedule of names, addresses, type of service and
   amounts. Enter here the total of all payments to all independent contractors. . . . . 15a $_____

16 If you incurred or paid any of the following taxes and/or related penalties, enter the amounts in the
   blanks provided.

		Tax	Penalty
a Payroll (employer's portion of both federal and state)	16a		
b Sales (on items you sold)	16b		
c Personal Property	16c		
d Real Estate	16d		
e Unrelated Business Income	16e		

17 Were you named as a beneficiary to receive a portion of commercial transactions (commercial co- | Yes | No |
   ventures, joint venture marketing, or cause-related marketing)?
   If "yes", enter here the gross amount received . . . . 17a $_____

(18-30 not currently in use)

PAGE 2

T A B L E   B.6—*Continued*

PART III   ADDITIONAL INFORMATION FROM PRIVATE FOUNDATIONS ONLY

	Yes	No

31 Did you file a Form 4720 with the Internal Revenue Service? 31
      If "yes", "affix in sequence as Exhibit 31" a copy of Form 4720 and enter here the amount of total taxes paid
      with that return **31a**
  (32–39 not currently in use)

PART IV   FUNDRAISING CONSULTANT OR COMMERCIAL FUNDRAISER (FC-CFR)   (SEE QUESTION 11)

	EVENT # 1	EVENT # 2	EVENT # 3 **	TOTAL
40 Brief Description of Campaign, Drive or Event				
41 Date or Period Covered				
42 Name of FC-CFR				
43 Address of FC-CFR				
44 Total Public Donations *			44	
45 All Payments to FC-CFR			45	
46 All Other Fund-Raising Expenses			46	
47 Net Proceeds (Line 44 Less 45 and 46)			47	

(48–59 not currently in use)   * On line 44, do **not** deduct any costs from gross donations.
      ** NOTE: If more than three events, attach a schedule using the same format and include amounts in Part IV totals.

PART V   SUMMARY OF INVESTMENTS TOTALING $50,000 OR MORE   (SEE QUESTION 12)

60 Securities, beginning of year at cost (990, line 54(A) or 990-PF, Part II, lines 10a–c and 12 column (a)) . . . . 60 _____
61 Securities acquired, at cost or original basis . . . . 61 _____
62 Securities sold, at cost or original basis (may include sales expenses). . . . . 62 _____
63 Securities, end of year at cost (990, line 54(B) or 990-PF, Part II, lines 10a–c and 12 column (b)) . . . . 63 _____
64 Securities, end of year at market value . . . . 64 _____
65 Sum of all gains on sales during the year . . . . 65 _____
66 Sum of all losses on sales during the year. . . . . 66 _____
67 Dividends and interest from securities (990, line 5 or 990-PF, Part I, line 4, column (a)) . . . . 67 _____
68 Total return realized (line 65 less line 66, plus line 67) . . . . 68 _____
69 "Less all fees, salaries, and other costs incurred to earn investment income" . . . . 69 _____
70 Net return realized from investments in securities (line 68 less line 69). . . . . 70 _____

Has this organization engaged in, purchased, sold or held during the year:

		Yes	No
71 Investments (any type) which produce no current income? 71			
72 Investments (any type) worth one half or less of original basis? 72			
73 Securities on margin? 73			
74 Warrants, puts, calls, options, commodity futures, or short sales? 74			
75 Stocks rated "Speculative Grade" by Moody's, or ranked "B–" or lower by Standard & Poor's? 75			
76 Securities not publicly traded? 76			
77 Municipal bonds or similar tax-exempt securities which yield less than taxable securities? 77			
78 Stock in which an officer, director or trustee owns 10% or more of the outstanding shares?. 78			

If "yes" on any line from 71–78, affix in sequence as Exhibit 78 a full explanation including original basis and current value.

94 24777

T A B L E   B.6—*Continued*

INSTRUCTIONS FOR FILING FORM CT-2

Periodic Report to Attorney General of California

THE ATTORNEY GENERAL IS RESPONSIBLE UNDER CALIFORNIA LAW TO PROTECT THE PUBLIC INTEREST IN ASSETS HELD FOR CHARITABLE PURPOSES (PURPOSES BENEFITING THE PUBLIC INTEREST). THIS RESPONSIBILITY IS CARRIED OUT IN PART BY REQUIRING ORGANIZATIONS AND TRUSTS HOLDING SUCH ASSETS TO REGISTER AND FILE PERIODIC REPORTS.

GENERAL INSTRUCTIONS

WHO MUST FILE A PERIODIC REPORT, FORM CT-2

Every corporation, association or trustee holding assets for the public benefit is required to file Form CT-2, EXCEPT:

(1) a government agency,

(2) a religious corporation sole,

(3) a cemetery corporation regulated under Chapter 19 of Division 3 of the Business and Professions Code.

(4) a political committee defined in Section 82013 of the California Government Code which is required to and which does file with the Secretary of State any statement pursuant to the provisions of Article 2 (commencing with Section 84200) of Chapter 4 of Title 9.

(5) a charitable corporation organized and operated primarily as a religious organization, educational institution or hospital.

(6) a health care service plan licensed pursuant to Section 1349 of the Health and Safety Code.

(7) corporate trustees which are subject to the jurisdiction of the Superintendent of Banks of the State of California or to the Comptroller of Currency of the United States. However, for testamentary trusts, such trustees should file a copy of a complete annual financial summary which is prepared in the ordinary course of business. See Probate Code Sections 16060–16063.

Those required to file Form CT-2 are frequently exempt from tax under Section 501(c)(3) or 501(c)(4) of the Internal Revenue Code and Section 23701d or 23701f of the California Revenue and Taxation Code. The requirement for reporting, however, is not dependent upon such tax exemption.

ALL PRIVATE FOUNDATIONS are required by Federal Law to file a copy of Form 990-PF and 4720 with this office even though certain foundations may be exempt from filing Form CT-2.

A NONEXEMPT CHARITABLE TRUST described in Section 4947(a)(1) of the Internal Revenue Code, which also meets the definition of a private foundation under Section 509(a) of the Internal Revenue Code, must comply with the reporting requirements of a private foundation by filing Form CT-2 with Form 990-PF attached.

WHAT TO FILE

A copy of Internal Revenue Service Form 990, 990EZ or 990-PF is a REQUIRED attachment to Form CT-2. These forms are the only acceptable computer input documents. A FORM CT-2 FILED WITHOUT A COPY OF THE APPLICABLE FEDERAL RETURN DOES NOT MEET THE FILING REQUIREMENT. Additional attachments may be sent as supplements to, but not in lieu of entering applicable information on the pertinent lines of Form CT-2 and federal returns. Do not enter comments like, "See Attached Statements" in lieu of entering amounts on the pertinent lines. Such attachments cannot be computer processed.

A few organizations which are required to file Form CT-2 may not be filing Form 990 or 990-PF with the Internal Revenue Service. All organizations must complete all parts and all lines of Form 990 to meet the Attorney Generals filing requirement even though Internal Revenue Service requirements may permit certain small organizations to omit the form or some lines on the Form 990.

Blank Forms 990, 990EZ or 990-PF may be obtained from the Internal Revenue Service or other sources of federal tax forms. Single copies of these forms is also available from the Registry of Charitable Trusts.

Remove any confidential list required by Internal Revenue Service of your large donors before filing a copy of Form 990 attachments with the Registry of Charitable Trusts, to avoid inadvertent public disclosure.

Forms CT-2 not completed in accordance with these instructions are not acceptable and do not meet the filing requirement.

Page 1 of Instructions (continued on the last page)

EXTENDED REPORTING

Small registrants MUST FILE AN INITIAL REPORT and thereafter may file only once every tenth year. EXCEPTION—A REPORT IS REQUIRED IF ANY ONE OF THE FOLLOWING OCCURS FOR THE YEAR BEING CONSIDERED:

(1) gross revenue exceeds $25,000; or

(2) total assets at any time exceed $25,000; or

(3) the public benefit purposes are amended or modified; or

(4) self-dealing transactions occur as defined in Cal. Corp. Code section 5233;

(5) loans are made by the organization to a director or officer; or

(6) substantial assets are sold or transferred; or

(7) the organization becomes inactive, disbands or dissolves; or

(8) ten years have passed since the last Form CT-2 was filed.

You must notify us of any address change even though Form CT-2 need not be filed.

If a blank Form CT-2 was sent to you but is not required to be filed because all of the above conditions are met, please return Form CT-2 with Part 1A amounts completed and an explanation that the organization is excused from filing under the extended reporting provisions. This will permit a correction of our records.

REPRODUCTION OF FORM CT-2 AND IRS ATTACHMENTS

The Attorney General prefers that the Form CT-2 filed be on the form with the preaddressed label affixed which is mailed to each registrant. Reproduced copies will be accepted subject to the following conditions:

(1) Reproductions must have a high standard of legibility and permanence, both as to original form and filled-in data. (2) The preaddressed label or a reproduction thereof must appear on the copy filed. (3) Both sides of the paper should be used in making reproductions, resulting in the same head to foot tumble style page arrangement as that of the official form. (4) All signatures must be original signatures affixed subsequent to the reproduction process. (5) The Attorney General reserves the right to reject any Form CT-2 or attachments which do not meet these conditions.

WHEN AND WHERE TO FILE

Form CT-2 must be filed on or before the 15th day of the fifth month (within 4½ months) following the close of your accounting period with the Registry of Charitable Trusts, P.O. Box 903447, Sacramento, CA 94203-4470.

FAILURE TO FILE ON TIME

If an organization or trust fails to file Form CT-2 on or before the due date, it is subject to the disallowance of state income tax exemption and the assessment of a minimum tax of $800, plus interest, which cannot be cancelled when Form CT-2 is subsequently filed. Further action will follow until the required report is filed.

Those persons responsible for delinquent filing are personally liable for the payment of taxes and interest incurred. Charitable funds may not be used to pay such liabilities.

EXTENSION OF TIME FOR FILING

If Form CT-2 and the required attachment of Internal Revenue Service forms, cannot be filed within four and one-half months after the accounting period ends, the organization has up to an additional six months to file without telephoning or filing a written request for an extension of time. However, an organization is not granted this extension if it has not complied with registration or filed the prior report by the due date of the current report.

If the current report is not filed by the extended due date, tax exemption may be disallowed. An $800 minimum tax plus interest may be assessed, for which the persons responsible may be personally liable.

T A B L E B.7

New York State Department of Taxation and Finance	New York State and Local Sales and Use Tax **Application for an Exempt Organization Certificate**	**ST-119.2** (1/94)

Name of organization

Address (number and street)   City (town), state and ZIP code

Name and telephone number of person to be contacted (if the person is someone other than an officer, this application must be accompanied by a power of attorney executed by the officer)

(   )

Date organized   Date incorporated   Federal identification number

Check the appropriate boxes to indicate the section of law and the purpose for which you are claiming exempt status.

1a ☐ **Section 1116(a)(4)**

☐ Religious   ☐ Testing for public safety   ☐ Prevention of cruelty to children or animals

☐ Charitable   ☐ Scientific   ☐ Fostering national or international amateur

☐ Educational   ☐ Literary   sports competition

1b ☐ **Section 1116(a)(5)**   Posts, organizations and auxiliary of past or present members of the armed services

What percentage of your members are past or present members of the armed services of the United States?   _____ %

What percentage of your members are cadets or are spouses, widows or widowers of cadets or past or present members of the armed services?   _____ %

What percentage of your members do not fall within either of the above categories?   _____ %

2 Are you currently registered as a vendor with the Tax Department? ☐ Yes ☐ No If Yes, enter your Certificate of Authority number _____.

If you answer Yes to questions 3 through 7, attach an explanation.

3 Has any distribution of the organization's property ever been made to shareholders or members?   ☐ Yes ☐ No

4 Does any part of the net earnings of the organization go to the benefit of any private shareholder or individual?   ☐ Yes ☐ No

5 Has the organization ever advocated or opposed pending or proposed legislation?   ☐ Yes ☐ No

6 Has the organization ever participated in a political campaign or endorsed a candidate for public office?   ☐ Yes ☐ No

7 If the organization fosters national or international amateur sports competition, does it provide any facilities or equipment, either directly or indirectly, for the use of amateur athletes?   ☐ Yes ☐ No

8 Have you received an exemption from federal income tax? (If Yes, see instructions)   ☐ Yes ☐ No

9 If you are a branch or chapter, has your parent organization received an exemption from federal income tax that applies to subordinate branches or chapters? (If Yes, see instructions)   ☐ Yes ☐ No

10 Check the appropriate box to indicate your type of organization.

☐ Corporation - (attach a copy of articles of incorporation, including filing receipt, and bylaws)

☐ Trust - (attach a copy of Declaration of Trust and bylaws)

☐ Other (attach a copy of constitution and bylaws)

11 Attach the following to this application:

— **Statement of activities** fully describing all current and proposed activities.

— **Statement of receipts and expenditures** for your most recent fiscal year of operation, clearly reflecting the nature and amount of receipts and the purpose and amount of expenditures. (If you have been in existence less than a year, submit a statement to date and a proposed budget for the rest of the year.)

— **Statement of assets and liabilities** as of the end of your most recent fiscal year (if you have been in existence less than a year, as of the date of this application).

I declare that I have examined the information given in this application and all attachments and, to the best of my knowledge and belief, it is correct and complete. I understand that a willfully false representation is a crime punishable under the laws of New York State including but not limited to sections 175.30, 175.35 and 210.45 of the Penal Law and section 1817(b) of the Tax Law.

Signature of officer or trustee   Date

Name and title of officer of trustee (please print)

T A B L E   B.8

New York State Department of Taxation and Finance

CT-247
(7/94)

Application for Exemption from Corporate Franchise Taxes By a Not-for-Profit Organization

Mailing Name and Address	Taxpayer's business name		Employer identification number		For office use only
	Business name at location below *(if different from business name above)* C/O				
	Street or PO Box	City or town	State	ZIP code	

Principal business activity	Date tax exemption claimed from	For audit use only
Form of organization ☐ Corporation ☐ Association ☐ Trust ☐ Other	Business/officer telephone number ( )	☐ Taxable ☐ Exempt
Date of formation	State or country of incorporation	

Indicate exact name of the law under which the entity was formed *(general corporation, not-for-profit, membership, etc.)*. Cite statutory provisions.

Federal return filed on Form: ☐ 990 ☐ 990T ☐ 1120 ☐ Other _____

1   Is the entity organized and operated as a not-for-profit organization? .... ☐ Yes ☐ No

2   Is the entity authorized to issue capital stock? If *Yes*, check the appropriate box below .... ☐ Yes ☐ No

☐ Title holding company   ☐ Collective investment   ☐ Other: _____

List shareholder: _____

3   Does any part of the net earnings of the organization benefit any officer, director, or member? .... ☐ Yes ☐ No

4   Is the entity exempt from federal income tax? .... ☐ Yes ☐ No

If *Yes*, indicate date of exemption: _____ **Submit a copy of the federal exemption letter when filing this form**

If *No*, indicate reason why exemption disallowed: _____

5   Is the entity engaged in an unrelated business activity at a location in New York State? .... ☐ Yes ☐ No

6   List location and type of activity for each office and other places of business *(attach separate sheet if necessary)*.

Location	Nature of activity

7   List officers, employees, agents and representatives in New York State and briefly describe their duties *(attach separate sheet if necessary)*.

Name	Title	Duties

8   List type and use of real property owned in New York State *(attach separate sheet if necessary)*.

Type	How used

9   Describe any New York State activities not shown above *(attach separate sheet if necessary)*.

Certification. I certify that this return and any attachments are to the best of my knowledge and belief true, correct and complete.

Signature of elected officer or authorized person	Official title	Date

Paid Preparer's Use Only	Firm's name *(or yours if self-employed)*	ID number	Date
	Address	Signature of Individual preparing this return	

About the Disk

HOW TO USE THE DISKETTE

Financial Management for Nonprofits includes a *Microsoft Excel* spreadsheet diskette with a set of computer-aided tools for managing the finances of NPOs. All the files contained in the diskette are drawn directly from the examples discussed in the book, so that you can practice various financial tools hands-on with *Excel*. Note that these files can be easily used with other software (I.e., *Quattro Pro* and *Lotus 1-2-3*) since they are compatible with each other. Designed to be readily modified and adapted, the files are meant to save time and to help gain insights into various techniques to nonprofit financial management. First, install the diskette on your hard disk (perhaps keep the original diskette intact for future use). Then customize the files with your own input data and experiment with them.

DISK TABLE OF CONTENTS

File Name	Text Reference	Title
03-ex-1.xls	Example 3.1; Figures 3.1, 3.2	Break-Even and Surplus Volume Charts
03-ex-10.xls	Example 3.10	Break-Even Calculation
03-ex-11.xls	Example 3.11	Break-Even Calculation
03-ex-12.xls	Example 3.12	CVP Analysis (Goal Seeking)
03-ex-15.xls	Example 3.15	Multi-Program Break-Even Analysis
03-ex-16.xls	Example 3.16	Multi-Program CVP Analysis (Goal Seeking)
04-ex-1.xls	Example 4.1	Trend Analysis
		Liquidation Analysis
		Analysis of Solvency
		Analysis of the Statement of Activities
04-ex-2.xls	Example 4.2	Financial Ratio Analysis
05-ex-4.xls	Example 5.4	Scatter Diagram and Regression Analysis

File Name	Text Reference	Title
05-ex-13.xls	Example 5.13	Sheet 1. Annual Enrollment Data for Pep University with Current and Previous Advertising Budgets
		Sheet 2. Simple Regression Output
		Sheet 3. Multiple Regression Output
08-ex-1.xls	Example 8.1, 8.2	Example 1. Labor Cost Data
		Example 2. Regression Output
08-ex-4.xls	Example 8.4	Sheet 1. X-Ray Unit—Medical Service Corporation—Performance Report—Static Budget
		Sheet 2. X-Ray Unit—Medical Service Corporation—Flexible Budget
		Sheet 3. X-Ray Unit—Medical Service Corporation—Performance Report—Flexible Budget
08-ex-5.xls	Example 8.5	Sheet 1. Jon Jay Hospital—Flexible Budget for Department 1
		Sheet 2. Flexible Budget Variance for Department 1
13-ex-2.xls	Example 13.2	Revenue and Cost Report, January 19X7
13-ex-9.xls	Examples 13.9, 13.11	Discounted Cash Flow (DCF) Analysis and IRR
13-ex-15a.xls	Example 13.16	"What-If" Model for College Planning—Scenario 1
13-ex-15b.xls		"What-If" Model for College Planning—Scenario 2

Disk Sample
Break-Even and Surplus-Volume Charts (Figure 3.1, 3.2)

p	v	Volume	Revenue	VC	FC	TC	Surplus
$250.00	$50.00	1000	$ 250,000	$ 50,000	$650,000	$700,000	$(450,000)
$250.00	$50.00	2000	$ 500,000	$100,000	$650,000	$750,000	$(250,000)
$250.00	$50.00	300	$ 750,000	$150,000	$650,000	$800,000	$ (50,000)
$250.00	$50.00	4000	$1,000,000	$200,000	$650,000	$850,000	$ 150,000
$250.00	$50.00	5000	$1,250,000	$250,000	$650,000	$900,000	$ 350,000
$250.00	$50.00	6000	$1,500,000	$300,000	$650,000	$950,000	$ 550,000

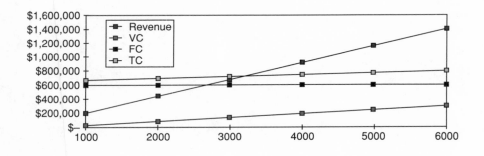

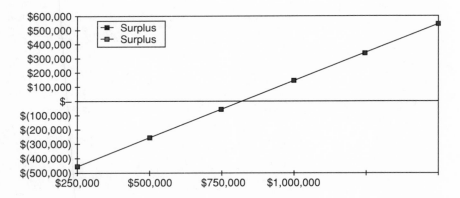

A List of Computer Software

There is a variety of computer software designed specifically for budgeting, forecasting, and activity-based costing. Some programs are *stand-alone* packages, others are *templates*, and still others are spreadsheet *add-ins*.

BUDGETING AND PLANNING SOFTWARE

Budget Express

Budget Express (add-in) "understands" the structure of financial worksheets and concepts (such as months, quarters, years, totals, and subtotals; speeding up budget; and forecast preparation). The program creates column headers for months, automatically totals columns and rows, and calculates quarterly and yearly summaries. For sophisticated "what-if" analyses, just specify your goal; Budget Express displays your current and target values as you make changes.

Up Your Cash Flow

This program (stand-alone) generates cash-flow, revenue, and expense forecasts; detailed income by service and payroll by employee forecasts; monthly balance sheets; bar graphs; ratio and break-even analyses; and more.

Cash Collector

This program (stand-alone) assists you in reviewing and aging receivables. You always know who owes what; nothing "falls through the cracks." What happens when collection action is required? Simply click through menu-driven screens to automatically generate letters and other professionally written collection documents (all included) that have been proved to pull in the payments.

Cash Flow Analysis

This software (stand-alone) provides projections of cash inflow and cash outflow. You input data into eight categories: sales, cost of sales, administrative expense, long-term debt, other cash receipts, inventory buildup/reduction, and capital expenditures (acquisition of long-term assets such as equipment). The program allows changes in assumptions and scenarios and provides a complete array of reports.

CapPLANS

This program (template) evaluates proposals based on net preset value (NPV), internal rate of return (IRR), and payout period. Runs up to four sensitivity analyses. It projects revenue over a 15-year horizon. In addition to preparing a complete report of your analysis, CapPLANS generates a concise, four-page executive summary—great for expediting approval. It can add ready-made graphs to illustrate revenue clearly, at a glance.

Project Evaluation Toolkit

This software (template) calculates the dollar value of your project based on six valuation methods, including discounted cash flow and impact on the balance sheet. It assesses intangibles such as impact on strategy or labor relations. It also uses scenario planning to show the effects of changing start dates, income forecasts, and other critical variables.

@Risk

How will a new competitor affect your market share? @Risk (add-in) calculates the likelihood of changes and events that affect your bottom line. First use @Risk's familiar "@" functions to define the risk in your worksheet. Then let @Risk run thousands of "what-if" tests, using one of two proven statistical sampling techniques—Monte Carlo and Latin Hypercube. You get a clear, colorful graph that tells you the likelihood of every possible bottom-line value. At a glance you'll know whether your risk is acceptable, or if you need to make a contingency plan.

CFO Spreadsheet Applications

These ready-to-use spreadsheet templates offer easy ways to make many financial decisions. They are divided into three modules: cash management, capital budgeting, and advanced topics.

What's Best!

If you have limited resources—for example, people, inventory, time, or cash—then What's Best! (stand-alone) can tell you how to allocate these resources in order to maximize or minimize a given objective, such as cost minimization. What's Best! uses a proven method—linear programming—to help you achieve your goals. This software can solve a variety of financial problems that cut across every industry at every level of decision making.

Inventory Analyst

Inventory Analyst (template) tells precisely how much inventory to order, and when to order it. Choose from four carefully explained ordering methods: economic order quantity (EOQ), fixed order quantity, fixed months requirements, and level load by work days. Inventory Analyst ensures that you'll always have enough stock to get you through your ordering period.

Just load up to 48 months worth of inventory history, and Inventory Analyst makes the forecast based on one of three forecasting methods: time series, exponential smoothing, and moving averages. It explains which method is best for you. Inventory Analyst will adjust your forecast for seasonality, too.

FORECASTING AND STATISTICAL SOFTWARE

There are numerous computer software packages that are used for forecasting purposes. They are broadly divided into two major categories: forecasting software and general purpose statistical software. Some programs are stand-alone, while others are spreadsheet add-ins. Still others are templates. A brief summary of some popular programs follows.

Forecast! GFX

This is a stand-alone forecasting system that can perform five types of time-series analysis: seasonal adjustment, linear and nonlinear trend, moving-average, exponential smoothing, and decomposition. Trend analysis supports linear, exponential, hyperbolic, S-curve, and polynomial trends. Hyperbolic trend models are used to analyze data that indicate a decline toward a limit, such as the output of an oil well or the price of a particular model of personal computer. Forecast! GFX can perform multiple-regression analysis with up to 10 independent variables.

ForeCalc

This software (add-in) features the following:

- It uses nine forecasting techniques and includes both automatic and manual modes.
- It eliminates the need to export or reenter data.

You can use it in either automatic or manual mode. In automatic mode, just highlight the historical data in your spreadsheet, such as income and expenses; then ForeCalc tests several exponential-smoothing models and picks the one that best fits your data.

Forecast results can be transferred to your spreadsheet with upper and lower confidence limits. ForeCalc generates a line graph showing the original data, the forecasted values, and confidence limits.

ForeCalc can automatically choose the most accurate forecasting technique:

- Simple one-parameter smoothing.
- Holt's two-parameter smoothing.
- Winters's three-parameter smoothing.
- Trendless seasonal models.
- Dampened versions of Holt's and Winters's smoothing.

ForeCalc's manual mode lets you select the type of trend and the seasonality—yielding nine possible model combinations. You can vary the type of trend (constant, linear, or dampened), as well as the seasonality (nonseasonal, additive, or multiplicative).

StatPlan IV

StatPlan IV is a stand-alone program for those who understand how to apply statistics to decision making. You can use it for market analysis, trend forecasting, and statistical modeling. StatPlan IV lets you analyze data by range, mean, median, standard deviation, skewness, kurtosis, correlation analysis, one- or two-way analysis of variance (Anova), cross tabulations, and t-test.

The forecasting methods include multiple regression, stepwise multiple regression, polynomial regression, bivariate curve fitting, autocorrelation analysis, trend and cycle analysis, and exponential smoothing.

The data can be displayed in X-Y plots, histograms, time-series graphs, autocorrelation plots, actual versus forecast plots, or frequency and percentile tables.

Geneva Statistical Forecasting

Geneva Statistical Forecasting, a stand-alone software package, can batch-process forecasts for thousands of data series, provided the series are all measured in the same time units (days, weeks, months, and so on). The software automatically tries out as many as nine different forecasting methods, including six linear and nonlinear regressions and three exponential-smoothing techniques, before picking the one that best fits your historical data.

The program incorporates provisions that simplify and accelerate the process of reforecasting data items. Once you complete the initial forecast, you can save a data file that records the forecasting method assigned to each line item. When it is time to update the data, simply retrieve the file and reforecast, using the same methods as before. Geneva Statistical Forecasting tries as many as nine forecasting methods for each line item.

SmartForecasts

SmartForecasts, a stand-alone forecasting software package, features the following:

- It automatically chooses the right statistical method.
- It lets you manually adjust forecasts to reflect your business judgment.
- It produces forecast results.

SmartForecasts combines the benefits of statistical and judgmental forecasting. It can determine which statistical method will give you the most accurate forecast, and can handle all the math. Forecasts can be modified using the program's EYEBALL utility. You may need to adjust a sales forecast to reflect an anticipated increase in advertising or a decrease in price. SmartForecasts summarizes data with descriptive statistics, plots the distribution of data values with histograms, plots variables in a scattergram, and identifies leading indicators.

You can forecast using single or double exponential smoothing, and simple or linear moving averages. This program even builds seasonality into your forecasts, using Winters's exponential smoothing, or you can eliminate seasonality by using times series decomposition and seasonal adjustment.

In addition, SmartForecasts features simultaneous multiseries forecasting of up to 60 variables and up to 150 data points per variable, offers multivariate regression to let you relate business variables, and has an Undo command for mistakes.

Tomorrow

Tomorrow, a stand-alone forecasting software package, uses an optimized combination of linear regression, single exponential smoothing, adaptive rate response single exponential smoothing, Brown's one-parameter double exponential smoothing, Holt's two-parameter exponential smoothing, Brown's one-parameter triple exponential smoothing, and Gardner's three-parameter damped trend. Some of the main features include:

- There's no need to reformat your existing spreadsheets. Tomorrow recognizes and forecasts formula cells (containing totals and subtotals, for example). It handles both horizontally and vertically oriented spreadsheets. It accepts historical data in up to 30 separate ranges.

- It allows you to specify seasonality manually, or it calculates seasonality automatically.
- It allows you to do several forecasts of different time series (for example, sales data from different regions) at once.
- It recognizes and forecasts time series headings (names of months, etc.).
- The forecast optionally becomes a normal part of your spreadsheet.
- It offers comprehensive context-sensitive on-line help.

Forecast Pro

Forecast Pro, a stand-alone forecasting software package, uses artificial intelligence. A built-in expert system examines your data, then guides you to exponential smoothing, Box-Jenkins, or regression—whichever method suits the data best.

MicroTSP

MicroTSP is a stand-alone software package that provides the tools most frequently used in practical econometric and forecasting work. It covers the following:

1. Descriptive statistics.
2. A wide range of single equation estimation techniques, including ordinary least squares (multiple regression), two-stage least squares, nonlinear least squares, and probit and logit.

Forecasting tools include:

1. Exponential smoothing including single exponential, double exponential, and Winters's smoothing.
2. Box-Jenkins methodology.

Forecast Plus

Forecast Plus, a stand-alone forecasting software package, uses artificial intelligence. A built-in expert system examines your data, then guides you to one of thirteen forecasting methods, including exponential smoothing, Box-Jenkins, and regression—whichever method suits the data best.

The software features the following:

- A simple-to-use menu system.
- High-resolution graphic capability.
- The ability to choose an appropriate forecasting technique.

- The ability to handle all phases of forecasting analysis.
- The ability to save forecast data.
- Optimization of smoothing constants.

General Purpose Statistical Software

There are numerous statistical software programs widely in use that can help you build a forecasting model. Some of the more popular ones include: (1) Systat, (2) SAS Application System, (3) Statgraphics, (4) SPSS, (5) PC-90, (6) Minitab, (7) RATS, and (8) BMD.

ACTIVITY-BASED COSTING (ABC) SOFTWARE

Numerous PC/network software packages are available for implementing ABC analysis. Following is a representative list.

1. Profit Manager, KPMG Peat Marwick, (800) 537–0047 or (313) 983–0225.
2. Activa, Price Waterhouse, (314) 425–0500.
3. ABCost Manager, Coopers & Lybrand, (312) 701–5783.
4. TR/ACM, Deloitte & Touche, (415) 247–4621 or (617) 261–8623.
5. Activity Analyzer, Lead Software, Inc., (708) 351–5155.
6. CMS-PC, ICMS, Inc., (800) 955–2233 or (817) 633–2873.
7. EasyABC Plus and EasyABC Quick, ABC Technologies, Inc., (503) 626–4895.
8. Profile ABC, Applied Computer Services, Inc., (203) 849–9557.
9. The Cost Blueprint, ProAct Corporation, (800) 892–4158.

APPENDIX E

Tables

T A B L E E.1

Present Value of $1

$$\frac{1}{(1+i)^n} = T_1(i,n)$$

Period	4%	6%	8%	10%	12%	14%	16%	18%	20%	22%	24%	26%	28%	30%
1	.962	.943	.926	.909	.893	.877	.862	.847	.833	.820	.806	.794	.781	.769
2	.925	.890	.857	.826	.797	.769	.743	.718	.694	.672	.650	.630	.610	.592
3	.889	.840	.794	.751	.712	.675	.641	.609	.579	.551	.524	.500	.477	.455
4	.855	.792	.735	.683	.636	.592	.552	.516	.482	.451	.423	.397	.373	.350
5	.822	.747	.681	.621	.567	.519	.476	.437	.402	.370	.341	.315	.291	.269
6	.790	.705	.630	.564	.507	.456	.410	.370	.335	.303	.275	.250	.227	.207
7	.760	.665	.583	.513	.452	.400	.354	.314	.279	.249	.222	.198	.178	.159
8	.731	.627	.540	.467	.404	.351	.305	.266	.233	.204	.179	.157	.139	.123
9	.703	.592	.500	.424	.361	.308	.263	.225	.194	.167	.144	.125	.108	.094
10	.676	.558	.463	.386	.322	.270	.227	.191	.162	.137	.116	.099	.085	.073
11	.650	.527	.429	.350	.287	.237	.195	.162	.135	.112	.094	.079	.066	.056
12	.625	.497	.397	.319	.257	.208	.168	.137	.112	.092	.076	.062	.052	.043
13	.601	.469	.368	.290	.229	.182	.145	.116	.093	.075	.061	.050	.040	.033
14	.577	.442	.340	.263	.205	.160	.125	.099	.078	.062	.049	.039	.032	.025
15	.555	.417	.315	.239	.183	.140	.108	.084	.065	.051	.040	.031	.025	.020
16	.534	.394	.292	.218	.163	.123	.093	.071	.054	.042	.032	.025	.019	.015
17	.513	.371	.270	.198	.146	.108	.080	.060	.045	.034	.026	.020	.015	.012
18	.494	.350	.250	.180	.130	.095	.069	.051	.038	.028	.021	.016	.012	.009
19	.475	.331	.232	.164	.116	.083	.060	.043	.031	.023	.017	.012	.009	.007
20	.456	.312	.215	.149	.104	.073	.051	.037	.026	.019	.014	.010	.007	.005
21	.439	.294	.199	.135	.093	.064	.044	.031	.022	.015	.011	.008	.006	.004
22	.422	.278	.184	.123	.083	.056	.038	.026	.018	.013	.009	.006	.004	.003
23	.406	.262	.170	.112	.074	.049	.033	.022	.015	.010	.007	.005	.003	.002
24	.390	.247	.158	.102	.066	.043	.028	.019	.013	.008	.006	.004	.003	.002
25	.375	.233	.146	.092	.059	.038	.024	.016	.010	.007	.005	.003	.002	.001
26	.361	.220	.135	.084	.053	.033	.021	.014	.009	.006	.004	.002	.002	.001
27	.347	.207	.125	.076	.047	.029	.018	.011	.007	.005	.003	.002	.001	.001
28	.333	.196	.116	.069	.042	.026	.016	.010	.006	.004	.002	.002	.001	.001
29	.321	.185	.107	.063	.037	.022	.014	.008	.005	.003	.002	.001	.001	.001
30	.308	.174	.099	.057	.033	.020	.012	.007	.004	.003	.002	.001	.001	
40	.208	.097	.046	.022	.011	.005	.003	.001	.001					

T A B L E   E.2

Present Value of an Annuity of $1 for N Periods

$$\frac{1}{i}\left[1 - \frac{1}{(1+i)^n}\right] = T_2(i,n)$$

n	1%	2%	3%	4%	5%	6%	7%	8%	9%	10%
1	.990	.980	.971	.962	.952	.943	.935	.926	.917	.909
2	1.970	1.942	1.913	1.886	1.859	1.833	1.808	1.783	1.759	1.736
3	2.941	2.884	2.829	2.775	2.723	2.673	2.624	2.577	2.531	2.487
4	3.902	3.808	3.717	3.630	3.546	3.465	3.387	3.312	3.240	3.170
5	4.853	4.713	4.580	4.452	4.329	4.212	4.100	3.993	3.890	3.791
6	5.795	5.601	5.417	5.242	5.076	4.917	4.767	4.623	4.486	4.355
7	6.728	6.472	6.230	6.002	5.786	5.582	5.389	5.206	5.033	4.868
8	7.652	7.326	7.020	6.733	6.463	6.210	5.971	5.747	5.535	5.335
9	8.566	8.162	7.786	7.435	7.108	6.802	6.515	6.247	5.995	5.759
10	9.471	8.983	8.530	8.111	7.722	7.360	7.024	6.710	6.418	6.145
11	10.368	9.787	9.253	8.760	8.306	7.887	7.499	7.139	6.805	6.495
12	11.255	10.575	9.954	9.385	8.863	8.384	7.943	7.536	7.161	6.814
13	12.134	11.348	10.635	9.986	9.394	8.853	8.358	7.904	7.487	7.103
14	13.004	12.106	11.296	10.563	9.899	9.295	8.746	8.244	7.786	7.367
15	13.865	12.849	11.938	11.118	10.380	9.712	9.108	8.560	8.061	7.606
16	14.718	13.578	12.561	11.652	10.838	10.106	9.447	8.851	8.313	7.824
17	15.562	14.292	13.166	12.166	11.274	10.477	9.763	9.122	8.544	8.022
18	16.398	14.992	13.754	12.659	11.690	10.828	10.059	9.372	8.756	8.201
19	17.226	15.679	14.324	13.134	12.085	11.158	10.336	9.604	8.950	8.365
20	18.046	16.352	14.878	13.590	12.462	11.470	10.594	9.818	9.129	8.514
21	18.857	17.011	15.415	14.029	12.821	11.764	10.836	10.017	9.292	8.649
22	19.661	17.658	15.937	14.451	13.163	12.042	11.061	10.201	9.442	8.772
23	20.456	18.292	16.444	14.857	13.489	12.303	11.272	10.371	9.580	8.883
24	18.244	18.914	16.936	15.247	13.799	12.550	11.469	10.529	9.707	8.985
25	22.023	19.524	17.413	15.622	14.094	12.783	11.654	10.675	9.823	9.077
30	25.808	22.397	19.601	17.292	15.373	13.765	12.409	11.258	10.274	9.427
40	32.835	27.356	23.115	19.793	17.159	15.046	13.332	11.925	10.757	9.779
50	39.197	31.424	25.730	21.482	18.256	15.762	13.801	12.234	10.962	9.915

T A B L E   E.3

Critical Values for the *t* Statistic

			Values of t			
d.f.	$t_{0.100}$	$t_{0.050}$	$t_{0.025}$	$t_{0.010}$	$t_{0.005}$	**d.f.**
1	3.078	6.314	12.706	31.821	63.657	1
2	1.886	2.920	4.303	6.965	9.925	2
3	1.638	2.353	3.182	4.541	5.841	3
4	1.533	2.132	2.776	3.747	4.604	4
5	1.476	2.015	2.571	3.365	4.032	5
6	1.440	1.943	2.447	3.143	3.707	6
7	1.415	1.895	2.365	2.998	3.499	7
8	1.397	1.860	2.306	2.896	3.355	8
9	1.383	1.833	2.262	2.821	3.250	9
10	1.372	1.812	2.228	2.764	3.169	10
11	1.363	1.796	2.201	2.718	3.106	11
12	1.356	1.782	2.179	2.681	3.055	12
13	1.350	1.771	2.160	2.650	3.012	13
14	1.345	1.761	2.145	2.624	2.977	14
15	1.341	1.753	2.131	2.602	2.947	15
16	1.337	1.746	2.120	2.583	2.921	16
17	1.333	1.740	2.110	2.567	2.898	17
18	1.330	1.734	2.101	2.552	2.878	18
19	1.328	1.729	2.093	2.539	2.861	19
20	1.325	1.725	2.086	2.528	2.845	20
21	1.323	1.721	2.080	2.518	2.831	21
22	1.321	1.717	2.074	2.508	2.819	22
23	1.319	1.714	2.069	2.500	2.807	23
24	1.318	1.711	2.064	2.492	2.797	24
25	1.316	1.708	2.060	2.485	2.787	25
26	1.315	1.706	2.056	2.479	2.779	26
27	1.314	1.703	2.052	2.473	2.771	27
28	1.313	1.701	2.048	2.467	2.763	28
29	1.311	1.699	2.045	2.462	2.756	29
Inf.	1.282	1.645	1.960	2.326	2.576	Inf.

Note:The *t* value describes the sampling distribution of a deviation from a population value divided by the standard error.

Degrees of freedom (*d.f.*) are in the first column. The probabilities indicated as subvalues of *t* in the heading refer to the sum of a one-tailed area under the curve that lies outside the point *t*. For example, in the distribution of the means of samples of size $n = 10$, $d.f. = n - 2 = 8$; then 0.0025 of the area under the curve falls in one tail outside the interval $t \pm 2.306$.

I N D E X